Arthuriana

Arthuriana
Early Arthurian Tradition and the Origins of the Legend

Thomas Green

THE LINDES PRESS

As with everything, so with this:
For Frances and Evie.

First published 2009

The Lindes Press
Louth, Lincolnshire

www.arthuriana.co.uk

A catalogue record for this book is available from the
British Library.

ISBN 978 1 4452 2110 6

Contents

Preface

This book collects together the academic and popular articles which have appeared on my 'Arthurian Resources' website – *www.arthuriana.co.uk* – since 1998.* It has been created in response to requests from readers for a print version of the site, in order to ease both the reading and referencing of the material archived there; as such, the articles from the website are reproduced here with the minimum of alteration, aside from some necessary reformatting.

'The Historicity and Historicisation of Arthur' was the first piece to appear on the website; it takes the form of an extensive review article which gathers together and critiques scholarship on the sources for a 'historical Arthur'. Although an up-to-date expansion, development and revision of the views presented there can be found in my *Concepts of Arthur* (Tempus, 2007), the article continues to be made available due to its long independent existence and the fact that has been cited in current scholarship on the early Arthurian legend, for example in N. J. Higham, *King Arthur, Myth-Making and History* (Routledge, 2002), and in N. J. Lacy (ed.), *The History of Arthurian Scholarship* (Boydell, 2006).

'A Bibliographic Guide to Welsh Arthurian Literature' and 'A Gazetteer of Arthurian Onomastic and Topographic Folklore' represent detailed guides to their respective topics. The first offers a discussion of virtually every piece of early Welsh Arthurian literary material, including an indication of its content, recent scholarship, and the availability of editions and translations. The second provides a discussion of the early evidence for Arthur and his companions appearing in local topographic and onomastic folklore, along with a detailed gazetteer (with grid references) of all such items which take the form 'Arthur's X'. In contrast, 'Lincolnshire and the Arthurian Legend' is a more speculative piece, a 'what-if'. If we *were* to make the assumption that Arthur did actually exist, then who might he have been? This piece attempts to answer this question in light of recent academic work on both the Arthurian sources and the archaeology and history of post-Roman Britain, before noting the essential caveats which must accompany any such 'identification'.

The last two sections encompass a number of different articles and

---

* The website was first located at *www.users.globalnet.co.uk/~tomgreen/Arthuriana.htm* but moved to its current location in 2001.

pieces within them. 'Arthur and Jack the Giant-Killer' begins with an introduction to the tale of Jack the Giant-Killer and an analysis of the links between this character and the Welsh and Cornish 'folkloric' Arthur. It then goes on to include transcripts of several early versions of Jack's tale and examples of analogous Arthurian giant-killings. Finally, 'Miscellaneous Arthuriana' consists of a variety of more informal thoughts on Arthurian issues which have appeared on the site over the last decade, along with answers to some of the most common questions.

All told, the collection provides a guide to a significant proportion of the early Arthurian legend and it is hoped that it will be found to be of some value. It should be noted, incidentally, that no attempt has been made to harmonise the different referencing systems used by the articles. Not only was it the aim of the present work to reproduce the website articles as closely as possible, but the different methods of referencing do to some degree reflect the different aims of the pieces, so that the bibliographic essays give full references, analyses use parenthetical references, and the edited transcript of a 1787 chapbook uses footnotes.

Thomas Green
October 2009

1

The Historicity and Historicisation of Arthur

The Historicity and Historicisation of Arthur

1. Introduction

Many different theories are available as to the 'identity' of Arthur and some brief methodological notes will be found here regarding the making of such identifications. While these theories are interesting, they fail to address fully one important question – was there a historical post-Roman Arthur? Many books, articles and web-pages simply make the *a priori* assumption that there has to be a historical figure behind the Arthurian legends. Such an assumption is totally unjustified. As anyone at all familiar with medieval literature in general will know, the historicisation of non-historical/mythical personages – often through association with some important event of the past – is not in any way an unusual occurrence. Some examples of this that will probably particularly interest readers of this article are Hengest and Horsa, who were Kentish totemic horse-gods historicised by the eighth century with an important role in the fifth-century Anglo-Saxon conquest of eastern Britain (see Turville-Petre, 1953-7; Ward, 1969; Brooks, 1989; Yorke, 1993); Merlin (Welsh *Myrddin*), who was an eponymous founder-figure derived from the place-name *Caer-fyrddin* and historicised with the deeds of one Lailoken (see Jarman, 1991); and the Norse demigod Sigurd/Siegfried who was historicised by being associated with a famous historical battle between the Huns and the Burgundians dated A.D. 437, in the *Nibelungenlied* (Thomas, 1995: 390).[1] Given this, no *a priori* judgements can be made as to whether a figure is, in origin, historical, mythical or fictional – each individual case must (and can only) be decided by a close examination of all the relevant material. When we have figures such as Arthur being portrayed as historical we are therefore, on a very basic level, looking at *either* a historical figure *or* a legendary figure who became historicised, with neither explanation enjoying priority on *a priori* grounds – it must be recognised that one can only say that there has to have been a historical Arthur once all the material has been evaluated and this has been shown to be the case; there is no possible justification for simply assuming this. The following article is intended to provide a summary account and bibliography of the latest academic research into Arthur with a particular focus on the question of historicity. Aside from the various articles and books cited, much of what is below has been discussed in detail on the discussion list of the International Arthurian Society, *Arthurnet*, in a moderated debate that I had the great pleasure of chairing. The results of this discussion, including all posted comments, can be found in the *Arthurnet* archives.

2. The Historical Arthur: an Analytical and Bibliographic Survey

Any inquiry into the 'historical' Arthur must proceed from the sources. One of the most important sources for the student of post-Roman Britain is archaeology and, indeed, the case is sometimes made that it is our only reliable source (see, for example, Arnold, 1984). When looking at Arthur's possible historicity however, archaeology cannot really help as it deals with sites not people – it can show that a site was occupied in the right period but only very rarely (that is, when we have an inscription) can it tell us who the occupier was. The only piece of archaeological data which might have been significant to the debate is the Glastonbury cross naming King Arthur as the occupant of the grave it was supposedly found in by the monks of Glastonbury in 1191. Some have suggested a mid-tenth- or eleventh-century date for this (for example, Radford, 1968; Alcock, 1971) but it is now clear that it was the product of a late twelfth-century fraud and derivative of Geoffrey of Monmouth's *Historia Regum Britanniae,* and thus of no use in the search for a historical Arthur (see Rahtz, 1993; Carey, 1999; Carley, 1999; Gransden, 1976; *Somerset and Dorset Notes & Queries* for 1984; there was a copy of Geoffrey's *Historia* at Glastonbury from *c.* 1170. The early sixth-century inscribed stone that has recently been found at Tintagel does *not* refer to Arthur, contrary to reports by English Heritage and the media). Given the above, any conclusions regarding Arthur's historicity, or lack thereof, must be drawn from the textual references to him.

The King Arthur we encounter in the later medieval texts (and with which people are often most familiar) is not the Arthur of earlier works – shortly before A.D. 1139 Geoffrey of Monmouth (*Galfridus Monemutensis*) completed his *Historia Regum Britanniae* ('History of the Kings of Britain') which glorified Arthur and made him an international warlord. This work quickly became influential throughout western Europe and affected the Arthurian legend in all areas with the result that, in general, scholars look to sources written before Geoffrey's *Historia* for the 'original' Arthur (that is, in the 'pre-Galfridian' sources). One well known dissenter from this is Geoffrey Ashe (1981; 1985; 1995) who argues that Riotamus, a fifth-century 'king' of the Britons who campaigned on the continent, is the actual historical prototype of Arthur and Geoffrey of Monmouth drew on this tradition when writing his *magnum opus*. While this theory is quite popular it is rightly dismissed by academic commentators as nothing more than 'straws in the wind' (Bromwich *et al*, 1991: 6. See also Padel, 1994: 31, n. 113; Hanning, 1995; Padel, 1995) on the grounds that, while Riotamus (or Breton traditions about this figure) could be the (partial) inspiration for Geoffrey's *portrayal* of Arthur, he has nothing at all in common with the insular traditions of Arthur and thus cannot be the prototype for Arthur as a whole (indeed, he doesn't even have the correct name – Ashe explains this by saying that Riotamus was a title and Arthur was his real name but a recent reviewer (Padel, 1995) has shown this to be untenable). The above means that the historical Arthur, if he existed, will be found in the pre-Galfridian texts and it is to these we must now turn.

The pre-Galfridian sources for Arthur can be most conveniently read in Coe and Young (1995), which provides facing text and translation. Some earlier historians, such as John Morris (1973), tried to make use of, as historical texts, all the sources which mentioned Arthur including, for example, the Saints' Lives and late poetry. This tendency has been correctly and heavily criticised by David Dumville (1977a), amongst others, mainly because these sources cannot be seen as in any way historically reliable – we are therefore, when looking at a possibly historical Arthur and in the light of Dumville's comments, essentially confined to four pieces of evidence which might contain information of real historical value: the *Annales Cambriae* (Phillimore, 1888; Morris, 1980); the *Historia Brittonum* (Morris, 1980; Dumville, 1985; Koch and Carey, 1995); the collection of heroic death-songs known as *Y Gododdin* (Jackson, 1969; Jarman, 1988; Koch, 1997); and the four or five occurrences of the name Arthur in sixth- and seventh-century contexts (Barber, 1972; Bromwich 1975-6; Coe and Young, 1995: 156-65).

Dealing with the last of these first, the occurrence of four (or possibly five) people named 'Arthur' in sixth- and seventh-century western Scotland and Wales has often been seen as one of the best pieces of evidence for a historical Arthur – the argument is, essentially, that the appearance of these names reflects the commemoration of an earlier historical figure (see, for example, Chadwick and Chadwick, 1932).[2] However such a commemoration by name of an earlier historical hero would be totally unparalleled in the Celtic world and as such cannot be at all supported as an explanation of these names (see Bromwich, 1975-6: 178-79). Thus these names cannot be used as evidence for a historical Arthur and as long as we continue to see Arthur as genuinely historical they are likely to remain a lasting crux (at present there is only one viable explanation of these names, that proposed by Oliver Padel (1994: 24) – see below on this. It is worth noting that none of these 'Arthurs' can be seen as the 'original' Arthur, *pace* Barber, 1972 – see Bromwich, 1975-6: 179; Jackson, 1973; Roberts, 1973-4).

The second source for consideration is the collection of heroic death-songs known as *Y Gododdin*, relating to a battle fought in the late sixth century. In recent years there has been considerable debate over the statement in *Y Gododdin* that Gordur 'fed black ravens on the rampart of a fort, although he was no Arthur' (B.38. Koch (1997) numbers this B².38). Thomas Charles-Edwards (1991: 14), building on his theory of textual transmission (set forth in Charles-Edwards, 1978), concluded that, as the reference only occurs in the B version and not the A version of *Y Gododdin*, it need be no older than the ninth or tenth century. Recently, however, Koch (1997) has attempted a 'reconstruction' of the 'original' text of *Y Gododdin* and includes the 'Arthurian' reference in this text, dated by him to pre-A.D. 638. Whilst his is certainly an interesting exercise in discovering how *Y Gododdin* might have looked if it was of sixth- or seventh-century date, the limitations of this 'reconstruction' must be recognised. As one reviewer has noted, Koch's text is, in reality, a *translation* of *Y Gododdin* into the language of *c.* A.D. 600 and in this it must be seen in the same light as Jarman's earlier translation of this text into modern Welsh (Jarman, 1988) – Koch has not shown that *Y Gododdin* was composed in this period, only what it might have looked like *if* it had been (Padel, 1998). Indeed, Isaac has demonstrated that Koch's whole theory of the creation and transmission of *Y Gododdin*, including the idea that B² represents the Ur-text, cannot be at all supported (Isaac, 1999). Similar caveats have been shown to apply to Koch's 'reconstruction' of the poem *Gweith Gwen Ystrat*, with Isaac demonstrating that whilst one can undertake such a exercise and show how this poem would have looked if it had been composed *c.* A.D. 600, such a reconstruction is entirely unwarranted and there is no reason to think that the text was composed in this period (Isaac, 1998). Given the above, it seems clear that, despite Koch's assertions, '[t]he date of composition [of *Y Gododdin*] remains as unclear as ever' (Padel, 1998: 55). Indeed Isaac (1996; 1999) has recently followed D. Simon Evans (1978) in arguing that there is no linguistic evidence that would necessitate dating *Y Gododdin* as a whole before the ninth or tenth century and, in light of all of this, Charles-Edwards' comments on the antiquity of the Arthurian references in this text must stand.

Turning to the 'Arthurian' *awdl* ('stanza') of *Y Gododdin*, how does this reference affect the question of Arthur's historicity, given that Arthur only appears as a comparison to a warrior of (supposedly) the late sixth century? One common argument is that in works such as *Y Gododdin* the figures named are always believed to be historical and therefore the Arthurian *awdl* would seem to indicate that by the ninth or tenth century Arthur was believed to have been a historical personage, at least by the author of *Y Gododdin* (see Jarman, 1989-90; Bromwich *et al*, 1991). Whilst superficially convincing, there are considerable problems with such a judgement. First, the simple fact of the matter is that we can only identify a few of the characters that appear in early Welsh heroic poetry; many of the people in the poems appear only there, so that we have no knowledge of whether they were (or were thought to be) historical or not – it is an assumption, nothing more, that everyone in these poems was a real historical figure and as such we cannot take Arthur's presence in *Y Gododdin* as evidence either for his historicity or a belief in his historicity. Second, the assumption may well not have a sound basis as Rowland has recently noted that the people who appear in these works (and are recognisable) are *nearly* all historical figures, that Gereint like *most of the heroes* identifiable in this type of poetry is a historical figure (Rowland, 1990). Given this, there is no reason for making any such assumptions. Third, in *Y Gododdin* Arthur is in the remarkable position of appearing 'only not to appear' (Padel, 1994: 14). Unlike Gordur or the other warriors he is not actually present at the battle: 'In the allusion, Arthur is presented as the unrivalled paragon of martial valour and is thus used to form a highly unusual comparison by rendering explicitly inferior the honorand of the *awdl* ("stanza"). Therefore, if the relevant *awdl* and lines can be sustained as Aneirin's original, this would tell us that by the later sixth century there existed in North Britain a tradition of a Brittonic superhero Arthur...' (Koch, 1996: 242). Whilst we might not be able to accept Koch's assertions on dating, we can say that Arthur is essentially a 'highly unusual comparison', not a warrior who is being honoured; he is not envisaged as being present at the battle and he is a military 'superhero', someone to whose heights of valour not even a man who killed 300 in one rush could compare. He is therefore in a different league to the rest of the figures who appear in *Y Gododdin* and, as such, there is no reason to think that assumptions drawn from the identifications of a few characters in the text as a whole, even if they were viable, would apply to him. All the *Y Gododdin* reference tells us is that Arthur was seen, by the ninth or tenth century, as 'the impossible comparison' (Padel, 1994: 14), a 'superhero' to whom not even the greatest living warrior could compare; it does *not* tell us whether this reflects a mythical 'superhero' named Arthur or a historical Arthur mythicised and Arthur is, in the text, in no way associated with the defence of post-Roman Britain or any specific period of history.[3]

In light of the fact that neither of the above can help in the investigation of Arthur's possible 'historicity', the case for a historical Arthur rests entirely on two sources, the *Historia Brittonum* and the *Annales Cambriae*, both of which would appear to have a concept of Arthur that is (at least partly) unequivocally historical. The *Historia Brittonum* was written anonymously in A.D. 829/30, the ascription to one 'Nennius' now being regarded as false (Dumville, 1974; 1975-6, though see Field, 1996). There is considerable debate over the nature of the text (see, for example, Dumville, 1986; Charles-Edwards, 1991; Dumville, 1994; Koch, 1997; Howlett, 1998) but it now seems clear that the writer of the *Historia* was not an ignorant and incompetent compiler who simply 'made a heap' of earlier sources but rather an 'author' who wrote the *Historia Brittonum* with a unity of structure and outlook and engaged in the active processing of his sources, and this conclusion is endorsed by the researches of David Howlett who sees the *Historia* as a work of architectonic genius making use of the sophisticated 'Biblical style' in its construction (Howlett, pers. comm.; 1998: chapter 5. For the Celtic-Latin tradition of Biblical style see Howlett, 1995).

Given the above, we must question to what extent the author altered his sources for his own purposes, what were the nature of his sources, and thus how far can we trust what we read in the *Historia*? Dumville (1986) took a very pessimistic line on this, arguing that it was a source only for the ninth century and its concerns. While this view has been challenged by Thomas Charles-Edwards (1991), who identifies the *Historia* as a fusion of the two historical genres, *historia gentis* and *historia ecclesiastica*, it is still clearly the case that 'even where credit might be given to the supposed source [of a section of the *Historia*], the author's methods... do not encourage us to be confident about the possibility of recovering usable information about the period whose history he was narrating. His procedures were synthetic and interpretive, his sources overwhelmingly non-contemporaneous with the events which they purport to describe' (Dumville, 1994: 419).[4] As such the *Historia* is of very dubious historical value, for example, in addition to many of its sources being of a similar date to itself and suspect in nature, the *Historia* can be shown to portray characters who are decidedly mythical in origin, such as Hengest and Horsa (see Turville-Petre, 1953-7; Ward, 1969; Brooks, 1989; Yorke, 1993), as genuinely historical. Indeed, as a number of recent commentators have recognised, the *Historia Brittonum* is in fact a synchronising and synthetic history of the type well known from medieval Ireland, fusing sources for its own political ends and involved in the creation of a full national pseudo-history, a process which was closely allied with the historicising of legend (Padel, 1994: 23; Carey, 1994; Dumville, 1994; Coe and Young, 1995: 6). Directly relevant to this question of the 'historical value' of the *Historia Brittonum* is the fact that the author of the *Historia* was not writing 'history' as we know it today but was rather engaging in something more akin to that which we would call sermonising, and this must be remembered in any analysis of the *Historia*. To try and read such works as the *Historia* as linear history is completely false to the methods and assumptions with which they were composed (see Hanning, 1966; Howlett, 1998; N. Hinton, pers. comm.).

This leads us to Chapter 56 of the *Historia Brittonum*, which contains the references to a 'historical' Arthur. This is 'a pseudo-historical account of a suspiciously formulaic list of twelve battles against Germanic invaders' (Coe and Young, 1995: 6), supposedly fought by Arthur. Some have suggested (for example, Chadwick and Chadwick, 1932; Jones, 1964) that Chapter 56 could have been based on a poem written in Welsh that was translated into Latin by the author of the *Historia*. Whilst this is an interesting suggestion it has to be recognised that such a notion is speculation and it does not allow us to give this section of the *Historia* an early date. Indeed, various considerations indicate that any such hypothetical poem would date to much the same period as the *Historia* anyway (see Jackson, 1945-6: 57; Jackson, 1959a: 7-8; Dumville, 1977a: 188; Jarman, 1981: 2-3; Dumville, 1986: 13-14; Charles-Edwards, 1991: 21-29; Padel, 1994).[5] Furthermore it must not be forgotten that, with the writer of the *Historia Brittonum* now seen as an author actively manipulating his text to create a synthetic pseudo-history rather than a simple compiler, Chapter 56 was, to some large extent, his creation. This is underlined by Howlett's (1998: chapter 5) discovery that this section is written in the highly complex 'Biblical style', showing that Chapter 56 was an integral part of the *Historia* that was created, engineered and planned by the author in accordance with his aims and methodology. As such the notion that Chapter 56 might represent anything like a postulated earlier source incorporated bodily into the text of the *Historia* can be rejected. Instead it seems clear that this chapter, along with its concept of Arthur, cannot be separated from the *Historia* as a whole, the aims, methodology, unity of structure and outlook with which this was created, or, indeed, the general comments of Dumville and others on the nature of the *Historia* and its sources noted above (see further Hanning, 1966; Barber, 1972: 101 ff.; Charles-Edwards, 1991: 21 ff. on Chapter 56 as an integral and inseparable part of the *Historia*). The best we can therefore honestly say is that in the *Historia Brittonum*, a source of very dubious historical value (which can be shown to portray mythical figures as genuinely historical), we have evidence for the idea that Arthur was a historical figure being current by A.D. 829/30 at the latest.

Our last source, the *Annales Cambriae*, was compiled in 950s and is sometimes seen as providing good evidence for Arthur being a historical figure (see Grabowski and Dumville, 1984 for the dating. Studies and commentaries on the text include Jones, 1964; Alcock, 1971; Hughes, 1980; Grabowski and Dumville, 1984; Dumville, 1990; Charles-Edwards, 1991 and Koch, 1996. Dumville apparently has a new study of the *Annales* forthcoming). It mentions Arthur in two entries: that for A.D. 516 which tells of the 'battle of Badon, in which Arthur carried the cross of our Lord Jesus Christ on his shoulders for three days and three nights, and the Britons were the victors' and that for A.D. 537 concerning 'the battle of Camlann, in which Arthur and Medraut fell'. In assessing the value of these entries, considerable attention should be paid to the date of these annals. Jones (1964) and Alcock (1971) were both inclined to see at least one of these annals as a contemporary record of Arthur and, if it could be accepted, such a conclusion would 'prove' Arthur's historicity. However, Hughes (1980) in her important and extensive studies of the *Annales* reached a rather different (and convincing) conclusion, and this has been built upon by Dumville (in Grabowski and Dumville, 1984) and Charles-Edwards (1991) – the *Annales Cambriae* to 613 is basically a version of the 'Chronicle of Ireland', with the sections from 613 to 777 being based on North British materials; there is absolutely no justification for thinking that any of the pre-613 British entries are drawn from contemporary or even near-contemporary sources and, rather, they should be seen as retrospective interpolations dating from between the very late eighth century (the period in which the 'Chronicle of Ireland' was first brought together with the post-613 North British materials at St David's in order to extend backwards a chronicle kept by that community from the closing years of the eighth century onwards) and the mid-tenth century (when the *Annales* reached something like its final form). Indeed, in light of Dumville's further researches into the date of this bringing together, the above *terminus post quem* for the interpolations might well be shifted forward to the early-mid-tenth century.

Looking at the annals themselves, one very important point must be made: the Badon entry in the *Annales* is not an independent witness to Arthur's historicity. Instead it is clearly related to the *Historia Brittonum*'s account (Chapter 56) of Arthur's eighth battle at *Guinnion* Castle, in which Arthur carries an icon on his shoulders into battle with him, and as such the *Annales* account either derives from the *Historia Brittonum* or its source. Thomas Charles-Edwards has suggested (1991: 25-28) that they be seen as dual elaborations of single original, the entry in neither case being very much older than the text it is contained in (829/30 for the *Historia* and the 950s for the *Annales*). However, a more convincing explanation has been provided by John Koch. Koch observes that both the *Historia Brittonum* and the *Annales Cambriae* have the probable confusion of Old Welsh *scuit* 'shield' and *scuid* 'shoulder' in them and notes that 'that error of transmission is hardly likely to have come about twice'. He goes on to say that 'In all details, the *Annales Cambriae* entry is more easily understood as derived from *Historia Brittonum*'s account', which would appear to be the most probable scenario on the present evidence and is sound even without the support of the *scuit/d* confusion (see Koch, 1996: 252-53 for discussion; also Barber, 1972: 105). Similarly the second entry regarding Camlann is best viewed as non-traditional and as having mid-tenth-century origins (see Charles-Edwards, 1991: 25-27, 28; Ashe, 1986: 76-78; Wood, 1981: 59-60; Bromwich, 1978a: 487; Jarman, 1983: 109), with the consequence that the *Annales Cambriae* cannot really be seen to be of any independent value in making the case for a 'historical Arthur'. As a result we are forced to return to the text of the *Historia Brittonum*.

Whilst general comments on Chapter 56 of the *Historia Brittonum* have been made, a more detailed examination of the information contained within it may prove enlightening. It is easy to assume that all the battles mentioned in Chapter 56 were remembered as being those fought by Arthur but such assumptions may well be incorrect. Perhaps the most famous

'Arthurian' battle is that of Badon (*in montis badonis*) but the reference to this has serious problems. It has long been accepted that this is the same battle as the *obsessio Badonici montis* of Gildas's *De Excidio Britanniae* § 26 (see Winterbottom, 1978 for an edition and translation. The date of publication of this work, and thus the date of Badon, has been much discussed – see for example Miller, 1975; O'Sullivan, 1978; Sims-Williams, 1983; Lapidge and Dumville (edd.), 1984; Higham, 1994; Howlett, 1998)[6] and one of the arguments against Arthur's historicity has always been that Gildas fails to mention Arthur in his reference to the battle.[7] It is usually countered (as Jackson 1959a) that he was deliberately omitted, either because Gildas didn't approve of him or because his contribution to the victory was too well known, but recent work suggests that the reason Arthur was not mentioned was indeed because he was not associated with the battle when Gildas wrote. Rather than not naming anyone as the British leader at Badon, Gildas does indeed assign Badon a victor – Ambrosius Aurelianus. The idea that this figure was the true victor has been previously dismissed on the grounds that the manuscript (British Library, Cotton Vitellius A.vi) implies a major interval between Ambrosius and Badon. Oliver Padel has returned to the original manuscript however and has been able to show that the break evident in Winterbottom's edition (1978) has no manuscript authority and rather that Mount Badon now 'reads naturally as the victory that crowned the career of Ambrosius Aurelianus' (Padel, 1994: 16-18 at p. 17. For further very good reasons to doubt the attribution of Badon to Arthur see Jones, 1964; Bromwich, 1978a: 276; Bromwich *et al*, 1991: 3-4. There seems to be good evidence for the existence of traditions about Badon which did not associate it with Arthur – see Bromwich, 1978a). This is all, of course, of the utmost significance as it further undermines our faith in the 'traditions' recorded in the *Historia Brittonum* – it seems very probable that in the case of Badon we are seeing a battle that had originally been fought by another leader being attributed to Arthur by the ninth century (It is interesting to note that this conclusion has also recently been reached – apparently without knowledge of Padel's work – by Woods (1999: 34-38) who, like Padel, returns to the original manuscript and finds the un-edited text clearly indicating that Gildas saw Badon as being won by Ambrosius). This tendency would appear not to be restricted to the battle of Badon – similar cases can be made for the eleventh, ninth and seventh battles (see Jackson, 1945-6; Jackson, 1949; Bromwich 1975-6 and Padel, 1994: 18-19). The other battles are largely unidentifiable,[8] though the tenth, the 'battle on the bank of a river which is called Tribruit', is recorded elsewhere in very early sources as a traditional battle against werewolves, thus casting further doubt on the *Historia*'s value; similarly a good case can be made for seeing *Cat Coit Celidon* in Chapter 56 as the entirely mythical battle of trees recorded in the archaic poem from the Book of Taliesin, *Kat Godeu*.

Other elements within the body of Chapter 56 appear similarly suspect.

For example, Hanning (1966: 119-20) and Charles-Edwards (1991: 24-25 and 28) have respectively shown that both the number of battles and the reference to Arthur as *dux bellorum* would seem to reflect the needs of the author of the *Historia* rather than any postulated earlier source. Whether or not all of the above conclusions regarding the identification of the battles are accepted it can be said, bringing all this together, that in the *Historia Brittonum,* our only really usable source for a 'historical' Arthur, we have a text which cannot be at all relied upon to pre-date the ninth century and the contents of which can be described as being, at the very least, suspect – as such it can tell us virtually nothing certain about any possible 'historical' Arthur. Indeed, the whole portrayal of Arthur in the *Historia Brittonum* might be seen to reflect the needs and aims of the ninth-century author rather than genuinely ancient tradition, as we might expect given the nature of the text as a whole (see Hanning, 1966; Dumville, 1986; Charles-Edwards, 1991: 21-29; Dumville, 1994; Coe and Young, 1995: 6-7; Howlett, 1998). The failure of the *Historia* as a source of information regarding any historical Arthur and the consequent intangibility of this 'historical' Arthur is a fact which has often been remarked upon: as Dumville has written, 'This is not the stuff of which history can be made' (1977a: 188. See further Jackson, 1945-6; Jackson, 1959a; Jones, 1964; Bromwich, 1974-5; Dumville, 1977a; Charles-Edwards, 1991; Padel, 1994, and also Dumville's (1994) comments on the *Historia* as a whole).

What then of the case for Arthur's historicity? It should be obvious that, even when we restrict ourselves to the best sources for a 'historical' Arthur, as discussed above, we can come to no solid conclusions regarding historicity. The four occurrences of the name Arthur in southern Scotland and southern Wales in the sixth and seventh centuries cannot be seen as evidence for a historical Arthur; indeed they defy interpretation if we have a historical Arthur. The *Y Gododdin* reference clearly reflects a ninth- or tenth-century (and possibly earlier) concept of Arthur as a military 'superhero' but this concept of Arthur could result either from a mythical figure being used as 'the impossible comparison' or a historical figure being mythicised as a paragon of valour – thus this reference cannot help us to reach any solid conclusions. The case for a historical Arthur must therefore be based on only two sources, the *Historia Brittonum* and the *Annales Cambriae*, and neither of these can be seen as a reliable witness to historicity, both being late in date and suspect in content, with the latter very probably being derivative of the former and the former being a synthetic pseudo-history known to portray mythical figures as historical – as such, these sources cannot in any way prove that there was a historical fifth-/sixth-century Arthur and no contemporary or near-contemporary source makes any mention of him.[9] The best we can say is that there existed by the ninth-century at the latest a concept of Arthur as a historical figure; our sources are simply not of the quality that would allow us to come to any firmer conclusion than this.[10]

Against this we have to set the evidence for the existence of a concept of Arthur as a legendary figure. Whatever else we might say about it, *Y Gododdin* (and, it might be added, *Marwnad Cynddylan*) very clearly possesses a concept of Arthur as a mythical 'superhero', not a historical figure. Similarly in the *Historia Brittonum*, the earliest source to portray Arthur as 'historical', Arthur appears not only in the 'historical' light of Chapter 56 but also in a manifestly legendary folkloric light in Chapter 73 (an important point that is too often overlooked, particularly as the legends recorded here are considered to pre-date the ninth century, see Bromwich and Evans, 1992: lxvi), and this same concept of Arthur as a mythical hero is found in a number of other early sources, such as the eighth-century *Preideu Annwfyn* (Padel, 1994; Koch, 1996: 263-65, etc.. See further below). Given this, a concept of Arthur as a figure of myth and legend can be demonstrated to be present as early as (and, indeed, earlier than) a concept of Arthur as a historical figure. Here we must return to the methodological comments made at the beginning of this study. As was there noted, there are numerous examples of mythical or fictional figures being historicised, often in association with some important event of the past, and consequently 'no *a priori* judgements can be made as to whether a figure is, in origin, historical, mythical or fictional – each individual case must (and can only) be decided by a close examination of all the relevant material.' Each of these possibilities is equally as likely to be true, on *a priori* grounds, as the others; the burden of proof lies with all sides. In the absence of such proof we simply cannot assume – in the 'no smoke without fire' mould – that one explanation of figures such as Arthur enjoys priority over the others: it does not. Thus whilst the above 'legendary Arthur' might be the result of a historical figure being mythicised, it is at least equally as likely that, in the absence of good evidence either way, the above 'historical Arthur' was a result of a legendary figure being historicised (it is perhaps worth noting with regards to this that the 'process of historicising legends was a widespread feature of Celtic literary activity in the Middle Ages' (Padel, 1994: 23)).

Hence in answer to the question 'Was there a historical Arthur?', the sources being questioned (*i.e.* the *Historia Brittonum* and the *Annales Cambriae*) can only answer 'perhaps, maybe' – they cannot say 'no there wasn't' for obvious reasons but equally they cannot say 'yes there was': the nature and quality of the sources for a 'historical' Arthur is quite simply such that they neither show nor demand a historical figure to lie behind them and we most definitely cannot assume one in the absence of this. Whilst it is possible that Chapter 56 of the *Historia* reflects, to some extent, the distorted but genuine traditions of a 'historical Arthur', it is at least equally as likely, given the nature of our sources, their claims to reliability and the fact that a concept of Arthur as a mythical hero existed from at least the eighth century, that the opposite is true and that these references simply reflect a legendary figure (such as that of Chapter 73 of the *Historia*) historicised by the ninth century. Arthur could well be a mythical figure portrayed as historical by the author of the *Historia Brittonum* in just the same way as Hengest and Horsa were mythical figures portrayed as historical by both Bede and the author of the *Historia*. In the absence of *a priori* assumptions regarding historicity, a detailed investigation of the 'relevant material' (as required by the above methodology) has left us with a situation in which the information contained within these late references could still reflect *either* a historical figure *or* a legendary figure historicised with no convincing reason, from the internal evidence of these few sources, for accepting one alternative over the other. To put it another way, there is no obvious reason from the material discussed above to prefer the portrayal of Arthur in Chapter 56 of the ninth-century *Historia Brittonum* over that in Chapter 73, or vice versa.[11]

Part of the problem, of course, lies with methodology. When the case for a historical fifth-/sixth-century Arthur is made, it involves trawling the pre-Galfridian source material for anything that might be used to back it up. The interest is not with the pre-Galfridian material itself and with what it tells us but rather with what it can tell us about a possibly historical figure called Arthur. The texts selected to answer this question, as in the above analysis, are thus divorced from the context of the whole body of pre-Galfridian material in which they must surely be viewed and of which they form an integral part. By asking 'Was there a historical Arthur?' one *forces* the texts to answer 'perhaps, maybe'; they have no other choice because, on the basis of the few sources selected and the viewing of these few sources in isolation, they are incapable of denying that there was such a figure just as they are incapable of confirming it. As such this 'perhaps, maybe' is in reality valueless. What this means is that conclusions regarding Arthur's historicity can and should only be drawn via a sound methodology, namely by looking at *all* the available evidence and allowing it to 'lead', not forcing it to conform to preconceived notions. The *Historia Brittonum* and *Annales Cambriae* references must be seen in the context of all the early Arthurian material, not as discrete pieces of information that can be mined for 'facts'. No judgements of any value can be made by attacking the pre-Galfridian corpus in a piecemeal fashion – one has to look at the weight of the body of evidence as a whole. To quote Padel, 'the nature of the inquiry, which hitherto has always started with the natural question "was there a historical Arthur?", has determined its outcome ("Yes, perhaps")' (Padel, 1994: 2. Ashe (1995) also makes this point). By commencing an examination of the pre-Galfridian material with a view to discovering (or, at least, investigating) a truly historical figure of the post-Roman period the conclusions reached are unavoidably biased and the investigation ignores the majority of the available early evidence.

We must therefore ask, what is the nature of Arthur in the pre-

Galfridian sources with which we are here primarily concerned with? Where does the 'weight' of the evidence 'lead' us? What is the context of the 'historical' sources? The most recent attempt to define this 'nature' (which then proceeds, after doing this, to adopt the above methodology and look at the *Annales* and *Historia* references in the context of this nature) is by Oliver Padel.[12] The conclusion reached is that, when the pre-Galfridian sources are approached without such preconceived agendas and *a priori* assumptions as described above, the results prove to be most interesting: 'if the collective evidence is first allowed to speak for itself, its weight is quite different.' (Padel, 1994: 2). In non-Galfridian tradition, Arthur was very clearly 'the leader of a band of heroes who live outside of society, whose main world is one of magical animals, giants and other wonderful happenings, located in the wild parts of the landscape.' (Padel, 1994: 14); Arthur is portrayed as a figure of pan-Brittonic[13] folklore and mythology, associated with the Otherworld, supernatural enemies and superhuman deeds, not history. This concept of Arthur occurs in both the very earliest of these sources (earlier than and contemporary with the earliest references to a possibly 'historical Arthur') and, indeed, in the vast majority of the non-Galfridian sources, with these sources consistent in their portrayal of Arthur. For example, it appears in the eighth-century or earlier mythological poem *Preideu Annwfyn* (see Koch, 1996: 263-65), the very early mythological poem *Kat Godeu* (see Ford, 1977 for a translation), Chapter 73 of the *Historia Brittonum* (the folklore contained in which is considered to be 'already ancient by the ninth century' (Bromwich and Evans 1992: lxvi)), *Pa gur yv y porthaur?* (which might be as early as the ninth century, or even the eighth, and is, itself, simply a summary of many earlier entirely mythical Arthurian tales (Bromwich, 1978b: 21; Koch, 1996; Koch, 1994: 1127; Edel, 1983)), and *Culhwch ac Olwen* (which was written in the eleventh century but is a literary composition based on a number of earlier legendary Arthurian tales brought together with the 'giant's daughter' folklore tale-type – the Arthurian material is generally considered to represent the same body of very early non-historical tales as *Pa gur yv y porthaur?*, *Historia Brittonum* Chapter 73 and *Preideu Annwfyn* do: see Edel, 1983; Bromwich and Evans, 1992).

Padel is not at all alone in seeing this as the context of the *Historia Brittonum* and *Annales Cambriae* references, though he has given the subject its fullest treatment. Two of the foremost authorities on early Arthurian literature, Rachel Bromwich and D. Simon Evans, have recently written that 'Arthur was above all else... a defender of his country against every kind of danger, both internal and external: a slayer of giants and witches, a hunter of monstrous animals – giant boars, a savage cat monster, a winged serpent (or dragon) – and also, as it appears from *Culhwch* and *Preiddeu Annwn*, a releaser of prisoners. This concept of Arthur is substantiated from all the early sources: the poems *Pa Gur* and *Preiddeu Annwn*, the Triads, the Saints Lives, and the *Mirabilia* attached to the *Historia Brittonum*... in early literature he belongs, like Fionn, to the realm of mythology rather than to that of history.' (Bromwich and Evans (edd.) 1992: xxviii-xxix. See Ford (1983) for some very interesting supplementary evidence for the view that the pre-Galfridian Arthur belongs to the realms of mythology. The above comments on the 'nature of Arthur' in early literature represent the general view among Celticists of this question, see for example Ford 1986; Jarman, 1983; Ross, 2001, chapter 4; and note 14 below). In essence, the vast majority of the non-Galfridian material, including the earliest sources, paints a notably consistent picture of Arthur as a pan-Brittonic folkloric hero, a peerless warrior of giant-like stature who leads a band of superhuman heroes that roam the wild places of the landscape, who raids the Otherworld whilst being intimately associated with it, who fights and protects Britain from supernatural enemies, who hunts wondrous animals and who takes part in mythical battles, and hence the 'weight' of this evidence indicates not a historical origin for Arthur but rather a legendary one (it is particularly worthy of note that Arthur is *never* associated with either the Saxons or Badon in the vast majority of the material, despite the fact that such an association is usually said to be the reason for his fame, and when this association does appear it is *only* present in those sources which are directly derivative of *Historia Brittonum* Chapter 56). In fact, the Fionn parallel in the above quote is also noted by Padel in his article – it is his convincing conclusion that the nature of Arthur evidenced in the pre-Galfridian sources is *very* similar indeed to the nature of Fionn in Gaelic literature, this Fionn being an entirely mythical character (originally a god) who became associated (*i.e.* historicised) with the repelling of the Viking invasions of Ireland and who had a list of battles against his 'foes' attached to his name (for Fionn see Ó hÓgáin, 1988; Padel (1994) summarises some of the parallels on pp. 19-23). Van Hamel made some very similar observations regarding the nature of Arthur in the early sources and the very close parallels between him and Fionn, noting that it was but a natural, logical step 'to represent a hero of this type [*i.e.* a protector of Britain against supernatural threats] as a victor over the Saxons' (1934, quote at p. 231. See also Murphy, 1953: 213-17; MacKillop, 1986: 63-64; Koch, 1996: 261; Ross, 2001: chapter 4).[14]

How does this affect the question of Arthur's historicity? What then of those references to a 'historical' Arthur which, when viewed in isolation, can only answer the question 'Was there a historical Arthur?' with 'perhaps; maybe' and could at least just as easily represent a legendary figure historicised as the distorted remembrances of a 'genuinely' historical figure? To recapitulate, the conclusions resulting from the above discussion are:

> (A) that one cannot assume that a character is historical simply because a medieval source claims that this is the case: such *a priori*

assumptions are demonstrably false (Hengest & Horsa and Fionn being good examples of mythical figures historicised by later writers) and are thus unacceptable. One can only say that there was/has to have been a historical Arthur once all the material has been evaluated and this is shown to be the case. There is no possible justification for simply assuming this to be the case – 'historical' explanations of figures such as Arthur do not, on *a priori* grounds, enjoy priority over other explanations. Indeed, it should be remembered that the 'process of historicising legends was a widespread feature of Celtic literary activity in the Middle Ages.' (Padel, 1994: 23).

(B) that the few usable sources that we have which portray Arthur as 'historical' could very easily represent *either* a legendary figure historicised *or* the distorted traditions of a genuinely historical Arthur. Each possibility is equally as likely as the other judging from the internal evidence of the sources and, as such, no conclusions can be reached on the matter of historicity – there may have been a historical Arthur but at least equally as well there may not have been.

(C) that whilst it is true to say, as in (B) above, that *Historia Brittonum* Chapter 56 etc. could just as easily reflect a legendary figure historicised as a genuinely historical personage, this method of analysis fails to answer the question of Arthur's historicity satisfactorily. By treating the 'historical Arthur' sources in isolation rather than in the context of the whole body of non-Galfridian Arthurian literature of which they form an integral part, valuable information is ignored that is essential to the interpretation of these sources and, as such, no conclusions of any value can be drawn. To give an example, we might have a charter purporting to be a grant of land to a monastery from a king. When this charter is viewed on its own the evidence internal to the charter may be such that no decision can be made over whether it is genuine or a forgery – in the absence of convincing evidence for either option each possibility might be said to be equally as likely. If, however, this charter is looked at in the context of all the other charters from that monastery then the situation is rather different: thus if, for example, all the other charters from that monastery appear to be forgeries then it seems very likely indeed that this charter too is a forgery. In the context of the body of material of which it forms an integral and inseparable part, it becomes clear that the two possibilities allowed by the internal evidence are not in fact equally as likely – when viewed in light of all the other material it remains remotely possible that the charter may be genuine but it is infinitely more probable that it is a forgery. In other words, the serious possibility that the charter is genuine only really existed because the charter was being analysed outside of the body of material of which it is an integral part, something which caused information essential to the interpretation of the charter to be ignored – when it is viewed within the context of all the material, there is simply no reason to think that it might be genuine; the charter's context is such that this is not, in the absence of evidence in its favour, a serious possibility. In the same way, conclusions regarding historicity can only be drawn from looking at the 'historical Arthur' texts in the context of the whole body of early material. The *Historia Brittonum* and *Annales Cambriae* references must be seen in the context of all the early Arthurian material, not as discrete pieces of information that can be mined for 'facts'; no judgements of any value can be made by attacking the pre-Galfridian corpus in a piecemeal fashion – one has to look at the weight of the body of evidence as a whole and allow it to 'lead'. To do otherwise simply biases the conclusions and ignores the vast majority of the available early evidence.

(D) that the weight of the non-Galfridian material (early and late) provides, as numerous scholars have noted, a very clear and consistent picture of Arthur as a thoroughly legendary figure of folklore and myth not associated in any way with either the Saxons or Badon, and with this figure resembling in many of its characteristics (and, indeed the development of its legend) the Gaelic Fionn who was a mythical figure – originally a god – later historicised with battles against foreign invaders.

These four relatively uncontroversial conclusions have, as should be obvious, some very interesting consequences for the question of Arthur's historicity. Following them through, it seems clear that if those few references which portray Arthur as historical are seen in the context of the material as a whole – as they have to be – then the weight of the material is such that there is absolutely no justification for believing there to have been a historical figure of the fifth or sixth century named Arthur who is the basis for all later legends. When the 'historical' references are pulled out of their context and viewed in isolation then, as we have seen, they *may possibly* represent the distorted traditions of a historical figure but at least equally as well they may not. However, when they are viewed, as they must be, in the context of the body of material of which they are an integral part this 'maybe' evaporates. All the other evidence, the vast majority of the early material, portrays Arthur as an entirely legendary figure from the same mould as the Gaelic Fionn, and he is never connected in this material in any way with either the Saxons or Badon. As such there is simply no reason to think that there was a historical Arthur. The 'maybe' only appears when it is forced to, when the few references to a 'historical' Arthur are divorced from their context and made to answer questions regarding the possibility of a historical Arthur. If we ask what the material actually says rather than try and force any preconceived notions upon it then it appears, as Padel has observed, to very clearly tell of a legendary figure of folklore named *Art(h)ur* who was historicised in much the same way as Hengest or Fionn were – the serious possibility of there ever having been a 'historical Arthur' who was the 'original' from whom all the later tales spring is simply a construct based on a misuse of the sources. Therefore, rather than the folkloric Arthur evidenced in the *Historia Brittonum* Chapter 73 being an elaboration of the 'historical' Arthur of Chapter 56, this 'legendary' Arthur would appear to be 'the true one, and the "historical" Arthur... the secondary development.' (Padel, 1994: 30), a logical extension of his folkloric role, with not only the existence of Arthur but also his association with the fifth and sixth centuries being seen as most probably spurious (with regards to this, it should be noted that the post-Roman period was not the only period into which Arthur was historicised – see below). To put it another way, the context of the few 'historical' references is such that the onus of proof would seem to come to lie firmly on the shoulders of those who would have a historical fifth-/sixth-century Arthur as the basis for all the later legends – in the absence of proof of historicity (and in the absence of *a priori* assumptions and the forcing of preconceived agendas onto the sources) there is simply no reason to think that a 'historical Arthur' is a serious possibility.

We must consequently ask, can the 'evidence' for a 'historical' Arthur of the fifth/sixth century live up to this burden of proof? Does it provide any reason to believe that there was a fifth- or sixth-century figure named Arthur? Taken on its own, it can be legitimately said that the answer to this is 'no'. Even when viewed outside of the context of the whole body of early material, thus in the most advantageous circumstances, it could (as has been seen above) only produce the answer 'perhaps; maybe'; the Arthur portrayed in the *Historia Brittonum* and the *Annales Cambriae* could be easily understood as *either* a historical figure *or* a legendary one historicised. In the context of the pre-Galfridian material this answer becomes meaningless due to the shifting of the burden of proof – as such the 'maybe' has to be taken as a 'no'. The *Historia* and the *Annales* do not provide the necessary proof that would allow us to disregard the context of the pre-Galfridian material (particularly as the latter is very probably derivative of the former, and the former is known to portray mythical figures as historical) and thus on the basis of these pieces of evidence we are forced to conclude that there is, at present, no cogent reason to think that there was a historical post-Roman Arthur. Instead he is best seen, like Fionn for the Gaelic regions, as a folkloric hero, living in the wilds of the landscape and protecting Britain from all kinds of supernatural threats, just as the vast majority of the evidence suggests.[15] Indeed it is worth pointing out once more that the *Historia Brittonum*'s account of Arthur in Chapter 56 not only appears to include deeds of a number of earlier warriors such as Urien of Rheged and Ambrosius Aurelianus, but also identifiable mythical elements which have been historicised in this text – the possibly very early poem *Kat Godeu* would appear to be concerned with a mythical battle in which Arthur plays some (perhaps major) part and in which the trees of *Coed Celyddon* are magically animated to fight, thus showing the battle of *Coit Celidon* ('the Caledonian Forest') recorded in Chapter 56 of the *Historia Brittonum* in a very interesting light. Similarly, the 'battle on the bank of a river which is called Tribruit' in Chapter 56 of the *Historia* appears elsewhere, in the early *Pa gur yv y porthaur?* (which summarises a number of pre-existing Arthurian tales) as an entirely mythical battle against werewolves (With regards to the battles named in the *Historia Brittonum*, it should perhaps be emphasised that there is no reason to think that all of the battles used to historicise Arthur were real historical battles – at least some of the battles used to historicise Fionn seem to have been invented spontaneously for the purposes of historicisation and this could well be the case here (a fact that may well explain some of the problems in identifying the battles in *Historia Brittonum* Chapter 56, see Padel, 1994: 21; Jackson, 1945-6)).

The above conclusions may well help explain certain puzzling features of the Arthurian legend, in particular the strange absence which has often been noted (*e.g.* Bromwich, 1978a: 274; Thomas, 1995: 389) of Arthur from the early Welsh genealogies. Such texts are perhaps best understood as dynastic 'propaganda' (see Dumville, 1977a; 1977b) and if Arthur was generally held to have been a great historical leader at the time of their compilation, his absence would be very puzzling; if, on the other hand, he was not viewed in this light but instead as a pan-Brittonic folkloric hero then his absence is entirely comprehensible (see Gowans, 1988 for a similar situation involving Cai). This notion, of a reluctance to use the name of a national folkloric hero, can also provide the only viable explanation of one of the first pieces of evidence examined here, that is the four (or five) occurrences of the name *Arthur* in sixth- and seventh-century contexts, as Padel has recently noted (1994: 24). Padel observes, as others have done before him, that all the occurrences of the name 'Arthur' are recorded in Gaelic sources and occur in the context of the Irish settlers in western Wales and Scotland (see Bromwich 1975-6; Barber, 1972) and he suggests that the absence of this name in British contexts is due to Arthur being regarded 'with exceptional awe' as a legendary hero and Protector of Britain, whilst the Irish 'when they came into contact with the folklore as a result of their settlements in western Britain, need not have felt such reverence or reluctance' (Padel, 1994: 24) and consequently they made use of this name (the date of adoption of this name would, of course, be dependent on complex cultural interactions and developments and thus the fact that it was not immediately adopted should not be seen as significant). As well as explaining satisfactorily all the available evidence this suggestion gains a considerable amount of credence from the fact that detailed study of the Welsh genealogical tracts reveals that not one single person of British descent in Wales bore the name 'Arthur' in the genealogies until the late sixteenth century at the earliest, a situation Bartrum suggests may well be because the name carried some sort of superstition with it (Bartrum, 1965). If Arthur was to be viewed as historical rather than legendary, then explanation of these three pieces of information (the absence of Arthur from the early royal genealogies; the sudden occurrence of four people named Arthur in the context of the Irish settlers in Wales and Scotland; the fact that not one single person in Wales of British descent can be shown to bear the name Arthur until at least the late sixteenth century) would be a very difficult problem.

Another 'puzzling' feature particularly worthy of note is the fact that, outside of the *Historia Brittonum* Chapter 56, the *Annales Cambriae* (which is derivative of the *Historia Brittonum*), the possibly eleventh-century Breton *Life of Saint Goueznou* (which paraphrases the *Historia Brittonum*) and William of Malmesbury's twelfth-century *Gesta Regum* (which again paraphrases the *Historia Brittonum* and the *Annales Cambriae*), Arthur is *never* associated in the whole body of pre-Galfridian literature with the post-Roman defeat of the Saxons – a very strange situation surely for one who is supposed to be famed *because* of such an association. However, it fits with the fact that there seems to be good reason to believe that there was a separate non-Arthurian tradition regarding the battle of Badon (which, again, is only ever associated with Arthur in the few sources (above) that are directly derivative of the *Historia Brittonum* – in sources that are not connected with the *Historia*, Badon is not linked with Arthur nor is Arthur linked with Badon, see Bromwich, 1978a), the single event which puts Arthur's supposed victories into the realms of history and which, in essence, defines his role as defeater of the Saxons. Both of these features, especially when taken together, appear highly suggestive. One has to ask, why, if the reason that Arthur was so honoured in Welsh tradition was that he led the British resistance and won the famous battle of Badon, this is ignored and even perhaps doubted by the 'guardians of Welsh tradition'? Why, in the vast majority of cases, both early and late, did they instead paint a consistent picture of Arthur as a figure of folklore who was very similar indeed to the Gaelic Fionn, an entirely mythical figure who came to be historicised with great battles against the Viking invaders of Ireland? Indeed, one might further ask why, if Arthur was universally famous not for being a folkloric Protector of Britain but rather the defeater of the Saxons, the Cornish felt perfectly able to *totally* ignore his Saxon associations and instead historicise him into distant antiquity *and* into the period of the *Viking* incursions (see Hunt, 1881; Courtney, 1890)?[16]

Such considerations as those above, quite apart from the fact that the adoption of a sound methodology forces us to conclude that Arthur was in all probability a folkloric 'Protector of Britain', suggest that such an interpretation is the correct one.[17] A historical fifth- or sixth-century Arthur is not in anyway necessary to the understanding of the pre-Galfridian Arthur and the evidence we have makes the postulation of such a figure not only unnecessary but also completely unjustifiable.

3. The Historicisation of Arthur

Whatever else Arthur is, he is a composite figure. Through the centuries the concept of Arthur did not stay the same – there is no 'standard' Arthurian legend as this legend is the result of Arthur attracting to himself both the deeds and characteristics of other tales and characters. This bears directly on the above question – we cannot conclude that there was no historical Arthur as there was, to the extent that certain texts, notably the *Historia Brittonum*, the *Annales Cambriae* and Geoffrey's *Historia Regum Britanniae*, have a concept of Arthur that is clearly historical. While the Arthur they portray cannot be seen, in light of the above, as the 'original', it is surely still a valuable exercise to inquire as to whose deeds were being later attributed to Arthur, as these deeds are an integral part of many later portrayals of Arthur and as such do constitute part of the origins of Arthur.

What then of the Arthur of *Historia Brittonum* Chapter 56? While we might legitimately look for an 'original' for each of the battles, we also have to ask whether the whole concept presented in Chapter 56 of the *Historia* is based on a single figure. The prime candidate for this 'honour' has to be, naturally, Ambrosius Aurelianus. In Gildas's *De Excidio Britanniae* Ambrosius is given prominence as the initiator of the British counter-attack which, after the fighting of several battles, culminates in the battle of Badon, just as Arthur in the *Historia Brittonum* initiates the British counter-attack which, after the fighting of several battles, culminates in the battle of Badon. On the basis of this we may well be able to say that, to some extent, we do have a historical Arthur – Ambrosius – in the sense that the concept of Arthur as a historical figure and the framework for historicisation was based on his deeds.[18]

With regards to the individual battles, this is perhaps more difficult. As noted in the preceding discussion, the 'battle on the bank of a river which is called Tribruit' and *Cat Coit Celidon* may well be actual Arthurian mythic battles. Others may be 'real' or they could be invented: Badon, as has been argued above, can be easily associated with Ambrosius, just like the whole framework of historicisation, and *Breguoin* appears elsewhere in very early sources as a battle fought by Urien of Rheged. Others however could simply be made up, as is thought to be the case for the battles used to historicise Fionn in his battle-list and as has been suggested earlier in this study. The problem with undertaking any exercise of this kind is the fact that the names given to the battles could represent many areas – only a few can actually be called certain and on the basis of this list theories of a Southern Arthur, a Midland Arthur and a Northern Arthur have all been constructed. A partial solution is to split the list up into separate characters as above but it should be remembered that it can only be taken so far. The desire to identify these battles is often great but this should not prevent us from recognising that with sufficient 'ingenuity' they can be made to fit just about any area and many may not, in fact, be identifiable or even have identifications.

With regards to the whole question of historicity and historicisation, it has been suggested that, rather than ask whether there is any justification for postulating a historical Arthur, we should ask whether any candidate fits the 'facts' – certainly the undertaking of such an exercise is very beneficial but it probably doesn't actually show anything, at least with regards to historicity. To take an example, several people have suggested, over the years, that Ambrosius is Arthur on the basis of *Historia Brittonum* Chapter 56. However, what they see can be one of two things – either they are seeing the 'truth', that Ambrosius was Arthur, or they are seeing a partial truth, that the portrayal of Arthur in these sources was based on Ambrosius but that this is a secondary development of a folkloric Arthur; in a sense Ambrosius was Arthur but not in the sense that most people would mean when seeking an answer to this question. How does one get away from this? The only way I can see is by adopting the above methodology, by asking what justification there is for postulating a historical Arthur. Indeed, it should further be pointed out that there are certain dangers in looking for characters who 'fit the facts' – to take the example of Chapter 56 of the *Historia Brittonum* once more, with sufficient 'imagination' and linguistic gymnastics, as has been noted, the list of battles in this Chapter can be made to fit just about any locality one can think of and as such these theories are mutually cancelling and methodologically indefensible – thus Collingwood (1929) succeeded in 'discovering' all the battles in the south-east, which happily fitted his theory that Arthur only fought the Jutes; Anscombe (1904) 'found' that all the battles were fought in the Midlands; and Skene (1868: I, 52-58) 'discovered' that all the battles could be identified with places in Scotland! The above methodological considerations hold whether one is looking at models for historicisation or 'Arthurian originals' – a vast literature has been generated, both online and offline, by the search for historical characters who 'fit the facts' but the simple truth of the matter is that the vast majority of these efforts are methodologically indefensible. While internally consistent, these theories are all mutually cancelling, explain only a tiny portion of the legend, if any of it, and an almost infinite number of such identifications can be made (especially when a shot of 'ingenuity' is added to the mix), all impossible to disprove but equally nearly all invalid.

Another aspect of the Arthurian legend that has been much discussed is the Gallic invasion. This aspect of Arthur's character first appears in Geoffrey of Monmouth's *Historia Regum Britanniae*, the Breton *Life of Saint Goueznou* and *Culhwch ac Olwen* (though the reference in the latter is probably either Galfridian in origins or simple fantasy, see Bromwich and Evans, 1992: 58-59). Some, notably Geoffrey Ashe (1981; 1985; 1995) and C. Scott Littleton and Linda Malcor (1994), would see this as an original element of the Arthurian tradition. However, as Padel (1995: 109-10), Bromwich (1991: 5-6) and others have noted, there is nothing at all suggestive of such a notion of Arthur as a Gallic adventurer in the early insular sources (except for *Culhwch*, but see above) and therefore if it is an early element it should be seen as absent from the insular tradition and thus continental in origin (as is suggested by its appearance in the Breton life). Perhaps the best explanation is to see the Gallic campaign as a non-insular (Breton?) historicisation of the pan-Brittonic folkloric Arthur in much the same way as suggested for *Historia Brittonum* Chapter 56 but in this case with a composite remembrance of British campaigns on the continent – attention might be particularly drawn to Riotamus (on the basis of Ashe's evidence) and the powerful legend of the Emperor Maximus, the Welsh *Maxen Wledig*, who was believed to have conquered Rome and afterwards to have left his troops as the first colonisers of Brittany, as candidates for such a 'historicisation'.

4. The Origins of Arthur

The origins of Arthur are always going to be controversial. Given the above conclusion that there is no reason to believe that the concept of Arthur as a fifth-/sixth-century warrior is anything other than a secondary development of the legendary/mythical Arthur seen in (for example) *Preideu Annwfyn*, *Pa gur yv y porthaur?*, *Historia Brittonum* Chapter 73 and *Culhwch ac Olwen*, the origins of Arthur are essentially open. While many theories of origins, each internally consistent, can and probably will be constructed, at present there are two main theories for the origins of any legendary Arthur [though see now Green, 2007: chapter 5 for a thorough discussion].

The first has been supported over the years by Kemp Malone (1924-5), Oliver Padel (1994: 31; 1995: 111-12), and C. Scott Littleton and Linda Malcor (1994), and suggests that the second-century Lucius Artorius Castus is the original Arthur (see Malone, 1924-5 on this figure), though Padel supports this only very tentatively. Malone based his theory on the fact that the Latin personal name *Artorius* ('plowman') would have developed into *Art(h)ur* in the vernacular quite regularly (the long *o* of Latin loan-words regularly appears as *u* in Welsh and such endings as *-ius* are dropped, thus changing *Artorius* into *Art(h)ur*), and on the Gallic campaign as evidenced in Geoffrey of Monmouth. On the latter argument, one would have to say that not all would accept its validity, with alternative explanations being available for the existence of this element in Geoffrey's work (see above). Therefore the case, as set out by Malone and nodded at by Padel, for Lucius Artorius Castus as the 'original' Arthur is, initially at least, based on the name alone. If the *Artorius* derivation is accepted as the only likely etymology of the name Arthur then this identification does seem to be the most reasonable and it would help explain the continental invasion tale (though it is not necessary to any such explanation). However, it requires us to see Arthur as a figure who was first of all historical, then became totally absorbed into Celtic folklore and then, at a later point, was historicised into a entirely different era from that in which he had his origins. Whilst not impossible, some might think it a little over complicated. In recent years though, an alternative argument in favour of Lucius Artorius Castus has emerged – Littleton and Malcor (1994) have argued that in post-Galfridian Romance a number of features can be discerned in the legend which could be Scythian in origins, and the only evidence of Scythians in Britain comes from the second century, when a group of Sarmatians were brought over to northern Britain as Roman cavalry by one Lucius Artorius Castus. Essentially the authors argue that the 'most important' of Arthurian figures and themes (which include, according to Littleton and Malcor, the sword in the stone, the Holy Grail and the return of Arthur's sword to the lake), on the basis of the parallels they observe, originated in the culture of the nomadic horse-riding peoples who inhabited the Eurasian steppes, an area known as Scythia to the Romans and Greeks, and that they were imported into western Europe by two of these tribes, the Sarmatians and the Alans – in their eyes Arthur is simply a different name attached to the the legend of Batraz, the hero of the Scythian Narts tales (Lancelot is seen in almost identical terms, with 'Arthur' being the insular British development of this Batraz, via the Sarmatians, and Lancelot the continental development, via the Alans).

Certainly such a view of the process is intriguing, the parallels identified are very interesting, and by simply having Lucius Artorius Castus give his name to a pre-existing folkloric cycle one can avoid the problems of having him as the origins of such a cycle (though one could object that he could have just as easily simply given his name to a pre-existing *insular Celtic* folkloric cycle, perhaps related to the Fionn cycle). The main problem with this theory is, however, the 1000 years of silent transmission of these Scythian folktales as central to the Arthurian legend that the authors require us to accept, both in Britain and on the continent – all the 'Scythian' elements appear in the post-Galfridian works, from Chrétien de Troyes onwards, and some of the most striking apparent parallels between the Arthurian legend and the eastern Batraz story make their very first appearances in Malory's *Le Morte Darthur*! There is simply no trace of Lancelot in continental literature before Chrétien de Troyes in the twelfth century and none of the 'most important of Arthurian themes' are even hinted at in the reasonably large body of insular Arthurian traditions that we have preserved in *Culhwch*, *Pa gur?*, the Triads etc. – Arthur, as he appears in non-Galfridian tradition, looks like an entirely insular figure with an insular cycle (see Padel, 1994, 1995; Bromwich and Evans, 1992; Ford, 1983; Edel, 1983; etc.) and it is only in post-Galfridian materials that he gains what Littleton and Malcor see as the 'essential elements' of his legend when making him simply Batraz by another name (with regards to Lancelot, a large part of their thesis depends on, aside from 1000 years of silent transmission, their etymologising his name from *(A)lanz-lot*, 'the Alan's parcel of land' etc., the validity of which has been questioned by a recent reviewer (Wood, 1995: 126)). Certainly the evidence that Littleton and Malcor present is highly suggestive of *some sort* of connection between the post-Galfridian Arthurian legend and Scythian legend but the parallels they observe should, in the absence of any evidence for its presence in non-Galfridian tradition in Britain and previous to the twelfth century on the continent, very probably be seen as late additions to the Arthurian legend, not elements that are both early and central to the tradition, whatever the ultimate origins of these elements are in western Europe (see Wadge, 1987 and Kennedy, 1995: 129-30 for alternative methods of transmission, including common Indo-European heritage). As such, the 'evidence' of Scythian parallels cannot realistically be used to support the theory that Lucius Artorius Castus supplied Arthur with his name and, consequently, this notion rests entirely on the derivation of *Art(h)ur* from the Latin *Artorius*.

The second theory represents a challenge to this by suggesting that, while the *Artorius* derivation of Arthur is perfectly acceptable, so too is a native derivation. Old Welsh *Arthur* would regularly develop in the vernacular from Brittonic **Arto-uiros*, 'bear-man' > Archaic Welsh *Art(u)ur* > *Arthur*, although for the Middle Welsh period and later we would have to rely on petrification in this form [something which is not entirely unheard of – see now Green, 2007: 190]. The suggestion of a native derivation gains additional support from the fact that, in Latin documents, the name 'Arthur' is always written *Art(h)ur*/*Art(h)urus* etc. and never in the form *Artorius* (the form *Art(h)urus* is, of course, fully in keeping with the British derivation as non-Latin names often had the normal ending *-us* added to give them a Latin appearance and to provide them with a basis for Latin case endings – thus British *Art(h)ur* would have been Latinised as *Art(h)urus*. It should of course be noted that, while suggestive, the absence of *Artorius* forms could simply reflect the total absorption of the name *Artorius* into pan-Brittonic folklore). A British origin for the name Arthur is further given credence by the frequent use of Welsh *art(h)* ('bear') figuratively to denote a warrior, thus making the name appropriate for a figure who is, in non-Galfridian tradition, a ferocious (bearlike?) fighter and a 'peerless military superhero' (see Bromwich *et al*, 1991: 5-6; Griffin, 1994). The connection between Arthur and the bear was certainly made by medieval authors. Thus in the non-Galfridian Welsh poem *Ymddiddan Arthur a'r Eryr* ('The Dialogue of Arthur and the Eagle'), Arthur is repeatedly described as 'bear of men' (*arth gwyr*), 'bear of the host', and so forth. Similarly the Sawley Glosses, which are marginal additions to a late twelfth- or early thirteenth-century manuscript of the *Historia Brittonum*, comment that '"Arthur" translated into Latin means "horrible bear"...' (Coe and Young, 1995: 11). Finally, Rachel Bromwich has shown that that *Arcturus*, deriving from the Greek word for 'Keeper of the Bears' and denoting a bright star associated with the Great Bear (Ursa Major) constellation (see Rogers, 1998: 86; Griffen, 1994: 83-84), was a genuine non-Galfridian variant form of Arthur's name,

> and one for which there is good reason to believe there was traditional authority. *Arcturus*, like *Arctos* (=Ursa Major or 'the bear') was often used to denote the polar region, the far north, and there are references in Latin literature to the savage and tempestuous weather associated with the rising and setting of the star *Arcturus*. By extension, the name of the star gave rise to the adj. used by Lucan for the Gauls as *arctoas gentes* 'people of the (far) north', *Bellum Civile* V, 661. To name a hero *Arcturus* could therefore be taken to imply that he belonged to the north (*i.e.* to north-west Europe), and that he was 'bear-like' in his characteristics. (Bromwich, 1978a: 544-45. See also Griffen, 1994: 82ff.)

The above references would appear to favour a native derivation and such a derivation would seem to be most in harmony with the nature of the pre-Galfridian Arthur as a pan-Brittonic legendary hero, a peerless warrior associated with local topographic folklore, avoiding the need to postulate the complicated scenario of having a historical figure totally mythicised and then historicised into a period with which he was previously unrelated.[19] Indeed, even if we were to reject a derivation from Brittonic **Arto-uiros* on the basis of the need for petrification in the Old Welsh form, it needs to be remembered that other derivations than *Artorius* are still possible, some similarly involving Brittonic *Arto-*, 'bear, warrior, hero'. In fact, even if the *Artorius* derivation is correct it may well not carry with it any implications of possible historicity, given the tendency for the Romanisation of nomenclature seen in both personal and divine names from Britain and

Gaul, either through wholesale replacement or new suffixes [there is now a full discussion of all this in Green, 2007: 178-94].

If a derivation involving Brittonic *Arto-* is accepted as possible and fitting, one might point not only to the figurative uses of British *art(h)*, Brittonic *Arto-*, but also, very tentatively, to the evidence for Celtic 'bear-cults', including divinities such as *Dea Artio* ('bear goddess'), *Andarta* ('the powerful bear'), *Artgenos* ('son of the bear god') and *Artaios* ('bearlike') (Ford, 1986: 94; MacCulloch, 1911: 212-13; Ross, 1992: 434-35). With regards to this, it is interesting to note that many of the 'bear-gods' appear to have been forest gods (see Olmsted, 1994: 429-30, 431) – Arthur was associated from possibly a very early period with a mythical battle of the trees of the great Caledonian forest (in the poem *Kat Godeu*) and his court, in pre-Galfridian tradition, was at *Kelli wic*, 'forest grove', though one wouldn't wish to press this point. Whilst he need be no more than a legendary 'hero', there is no bar to Arthur actually having originally been a god, just as Fionn was (see Ó hÓgáin, 1988). It all depends on how far one is willing to go, though *if* Arthur was *originally* such a mythological figure then there may well be a more plausible divine origin for him than as a bear-god, and one which still explains the name [see Green, 2007: 229-40]. Indeed, mythologist Ann Ross has recently come out in support of Arthur originally being a 'Celtic deity of an all purpose type', a warrior and protective god – the 'divine protector' – of the Britons, who closely paralleled the Gaelic Fionn (Ross, 2001: chapter 4).

There are, naturally, many other possible native derivations and mythological origins for Arthur that have been proposed over the years and which may, in the light of all the above, deserve re-examination, for example, Sir John Rhys's championing of Arthur as a culture-hero (Rhys, 1891); Kemp Malone's suggestion that Arthur and Uthr (the latter *was* a pre-Galfridian character) were one and the same person, both being a Celtic god (Malone,1924); and the intriguing evidence for a folkloric belief that Arthur is a crow, raven or a Cornish Chough ('a red-legged crow'). This latter is well-documented in the folklore of south-western Britain and Brittany (see Hunt, 1881: II, 308-09; Courtney, 1890: 58; Loomis, 1958: 16; Bruce, 1923: I, 34, n. 74), the earliest occurrences being in the 1582 Chronicle of Julian del Castillo and three times in the works of Cervantes,[20] casting some suggestive light on the *Y Gododdin* reference that '[Gorddur] used to entice down black ravens in front of the wall of the fortified town – though he was no Arthur' and the possible derivation of Arthur's name from *arddhu* 'very black' (see MacKillop, 1998 and Spence, 1945: 146 [the connection with the crow/raven/chough may have a more plausible explanation than this, however – Green, 2007: 145-51, 237]). However, caution must once more be urged – just as an almost infinite number of *historical* prototypes for Arthur can be identified with enough enthusiasm, it seems very likely that a similar number of *mythical* prototypes can also be identified and, as such, the methodological comments made with regards to the identification of 'historical Arthurs' must be applied to this problem also.

5. Endnotes

[1] Another example of a non-historical personage who is often mistakenly thought to be historical is, as Geoffrey Ashe has recently pointed out ('The Origins of the Arthurian Legend', *Arthuriana*, 5.3 (1995), pp. 1-24 at p. 6), Sherlock Holmes: 'He is so vivid that countless people have taken his existence for granted. For many years the office on the site of his Baker Street lodgings (not really identifiable, but given a street number) received a steady trickle of letters addressed to him... Yet we know how his saga began, and it was in Conan Doyle's imagination, not in the biography of a real detective.' It needs to be said that the above are only interesting *examples* of the historicisation of mythical/fictional characters and that the question of whether such historicisation occurs does not by any means rest on these few examples alone (or even primarily). That historicisation could and did happen is beyond doubt – not everything we are told by medieval authors about events many centuries in the past need be the complete 'truth', even if the authors themselves might have believed it.

[2] Only names in the form *Art(h)ur* and its Latinisations concern us here as they are the only relevant forms. The case is occasionally made (though not in academic literature) that all names with the element *art(h)* should be considered – this is, however, simply a very common personal and place name element (in early Gaul, Ireland and Britain) meaning 'bear' and, as such, there is absolutely no reason to think that there is any special relationship between the large number of names with *art(h)* as an element and the name *Art(h)ur* – they are all separate and distinct names. This important fact relates directly to a very recent find during the excavations at Tintagel of a sixth-century stone inscribed *PATER COLIAVI FICIT ARTOGNOV*, which translates as 'Artognou, father of a descendant of Coll, has had (this) made/built/constructed.' (*English Heritage press release*, Thursday, 6 August 1998; S. de Bruxelles, 'Arthur: is this where myth meets history?' in *The Times*, Friday, 7 August 1998, p. 5). English Heritage have chosen (despite the strong and perfectly understandable reservations of the archaeologists in charge of the dig) to milk this find for publicity by pushing the notion of an association between the names Arthur and Artognou – *Artognou* is, however, *not in any way* the same name as *Art(h)ur*, the only thing they have in common is the apparent presence of the very common personal- and place-name element *art(h)* (a relationship that the name *Art(h)ur* shares with many other names, from many different periods and places) and, as such, claims that this stone refer to a 'historical Arthur' are completely unjustified, a position which would seem to be in line with that taken by those scholars in the best position to evaluate the evidence: Chris Morris, in charge of the excavations, has (in an online statement made by the archaeologists rather than English Heritage) said that 'we must dismiss any idea that the name on this stone is in any way to be associated with the legendary and literary figure Arthur... As

Professor Thomas states, 'All this stone shows in the name ARTOGNOU, is the use of this (Celtic) element [art(h)].'' (*http://www.gla.ac.uk/Acad/Archaeology/*, Friday, 15 August 1998). The following sensible comment was posted on *alt.legend.king-arthur*.

> I find it amusing that the news has already switched to claiming that the inscription mentions the name 'Arthur'. There are any number of early Brythonic names with the initial element 'Art(h)-', including several examples of the name 'Artgen' (see Bartrum 'Early Welsh Genealogical Tracts'), which contains the same basic elements as the inscription's 'Artognou' except that the latter has the zero-grade form of the second element (see Evans 'Gaulish Personal Names' for '-gno-'). Unless the legendary Arthur wasn't really named Arthur, I don't see how the inscription can have anything to do with him. It's a different name. (Heather Rose Jones, *alt.legend.king-arthur* posting, 07 August 1998 17:42).

It should also be noted that Adrian Gilbert, in *The Holy Kingdom* (London, 1998), has claimed that Arthwys, a king from southern Wales, is Arthur, on the assumption that *Arthwys* is the Welsh form of *Art(h)ur* and some highly dubious archaeological 'finds'. This is demonstrably false, at least with regards to the name, as the Welsh form of *Art(h)ur* is very clearly *Art(h)ur*! Arthur is never referred to as *Arthwys* in vernacular sources and, indeed, 'Arthwys' is an entirely separate and well documented Welsh personal name that cannot be in any way associated with the name *Art(h)ur* or with the Latin name *Artorius* that is often assumed to lie behind the name Arthur, as asserted by Gilbert. Indeed, the correct form of the name is actually *Athrwys*, not the more Arthur-like misspelling *Arthwys*, in any case.

[3] The mid-seventh-century poem *Marwnad Cynddylan* refers to Arthur in much the same way as does *Y Gododdin*, this text implying that the military deeds of Cynddylan and his brothers are of such great valour that these warriors might be seen as *canawon Artur fras, dinas dengyn*, 'whelps of great/stout Arthur, a mighty fortress' (see R. Bromwich, 'Concepts of Arthur', *Studia Celtica*, 10/11 (1975-6), pp. 163-81 at p. 177; R. Bromwich *et al*, 'Introduction', in R. Bromwich *et al* (edd.) *The Arthur of the Welsh. The Arthurian Legend in Medieval Welsh Literature* (Cardiff, 1991), pp. 1-14 at p. 5; A.O.H. Jarman, 'The Delineation of Arthur in Early Welsh Verse', in K. Varty (ed.) *An Arthurian Tapestry: Essays in Memory of Lewis Thorpe* (Glasgow, 1981), pp. 1-21 at p. 4. 'Fortress', *dinas*, here has the sense of 'defence, defender'). If this is accepted – Rowland in her *Early Welsh Saga Poetry: a Study and Edition of the Englynion* (Cambridge, 1990), p. 186, suggests an alternate reading for the text of the poem but this doesn't seem to have gained general acceptance – then it shows that the concept of Arthur as a 'peerless warrior'/'superhero' was present in East Powys (roughly modern Shropshire) in the seventh century (its contribution to the historicity debate would, of course, be the same as that of *Y Gododdin*, just discussed). Whatever the case, *Y Gododdin*'s concept of Arthur as the 'paragon of military valour' is clearly shared by other non-Galfridian Welsh sources too, such as the poems *Kadeir Teyrnon*, *Gereint fil[ius] Erbin*, *Ymddiddan Arthur a'r Eryr*, and *Marwnat vthyr pen[dragon]*.

[4] Whilst Charles-Edwards is right to point to similarities between the works of Bede and Paul the Deacon and the *Historia Brittonum*, the reputations of the former as 'reliable' historians are solely a result of the fact that they deal mainly with near-contemporary events. The author of the *Historia* was, however, dealing with events 300 years or more in the past and for such distant periods both Bede and Paul the Deacon are equally unreliable (see D.N. Dumville, '*Historia Brittonum*: an Insular History from the Carolingian Age', in A. Scharer and G. Scheibelreiter (edd.) *Historiographie im frühen Mittelalter* (Wien/München, 1994), pp. 406-34 at pp. 418-19).

[5] It is worth noting that it has been argued that the tale of Arthur carrying an icon of the Virgin Mary into battle – which is often taken as part of any hypothetical poem, most recently by Koch – must have had its origins in the ninth century and quite possibly in a monastic context (see R. Barber, *The Figure of Arthur* (London, 1972), p. 101ff.), like that in which the author of the *Historia* was working, implying at the very least a similar origin for the poem that supposedly contained it.

[6] Howlett, in his book *Cambro-Latin Compositions, Their Competence and Craftsmanship* (Dublin, 1998), argues convincingly that the date A.D. 496 for Badon is inset into the Latin of early medieval texts as part of the Celtic-Latin tradition of Biblical style (see D.R. Howlett's *The Celtic-Latin Tradition of Biblical Style* (Dublin, 1995) on this), with A.D. 540 being inset as the date that Gildas's *De Excidio Britanniae* was completed.

[7] It is sometimes claimed, deriving the name Arthur from the Welsh word *arth* 'bear', that Gildas does mention Arthur when he refers to Cuneglasus as *urse* – such an interpretation of Gildas is, however, wildly speculative and unacceptable (see K.H. Jackson's '*Varia*: II. Gildas and the Names of the British Princes', *Cambridge Medieval Celtic Studies*, 3 (1982), pp. 30-40 at pp. 32-34 for a full investigation of this passage, which is entirely understandable within the context of Gildas's text).

[8] In fact, it is worth remembering that some of the unidentifiable names look like they may well have been invented, thus further casting doubt on the *Historia* (see K.H. Jackson, 'Once Again Arthur's Battles', *Modern Philology*, 43 (1945-6), pp. 44-57). A brief word should be said regarding the very many theories of a 'local' Arthur (a good example is W.G. Collingwood's 'Arthur's battles', *Antiquity*, 3 (1929), pp. 292-98) which have been based on the list of battles in Chapter 56 of the *Historia Brittonum*. With sufficient 'imagination' and linguistic gymnastics the list of battles can be made to fit just about any locality one can think of and as such these theories are mutually cancelling and methodologically indefensible – thus Collingwood succeeded in 'discovering' all the battles in the south-east, which happily fitted his theory that Arthur only fought the Jutes; Anscombe ('Local names in the "Arthuriana" in the "Historia Brittonum"', *Zeitschrift für celtische Philologie*, 5 (1904), pp. 103-23) 'found' that all the battles were fought in the Midlands and Skene (*The Four Ancient Books of Wales* (Edinburgh, 1868), I, pp. 52-58) 'discovered' that all the battles could be identified with places in Scotland! Such conclusions can only increase our concerns regarding the contents of the *Historia*. For a scholarly and level-headed approach see Kenneth Jackson's articles 'Once Again Arthur's Battles', *Modern Philology*, 43 (1945-6), pp. 44-57; 'Arthur's Battle of Breguoin',

Antiquity, 23 (1949), pp. 48-49; and 'The Site of Mount Badon', *Journal of Celtic Studies*, 2 (1953-8), pp. 152-55 (the site of Badon is much disputed though). Incidently, it should be noted that Peter Field ('Gildas and the City of the Legions', *The Heroic Age*, 1 (1999)) has argued for an identification of the ninth battle differing from that which is usually accepted. Whilst an interesting suggestion, it is no more than a possibility and not necessarily the most plausible one. More importantly, even if it were to be accepted, his notions with regards to the nature of modern criticism of the *Historia Brittonum* and the significance of his suggestion to this cannot be endorsed.

[9] This last point is, in fact, a very important one. If any investigation into the history of the post-Roman period in Britain is to have any validity at all (and appear acceptable to academic historians) then it must be done with a sound methodology. This impinges directly on the problem of Arthur in view of the fact that 'no contemporary or near-contemporary source makes any mention of him [Arthur]': Dumville has made the important observation that 'History must be written from contemporary sources or with the aid of testimony carried to a later era by an identified and acceptable line of transmission' or 'it will not be worth the paper it is printed on' (D.N. Dumville, *Histories and Pseudo-Histories of the Insular Middle Ages* (Aldershot 1990), X, 55); he rightly rejects 'the old foolish game of trying to write narrative history of an effectively pre-historic period with the aid of unhistorical and non-contemporary sources' (*ibid.*, IV, 4). As Chris Snyder has recently written, 'If you are trying to argue for an historical Arthur..., you cannot stray from the primary sources for the period: *i.e.* Patrick, the Gallic Chronicles, Constantius of Lyon, Gildas, etc. NONE of these sources mention Arthur. Therefore, building an Arthur theory by starting with later sources (*e.g.* 'Nennius,' the Welsh Annals, the Gododdin, the Anglo-Saxon Chronicle, Welsh genealogies, Geoffrey of Monmouth) and then trying to argue backwards to Gildas and Badon is an unsound methodology according to modern historiographic principles.' (*Arthurnet* posting, 02 June 1998, 17:55).

[10] With regards to the comment that 'our sources are simply not of the quality...', this refers exclusively to their value as historical sources for the post-Roman centuries. As Howlett has observed, 'The *Historia Brittonum* has received harsh criticism from modern historians,' but such criticism can deflect our attention from the intrinsic quality of the *Historia* as a text of the ninth century: 'His work shows that an early-ninth-century Welsh scholar could cope with the difficult sixth-century prose of Gildas... He could interweave multiple arithmetic features into his prose, each different from the others, each discretely perfect, none impeding or thwarting any other, none drawing attention to itself flamboyantly, all contributing to the harmony of a richly polyphonic narrative. The *Historia* has for a long time been misprised and undervalued. It is time now to read and appreciate it properly.' (D.R. Howlett, *Cambro-Latin Compositions, Their Competence and Craftsmanship* (Dublin, 1998), chapter 5).

[11] Such considerations have, to a large extent, led to the adoption of Dumville's concluding remarks on Arthur by academic historians, namely that 'The fact of the matter is that there is no historical evidence about Arthur; we must reject him from

our histories and, above all, from the titles of our books' ('Sub-Roman Britain: History and Legend', *History*, 62 (1977), pp. 173-92 at p. 188), and Arthur is noticeably absent from (or dismissed in) the latest research concerned with the post-Roman period (for example, S. Bassett (ed.), *The Origins of Anglo-Saxon Kingdoms* (London, 1989); A.S. Esmonde-Cleary, *The Ending of Roman Britain* (London, 1989); N.J. Higham, *Rome, Britain and the Anglo-Saxons* (London, 1992); K.R. Dark, *Civitas to Kingdom: British Political Continuity 300-800* (London, 1993); B.A.E. Yorke, *Wessex in the Early Middle Ages* (London, 1995); C.A. Snyder, *An Age of Tyrants. Britain and the Britons A.D. 400-600* (Pennsylvania/Stroud, 1998)). Whilst Dumville's remarks may be a little harsh in places, even if one accepts the above 'perhaps' as a 'yes' then one can go no further: the evidence simply is not of the quality that it would allow us to say anything at all concrete about any possible historical Arthur. Charles Thomas perhaps summed up best the modern historian's attitude to such figures as Arthur, only recorded in very late and highly untrustworthy sources, when he wrote that 'Many will agree with Dr Dumville's *cri de coeur*. 'The fact of the matter is that there is no historical evidence about Arthur; we must reject him from our histories and, above all, from the titles of our books.' Any sane person would agree. These enticing Will-of-the-wisps have too long dominated, and deflected, useful advances in our study.' (*Christianity in Roman Britain to AD 500* (London, 1981), p. 245).

[12] In some ways Padel's approach to this problem is far preferable to my own and should be consulted by anyone at all interested in the question of Arthur. However, it was felt desirable to first provide a summary of the latest research into the texts that are usually turned to when looking at the 'historical Arthur' and make it clear that a historical Arthur cannot be assumed to have existed, before moving on to methodological issues etc.. Those already familiar with the methodological problems and Padel's important reassessment of the whole question will find much, of course, that is already familiar – I can only hope that a slightly different approach to the sources and a slightly fuller consideration of certain pieces of evidence and problems than Oliver Padel could give may be found to be of some small benefit to these readers.

[13] That is to say, not localised in any particular region. That Arthur was pan-Brittonic from the very first is clearly evidenced in the pre-Galfridian material which places him in southern Scotland, south-western Britain, Wales and Brittany (see Padel, 'The Nature of Arthur', *Cambrian Medieval Celtic Studies*, 27 (1994), pp. 1-14 for a demonstration of this) and is true even of the earliest references to him (the four or five people named 'Arthur' in the sixth and seventh centuries are to be found as far apart as south Wales and south Scotland, whilst *Marwnad Cynddylan* indicates a knowledge of Arthur in mid-seventh-century Shropshire).

[14] It should also be noted that this folkloric Arthur not only dominates the pre-Galfridian material but also appears in the later works – he is clearly present in non-Galfridian Welsh tradition that post-dates Geoffrey's work and, indeed, he is also to be seen in Galfridian and post-Galfridian materials. To quote no less authorities than Gwyn and Thomas Jones, 'What of Arthur himself? His nature is unmistakable: he is the folk hero, a beneficent giant, who with his men rids the land

of other giants, of witches and monsters; he undertakes journeys to the Otherworld to rescue prisoners and carry off treasures; he is rude, savage, heroic and protective... It is remarkable how much of this British Arthur has survived in the early twelfth-century *Historia* of Geoffrey of Monmouth and the mid-fifteenth-century *Morte Darthur* of Malory. Arthur setting off with Kaius and Bedeuerus to slay the swine-eating Spanish giant, and bursting out laughing when the monster crashes like a torn-up oak, or his battle with the beard-collecting Ritho, are cases in point... Behind the royal features in Geoffrey and Malory may be discerned the ruder lineaments of the folk hero...' (*The Mabinogion* (Dent 1949) p. xxv). It is in local folklore that the continuing dominance of this folkloric Arthur is most obvious however, as we might expect and as Padel has shown (see 'The Nature of Arthur', *Cambrian Medieval Celtic Studies*, 27 (1994), pp. 1-31, in particular pp. 25-30. See also Grooms' *The Giants of Wales. Cewri Cymrui*, Welsh Studies 10 (Lampeter, 1993)). Thus, for example, in Cornish folklore Arthur was, even as late as the nineteenth century, largely pre-Galfridian in nature, his name being attached to a large number of 'remarkable' topographic feature in just the same way as it was centuries before (with similar features that were not associated with Arthur being ascribed to giants) and Arthur was additionally renowned for ridding the area of the giants who compete with him for prominence in the topographic folklore (R. Hunt, *Popular Romances of the West of England. The Drolls, Traditions and Superstitions of Old Cornwall*, third edition (reprinted Felinfach, 1993), II, p. 307. This situation also existed within Welsh and Breton folklore, see C. Grooms, *The Giants of Wales. Cewri Cymru*, Welsh Studies 10 (Lampeter, 1993)).

[15] This is not to say, naturally, that a historical post-Roman Arthur is disproved – one can only very rarely prove that a particular figure never existed (just as one can never prove that aliens did not assist in the building of the Pyramids or Silbury Hill). Rather what is being said is that, by the adoption of a sound methodology and the consequent viewing of the very few 'historical' references in the context that they must surely be seen in, the burden of proof is transferred from both parties in the debate over historicity to that which would argue that Arthur was a historical fifth-/sixth-century personage; it is not simply that a historical Arthur is not needed to understand the legend but rather that, in the absence of proof, the postulation of a historical post-Roman figure behind the pre-Galfridian material is completely unjustified and we must follow the vast majority of the evidence in seeing Arthur as a legendary figure. What we have to do is decide what is reasonable and what is not, and while Arthur *could have been* a real fifth-century personage, on present evidence there is absolutely no reason to think that he was. Of course, some will be unwilling, despite the above, to let go of a historical Arthur for whatever personal reasons – in such circumstances one can only think of the following words by Bertrand Russell:

> I wish to propose for the reader's favourable consideration a doctrine which may, I fear, appear wildly paradoxical and subversive. The doctrine in question is this: that it is undesirable to believe a proposition when there is no ground whatever for supposing it true. I must, of course, admit that if such an opinion became common it would completely transform our social life and our political system; since both are at present faultless,

this must weigh against it. (Bertrand Russell, *Skeptical Essays*, I (1928))

[16] In Cornish oral tradition there is absolutely no trace of Arthur being renowned for fighting and defeating the Saxon invaders of post-Roman Britain – in fact he is not associated in any way with the Saxons. Rather he is renowned for defeating the Vikings in western Cornwall, on Vellan-drucher Moor (see R. Hunt, *Popular Romances of the West of England. The Drolls, Traditions and Superstitions of Old Cornwall*, third edition (reprinted Felinfach, 1993), I, p. 181, and II, pp. 305-08; M.A. Courtney *Cornish Feasts and Folklore* (1890), p. 74) and for driving the giants out of Cornwall in antiquity (this is, of course, in addition to the topographical folklore, of the type identified by Padel in his 'The Nature of Arthur', *Cambrian Medieval Celtic Studies*, 27 (1994), pp. 1-31 that is present in Cornish folklore. Arthur was renowned for driving out the giants in Welsh oral tradition also – see C. Grooms, *The Giants of Wales. Cewri Cymru*, Welsh Studies 10 (Lampeter, 1993), pp. xlix-l). The first is obviously a historicisation of Arthur into a period many centuries after that which the more commonly read sources refer to; the latter may require a little more explanation. Whilst, first and foremost, it quite clearly reflects the 'original', legendary Arthur's folkloric role as giant-killer, it would also seem to represent a historicisation, as the belief that giants inhabited Britain before 'normal' humans (and that they had to be vanquished) is well evidenced both in, for example, Geoffrey of Monmouth's *Historia Regum Britanniae* and Cornish and Welsh folklore (see, for example, C. Grooms, *The Giants of Wales. Cewri Cymru*, Welsh Studies 10 (Lampeter, 1993), Introduction) – thus the association of Arthur with this vanquishing of the giants is, at least partly, a historicisation of Arthur into distant antiquity.

[17] Geoffrey Ashe ('The Origins of the Arthurian Legend', *Arthuriana*, 5.3 (1995), pp. 1-24) has given several reasons why, in his opinion, Arthur has to be historical. These have been dealt with in full by Padel in his commentary on Ashe's article in the same journal ('Recent Work on the Origins of the Arthurian Legend: A Comment', *Arthuriana*, 5.3 (1995), pp. 103-14), who has shown that they do not offer anything like the proof of historicity that Ashe suggests they do.

[18] It is occasionally asked whether it is likely that the victor of an important battle such as Badon might be replaced, after several centuries, by someone else. In answer to this, four points need to be made. Firstly, the historicisation of legendary/mythical figures is, as has already been noted, often achieved through the association of these figure with some major event of the past. For instance, Hengest and Horsa were given as an example of mythical personages historicised at the beginning of this study and these were dioscuric horse-gods who were historicised with nothing less than a pivotal role in the Anglo-Saxon settlement of England by the eighth century, replacing the likely original players in this event (see, for example, D.J. Ward, *The Divine Twins, A Indo-European Myth in Germanic Tradition*, University of California Folklore Studies vol. 19 (1969); D.P. Kirby *The Earliest English Kings* (London, 1991))! As such, the replacement of an original victor of (or player in) a major battle/event by a mythical/legendary character in the centuries after this occurred is not in any way implausible. Secondly, Badon is not the only battle that is suspected of being attributed to Arthur in *Historia Brittonum* chapter 56

but originally fought by someone else, the significance of which should be obvious. For example, Arthur's supposed battle of *Breguoin* would seem to have been a battle originally won by Urien of Rheged but attributed to Arthur by the ninth century, with Urien being a very important figure of early Welsh literature (see O.J. Padel, 'The Nature of Arthur', *Cambrian Medieval Celtic Studies*, 27 (1994), pp. 1-31 at p. 18; K.H. Jackson, 'Arthur's Battle of Breguoin', *Antiquity*, 23 (1949), pp. 48-49; R. Bromwich, 'Concepts of Arthur', *Studia Celtica*, 10/11 (1975-6), pp. 163-81). Thirdly, as was demonstrated earlier in this study, the association of Badon with Arthur is present only in a very few sources, all of which would seem to be ultimately derived from the *Historia Brittonum* Chapter 56. Indeed, as was also earlier noted, there are good reasons to believe in the existence of early medieval traditions regarding Badon which did not associate it with Arthur and which were originally more widely acknowledged than the those that did. In light of this it is clear that any replacement that occurred was not by any means universally accepted.

Finally, there is the question of the status of the Battle of Badon. Historians are used to giving it a pivotal role in the history of post-Roman Britain, based on the fact that Gildas mentions this battle and no other. Whether this is justified or not is to be debated, given that Gildas dates it by saying that it was fought in the year of his birth. However, even if it was pivotal, we have to acknowledge that the Britons of later centuries were not inclined to view it as particularly significant. Whilst non-Arthurian Welsh sources do mention Badon (though not in association with Arthur), as a whole it was clearly not seen as that important. Their main interest was rather with the sagas of later sixth- and seventh-century heroes such as Urien of Rheged and Badon is rarely mentioned (see R. Bromwich, *Trioedd Ynys Prydein. The Welsh Triads*, second edition (Cardiff, 1978)). Probably the most interesting evidence comes from the poem *Armes Prydein*, composed in the tenth century and in which the creation of a confederacy (of the Welsh, the Irish, and the men of Strathclyde, Cornwall, Brittany and Dublin) to defeat the 'English' is both advocated and prophesied. This featured a number of important people from the past designed to rally the Britons and their allies against the Anglo-Saxons, including the seventh-century Cynan and Cadwaladr, who are expected to return to lead the Britons in their confederacy, but neither Badon itself nor the victor of Badon (be he Ambrosius or Arthur) gets any mention whatsoever, surely a damning comment on the place of this much lauded victory against the Saxons in the British consciousness at this point (roughly the same point that it is suggested that Arthur's name becomes attached to the battle of Badon). Given all the above, it can be concluded that the replacement of Ambrosius as victor of Badon by Arthur in a few texts all related to the ninth-century *Historia Brittonum* is in no way implausible.

[19] As Kemp Malone long ago wrote, 'It will not do to take the name Arthur in all isolation, and look for a phonetically possible etymology. We must consider the name in connexion with the entire body of Arthurian material. The etymology which fits with this material is the etymology that we must adopt.' (K. Malone, 'The Historicity of Arthur', *The Journal of English and Germanic Philology*, 23 (1924), pp. 463-91 at p. 468).

[20] The earliest mention comes from a Spanish Chronicle of 1582 which asserts that it was common talk (*fama cumun*) that Arthur had been enchanted to the form of a

crow and that many penalties were inflicted on anyone who killed one of these birds. Cervantes also refers to this belief three times in his *Don Quixote* (Vol. 1, 1605; Vol. 2, 1615) and his posthumously published *Persiles y Sigismunda* (1617). The following quote from R. Hunt's nineteenth-century *Popular Romances of the West of England. The Drolls, Traditions and Superstitions of Old Cornwall*, third edition (reprinted Felinfach, 1993), II, pp. 308-09, based itself largely around an eighteenth-century note, brings some of these elements together nicely:

I quote the following as it stands:– [from *Notes and Queries*, vol. viii, p. 618]

"In Jarvis's translation of 'Don Quixote,' book ii. chap. v., the following passage occurs:–

"'Have you not read, sir,' answered Don Quixote, 'the annals and histories of England, wherein are recorded the famous exploits of King Arthur, whom, in our Castilian tongue, we always call King Artus; of whom there goes an old tradition, and a common one, all over the kingdom of Great Britain, that this king did not die, but that, by magic art, he was turned into a raven; and that, in process of time, he shall reign again and recover his kingdom and sceptre, for which reason it cannot be proved that, from that time to this, any Englishman has killed a raven?'

"My reason for transcribing this passage is to record the curious fact that the legend of King Arthur's existence in the form of a raven was still repeated as a piece of folklore in Cornwall about sixty years ago. My father, who died about two years since, at the age of eighty, spent a few years of his youth in the neighbourhood of Penzance. One day he was walking along Marazion Green with his fowling piece on his shoulder, he saw a raven at a distance and fired at it. An old man who was near immediately rebuked him, telling him that he ought on no account to have shot at a raven, for that King Arthur was still alive in the form of that bird. My father was much interested when I drew his attention to the passage which I have quoted above.

"Perhaps some of your Cornish or Welsh correspondents may be able to say whether the legend is still known among the people of Cornwall or Wales.   EDGAR MACCULLOCH

"Guernsey."

I have been most desirous of discovering if any such legend as the above exists... Nowhere do I find the raven associated with him, but I have been told that bad luck will follow the man who killed a Chough [a red-legged crow], for Arthur was transformed into one of these birds.

6. Bibliography and Further Reading

Alcock, L. 1971, *Arthur's Britain: History and Archaeology AD 367-634* (Harmondsworth)

Anscombe, A. 1904, 'Local names in the "Arthuriana" in the "Historia Brittonum"', *Zeitschrift für celtische Philologie*, 5, pp. 103-23

Arnold, C.J. 1984, *Roman Britain to Saxon England* (London)

Ashe, G. (ed.) 1968, *The Quest for Arthur's Britain* (London)

Ashe, G. 1981, '"A certain very ancient book": Traces of an Arthurian Source in Geoffrey of Monmouth's *History*', *Speculum*, 56, pp. 301-23

Ashe, G. 1985, *The Discovery of King Arthur*

Ashe, G. 1986, 'Camlann (Camlan)', in N.J. Lacy (ed.) *The Arthurian Encyclopedia* (New York), pp. 76-8

Ashe, G. 1995, 'The Origins of the Arthurian Legend', *Arthuriana*, 5.3, pp. 1-24

Barber, R. 1972, *The Figure of Arthur* (London)

Bartrum, P.C. 1965, 'Arthuriana in the Genealogical MSS', *The National Library of Wales Journal*, 14, pp. 243-45

Bassett, S. (ed.) 1989, *The Origins of Anglo-Saxon Kingdoms* (London)

Bromwich, R. 1975-6, 'Concepts of Arthur', *Studia Celtica*, 10/11, pp. 163-81

Bromwich, R. 1978a, *Trioedd Ynys Prydein. The Welsh Triads* (Cardiff: second edition)

Bromwich, R. 1978b, 'Introduction', in R. Bromwich and R.B. Jones (edd.) *Astudiaethau ar yr Hengerdd, Studies in Old Welsh Poetry* (Cardiff), pp. 1-24

Bromwich, R. 1983, 'Celtic Elements in Arthurian Romance: A General Survey', in P.B. Grout, R.A. Lodge, C.E. Pickford and E.K.C. Varty (edd.) *The Legend of Arthur in the Middle Ages* (Cambridge), pp. 41-55

Bromwich, R., Jarman, A.O.H. and Roberts, B.F. (edd.) 1991, *The Arthur of the Welsh. The Arthurian Legend in Medieval Welsh Literature* (Cardiff)

Bromwich, R., Jarman, A.O.H., Roberts, B.F. and Huws, D. 1991, 'Introduction' in Bromwich *et al* (edd.) 1991, pp. 1-14

Bromwich, R. and Evans, D.S. 1992, *Culhwch and Olwen. An Edition and Study of the Oldest Arthurian Tale* (Cardiff)

Brooks, N.P. 1989, 'The Creation and early structure of the Kingdom of Kent', in S. Basset (ed.) *The Origins of Anglo-Saxon Kingdoms Studies in the Early History of Britain* (London), pp. 55-74

Bruce, J.D. 1923, *The Evolution of Arthurian Romance* (Baltimore)

Carey, J. 1994, *The Irish National Origin-Legend: Synthetic Pseudohistory*, Quiggin Pamphlets on the Sources of Medieval Gaelic History, 1 (Cambridge)

Carey, J. 1999, 'The Finding of Arthur's Grave: A Story from Clonmacnoise?', in J. Carey *et al* (edd.) *Ildánach Ildírech. A Festschrift for Proinsias Mac Cana* (Andover & Aberystwyth), pp. 1-14

Carley, J.P. 1999, 'Arthur in English History', in W.R.J. Barron (ed.) *The Arthur of the English* (Cardiff), pp. 47-57

Chadwick, H.M. and Chadwick, N.K. 1932, *The Growth of Literature*, I, (Cambridge)

Chambers, E.K. 1927, *Arthur of Britain* (London)

Charles-Edwards, T.M. 1978, 'The Authenticity of the *Gododdin*: A Historian's View', in R. Bromwich and R.B. Jones (edd.) *Astudiaethau ar yr Hengerdd, Studies in Old Welsh Poetry* (Caerdydd), pp. 44-71

Charles-Edwards, T.M. 1991, 'The Arthur of History', in R. Bromwich *et al* (edd.) 1991, pp. 15-32

Coe, J.B. and Young, S. 1995, *The Celtic Sources for the Arthurian Legend* (Felinfach)

Collingwood, W.G. 1929, 'Arthur's battles', *Antiquity*, 3, pp. 292-98

Courtney, M.A. 1890, *Cornish Feasts and Folklore* (reprinted Penzance, 1998)

Dark, K.R. 1993, *Civitas to Kingdom: British Political Continuity 300-800* (London)

Dumville, D.N. 1974, 'Some Aspects of the Chronology of the *Historia*

Brittonum', *Bulletin of the Board of Celtic Studies*, 25, pp. 439-45

Dumville, D.N. 1975-6, 'Nennius and the *Historia Brittonum*', *Studia Celtica*, 10/11, pp. 78-95

Dumville, D.N. 1977a, 'Sub-Roman Britain: History and Legend', *History*, 62, pp. 173-92

Dumville, D.N. 1977b, 'Kingship, Genealogies and Renal Lists', in P.H. Sawyer and I.N. Wood (edd.) *Early Medieval Kingship* (Leeds), pp. 72-104

Dumville, D.N. 1985, *Historia Brittonum: iii. The Vatican Recension* (Cambridge)

Dumville, D.N. 1986, 'The Historical Value of the *Historia Brittonum*', *Arthurian Literature*, 6, pp. 1-26

Dumville, D.N. 1990, *Histories and Pseudo-Histories of the Insular Middle Ages* (Aldershot)

Dumville, D.N. 1994, '*Historia Brittonum:* an Insular History from the Carolingian Age', in A. Scharer and G. Scheibelreiter (edd.) *Historiographie im frühen Mittelalter* (Wien/München), pp. 406-34

Edel, D. 1983, 'The Arthur of "Culhwch and Olwen" as a figure of Epic-Heroic Tradition', *Reading Medieval Studies*, 9, pp. 3-15

Esmonde-Cleary, A.S, 1989, *The Ending of Roman Britain* (London)

Evans, D.S. 1978, 'Iaith y *Gododdin*', in R. Bromwich and R.B. Jones (edd.) *Astudiaethau ar yr Hengerdd, Studies in Old Welsh Poetry* (Cardiff), pp. 72-88

Field, P.J.C. 1996, 'Nennius and his History', *Studia Celtica*, 30, pp. 159-65

Ford, P.K. 1977, *The Mabinogi and Other Medieval Welsh Tales* (Los Angeles)

Ford, P.K. 1983, 'On the Significance of some Arthurian Names in Welsh', *Bulletin of the Board of Celtic Studies*, 30, pp. 268-73

Ford, P.K. 1986, 'Celtic Arthurian Literature', in N.J. Lacy (ed.) *The Arthuriana Encyclopedia* (New York), pp. 90-94

Gowans, L.M. 1988, *Cei and the Arthurian Legend*, Arthurian Studies xviii (Cambridge)

Grabowski, K. and Dumville, D.N. 1984, *Chronicles and Annals of Medieval Ireland and Wales* (Woodbridge)

Gransden, A. 1976, 'The Growth of Glastonbury Traditions and Legends in the Twelfth Century', *Journal of Ecclesiastical History*, 27, pp. 337-58

Green, T. 2007, *Concepts of Arthur* (Stroud)

Griffin, T.D. 1994, *Names from the dawn of British legend: Taliesin, Aneirin, Myrddin/Merlin, Arthur* (Felinfach)

Grooms, C. 1993, *The Giants of Wales. Cewri Cymru*, Welsh Studies Vol. 10 (Lampeter)

Hanning, R.W. 1966, *The Vision of History in Early Britain* (New York and London)

Hanning, R.W. 1995, '*Inventio Arthuri*: a comment on the essays of Geoffrey Ashe and D. R. Howlett', *Arthuriana*, 5.3, pp. 96-100

Higham, N.J. 1992, *Rome, Britain and the Anglo-Saxons* (London)

Higham, N.J. 1994, *The English Conquest* (Manchester)

Howlett, D.R. 1995, *The Celtic-Latin Tradition of Biblical Style* (Dublin)

Howlett, D.R. 1998, *Cambro-Latin Compositions, Their Competence and Craftsmanship* (Dublin)

Hughes, K. 1973, 'The *Annales Cambriae* and Related Texts', *Proceedings of the British Academy*, 59, pp. 233-58

Hughes, K. 1980, *Celtic Britain in the Early Middle Ages: Studies in Scottish and Welsh Sources* (Woodbridge)

Hunt, R. 1881, *Popular Romances of the West of England. The Drolls, Traditions and Superstitions of Old Cornwall*, third edition (reprinted Felinfach, 1993)

Isaac, G.R. 1996, *The Verb in the Book of Aneirin: Studies in Syntax Morphology*

42

and Etymology, Buchreihe der Zeitschrift für celtische Philologie, 12 (Tübingen)

Isaac, G.R. 1998, '*Gweith Gwen Ystrat* and the Northern Heroic Age of the Sixth Century', *Cambrian Medieval Celtic Studies*, 36, pp. 61-70

Isaac, G.R. 1999, 'Readings in the History and Transmission of the *Gododdin*', *Cambrian Medieval Celtic Studies*, 37, pp. 55-78

Jackson, K.H. 1945-6, 'Once Again Arthur's Battles', *Modern Philology*, 43, pp. 44-57

Jackson, K.H. 1949, 'Arthur's Battle of Breguoin', *Antiquity*, 23, pp. 48-49

Jackson, K.H. 1953-8, 'The Site of Mount Badon', *The Journal of Celtic Studies*, 2, pp. 152-55

Jackson, K.H. 1959a, 'The Arthur of History', in R. Loomis (ed.) *Arthurian Literature in the Middle Ages* (Oxford), pp. 1-11

Jackson, K.H. 1959b, 'Arthur in Early Welsh Verse', in R. Loomis (ed.) *Arthurian Literature in the Middle Ages* (Oxford), pp. 12-19

Jackson, K.H. 1969, *The Gododdin: The Oldest Scottish Poem* (Edinburgh)

Jackson, K.H. 1973, 'Review of R. Barber, *The Figure of Arthur*', *Medium Aevum*, 42, pp. 188-89

Jackson, K.H. 1982, '*Varia*: II. Gildas and the Names of the British Princes', *Cambridge Medieval Celtic Studies*, 3, pp. 30-40

Jarman, A.O.H. 1981, 'The Delineation of Arthur in Early Welsh Verse', in K. Varty (ed.) *An Arthurian Tapestry: Essays in Memory of Lewis Thorpe* (Glasgow), pp. 1-21

Jarman, A.O.H. 1983, 'The Arthurian Allusions in the Black Book of Carmarthen', in P.B. Grout, R.A. Lodge, C.E. Pickford and E.K.C. Varty (edd.) *The Legend of Arthur in the Middle Ages* (Cambridge), pp. 99-112

Jarman, A.O.H. 1988, *Aneirin: Y Gododdin, Britain's Oldest Heroic Poem* (Llandysul)

Jarman, A.O.H. 1989-90, 'The Arthurian Allusions in the Book of Aneirin', *Studia Celtica*, 24/5, pp. 15-25

Jarman, A.O.H. 1991, 'The Merlin Legend and the Welsh Tradition of Prophesy', in Bromwich *et al* (edd.) 1991, pp. 117-145

Jones, T. and Jones, G. 1949, *The Mabinogion* (London)

Jones, T. 1964, 'The Early Evolution of the Legend of Arthur', *Nottingham Medieval Studies*, 8, pp. 3-21

Kennedy, B. 1995, 'Review of C.S. Littleton and L.A. Malcor's *From Scythia to Camelot*', *Arthuriana*, 5.3, pp. 127-30

Kirby, D.P. 1991, *The Earliest English Kings* (London)

Koch, J.T. 1994, 'Review of R. Bromwich *et al* (edd.) *The Arthur of the Welsh*', *Speculum*, 69, pp. 1127-29

Koch, J.T. and Carey, J. 1995, *The Celtic Heroic Age : Literary Sources for Ancient Celtic Europe and Early Ireland and Wales* (Malden, Mass.)

Koch, J.T. 1996, 'The Celtic Lands', in N.J. Lacy (ed.) *Medieval Arthurian Literature: A Guide to Recent Research* (New York), pp. 239-322

Koch, J.T. 1997, *The Gododdin of Aneirin. Text and Context from Dark-Age North Britain* (Cardiff)

Lapidge, M. and Dumville, D.N. (edd.) 1984, *Gildas: New Approaches* (Woodbridge)

Littleton, C. Scott and Malcor, L. 1994, *From Scythia to Camelot: A Radical Reassessment of the Legends of King Arthur, the Knights of the Round Table, and the Holy Grail* (New York and London)

Loomis, R.S. 1958, 'Arthurian Tradition and Folklore', *Folklore*, 69, pp. 1-25

Loomis, R.S. (ed.) 1959, *Arthurian Literature in the Middle Ages* (Oxford)

MacCulloch, J.A. 1911, *The Religion of the Ancient Celts* (Edinburgh: repr. London, 1991)

MacKillop, J. 1986, *Fionn mac Cumhaill. Celtic Myth in English Literature* (Syracuse)

MacKillop, J. 1998, *Dictionary of Celtic Mythology* (Oxford)

Malone, K. 1924, 'The Historicity of Arthur', *Journal of English and Germanic Philology*, 23, pp. 463-491

Malone, K. 1924-5, 'Artorius', *Modern Philology*, 22, pp. 367-74

Miller, M. 1975, 'Relative and Absolute Publication Dates of Gildas's *De Excidio* in Medieval Scholarship', *Bulletin of the Board of Celtic Studies*, 26, pp. 169-74

Murphy, G. 1953, *Duanaire Finn iii* (London)

Morris, J. 1973, *The Age of Arthur* (London)

Morris, J. 1980, *Nennius: British History and the Welsh Annals* (Chichester)

Ó hÓgáin, D. 1988, *Fionn mac Cumhaill: Images of the Gaelic Hero* (Dublin)

O'Sullivan, T.D. 1978, *The De Excidio of Gildas, Its Authenticity and Date* (Leiden)

Olmsted, G.S. 1994, *The Gods of the Celts and the Indo-Europeans* (Budapest)

Padel, O.J. 1994, 'The Nature of Arthur', *Cambrian Medieval Celtic Studies*, 27, pp. 1-31

Padel, O.J. 1995, 'Recent Work on the Origins of the Arthurian Legend: A Comment', *Arthuriana*, 5.3, pp. 103-14

Padel, O.J. 1998, 'A New Study of the *Gododdin*', *Cambrian Medieval Celtic Studies*, 35, pp. 45-55

Phillimore, E. 1888, 'The "Annales Cambriae" and Old-Welsh Genealogies from "Harleian MS" 3859', *Y Cymmrodor*, 9, pp. 141-83

Rahtz, P. 1993, *English Heritage Book of Glastonbury* (London)

Radford, C.A.R. 1968, 'Glastonbury Abbey', in G.Ashe (ed.) *The Quest for*

Arthur's Britain (London), pp. 119-138

Rhys, J. 1891, *Studies in the Arthurian Legend* (Oxford)

Roberts, B.F. 1973-4, 'Review of R. Barber, *The Figure of Arthur*', *Studia Celtica*, 8/9, pp. 336-39

Roberts, B.F. 1991a, '*Culhwch ac Olwen*, The Triads, Saints' Lives', in Bromwich *et al* (edd.) 1991, pp. 73-95

Roberts, B.F. 1991b, 'Geoffrey of Monmouth, *Historia Regum Britanniae* and *Brut Y Brenhinedd*', in Bromwich *et al* (edd.) 1991, pp. 98-116

Rogers, J.H. 1998, 'Origins of the ancient constellations: II. The Mediterranean traditions', *Journal of the British Astronomical Association*, 108.2, pp. 79-89

Ross, A. 1992, *Pagan Celtic Britain* (London)

Ross, A. 2001, *Folklore of Wales* (Stroud)

Rowland, J. 1990, *Early Welsh Saga Poetry: a Study and Edition of the Englynion* (Cambridge)

Sims-Williams, P. 1983, 'Gildas and the Anglo-Saxons', *Cambridge Medieval Celtic Studies*, 6, pp. 1-30

Sims-Williams, P. 1991, 'The Early Welsh Arthurian Poems', in Bromwich *et al* (edd.) 1991, pp. 33-71

Skene, W.F. 1868, *The Four Ancient Books of Wales* (Edinburgh)

Snyder, C.A. 1998, *An Age of Tyrants. Britain and the Britons A.D. 400-600* (Pennsylvania/Stroud)

Spence, L. 1945, *The Magical Arts in Celtic Britain* (London)

Thomas, A.C. 1981, *Christianity in Britain to AD 500* (London)

Thomas, N. 1995, 'Arthurian Evidences: The Historicity and Historicisation of King Arthur', *Durham University Journal*, 87.2, pp. 385-92

46

Turville-Petre, J.E. 1953-7, 'Hengest and Horsa', *Saga Book of the Viking Society*, 14, pp. 273-90

Van Hamel, A.G. 1934, 'Aspects of Celtic Mythology', *Proceedings of the British Academy*, 20, pp. 207-48

Wadge, R. 1987, 'King Arthur: A British or Sarmatian Tradition?', *Folklore*, 98.2, pp. 204-15

Ward, D.J. 1969, *The Divine Twins, A Indo-European Myth in Germanic Tradition* University of California Folklore Studies vol. 19

Winterbottom, M. 1978, *Gildas, The Ruin of Britain and Other Works* (Chichester)

Wood, C.T. 1995, 'Review of C.S. Littleton and L.A. Malcor's *From Scythia to Camelot* and G. Phillips and M. Keatman's *King Arthur: The True Story*', *Arthuriana*, 5.3, pp. 124-27

Wood, M. 1981, *In Search of the Dark Ages* (London)

Wood, M. 1999, *In Search of England: Journeys Into the English Past* (London)

Yorke, B.A.E. 1993, 'Fact or Fiction? The written evidence for the fifth and sixth centuries AD', *Anglo-Saxon Studies in Archaeology and History*, 6, pp. 45-50

Yorke, B.A.E. 1995, *Wessex in the Early Middle Ages* (London)

2

A Bibliographic Guide to Welsh
Arthurian Literature

A Bibliographic Guide to Welsh Arthurian Literature

Contents

1. Introduction

The following is intended to provide a bibliographical guide to the Arthurian references found in medieval Welsh manuscripts. In addition to bibliographic data, it includes brief discussions of each text and its significance. Naturally, these short discussions are not intended replace those found in my *Concepts of Arthur* (Stroud, 2007), especially chapters two, three and four, which are necessarily considerably more detailed and involved. Nonetheless, it is hoped that the following will prove a useful and easily accessible handbook of those texts that are relevant to any study of the early Arthurian legend.

2. The Manuscripts

Most of the early references to Arthur are found in only a handful of manuscripts, briefly outlined below. In addition to the references cited in the individual sections, anyone seriously interested in Welsh manuscripts should consult Daniel Huws' *Medieval Welsh Manuscripts* (Cardiff, 2000).

a. The Black Book of Carmarthen

The 'Black Book of Carmarthen' (National Library of Wales, Peniarth MS 1) was compiled by a single scribe over a period of years in the latter half of the thirteenth century. It contains religious poetry, early praise-poems, prophetic verse belonging to the pre-Galfridian Merlin cycle and poems concerning Arthur and other 'legendary' heroes.

The most substantial Arthurian poem contained in the 'Black Book' is *Pa gur yv y porthaur?* ('What man is the gatekeeper/porter?'), which has been most recently translated and discussed in detail by Patrick Sims-Williams in 'The Early Welsh Arthurian Poems', in Bromwich *et al* (edd.) *The Arthur of the Welsh* (Cardiff, 1991), pp. 33-71 at pp. 38-46. The other references to Arthur are only brief allusions, for example in *Englynion y Beddau* ('Stanzas of the Graves'), though still important.

For the text see A.O.H. Jarman (ed.), *Llyfr Du Caerfyrddin* (Cardiff, 1982); for a general survey of the 'Black Book', its date and contents in English see A.O.H. Jarman, 'Llyfr Du Caerfyrddin: The Black Book of Carmarthen', *Proceedings of the British Academy*, 71 (1985), pp. 333-56. The manuscript, with a good introduction, is now available for viewing online at *http://www.llgc. org.uk/index.php?id=blackbookofcarmarthen*.

b. The Book of Taliesin

The 'Book of Taliesin' (NLW Peniarth MS 2), of which 38 folios survive, was written by a single scribe in the first quarter of the fourteenth century. Its contents (a mixture of religious, prophetic, mythical and historical poems) purport to comprise the collected works of the bard/sage Taliesin, as they were envisaged in the later Middle Ages. The case for a genuine early nucleus which might represent the authentic work of a sixth-century Taliesin is based on a group of archaic praise-poems addressed to Urien of Rheged and contemporary rulers: Ifor Williams, *Canu Taliesin* (Cardiff, 1960) and *The Poems of Taliesin*, translated by J.E. Caerwyn Williams (Dublin, 1968). Of more certain date is the tenth-century prophetic poem *Armes Prydein* (dating *c.* 930), which briefly mentions Myrddin (Merlin). The majority of the poems in the manuscript date from between the eighth and the eleventh centuries and are implicitly attributed to the fictional persona of the all-knowing, semi-divine Taliesin; for this legendary Taliesin and his relationship to the historical Taliesin of the sixth century, see Ifor Williams' *Lectures on Early Welsh Poetry* (Dublin, 1954) and *Chwedl Taliesin* (O'Donnell Lecture, 1957); P.K. Ford, *The Mabinogi* (1977); M. Haycock, '"Preiddeu Annwn" and the Figure of Taliesin', *Studia Celtica*, 18/19 (1983-4), pp. 52-78; P.K. Ford, *Ystoria Taliesin* (Cardiff, 1992); P.C. Bartrum, *A Welsh Classical Dictionary* (Aberystwyth, 1993), pp. 595-97; O. Davies, *Celtic Christianity in Early Medieval Wales* (Cardiff, 1996), chapter 4; J.T. Koch, *'De Sancto Iudicaelo Rege Historia* and Its Implications for the Welsh Taliesin', in J.F. Nagy and L.E. Jones (edd.) *Celtic Studies Association of North America Yearbook 3-4: Heroic Poets and Poetic Heroes in Celtic Tradition* (Dublin, 2005), pp. 247-62; M. Haycock (ed. and trans.), *Legendary Poems from the Book of Taliesin* (Aberystwyth, 2007), pp. 9-21.

The name of Arthur appears in only five of the poems in the 'Book of Taliesin' – *Kat Godeu, Kadeir Teyrnon, Kanu y Meirch, Marwnat vthyr pen[dragon]* and *Preideu Annwfyn*. Of these the most significant is *Preideu Annwfyn* ('The Spoils of Annwfyn'). The reason for the scarcity of references to Arthur is probably a matter of genre: 'that Arthur and Taliesin (like, say, Arthur and Charlemagne) were too important to share the same platform': P. Sims-Williams, 'The Early Welsh Arthurian Poems', in R. Bromwich *et al* (edd.) *The Arthur of the Welsh* (Cardiff, 1991), p. 51.

See M. Haycock, 'Llyfr Taliesin', *National Library of Wales Journal*, 25 (1988), pp. 357-86 for a discussion of the manuscript; a fuller study is provided by her unpublished 1983 doctoral dissertation. Further analysis of the manuscript and the poems can be found in Marged Haycock's published works, not least the article and book cited above; see also her 'Taliesin's Questions', *Cambrian Medieval Celtic Studies*, 33 (1997), pp. 19-79, and '"Some talk of Alexander and some of Hercules": three early medieval poems from the "Book of Taliesin"', *Cambridge Medieval Celtic Studies*, 13 (1987), pp.7-38.

Some debate exists over the links between the Taliesin poems and paganism, with John Koch suggesting that Haycock and others are wrong to argue that the Taliesin poems do not reflect in any way Celtic paganism and its struggles with Christianity: J.T. Koch, 'The Celtic Lands', in N.J. Lacy (ed.) *Medieval Arthurian Literature: A Guide to Recent Research* (New York, 1996), pp. 239-322 at pp. 263-65.

The text is available in J. Gwenogvryn Evans (ed.) *The Book of Taliesin: Facsimile and Text* (Llanbedrog, 1910) and the legendary poems are now edited, translated and discussed in Haycock's *Legendary Poems from the Book of Taliesin* (Aberystwyth, 2007). The Arthurian references are discussed – with further references – by Sims-Williams in his 'The Early Welsh Arthurian Poems', in R. Bromwich *et al* (edd.) *The Arthur of the Welsh* (Cardiff, 1991), pp. 33-71. A facsimile of the manuscript is also available online from the National Library of Wales at *http://www.llgc.org.uk/index.php?id=bookoftaliesin peniarthms2*.

c. The White Book of Rhydderch

The 'White Book of Rhydderch' (NLW Peniarth MSS. 4 and 5) is a remarkable and unprecedented compendium of medieval Welsh prose and poetry, written in the mid-fourteenth century, which is now bound in two volumes in the National Library of Wales. Peniarth 5, which originally preceded Peniarth 4, contains religious texts, the Welsh Charlemagne cycle and other matter. Peniarth 4 contains the earliest complete text of the 'Mabinogion' tales and, taken as a whole, the 'White Book' provides the earliest texts of much of the best of Welsh medieval secular prose.

A good recent discussion of the 'White Book' is Daniel Huws, 'Llyfr Gwyn Rhydderch', in D. Huws, *Medieval Welsh Manuscripts* (Cardiff, 2000), pp. 227-68 – a brief summary, by Huws, can also be read in R. Bromwich *et al* (edd.), *The Arthur of the Welsh* (Cardiff, 1991), pp. 9-11. The tales have been published in *The White Book Mabinogion* (Pwllheli, 1907) by J. Gwenogvryn Evans, reprinted as *Llyfr Gwyn Rhydderch* (Cardiff, 1973), as well as in numerous individual editions. Most relevant for present purposes is R. Bromwich and D. Simon Evans (edd.), *Culhwch and Olwen: An edition and study of the oldest Arthurian tale* (Cardiff, 1992). A full facsimile is available from the National Library of Wales at *http://www.llgc.org.uk/index.php?id= whitebookofrhydderchpeniart*.

d. The Red Book of Hergest

The 'Red Book of Hergest' (Jesus College, Oxford MS 111) is the largest of the of the Welsh medieval vernacular manuscripts and includes a copy of almost the whole of Welsh literature that dates pre-1400 (it was created by three sets of scribes working in collaboration sometime between 1382 and *c.* 1410), including the most extensive version of *Trioedd Ynys Prydein*, but with the exception of the materials in the 'Book of Aneirin', the 'Book of Taliesin', and the religious and legal texts. The chief scribe was one Hywel Fychan ap Hywel Goch of Builth and his hand has been identified in several other Welsh manuscripts, including in the 'White Book of Rhydderch', where the original scribe had left a space. There is a close correspondence between some of the texts in the 'Red' and 'White Books' (for example, their versions of the 'Mabinogion' and the Triads) and it is generally held that they derived independently from a lost common archetype.

The main texts of the 'Red Book' can be read in diplomatic editions in J. Rhys and J. Gwenogvryn Evans (edd.), *The Text of the Mabinogion and other Welsh tales from the Red Book of Hergest* (Oxford, 1887); J. Rhys and J. Gwenogvryn Evans (edd.), *The Texts of the Bruts from the Red Book of Hergest* (Oxford, 1890) and J. Gwenogvryn Evans, *The Poetry in the Red Book of Hergest* (Llanbedrog, 1911). A full facsimile of the 'Red Book of Hergest' is available online at *http://image.ox.ac.uk/show?collection=jesus&manuscript=ms 111*. For a description of the 'Red Book', see J. Gwenogvryn Evans, *Report on Manuscripts in the Welsh Language* (London, 1898-1910), II, pp. 1-29 and the references in R. Bromwich *et al* (edd.), *The Arthur of the Welsh* (Cardiff, 1991), p. 12.

e. *The Book of Aneirin*

The late thirteenth-century 'Book of Aneirin' (Cardiff MS 2.81) is a much-discussed manuscript of 38 small vellum pages, containing five poems (*Y Gododdin* and its four 'Additional Songs' or *Gorchanau*). Arthur is mentioned by name only once in the manuscript, in the B-text of *Y Gododdin*.

On the 'Book of Aneirin' see B.F. Roberts (ed.), *Early Welsh Poetry: Studies in the Book of Aneirin* (Aberystwyth, 1988) and for the text see I. Williams (ed.) *Canu Aneirin* (Cardiff, 1937). For *Y Gododdin* see the above and K.H. Jackson, *The Gododdin: The Oldest Scottish Poem* (Edinburgh, 1969), A.O.H. Jarman, *Aneirin: Y Gododdin, Britain's Oldest Heroic Poem* (Llandysul, 1988), and J.T. Koch, *The Gododdin of Aneirin: Text and Context from Dark-Age North Britain* (Cardiff, 1997). For a general overview of the 'Arthurian Allusions in the Book of Aneirin', see A.O.H. Jarman's article of the same name in *Studia Celtica*, 24/25 (1989/90), pp. 13-25. A full facsimile of the manuscript is available at the following website: *http://www.gtj.org.uk/en/small/item/GTJ10900//page/1/*.

3. The Texts

a. *Historia Brittonum §56 and the Annales Cambriae*

The Cambro-Latin *Historia Brittonum* was written anonymously in A.D. 829/30; whilst it has often been ascribed to one 'Nennius', this claim rests on very dubious evidence and is not really sustainable (see D.N. Dumville, 'Some Aspects of the Chronology of the *Historia Brittonum*', *Bulletin of the Board of Celtic Studies*, 25 (1974), pp. 439-45; D.N. Dumville, 'Nennius and the *Historia Brittonum*', *Studia Celtica*, 10/11 (1975/6), pp. 78-95. Cf. P.J.C. Field, 'Nennius and his History', *Studia Celtica*, 30 (1996), pp. 159-65). Although there has been considerable debate over the nature of the *Historia*, modern scholarship largely rejects the notion that it represents simply a 'heap' of earlier materials which can be mined for largely unaltered and genuinely ancient sources, brought together and preserved by a simple compiler in the ninth century, as promoted by L. Alcock, *Arthur's Britain: History and Archaeology AD 367-634* (Harmondsworth, 1973), p. 32. Instead, a detailed analysis of the text indicates that the author of the *Historia Brittonum* had, in the main, only very late and unreliable sources available to him; that he wrote with a unity of structure and outlook; and that he was engaged in the active processing of his sources. The result of this is that there seems little possibility of recovering usable information about the fifth and sixth centuries from his text. Furthermore, the claim that the twelve battles ascribed to Arthur in the *Historia Brittonum* §56 must have been taken from a pre-existing (and early) Welsh poem is merely an assumption, and one which recent academic commentators have rejected on a number of grounds. Given all of this, §56 of the *Historia Brittonum* can be only really considered to be evidence for the concept of Arthur possessed by the early ninth-century author of the *Historia*, nothing more. For a detailed discussions of all of this, see D.N. Dumville, 'The Historical Value of the *Historia Brittonum*', *Arthurian Literature*, 6 (1986), pp. 1-26; T.M. Charles-Edwards, 'The Arthur of History', in R. Bromwich *et al* (edd.) *The Arthur of the Welsh* (Cardiff, 1991), pp. 15-32; D.N. Dumville, '*Historia Brittonum*: an Insular History from the Carolingian Age', in A. Scharer and G. Scheibelreiter (edd.) *Historiographie im frühen Mittelalter* (Wien/München, 1994), pp. 406-34; T. Green, 'The Historicity and Historicisation of Arthur' (1998), archived at *http://www.arthuriana.co.uk/historicity/arthur.htm*; N.J. Higham, *King Arthur, Myth-Making and History* (London, 2002), pp. 119-69; T. Green, *Concepts of Arthur* (Stroud, 2007), pp.15-26, 30-44. The Arthurian battle-list in §56 runs as follows:

> At that time the Saxons increased their numbers and grew in Britain. On Hengest's death, his son Octha came down from the

north of Britain to the kingdom of the Kentishmen, and from him are sprung the kings of the Kentishmen. Then Arthur fought against them in those days, together with the kings of the British, but he was the *dux bellorum* ['leader in battles']. The first battle was at the mouth of the river called *Glein*. The second, the third, the fourth and the fifth were on another river, called the *Dubglas*, which is in the country of *Linnuis*. The sixth battle was on the river called *Bassas*. The seventh battle was in Celyddon Forest, that is *Cat Coit Celidon*. The eighth battle was in *Guinnion* Fort, and in it Arthur carried the image of the holy Mary, the everlasting Virgin, on his shoulders, and the heathen were put to flight this day, and there was a great slaughter upon them, through the power of Our Lord Jesus Christ and the power of the holy Virgin Mary, his mother. The ninth battle was fought in the city of the Legions. The tenth battle was fought on the bank of the river called *Tribruit*. The eleventh battle was on the hill called *Agned*. The twelfth battle was on *Badon* hill and in it nine hundred and sixty men fell in one day, from a single charge of Arthur's, and no one laid them low save he alone, and he was victorious in all his campaigns. (J. Morris, *Nennius: British History and The Welsh Annals* (Chichester, 1980), p. 35, with minor modifications)

The other important pre-Galfridian source which possesses a concept of Arthur as a historical figure who won battles against the Anglo-Saxons of *c.* A.D. 500 is the *Annales Cambriae*, 'The Welsh Annals'. This was compiled in the 950s and it contains the following references to Arthur:

[A.D. 516] *Bellum Badonis, in quo Arthur portavit crucem Domini nostril Jhesu Christi tribus diebus et tribus noctibus in humeros suos et Brittines victores fuerent...* [A.D. 537] *Guieth Camlann in qua Arthur et Medraut corruerunt, et mortalitas in Brittannia et in Hibernia fuit.* (Morris, 1980, p. 85)

[A.D. 516] The battle of Badon, in which Arthur carried the cross of our Lord Jesus Christ for three days and three nights on his shoulders, and the Britons were the victors... [A.D. 537] The battle of Camlann, in which Arthur and Medraut fell, and there was a great mortality [*i.e.* plague] in Britain and Ireland.

Although it has sometimes been maintained that these entries derive from much older British annals, this notion is extremely problematical in the light of the textual history of the *Annales Cambriae*: see especially K. Grabowski and D.N. Dumville, *Chronicles and Annals of Medieval Ireland and Wales*

(Woodbridge, 1984), pp. 209-26; Green, 2007, pp. 26-28. Furthermore, there seems to be some kind of relationship between the Badon entry and the *Historia Brittonum*'s account of Arthur's victory at *Guinnion*, with the result that a number of recent analyses have consider the *Annales* to be directly derivative of the *Historia Brittonum*'s account in terms of both its content and its concept of Arthur. See further J.T. Koch, 'The Celtic Lands', in N.J. Lacy (ed.) *Medieval Arthurian Literature: A Guide to Recent Research* (New York, 1996), pp. 239-322 at pp. 252-53; Higham, 2002, pp. 201-07; Green, 2007, pp. 28-30, 75-77, 216.

For a detailed discussion of both of these sources, and the context and reliability of their concepts of Arthur, see T. Green, *Concepts of Arthur* (Stroud, 2007), especially chapters one, two and six, and N.J. Higham, *King Arthur, Myth-Making and History* (London, 2002), especially pp. 119-69, 193-217. Latin texts with translations of both the *Historia Brittonum* and the *Annales Cambriae* can be most easily obtained in J. Morris (ed. and trans.) *Nennius: British History and The Welsh Annals* (Chichester, 1980). The best editions are, however, those of J. Stevenson (ed.) *Nennii Historia Britonum* (London, 1838), and E. Faral, *La Legende Arthurienne: Études et Documents, les plus Anciens Texts*, three volumes (Paris, 1929), III, pp. 1-62. The tenth-century Vatican Recension of the *Historia Brittonum* has been recently edited in D.N. Dumville (ed.), *Historia Brittonum: iii. The Vatican Recension* (Cambridge, 1985).

b. The Mirabilia of the Historia Brittonum

The *mirabilia* appear in §§67-75 of the *Historia Brittonum* (dated A.D. 829/30) and consist of twenty marvels. The first four are numbered (the rest simply begin *Aliud miraculum est*, 'Another wonder is' or *Est aliud mirabile*, 'There is another wonder') and are not located in Wales. Marvels 5 to 14 are located in Wales, generally in the south-east of the country and along the English border, and the last six marvels are those of Anglesey (15-18) and Ireland (19-20). The non-Welsh marvels appear to be drawn from pre-existing sources but the central group (5-14) seem to be of a somewhat different character – they seem to have had a much more popular context for the editor than the others in his list, and the nature of his account of them suggests that he was personally acquainted with these *mirabilia*. Of these 'Welsh' marvels, two (in §73 of the *Historia*) are associated with Arthur:

> There is another wonder in the country called Builth. There is a heap of stones there, and one of these stones placed on the top of the pile has the footprint of a dog on it. When he hunted Twrch Trwyth, Cafal (*Cabal*), the warrior Arthur's hound, impressed his footprint on the stone, and Arthur later brought together the pile of

stones, under the stone in which was his dog's footprint, and it is called Carn Cafal (*Carn Cabal*). Men come and take the stone in their hands for the space of a day and a night, and on the morrow it is found upon the stone pile. (J. Morris, *Nennius: British History and The Welsh Annals* (Chichester, 1980), p. 42, marvel no. 12)

Carn Cabal is a prehistoric cairn which gives its name to Corn Cafallt, a hill near Rhaeadr (Powys). The significance of this marvel lies mainly in the fact that it is a solid indication that the core of the tale of the hunting of *Twrch Trwyth*, told in detail in *Culhwch ac Olwen*, existed in the early ninth century at the latest and that Arthur was already associated with it; also significant is the fact that Arthur's hound is called *Cabal* 'horse', suggesting that the dog was perceived as being huge. There is an illustration and description of a candidate for the stone referred to in the *Historia* in Lady Charlotte Guest's *The Mabinogion* (London, 1849), II, p. 360 (p. 290 of the compact 1877 edition). This Arthurian 'marvel' has been considered to be already ancient by the ninth century (see Rachel Bromwich and D. Simon Evans (edd.), *Culhwch and Olwen. An edition and study of the oldest Arthurian tale* (Cardiff, 1992), p. lxvi, and T. Green, *Concepts of Arthur* (Stroud, 2007), pp. 67-70). The other Arthurian *mirabile* is number 13:

There is another wonder in the country called Ergyng (*Erging*). There is a tomb there by a spring, called Llygad Amr (*Licat Amr*); the name of the man who was buried in the tomb was Amr. He was the son of the warrior Arthur, and he killed him there and buried him. Men come to measure the tomb, and it is sometimes six feet long, sometimes nine, sometimes twelve, sometimes fifteen. At whatever measure you measure it on one occasion, you never find it again of the same measure, and I have tried it myself. (Morris, 1980, p. 42, marvel no. 13)

The region *Erging* is Archenfield (Herefordshire) and the usual identification of the spring *Licat Amr* 'the eye [or source] of *Amr*' is the river Gamber in Herefordshire and its source Gamber Head in Llanwarne, next to which is a now-destroyed prehistoric tumulus which is presumably the grave. Clearly this 'marvel' is, like the one above, an onomastic topographic tale drawn from local, popular folklore and here designed to explain the name *Licat Amr* and an associated grave. The story of Arthur killing Amr is otherwise unknown, although 'Amhar son of Arthur' appears in *Geraint* as one of Arthur's four chamberlains along with Bedwyr's son, Amhren: see Gwyn and Thomas Jones (trans.), *The Mabinogion* (London, 1949), p. 231. The milieu of the two Arthurian *mirabilia* is thus one of wonderful animals, supernatural events and remarkable features in the landscape that are explained by reference to Arthur and his attendant legends.

For a discussion of the *mirabilia* see O.J. Padel, 'The Nature of Arthur', *Cambrian Medieval Celtic Studies*, 27 (1994), pp. 1-31 particularly pp. 2-4; B.F. Roberts, '*Culhwch ac Olwen*, the Triads, Saint's Lives', in R. Bromwich, A.O.H. Jarman and B.F. Roberts (edd.), *The Arthur of the Welsh: The Arthurian Legend in Medieval Welsh Literature* (Cardiff, 1991), pp. 73-95 at pp. 88-93; Patrick K. Ford, 'On the Significance of some Arthurian Names in Welsh', *Bulletin of the Board of Celtic Studies*, 30 (1983), pp. 268-73; and T. Green, *Concepts of Arthur* (Stroud, 2007), pp. 67-72. A Latin text and translation of the *mirabilia* can be most easily had from J. Morris (ed. and trans.), *Nennius: British History and The Welsh Annals* (Chichester, 1980). The best editions of the *Historia Brittonum* are, however, those of J. Stevenson (ed.), *Nennii Historia Britonum* (London, 1838), and E. Faral, *La Legende Arthurienne: Études et Documents, les Plus Anciens Texts*, three volumes (Paris, 1929), III, pp. 1-62.

c. Y Gododdin

The collection of heroic death-songs known as *Y Gododdin* is found in the late thirteenth-century 'Book of Aneirin'. There has been much debate over the statement that the warrior Gwawddur 'fed black ravens on the rampart of a fort, though he was no Arthur' (B.38).[1] Thomas Charles-Edwards, building on his theory of textual transmission – set forth in T.M. Charles-Edwards, 'The Authenticity of the *Gododdin*: A Historian's View', in R. Bromwich and R.B. Jones (edd.) *Astudiaethau ar yr Hengerdd, Studies in Old Welsh Poetry* (Cardiff, 1978), pp. 44-71 – has concluded that, as the reference to Arthur only occurs in the B text and not the A text of *Y Gododdin*, it need be no older than the ninth or tenth century ('The Arthur of History', in R. Bromwich *et al* (edd.) *The Arthur of the Welsh* (Cardiff, 1991), p. 14). Recently, however, John Koch has attempted to 'reconstruct' the text of *Y Gododdin* (via principles of textual criticism and historical linguistics) to show how it would have looked if it was composed and written down pre-638, as he believes it to have been, and he argues that the *awdl* which mentions Arthur should be seen as part of this 'original' text of *Y Gododdin* (*The Gododdin of Aneirin: Text and Context from Dark-Age North Britain* (Cardiff, 1997), esp. Introduction and pp. 147-48). Whether he is right or not is, of course, to be debated; Graham Isaac, for example, has instead argued that there is no linguistic evidence which would necessitate dating *Y Gododdin* as a whole

---

1 J.T. Koch, *The Gododdin of Aneirin. Text and Context from Dark-Age North Britain* (Cardiff, 1997), numbers this *awdl* ('stanza') B².38 and reconstructs the Arthurian reference as *cït-nï·be em Arthür*. The word translated above as 'fed, glutted', *gochore*, is taken by Koch as 'sends down, draws down, entices' but this does not change the meaning of the passage.

before the ninth or tenth century: G.R. Isaac, *The Verb in the Book of Aneirin: Studies in Syntax Morphology and Etymology* (Tübingen, 1996), and G.R. Isaac, 'Readings in the History and Transmission of the Gododdin', *Cambrian Medieval Celtic Studies*, 37 (1999), pp. 55-78. See T. Green, *Concepts of Arthur* (Stroud, 2007), pp. 13-14, 50-52, for an overview and discussion of recent opinions.

Whatever the date of this *awdl*, the nature of the Arthurian reference and its concept of Arthur deserve comment. As Koch has observed, 'Arthur is presented as the unrivalled paragon of martial valour and is thus used to form a highly unusual comparison by rendering explicitly inferior the honorand of the *awdl*.' Arthur was clearly viewed by the poet as the impossible comparison, a 'Brittonic superhero' and legendary paragon of heroism to whose heights of valour not even a man who killed 300 in one rush could compare (J.T. Koch, 'The Celtic Lands', in N.J. Lacy (ed.) *Medieval Arthurian Literature: A Guide to Recent Research* (New York, 1996), pp. 239-322 at p. 242; see further O.J. Padel, 'The Nature of Arthur', *Cambrian Medieval Celtic Studies*, 27 (1994), p. 14; Green, 2007, pp. 14-15, 52). This concept of Arthur does not only appear in *Y Gododdin*; it is also to be found in a number of other non-Galfridian sources, including the mid-seventh-century *Marwnad Cynddylan* and the poetry of the twelfth- and thirteenth-century *Gogynfeirdd*.

Turning away from the reference to Arthur, there is one other significant 'Arthurian' allusion in *Y Gododdin*. This is the appearance of Myrddin (Merddin, Merlin) in the A text of *Y Gododdin* (stanza A.40), where it is said that *amuc Moryen / gwenwawt Mirdyn*, 'Morien defended the fair song [*or* blessed inspired verse] of Myrddin'. Unlike in the case of B².38, this *awdl* is found in both texts of *Y Gododdin* (A.40 and B¹.5), suggesting it may go back to the 'original' poem. However, whilst the *awdl* is present in both texts, the reference to *gwenwawt Mirdyn* is absent from the stanza in the more archaic B text and it has been excluded by Koch from his reconstruction of *Y Gododdin*. It is generally agreed that the Myrddin allusion cannot be seen as original to the poem and instead it should be considered as a relatively late interpolation to the text (*i.e.* belonging to perhaps the tenth to twelfth centuries, see Koch, 1996, pp. 242, 245; Koch, 1997, pp. lxxxv, ciii, cvi, 157-62; A.O.H. Jarman, 'The Arthurian Allusions in the Book of Aneirin', *Studia Celtica*, 24/25 (1989/90), pp. 20-23). It should, of course, be noted that this reference is, in any case, only tangentially 'Arthurian' as Myrddin and Arthur were not associated with each other in pre-Galfridian tradition.

For the text of *Y Gododdin*, see I. Williams (ed.) *Canu Aneirin* (Cardiff, 1938). For translations and reconstructed texts, see K.H. Jackson, *The Gododdin: The Oldest Scottish Poem* (Edinburgh, 1969); A.O.H. Jarman, *Aneirin: Y Gododdin, Britain's Oldest Heroic Poem* (Llandysul, 1988); and J.T. Koch, *The Gododdin of Aneirin: Text and Context from Dark-Age North Britain* (Cardiff, 1997).

d. Marwnad Cynddylan

The archaic heroic elegy *Marwnad Cynddylan* ('The Death-song of Cynddylan', a seventh-century prince of Powys) only survives in manuscripts dating from *c.* 1631 and later; the earliest is NLW 4973, p. 108ff., copied by Dr John Davies of Mallwyd. However these are believed to be accurate and reliable copies of much earlier originals and *Marwnad Cynddylan* has been shown to have been almost certainly composed in East Powys immediately after Cynddylan's death at *Winwæd* in A.D. 655 – see J. Rowland's *Early Welsh Saga Poetry: a Study and Edition of the Englynion* (Cambridge, 1990).

The poem would seem to refer to Arthur in much the same way as does *Y Gododdin* (Rowland, 1990, p. 186 suggests an alternate, non-Arthurian reading for the text of the poem, but this doesn't seem to have gained general acceptance). It implies that the military deeds of Cynddylan and his brothers are of such great valour that these warriors might be seen as *canawon Artur fras, dinas dengyn*, 'whelps of great Arthur, a mighty fortress' (see R. Bromwich, 'Concepts of Arthur', *Studia Celtica*, 10/11 (1975-6), pp. 163-81 at p. 177; T. Green, *Concepts of Arthur* (Stroud, 2007), pp. 53-54; R. Bromwich *et al*, 'Introduction', in R. Bromwich *et al* (edd.) *The Arthur of the Welsh: The Arthurian Legend in Medieval Welsh Literature* (Cardiff, 1991), pp. 1-14 at p. 5; J.T. Koch, 'The Celtic Lands', in N.J. Lacy (ed.) *Medieval Arthurian Literature: A Guide to Recent Research* (New York, 1996), pp. 239-322 at pp. 245-46. 'Fortress', *dinas*, here has the sense of 'defender, defence'). As such it shows that the concepts of Arthur as a 'peerless warrior' and the ultimate standard of comparison were present in East Powys (roughly modern Shropshire) by the mid-seventh century. This concept of Arthur as the 'paragon of military valour' is clearly shared by other non-Galfridian Welsh sources too, such as the poems *Kadeir Teyrnon*, *Gereint fil[ius] Erbin*, *Ymddiddan Arthur a'r Eryr*, and *Marwnat vthyr pen[dragon]*, and is also to be found in the works of the *Gogynfeirdd*.

See J. Rowland, *Early Welsh Saga Poetry: a Study and Edition of the Englynion* (Cambridge, 1990), for an edition, translation and discussion of the historical context of this poem; J.T. Koch and J. Carey, *The Celtic Heroic Age: Literary Sources for Ancient Celtic Europe and Early Ireland and Wales* (Malden, Mass., 1995), pp. 360-62 also has a translation of the whole poem.

e. Pa gur yv y porthaur?

Pa gur yv y porthaur? ('What man is the gatekeeper/porter?', also known as *Ymddiddan Arthur a Glewlwyd Gafaelfawr*, 'The Dialogue of Arthur and Glewlwyd Gafaelfawr') is an important pre-Galfridian Arthurian dialogue poem from the 'Black Book of Carmarthen'. It should most probably be dated to roughly the same period as the other Black Book *Ymddiddan*, that is the ninth or tenth century (R. Bromwich, 'Introduction', and B.F. Roberts, 'Rhai o Gerddi Ymddiddan Llyfr Du Caerfyrddin', in R. Bromwich and R.B. Jones (edd.) *Astudiaethau ar yr Hengerdd* (Cardiff, 1978), pp. 20-21, 281-325; B.F. Roberts, '*Culhwch ac Olwen*, The Triads, Saints' Lives', in R. Bromwich *et al* (edd.) *The Arthur of the Welsh* (Cardiff, 1991), pp. 73-95 at p. 78; see further T. Green, *Concepts of Arthur*, p. 80). However, as with much Old Welsh verse, a later date is impossible to rule out entirely and, indeed, Koch has pointed out that a date of composition in the eighth century is not implausible in the case of this poem (in *Speculum*, 69.4 (1994), pp. 1127-29).

The poem is, itself, simply a summary of many earlier mythical Arthurian tales, as Sims-Williams has pointed out ('The Early Welsh Arthurian Poems', in R. Bromwich *et al* (edd.) *The Arthur of the Welsh* (Cardiff, 1991), p. 38). In it Arthur is the head of a company of folkloric heroes and pagan gods who exercise marvellous and superhuman powers. It has 90 extant lines, the ending of the piece being lost due to a missing manuscript leaf (which unfortunately means that the poem breaks off in the middle of an extremely intriguing sentence). In the extant portion of the poem Bedwyr and Cai are Arthur's main henchmen and its general world is one in which Arthur and his men fight battles against human or supernatural enemies, including cynocephali (dog-headed men), witches, and Palug's Cat. The relationship between *Pa gur?* and *Culhwch ac Olwen* is problematical as there is some overlap – however, given the length of *Culhwch ac Olwen*, overlap is understandable and there are many points on which there is no overlap. It is thus unlikely that the compilers of *Culhwch* drew on a written text of *Pa gur?*, though they may well have known of it. Rather they both seem to draw from the same body of early Arthurian tradition, but with *Pa gur?* representing 'a stage prior to the merging of that tradition with the story of the wooing of the giant's daughter' and one at which Arthur and his heroes were outside the gate rather than inside the court (Koch, 1996, p. 261). The poem begins as a dialogue between Arthur and Glewlwyd:

> 'What man is the gatekeeper?'
> -'Glewlwyd Great Grasp;
> what man asks it?'
> - 'Arthur and [*or* with] Cai the fair.'
> - 'What [band] goes with you?'
> - 'The best men in the world.'
> -'Into my house you will not come
> unless you vouch for them'
> - 'I shall vouch for them,
> and you will see them,'
> (lines 1-10: Sims-Williams, 1991, p. 40)

This porter scene is probably a stock narrative formula of vernacular story-telling (analogous scenes are to be had in chapter 32 of the ninth-century *Historia Brittonum* and in *Culhwch ac Olwen*) which is derived from Celtic mythology (see Koch, 1996, p. 261, and 'Further to *Tongu Do Dia Toinges Mo Thuath*, &c.', *Études Celtiques*, 29 (1992), pp. 249-61). The word *gwared* that Sims-Williams translates as 'vouch for' can also be translated as 'disclose', 'discover'. Thomas Jones has plausibly suggested in light of this that the passage should be taken as indicating that when Arthur and his followers arrive at the gate they are invisible and that, 'since Arthur promises to reveal them,' one of Arthur's "endowments' or magical gifts in the background story was the power to make his men invisible' (T. Jones, 'The Early Evolution of the Legend of Arthur', *Nottingham Medieval Studies*, 8 (1964), pp. 3-21 at pp. 16-17). After the above passage the poem develops into a list of Arthur's men and their exploits recounted by Arthur, including deeds by Arthur himself:

> Though Arthur laughed [*or* ?played]
> he caused the/her blood to flow
> in Afarnach's hall,
> fighting with a witch.
> He pierced Cudgel(?) Head
> in the dwellings of Disethach.
> On the mountain of Edinburgh
> he fought with dogheads.
> By the hundred they fell;
> they fell by the hundred
> before Bedwyr the Perfect [*or* Perfect-Sinew].
> (lines 37-47: Sims-Williams, 1991, pp. 41-42)

The final conflict mentioned by the poem (lines 81-90) is a battle against *lleuon*, 'lions, wild-cats' and the monstrous sea-cat *Cath Paluc* ('Clawing Cat', later 'Palug's Cat') attributed to Cai. In other sources this features Arthur rather than Cai and it seems probable that all the sources are recounting a generally Arthurian battle, with Cai simply made prominent in *Pa gur?*'s telling and Arthur elsewhere. This might well apply to all the battles referred to in the poem and it is most interesting that the Arthurian battle against were-wolves at *Traeth Tryfrwyd*, mentioned in *Pa gur?* (lines 19-22, 48-51) as involving both Bedwyr and the sea-god Manawydan son of Llyr, is included in *Historia Brittonum* §56 as Arthur's tenth battle.

For a full discussion and translation of *Pa gur?* see P. Sims-Williams, 'The Early Welsh Arthurian Poems', in Bromwich *et al* (edd.) *The Arthur of the Welsh* (Cardiff, 1991), pp. 33-71 at pp. 38-46, and T. Green, *Concepts of Arthur* (Stroud, 2007), pp. 79-85, 100-2, 106, 112-13, 119-21. See also

A.O.H. Jarman, 'The Delineation of Arthur in Early Welsh Verse', in K. Varty (ed.) *An Arthurian Tapestry: Essays in Memory of Lewis Thorpe* (Glasgow, 1981), pp. 1-21 at pp. 7-10; A.O.H. Jarman, 'The Arthurian Allusions in the Black Book of Carmarthen', in P.B. Grout *et al* (edd.) *The Legend of Arthur in the Middle Ages* (Cambridge, 1983), pp. 99-112 at pp. 107-11; B.F. Roberts, 'Rhai o Gerddi Ymddiddan Llyfr Du Caerfyrddin', in R. Bromwich and R.B. Jones (edd.) *Astudiaethau ar yr Hengerdd* (Cardiff, 1978), pp. 281-325 (which includes the text of the poem); and B.F. Roberts, '*Culhwch ac Olwen*, the Triads, Saint's Lives', in R. Bromwich *et al* (edd.) *The Arthur of the Welsh* (Cardiff, 1991), pp. 73-95 at pp. 78-79. For an interesting comparison between this poem and the fragmentary English ballad 'King Arthur and King Cornwall', see O.J. Padel, *Arthur in Medieval Welsh Literature* (Cardiff, 2000), pp. 30-32.

f. Culhwch ac Olwen

Culhwch ac Olwen is the earliest tale in the so-called 'Mabinogion' and is preserved in two manuscripts: the 'White Book of Rhydderch' (Peniarth 4, cols.452-88) and the 'Red Book of Hergest' (cols.810-44), with the White Book only having the first two thirds of the story. The language of *Culhwch ac Olwen* appears to be Late Old Welsh and the composition of the extant redaction of the tale is generally placed in the late eleventh century, although one recent reviewer has suggested dating it to the mid-twelfth century: see R. Bromwich and D.S. Evans (edd.), *Culhwch and Olwen: An edition and study of the oldest Arthurian tale* (Cardiff, 1992), pp. xiv-xxv, lxxvii-lxxxiii; J.T. Koch, 'The Celtic Lands', in N.J. Lacy (ed.) *Medieval Arthurian Literature: A Guide to Recent Research* (New York, 1996), pp. 258-59; D. Edel, 'The Arthur of "Culhwch and Olwen" as a figure of Epic-Heroic Tradition', *Reading Medieval Studies*, 9 (1983), p. 3; S. Rodway, 'The Date and Authorship of Culhwch ac Olwen: A Reassessment', *Cambrian Medieval Celtic Studies*, 49 (2005), pp. 21-44. All of the above datings do, however, cause some significant problems if we choose to give a roughly similar date to the quintessentially Middle Welsh 'Four Branches of the Mabinogi' (as has often been the case) and Jones, Jackson and, most recently, Ford have all instead offered a mid to late tenth- or early eleventh-century date for the tale: T. Jones and G. Jones (trans.), *The Mabinogion* (London, 1949), p. ix; K.H. Jackson, *A Celtic Miscellany* (Harmondsworth, 1971), pp. 197-204; P.K. Ford, 'Culhwch and Olwen', in N.J. Lacy (ed.) *The New Arthurian Encyclopedia* (Garland, New York, 1996), pp. 104-06, also p. 508; see also Koch, 1996, pp. 258-59. Such a dating is also suggested by Koch, who has recently dated the tale tentatively to *c.* 1000 (J.T. Koch, *The Gododdin of Aneirin* (Cardiff, 1997), pp. civ, cv), and Edel, who supports a date in the second half of the tenth century for a written version of at least some parts of *Culhwch ac Olwen* (Edel, 1983, p. 3).

The concept of Arthur held by the tale is both that of a great overlord (he is the 'Chief of the Kings of Britain') and a renowned monster-slayer. Though *Culhwch ac Olwen* is most probably a literary composition it was clearly based on a number of earlier oral and legendary Arthurian tales which were brought together and fused with the 'giant's daughter' folklore tale-type to create the story as we now possess it – the Arthurian material is generally considered to represent the same body of very early non-historical tales as *Pa gur yv y porthaur?*, *Historia Brittonum* Chapter 73 and *Preideu Annwfyn* do. The two most obvious examples of such pre-existing tales incorporated into *Culhwch ac Olwen* are (1) the stories of the hunting of the divine great boar Twrch Trwyth – which is an event associated with Arthur from at least as early as the eighth century on the evidence of the *Historia Brittonum* (see Bromwich and Evans, 1992, p. lxvi: the concept of a mythical Giant Boar probably has its origins in pagan Celtic religious beliefs), and (2) the journey to Ireland by Arthur in his ship Prydwen to seize the cauldron of Diwrnach, which is clearly related to the journey to the Otherworld told in the eighth-century or earlier poem *Preideu Annwfyn*. Both would appear to partly derive in *Culhwch* from local onomastic folklore. Other early Arthurian tales which would seem to be preserved in the story of *Culhwch ac Olwen* include the killing of the Very Black Witch 'in the Uplands of Hell'; the killing of the giants Wrnach and Dillus the Bearded; the rescue by Arthur's warband of the pagan god Mabon ap Modron from an Otherworldly fortress; and Arthur's settling of a dispute between the divine Gwyn ap Nudd and Gwythyr ap Greidawl. See further particularly Bromwich and Evans, 1992, especially pp. xlvii-lxxv; T. Green, *Concepts of Arthur* (Stroud, 2007), especially pp. 57-59, 65, 68-69, 95-100, 107-08, 112-16, 159-62, 166, 173-75; Edel, 1983; and B.F. Roberts, '*Culhwch ac Olwen*, the Triads, Saint's Lives', in R. Bromwich *et al* (edd.) *The Arthur of the Welsh* (Cardiff, 1991), pp. 73-95 especially pp. 76-80).

At least some of the main characters of the tale (including both Culhwch and Olwen) may not have been traditional and have almost no recorded existence outside of the story itself, belonging to the 'giant's daughter' folk-legend that forms a frame for the pre-existing Arthurian tales rather than these tales themselves, although Yspaddaden Pen-kawr may have his origins in pre-500 oral tradition (see Koch, 1996, p. 256) and the name *Culhwch* is mentioned in a probably ninth-century *englyn* from a lament to Cynddylan of Powys. For the text with superb notes, a bibliography and a full discussion see Rachel Bromwich and D. Simon Evans (edd.) *Culhwch and Olwen: An edition and study of the oldest Arthurian tale* (Cardiff, 1992). See also T. Green, *Concepts of Arthur* (Stroud, 2007), chapters two, three and four; B.F. Roberts, '*Culhwch ac Olwen*, the Triads, Saint's Lives', in R. Bromwich *et al* (edd.) *The Arthur of the Welsh* (Cardiff, 1991), pp. 73-95; D. Edel 'The Arthur of "Culhwch and Olwen" as a figure of Epic-Heroic Tradition', *Reading Medieval Studies*, 9 (1983), pp. 3-15; and J.T. Koch, 'The Celtic Lands', in N.J.

Lacy (ed.) *Medieval Arthurian Literature* (New York, 1996), pp. 239-322 at pp. 256-62. Modern and reliable translations are available in T. Jones and G. Jones (trans.), *The Mabinogion* (London, 1949) and P.K. Ford (trans.), *The Mabinogi* (Berkeley, 1977).

g. Preideu Annwfyn

Preideu Annwfyn ('The Spoils of the Otherworld') is contained in the fourteenth century 'Book of Taliesin' (Poem XXX) and features the figures of Taliesin and Arthur. Haycock has suggested that the date of composition cannot easily be narrowed further than to the Old Welsh period in general but this has been challenged by Koch, who has shown that a mid to late eighth-century date would suit this poem, making it an earlier witness to the Arthurian legend than the *Historia Brittonum*: M. Haycock, '"Preiddeu Annwn" and the Figure of Taliesin', *Studia Celtica*, 18/19 (1983-4), p. 57; J.T. Koch, 'The Celtic Lands', in N.J. Lacy (ed.) *Medieval Arthurian Literature* (New York, 1996), pp. 263-65. Koch's research does, of course, confirm and vindicates Sir Ifor Williams' opinion that the poem should be dated to *c.* 900 or before (in R.S. Loomis, '"The Spoils of Annwn": An Early Welsh Poem', in R.S. Loomis, *Wales and the Arthurian Legend* (Cardiff, 1956), p. 131). It should be noted that the features Koch uses to date the poem to the mid to late eighth century would be present in earlier compositions also, and the mid to late eighth century might therefore be seen as a *terminus ante quem*.

The background to the poem is a story of an expedition by Arthur in his ship, Prydwen, to Annwfyn – the Celtic Otherworld – to seize a magical cauldron belonging to *Pen Annwfyn* ('The Chief of the Otherworld'), along with one or more remarkable/faery animals, from a fortress there, to which there are numerous analogues in Celtic literature (for example, the quest for Diwrnach the Irishman's cauldron in *Culhwch ac Olwen*). There also seems to be a story of the imprisonment of Gweir in the Otherworld and his release by Arthur, which again finds analogues in *Culhwch ac Olwen* (with the rescue by Arthur's warband of the pagan god Mabon ap Modron from an Otherworldly fortress) and elsewhere. Fuller versions of these stories must, by necessity, have been part of the mental furniture of the audience of *Preideu Annwfyn* in order that they might understand the now obscure allusions contained within it. As such, these stories must pre-date to some unknowable degree the composition of the poem: see Haycock, 1983-4, p. 55; T. Green, *Concepts of Arthur* (Stroud, 2007), pp. 54-67.

For discussion, text and translation see M. Haycock, '"Preiddeu Annwn" and the Figure of Taliesin', *Studia Celtica*, 18/19 (1983-4), pp. 52-78; M. Haycock (ed. and trans.), *Legendary Poems from the Book of Taliesin* (Aberystwyth, 2007), pp. 433-51. For detailed analyses of the poem see also T. Green, *Concepts of Arthur* (Stroud, 2007), especially pp. 54-67, 159-60; P.

Sims-Williams, 'The Early Welsh Arthurian Poems', in Bromwich *et al* (edd.) *The Arthur of the Welsh* (Cardiff, 1991), pp. 33-71 at pp. 54-57; A. Budgey, '"Preiddeu Annwn" and the Welsh Tradition of Arthur', in C.J. Burne, M. Harry and P. Ó Siadhail (edd.) *Celtic Languages and Celtic People* (Halifax, Nova Scotia, 1992), pp. 391-404; and R.S. Loomis, "The Spoils of Annwn' An Early Welsh Poem', in R.S. Loomis, *Wales and the Arthurian Legend* (Cardiff, 1956), pp. 131-78. Both Budgey and Loomis contain alternative translations of the text, as do J.B. Coe and S. Young (ed. and trans.), *The Celtic Sources for the Arthurian Legend* (Felinfach, 1995), and J.T. Koch and J. Carey (ed. and trans.), *The Celtic Heroic Age: Literary Sources for Ancient Celtic Europe and Early Ireland and Wales* (Malden, Mass., 1995).

h. *Englynion y Beddau*

The *Englynion y Beddau* ('Stanzas of the Graves') record, 'often with unexpected poetic power, the sites of the graves of once-famous heroes, testifying to the close association between heroes and places in early Welsh literature' (P. Sims-Williams, 'The Early Welsh Arthurian Poems', in R. Bromwich *et al* (edd.) *The Arthur of the Welsh* (Cardiff, 1991), p. 49), and 'the heroes named...belong to legend and folklore rather than to history' (A.O.H. Jarman, 'The Arthurian Allusions in the Black Book of Carmarthen', in P.B. Grout *et al* (edd.) *The Legend of Arthur in the Middle Ages* (Cambridge, 1983), pp. 99-112 at p. 111). Whilst the earliest extant manuscript containing them (the 'Black Book of Carmarthen') dates to the thirteenth century, there can be no doubt that the vast majority of the *englynion* are far older than this – Jenny Rowland has recently dated the Black Book text to the mid to late ninth century, but as antiquarian records of oral tales and topographic folklore they may well represent much older traditions: J. Rowland, *Early Welsh Saga Poetry: a Study and Edition of the Englynion* (Cambridge, 1990), p. 389; see also T. Jones, 'The Black Book of Carmarthen: Stanzas of the Graves', *Proceedings of the British Academy*, 53 (1967), pp. 97-137. Of the 73 stanzas in the Black Book, only three (8, 12 and 44) mention well-known Arthurian characters and of these the most important is no. 44 which names Arthur himself:

> [There is] a grave for March, a grave for Gwythur,
> a grave for Gwgawn Red-sword;
> the world's wonder (*anoeth*) [is] a grave for Arthur.
> (Sims-Williams, 1991, p. 49)

The poet's implication is that the graves of these Arthurian heroes are known but that of Arthur himself is *anoeth*, impossible to find/achieve, probably because he was rumoured not to be dead (a belief which is referred to elsewhere in the pre-Galfridian literature, see T. Green, *Concepts of Arthur* (Stroud, 2007), pp. 72-75). With regards to the other heroes in this passage, Gwythur is found associated with Arthur in *Culhwch ac Olwen* and *Kanu y Meirch*; Gwgawn appears in *Breuddwyd Rhonabwy*; and March is the cuckolded king of the semi-Arthurian Tristan stories. The following two stanzas (8 and 12, respectively) also concern characters and events from the early Arthurian legend:

> The grave of Gwalchmai is in Peryddon (*periton*)
> as a reproach to men;
> at Llanbardarn is the grave of Cynon.

> The grave of Osfran's son is at Camlann,
> after many a slaughter;
> the grave of Bedwyr is on Tryfan hill.
> (Sims-Williams, 1991, p. 50)

The grave of Gwalchmai, Arthur's nephew in *Culhwch ac Olwen*, is also referred to by William of Malmesbury *c.* 1125 in his *Gesta Regum Anglorum*, where is it placed upon the sea-shore 'in the province of Wales called R(h)os' and is said to be fourteen feet long (compare both the size of the grave and nature of the tale with the grave of Amr, Arthur's son, in the *mirabilia* of the *Historia Brittonum*). *Alld Tryvan* probably refers to Tryfan in Snowdonia but unfortunately no other non-Galfridian references to a tale of Bedwyr's death have survived to us; Camlann is obviously Arthur's last legendary defeat and the collocation with Tryfan in the above *englyn* suggests it was identified, at least by this ninth-century text, with Camlann near Mallwyd, Merionethshire.

See T. Green, *Concepts of Arthur* (Stroud, 2007), pp. 72-78, and P. Sims-Williams, 'The Early Welsh Arthurian Poems', in R. Bromwich *et al* (edd.) *The Arthur of the Welsh: The Arthurian Legend in Medieval Welsh Literature* (Cardiff, 1991), pp. 33-71 at pp. 49-51, for an examination of the *Englynion*. O.J. Padel's 'The Nature of Arthur', *Cambrian Medieval Celtic Studies*, 27 (1994), pp. 1-31 at pp. 8-12, has discussion of the belief that Arthur was not dead and would return, as does Green, 2007, chapter two. For the text and discussion see Thomas Jones, 'The Black Book of Carmarthen: Stanzas of the Graves', *Proceedings of the British Academy*, 53 (1967), pp. 97-137.

i. *Kat Godeu*

Kat Godeu ('The Battle of the Forest') is one of the so-called transformational poems from the fourteenth-century 'Book of Taliesin'. As it stands the poem itself certainly dates from later than the sixth century but contains elements which may reflect much older sources, for example the possible survival of pagan tree-lore (John B. Coe and Simon Young (ed. and trans.), *The Celtic Sources for the Arthurian Legend* (Felinfach, 1995), p. 141). The bulk of the poem is concerned with a great mythological battle – also mentioned in a variety of other non-Galfridian sources – fought by the divine sons of Dôn via an army of magically animated trees, the forest thus animated, it has been argued, being the famed *Coed Celyddon*, 'the Caledonian Forest': Ifor Williams, *The Poems of Taliesin* (Dublin, 1968), pp. xliii-xliv; R. Bromwich (ed. and trans.), *Trioedd Ynys Prydein. The Welsh Triads* (Cardiff, 1978), pp. 207-08, 540; M. Haycock, 'The Significance of the "Cad Goddau" Tree-List in the Book of Taliesin', in M.J. Bell *et al* (edd) *Celtic Linguistics: Readings in the Brythonic Languages for T. Arwyn Watkins* (Amsterdam, 1990), pp. 297-331 at pp. 308-09.

Arthur himself is named only once, when the 'druids of the wise one' are commanded to 'prophesy [to] Arthur' (lines 237-238). The text here could mean either 'of Arthur' or 'to Arthur', but it seems more likely that they are to prophesy to him and that he was therefore present (P. Sims-Williams 'The Early Welsh Arthurian Poems', in R. Bromwich *et al* (edd.) *The Arthur of the Welsh* (Cardiff, 1991), pp. 33-71 at pp. 51-52). In addition, near the beginning of the poem the 'lord of Britain' is mentioned in the context of the battle and Haycock has argued that this should probably be seen as a reference to Arthur too (see Haycock 1990, p. 298):

> *Keint yg kat godeu bric / Rac Prydein wledic*

> I sang in the van of the tree-battalion (or 'in the battle of the branchy trees') before the lord of Britain. (lines 26-7: Sims-Williams 1991, p. 52)

Therefore in *Kat Godeu* we seem to have a potentially early poem that features a mythical battle fought by the trees of *Coed Celyddon*, which is in some – perhaps major – way associated with Arthur; for a full discussion of all this, including the potential date of *Kat Godeu* itself, see T. Green, *Concepts of Arthur* (Stroud, 2007), pp. 62-67. The association of this battle with Arthur – henceforth called *Cad Goddau* to distinguish it from the poem of the same name – is, to some large degree, confirmed by an examination of other early sources. Thus, in the poem *Kat Godeu*, at least part of the fighting – coming immediately after the reference to 'the lord of Britain' – is focussed around a fort called *Kaer Nefenhir.*

> I wounded a great scaly animal: a hundred heads on him
> And a fierce host beneath the base of his tongue,
> And another host is on his necks.

A black, forked toad: a hundred claws on him.
An enchanted, crested snake in whose skin a hundred souls are
    punished.
I was in *Kaer Nefenhir* where grass and trees attacked,
Poets sang, warriors rushed forth.
(lines 30-44: P.K. Ford, *The Mabinogi and Other Medieval Welsh Tales*
(Berkeley, 1977), p. 184)

There is only one other reference in medieval Welsh literature to this fortress – it is named as one of the places conquered in the past by Arthur in *Culhwch ac Olwen* (see Green, 2007, p. 65). This is obviously suggestive of Arthur indeed being the *Prydein wledic*, 'lord of Britain', at the head of the army of trees in *Kat Godeu*. Similarly, later Welsh manuscripts state that an alternate name for the battle *Cad Goddau* was *Cad Achren*, a name which is highly suggestive of the name of one of the forts – *Caer Ochren* – that Arthur lead the attack on in the early poem *Preideu Annwfyn*: see for this identification, Green, 2007, p. 63; A. Budgey, '"Preiddeu Annwn" and the Welsh Tradition of Arthur', in C.J. Burne, M. Harry and P. Ó Siadhail (edd.) *Celtic Languages and Celtic People* (Halifax, Nova Scotia, 1992), pp. 391-404 at p. 396, and M. Haycock, '"Preiddeu Annwn" and the Figure of Taliesin', *Studia Celtica*, 18/19 (1983-4), pp. 52-78 at p. 75. Such a link between *Cad Achren* and Arthur's assault on *Caer Ochren* gains considerable support from the fact that *Trioedd Ynys Prydein* and other Welsh texts describe the battle of *Cad Goddau* as a 'futile/pointless battle' which was caused by a roebuck and a dog, identified as a greyhound in one text. This accords well with the description of Arthur's assault on *Caer Ochren* in *Preideu Annwfyn* as a 'woeful conflict' which seems to have been undertaken in order to retrieve the 'beast they keep with a silver head' (Green, 2007, p. 63; Budgey, 1992, p. 396).

Given all this, and the fact that the forest animated in *Kat Godeu* is considered to have been *Coed Celyddon*, it is difficult to avoid connecting this apparently mythical Arthurian battle with the *Cat Coit Celidon* ('the battle of *Coed Celyddon*') attributed to Arthur in §56 of the early ninth-century *Historia Brittonum* (Green, 2007, p. 67). As with the *Historia's* tenth battle, which appears as a battle against were-wolves involving the former sea-god Manawydan son of Llyr in *Pa gur yv y porthaur?*, we appear to have a situation in which a mythical Arthurian battle has been borrowed and historicised by the author of the *Historia* (or his hypothetical source) for his list of Arthur's supposed victories against the Saxons.

See further on this battle, T. Green, *Concepts of Arthur* (Stroud, 2007), pp. 62-67. The full text of the poem can be found in J. Gwenogvryn Evans (ed.), *The Book of Taliesin: Facsimile and Text* (Llanbedrog, 1910) and M. Haycock (ed. and trans.), *Legendary Poems from the Book of Taliesin* (Aberystwyth, 2007), pp. 167-239; it has been translated by Haycock in the above volume and by P.K. Ford as an appendix to his *The Mabinogi* (Berkeley, 1977), pp. 183-87.

j. *Marwnat Uthyr Pen[dragon]*, *Kadeir Teyrnon*, *Mad[awg] drut ac Erof*, and *Kanu y Meirch*

Aside from *Preideu Annwfyn* and *Kat Godeu* there are four other Arthurian references in the 'Book of Taliesin'. These are found in the poems *Marwnat Uthyr Pen[dragon]* ('The Death-Song of Uthyr Pendragon' – *Pendragon* is abbreviated in the manuscript); *Kadeir Teyrnon* ('The Chair of a Prince' or 'The Chair of Teyrnon'); *Mad[awg] drut ac Erof* ('Mad[awg] the fierce and Herod' – *Madawg* is abbreviated in the manuscript); and *Kanu y Meirch* ('Poem of the Horses'). None of these poems are usually dated any more precisely than to the Old Welsh period in general, roughly the ninth to eleventh centuries. *Marwnat Uthyr Pendragon* is a wholly Arthurian piece, being probably envisaged as being spoken by Arthur's father, Uthyr Pendragon, who seems, from *Trioedd Ynys Prydein* no. 28 and Geoffrey's *Historia Regum Britanniae*, to have been a Taliesin-like figure, a magician and shape-changer in Welsh tradition: P. Sims-Williams, 'The Early Welsh Arthurian Poems', in R. Bromwich *et al* (edd.) *The Arthur of the Welsh* (Cardiff, 1991), p. 53. The lines that are of particular significance for Arthur are as follows:

> A victorious sword-stroke before the sons of Cawrnur.
> I shared my shelter,
> a ninth share in Arthur's valour.
> I broke a hundred forts.
> I slew a hundred stewards.
> I bestowed a hundred mantles.
> I cut a hundred heads.
> I gave to an old chief
> very great swords of protection.
> [???]
> An iron protection ...[???]... mountain-top.
> To my deprivation, to my sorrow, ?[sinew was brave].
> The world would not exist were it not for my offspring.
> (lines 12-24: J.B. Coe and S. Young (ed. and trans.), *The Celtic Sources for the Arthurian Legend* (Felinfach, 1995), pp. 150-51)

Lines 13-14 are clearly to be related to the concept of Arthur as a mighty warrior, and Sims-Williams has suggested that Uthyr here means that he has passed on his qualities to his son (1991, p. 53). This is reinforced by the proud and intriguing boast (reflecting perhaps the non-Galfridian concept of Arthur as the 'Protector of Britain' against supernatural threats) in line 24 that 'The world would not exist were it not for my offspring'. With regards to Uthyr he is clearly conceived of as a powerful warrior and protector himself in the above lines, whilst the earlier parts of the poem have sometimes been used to argue that Uthyr was a pagan Celtic God (see K. Malone, 'The Historicity of Arthur', *Journal of English and Germanic Philology*, 23 (1924), pp. 463-91 at pp. 469-71; R. Loomis *Celtic Myth and Arthurian Romance* (London, 1926), p. 352). It is interesting in this context that the god Mabon ap Modron is described as Uthyr's servant in lines 13-14 of *Pa gur yv y porthaur?*. For a full analysis of this poem, see now T. Green, *Concepts of Arthur* (Stroud, 2007), pp. 145-50.

Kadeir Teyrnon is an obscure boasting poem uttered by the legendary, semi-divine Taliesin before he releases his patron Elffin from imprisonment. He begins by praising a certain *Teyrnon* who, if this is taken as the common-noun *teyrnon*, 'a prince', may well be Arthur himself: Sims-Williams, 1991, p. 52; T. Green, 'A Note on *Aladur*, *Alator* and *Arthur*', *Studia Celtica*, 41 (2007), pp. 237-41; M. Haycock (ed. and trans.), *Legendary Poems from the Book of Taliesin* (Aberystwyth, 2007), pp. 293-94, 300. Unfortunately as a whole the poem remains difficult but the following lines deserve comment:

> He brought them from Cawrnur,
> pale horses under saddle...
>
> The third deep matter for the wise one:
> the blessing of Arthur
> – Blessed Arthur –
> with harmonious song:
> the defender in battle,
> the trampler on nine.
> (lines 13-14, 17-22: Coe and Young, 1995, pp. 148-49 and Sims-Williams, 1991, p. 52)

Clearly the latter lines tell us something about how the tales of Arthur were viewed by the bards, as well as confirming again the concept of Arthur as a great warrior and defender. The former lines (lines 13-14) recall line 12 of *Marwnat Uthyr Pendragon*, which refers to Uthyr's attack on the 'sons of Cawrnur'. Viewed together these two references can probably be taken to imply the existence of a lost Arthurian tale in which Arthur and Uthyr warred against Cawrnur and his sons (who were probably giants, Welsh *cawr*). Further discussion of this poem can be found in Green, 2007 ('A Note'), and Green, 2007 (*Concepts*), pp. 118, 197.

The other two references are less significant but still interesting. *Madawg drut ac Erof* is a fragment of a poem:

> Madog, the rampart of rejoicing.
> Madog, before he was in the grave,
> he was a fortress of generosity
> [consisting] of feat(s) and play.
> The son of Uthyr, before death
> he handed over pledges.
> (Sims-Williams, 1991, pp. 53-54)

This Madog is also mentioned in *Ymddiddan Arthur a'r Eryr* and it seems clear that he was Arthur's brother in non-Galfridian tradition. The above however is all that really remains of whatever stories were current in early Welsh tradition regarding Madog, aside from two lines from a late twelfth-century religious poem ('Madog, famous leader, was false; he had great profit: wretched sorrow!': Sims-Williams 1991, p. 54). Finally there is the untitled poem generally called *Kanu y Meirch*, a long list of the horses of traditional heroes:

> And Gwythur's horse;
> And Gwawrddur's horse;
> And Arthur's horse,
> boldly bestowing pain;
> ...
> And Llamrei, full valuable,
> wide-nostrilled and powerful;
> (lines 30-33, 50-51: Coe and Young, 1995, pp. 148-49)

The grouping of the heroes was clearly dictated by rhyme but it is interesting that Gwythur and Gwawrddur are found elsewhere associated with Arthur (in *Englynion y Beddau* and *Y Gododdin* respectively). Arthur's horse is not given a name in this poem, but in *Culhwch ac Olwen* it is named as *Llamrei* – intriguingly, a horse so named appears later *Kanu y Meirch*, though without the name of its owner.

The text of these poems can be found in J. Gwenogvryn Evans (ed.) *The Book of Taliesin: Facsimile and Text* (Llanbedrog, 1910), and M. Haycock (ed. and trans.), *Legendary Poems from the Book of Taliesin* (Aberystwyth, 2007), pp.167-239, 293-311, 387-403, 459-62, 503-13. Haycock's edition includes translations of all of these poems; partial translations, along with the corresponding text, are also given by P. Sims-Williams, 'The Early Welsh Arthurian Poems', in R. Bromwich *et al* (edd.) *The Arthur of the Welsh: The Arthurian Legend in Medieval Welsh Literature* (Cardiff, 1991), pp. 33-71 at pp. 52-54, and Coe and Young (ed. and trans.), *The Celtic Sources for the Arthurian*

Legend (Felinfach, 1995), pp. 141-51. W.F. Skene, *The Four Ancient Books of Wales* (Edinburgh, 1868) gives full translations of the poems, but these are not reliable.

k. *Ymddiddan Arthur a'r Eryr*

The *Ymddiddan Arthur a'r Eryr* ('Dialogue of Arthur and the Eagle') is found in numerous manuscripts of the fourteenth century and later. On linguistic and thematic grounds it should probably be dated *c.* 1150 and considered non-Galfridian in content. The poem is a religious one, with Arthur portrayed as a pagan warrior-hero who gains religious enlightenment from the eagle, which is revealed to him as the reincarnation of his dead nephew Eliwlad, son of Madog, son of Uthyr:

> Arthur of surpassing far-flung fame,
> bear of the host, joy of shelter
> the eagle has seen you before.
> ...
> Arthur of the terrible sword,
> your enemies stand not before your rush.
> I am the son of Madog son of Uthyr.
> (stanzas 2 and 6: J.B. Coe and S. Young (ed. and trans.), *The Celtic Sources for the Arthurian Legend* (Felinfach, 1995), p. 105)

The concept of Arthur is clearly to be compared with that of *Y Gododdin* and *Marwnad Cynddylan* – he is not 'King Arthur' but rather a peerless warrior-hero, *gwryt gadarnaf*, 'strongest in valour', and *penn kadoed Kernyw*, 'chief of the battalions of Cornwall'. Indeed, the dialogue seems to occur on the coast of Cornwall, with Arthur speaking *o tu myr*, 'beside the seas', and addressing the eagle as one who *a dreigla glyncoet Kernyw*, 'roams the valley-woods [=the wooded Glynn valley near Bodmin?] of Cornwall'. We also find, in the first stanza, Arthur describing himself thus:

> I am amazed for I am a bard;
> from the top of the oak with its beautiful branches,
> why does the eagle stare, why does he laugh?
> (Coe and Young, 1995, p. 105)

This notion of Arthur as a bard is found elsewhere too, in the non-Galfridian *Trioedd Ynys Prydein* (nos. 12 and 18W), *Culhwch ac Olwen*, and also in an *englyn* and prose fragment from MS Mostyn 131, p. 770, which though late (perhaps fifteenth-century?) is clearly working in the native non-Galfridian tradition of Arthur:

Sandde Bryd Angel drive the crow
off the face of ?Duran [son of Arthur].
Dearly and belovedly his mother raised him.
     Arthur sang it
(J. Rowland, *Early Welsh Saga Poetry: a Study and Edition of the*
Englynion (Cambridge, 1990), pp. 250-51)

Another nod to pre-Galfridian concepts of Arthur comes later in the poem, when Arthur asks if he should mount a campaign against God and Heaven to retrieve Eliwlad from the afterlife, to which the eagle replies *Arthur, bendefig haelion... a Duw nithycia ymryson*, 'Arthur, chief of generous men... it is of no use to strive against God'. In this exchange we would seem to have a reference to Arthur's role as the liberator of prisoners from the Otherworld, encountered in *Preideu Annwfyn* and *Culhwch ac Olwen*, though here such an expedition is dismissed due to the power of the Christian God (compared to that of the pagan gods?).

With regards to the eagle itself, the identification of this bird as Arthur's nephew Eliwlad mab Madog mab Uthyr confirms that, in non-Galfridian tradition, Uthyr was indeed Arthur's father and that Arthur had a brother named Madog. Eliwlod ap Mad(og) ap Uthur also appears in the mid-fifteenth-century *Pedwar Marchog ar Hugain Llys Arthur* ('Twenty-Four Knights of Arthur's Court') as one of the 'Three Golden-Tongued Knights' of Arthur's Court: see R. Bromwich (ed. and trans.), *Trioedd Ynys Prydein. The Welsh Triads* (Cardiff, 1978).

See further on this poem P. Sims-Williams, 'The Early Welsh Arthurian Poems', in Bromwich *et al* (edd.) *The Arthur of the Welsh: The Arthurian Legend in Medieval Welsh Literature* (Cardiff, 1991), pp. 33-71 at pp. 57-58; O.J. Padel, *Arthur in Medieval Welsh Literature* (Cardiff, 2000), pp. 64-67; A.O.H. Jarman, 'The Delineation of Arthur in Early Welsh Verse', in K. Varty (ed.) *An Arthurian Tapestry* (Glasgow, 1981), pp. 1-21 at pp. 15-16; and M. Haycock, 'Ymddiddan Arthur a'r Eryr', in M. Haycock (ed.) *Blodeugerdd Barddas o Ganu Crefyddol Cynnar* (Abertawe, 1994), pp. 297-312. For text see I. Williams, 'Ymddiddan Arthur a'r Eryr', *Bulletin of the Board of Celtic Studies*, 2 (1925), pp. 269-86.

1. *Ymddiddan Melwas ac Gwenhwyfar*

The *Ymddiddan Melwas ac Gwenhwyfar* ('Dialogue of Melwas and Gwenhwyfar', also known as *Ymddiddan Arthur ac Gwenhwyfar*) is extant principally in two manuscripts of the sixteenth and seventeenth century (Wynnstay 1, p. 91 and Llanstephen 122, p. 426) and should be seen as non-Galfridian in origin, dating from perhaps as early as the mid-twelfth century: R. Bromwich (ed. and trans.), *Trioedd Ynys Prydein: The Welsh Triads* (Cardiff,

1978), pp. 383-84; P. Sims-Williams, 'The Early Welsh Arthurian Poems', in R. Bromwich *et al* (edd.) *The Arthur of the Welsh* (Cardiff, 1991), p. 57. The dialogue begins in the A-text at a feast, where Gwenhwyfar is waiting on the guests, among them Melwas:

> 'Who is the man who sits in the common part of the feast,
> without for him either its beginning or end,
> sitting down there below the dais?'

> 'The Melwas from Ynys Wydrin (Isle of Glass);
> you, with the golden, gilded vessels,
> I have drunk none of your wine.'

> 'Wait a little...
> I do not pour out my wine
> for a man who cannot hold out and would not stand in battle
> [and] would not stand up to Cai in his wine.'
> (Sims-Williams, 1991, p. 59)

In the following *englynion* Gwenhwyfar continues to taunt Melwas, while he proclaims his valour versus that of Cai. In both texts there is a reference to Gwenhwyfar and Melwas having met at a court in *Dyfneint*, 'Devon', but the nature of this meeting isn't clear. The background to this poem is a pre-Galfridian Welsh story concerned with the rescue of Gwenhwyfar ('white fairy/enchantress') by Arthur from an Otherworld Island of Glass controlled by Melwas ('honey-youth') – who appears in other works as a magician who was a 'thief that by magic and enchantment took a girl [presumably Gwenhwyfar] to the end of the world' – similar to *Preideu Annwfyn* and its analogues.

See further the *Vita Gildae* of Caradoc of Llancarfan, discussed briefly below, and P. Sims-Williams, 'The Early Welsh Arthurian Poems', in R. Bromwich *et al* (edd.) *The Arthur of the Welsh* (Cardiff, 1991), pp. 33-71 at pp. 58-61; also see T. Green, *Concepts of Arthur* (Stroud, 2007), pp. 59-60, 151; B.F. Roberts, '*Culhwch ac Olwen*, the Triads, Saints' Lives', in R. Bromwich *et al* (edd.) *The Arthur of the Welsh* (Cardiff, 1991), pp. 73-95 at p. 83; O.J. Padel *Arthur in Medieval Welsh Literature* (Cardiff, 2000), pp. 67-69; and R. Bromwich (ed. and trans.), *Trioedd Ynys Prydein: The Welsh Triads* (Cardiff, 1978), pp. 380-85. For texts and translations of both versions see J.B. Coe and S. Young (ed. and trans.), *The Celtic Sources for the Arthurian Legend* (Felinfach, 1995), pp. 110-15, and M. Williams, 'An Early Ritual Poem in Welsh', *Speculum*, 13 (1938), pp. 38-43.

m. *Ymddiddan Gwyddno Garanhir ac Gwyn ap Nudd*

The Arthurian interest in the 'Black Book of Carmarthen' poem *Ymddiddan Gwyddno Garanhir ac Gwyn fab Nudd* ('The Dialogue of Gwyddno Garanhir and Gwynn ap Nudd') is found near to the end, in seven stanzas that are sometimes considered as a separate work, *Mi a Wum* ('I have been'). The poem dates from perhaps the tenth century, although it could be a little later or a little earlier than this: R. Bromwich, 'Introduction', and B.F. Roberts, 'Rhai o Gerddi Ymddiddan Llyfr Du Caerfyrddin', in R. Bromwich and R.B. Jones (edd.) *Astudiaethau ar yr Hengerdd* (Cardiff, 1978), pp. 20-21, 281-325; A.O.H. Jarman, 'The Delineation of Arthur in Early Welsh Verse', in K. Varty (ed.) *An Arthurian Tapestry* (Glasgow, 1981), p. 6. The Arthurian reference is as follows:

> I have been where Llacheu was slain
> the son of Arthur, awful [/marvellous] in songs
> when ravens croaked over blood.
> (J.B. Coe and S. Young (ed. and trans.), *The Celtic Sources for the Arthurian Legend* (Felinfach, 1995), p. 125)

Llacheu son of Arthur is also mentioned in the pre-Galfridian *Trioedd Ynys Prydein* (no. 4) and *Pa gur yv y porthaur?* and thus can be considered 'a figure of considerable importance in the early Arthurian saga', belonging like Cai and Bedwyr 'to the oldest stratum of Arthurian tradition': R. Bromwich (ed. and trans.), *Trioedd Ynys Prydein. The Welsh Triads* (Cardiff, 1978), p. 416; see further T. Green, *Concepts of Arthur* (Stroud, 2007), pp. 168-69. A thirteenth-century elegy by Bleddyn Fardd records that 'Llachau was slain below Llech Ysgar' and, whilst the place is unidentified (though it was the site of one of the courts of Madog ap Maredudd, d. 1160), Sims-Williams suggests that there may have been a local legend underlying the above stanza like that of the *Historia Brittonum* chapter 73 ('The Early Welsh Arthurian Poems', in R. Bromwich *et al* (edd.) *The Arthur of the Welsh* (Cardiff, 1991), p. 44; O.J. Padel, *Arthur in Medieval Welsh Literature* (Cardiff, 2000), p. 99, suggests that 'below Llech Ysgar' might refer to Crickheath Hill south of Oswestry, Shropshire).

The slayer of Llacheu is not named in non-Galfridian sources; in *Y Seint Greal* he is said to have been slain by Cai, but this is due to a mistaken equation between Llacheu and Loholt of the *Perlesvaus* (Bromwich, 1978, pp. 417-18; C. Lloyd-Morgan, '*Breuddwyd Rhonabwy* and later Arthurian Literature', in R. Bromwich *et al* (edd.) *The Arthur of the Welsh* (Cardiff, 1991), pp. 183-208 at p 197). For some analysis of its Arthurian content, see T. Green, *Concepts of Arthur* (Stroud, 2007), pp. 61, 160-61, 168-69. For the text, see B.F. Roberts, 'Rhai o Gerddi Ymddiddan Llyfr Du Caerfyrddin', in R.

Bromwich and R.B. Jones (edd.) *Astudiaethau ar yr Hengerdd* (Cardiff, 1978), pp. 281-325; J. Rowland, *Early Welsh Saga Poetry: a Study and Edition of the Englynion* (Cambridge, 1990), and J.B. Coe and S. Young (ed. and trans.), *The Celtic Sources for the Arthurian Legend* (Felinfach, 1995), pp. 124-25.

n. Gereint fil[ius] Erbin

Gereint fil[ius] Erbin ('Geraint, son of Erbin') is found in three of our manuscripts; in the 'Black Book of Carmarthen', the 'White Book of Rhydderch', and the 'Red Book of Hergest'. The date of this poem is usually given as falling between the ninth and mid-twelfth centuries, though Rowland would seem to consider a mid to late ninth-century date as defensible: J. Rowland, *Early Welsh Saga Poetry: a Study and Edition of the Englynion* (Cambridge, 1990), pp. 241, 389; P. Sims-Williams, 'The Early Welsh Arthurian Poems', in R. Bromwich *et al* (edd.) *The Arthur of the Welsh* (Cardiff, 1991), p. 46; see also R. Bromwich, 'Introduction', and B.F. Roberts, 'Rhai o Gerddi Ymddiddan Llyfr Du Caerfyrddin', in R. Bromwich and R.B. Jones (edd.) *Astudiaethau ar yr Hengerdd* (Cardiff, 1978), pp. 20-21, 281-325. The poem concerns a battle fought at 'Llongborth' and takes the form of a eulogy to one Geraint. Geraint himself is usually identified as a Dumnonian prince from the late sixth century, whilst Llongborth could be Langport (Somerset) or some miscellaneous *llongborth*, 'ship harbour' (A.O.H. Jarman, 'The Arthurian Allusions in the Black Book of Carmarthen', in P.B. Grout *et al* (edd.) *The Legend of Arthur in the Middle Ages* (Cambridge, 1983), pp. 99-112 at p. 106; Cf. Sims-Williams, 1991, pp. 46-47).

The Arthurian reference comes in the eighth stanza (see Sims-Williams, 1991, pp. 47-48, for the solution to the different readings in the Black Book and the Red Book): 'At Llongborth were slain brave men of Arthur – (they) hewed with steel – the emperor [*ameraudur*], (the) ruler of battle.' This might be interpreted literally, that is to say that the poet was envisaging that Arthur's 'brave men' (if not Arthur himself) were present at this battle, assisting Geraint. In this case the reference should probably be seen as another case of honouring the subject of a poem by associating him directly with Arthur the 'paragon of military valour', here through making Arthur's men present at his final battle (in *Marwnad Cynddylan* the subject is honoured by being made a 'whelp of great Arthur'). Alternatively, and better to my mind, the formula 'brave men of Arthur,... the emperor, the ruler of battle' might be taken like 'whelps of great Arthur, a mighty defender' as simply a comparison honouring (and referring to) the subject(s) of the poem, in this case Geraint and his slain brothers-in-arms referred to in the next stanza, which forms a doublet with this one (*i.e.* they were so valorous that they might be called/likened to 'brave men of Arthur', just as Cynddylan and his brothers are of such great valour that they might be called/likened to 'whelps of great Arthur'). For a full discussion, see T. Green, *Concepts of Arthur* (Stroud, 2007), pp. 78-79.

With regards to the concept of Arthur it is clearly again that of the 'peerless warrior'; the reference to him as 'emperor', *ameraudur* (< Latin *imperator*) might foreshadow Geoffrey of Monmouth's Arthur in the *Historia Regum Britanniae*, though as Jarman notes the "'imperial' character of the portrait [of Arthur in this poem] should not, however, be overemphasised, for the strict meaning of the word is probably closer to 'general, commander', etc.' (1983, p. 106).

Text and translations of the poem can be found in A.O.H. Jarman (ed.), *Llyfr Du Caerfyrddin* (Cardiff, 1982); R. Bromwich and R.B. Jones (edd.), *Astudiaethau ar yr Hengerdd* (Cardiff, 1978), pp. 286-96; J. Rowland, *Early Welsh Saga Poetry: a Study and Edition of the Englynion* (Cambridge, 1990), pp. 457-61, 504-05, 636-39; and J.B. Coe and S. Young (ed. and trans.), *The Celtic Sources for the Arthurian Legend* (Felinfach, 1995), pp. 116-21.

o. The Latin Saints' Lives

Arthur appears in the eleventh- to thirteenth-century *Lives* of Padarn, Carannog, Illtud, Gildas, Cadog, Goueznou and Euflamm; texts and translations of these can be most readily accessed in John B. Coe and Simon Young (ed. and trans.), *The Celtic Sources for the Arthurian Legend* (Felinfach, 1995), pp. 14-43. Perhaps the most notable feature of the majority of these texts is that Arthur is usually portrayed not in the heroic terms encountered in other early texts, but as a tyrant – in fact what we are seeing is the use of Arthur as a 'foil' for the saint. The *Vitae* are ecclesiastical hero-tales that share many features with their secular counterparts and as such require conflict, this conflict being generally between the religious hero and the secular power, with the ruler being belittled in defeat. Thus Arthur is 'an arrogant, grasping tyrant who is humbled in ignominious defeat, not in any armed struggle but in his childish greed and even in his failure to fulfil his traditional role as giant or dragon-slayer... the Arthurian episodes appear to be genuine fragments of Arthurian legend [consistent with the portrayal of Arthur found in *Culhwch ac Olwen* etc.], manipulated so that they may display Arthur in the worst possible light': B.F. Roberts, 'Culhwch ac Olwen, the Triads, Saints' Lives', in R. Bromwich *et al* (edd.) *The Arthur of the Welsh* (Cardiff, 1991), pp. 73-95 at p. 83. However, it is worth noting that Arthur's wrong-doings in the other *Vitae* are not seen as irredeemable or malicious, as the deeds of other rulers that act as foils for saints are.

In the *Vita Gildae* of Caradoc of Llancarfan (1120s or 1130s) we find a version of the pre-Galfridian Welsh tale of the rescue of Gwenhwyfar from an Otherworldly Island of Glass controlled by Melwas, which is the background to *Ymddiddan Melwas ac Gwenhwyfar*, as well as a tale of conflict between Arthur and Huail ap Caw, which is referred to in *Culhwch ac Olwen* and would seem to reflect the concept of Arthur as 'Protector of Britain': T. Green, *Concepts of Arthur* (Stroud, 2007), pp. 59-60, 123-27, 151; P. Sims-Williams, 'The Early Welsh Arthurian Poems', in Bromwich *et al* (edd.) *The Arthur of the Welsh* (Cardiff, 1991), pp. 33-71 at pp. 58-61; Roberts, 1991, p. 83. In Lifris' *Vita Sancti Cadoci*, written between 1061 and 1104, we find two tales that are not known from any other source, one seeming to reflect a topographic folktale involving the exchange of magical or Otherworldly animals at a ford, and another that looks to be a folktale in which Arthur is a mighty warrior, protector, and defender of the realm/guardian of the border who exists outside of normal society: see O.J. Padel, 'The Nature of Arthur', *Cambrian Medieval Celtic Studies*, 27 (1994), pp. 1-31 at pp. 7-8; Green, 2007, pp. 128, 199-200; K. Malone, 'The Historicity of Arthur', *Journal of English and Germanic Philology*, 23 (1924), pp. 463-91 at pp. 481-82.

Also otherwise unknown are the tales of Arthur slaying dragons which have been manipulated by the authors of the Welsh *Vita Prima Sancti Carantoci* (*c.* 1100?) and the twelfth-century Breton *Vita Euflami*. In the case of the latter, the story would seem to have already been in existence by *c.* 1110 from the evidence of the Perros Relief and it shows clear signs of deriving from local topographic lore; it is also interesting for its description of Arthur as having 'armed himself with the triple-knotted club and defended his eager torso with the shield which a lion-skin covered' (Coe and Young, 1995, p. 39) and the fact that the author seems to have known of other stories of Arthur hunting monsters in Brittany, though he does not give details of these.

For discussion of the Saints' Lives see B.F. Roberts, '*Culhwch ac Olwen*, the Triads, Saints' Lives', in R. Bromwich *et al* (edd.) *The Arthur of the Welsh* (Cardiff, 1991), pp. 73-95 at pp. 82-84; T. Green, *Concepts of Arthur* (Stroud, 2007), particularly within chapters three to six; O.J. Padel, 'The Nature of Arthur', *Cambrian Medieval Celtic Studies*, 27 (1994), pp. 1-31 at pp. 6-8; O.J. Padel, *Arthur in Medieval Welsh Literature* (Cardiff, 2000), pp. 37-47; J.T. Koch, 'The Celtic Lands', in N.J. Lacy (ed.) *Medieval Arthurian Literature: A Guide to Recent Research* (New York, 1996), pp. 239-322 at pp. 268-69, 292; and G. Ashe, 'Saints' Lives', in N.J. Lacy (ed.) *The New Arthurian Encyclopedia* (New York, 1996), pp. 394-95.

p. De Miraculis Sanctae Mariae Laudensis, Liber Floridus, and Gesta Regum Anglorum

Although not strictly 'Welsh', these three Latin texts do contribute significantly to our knowledge of pre-Galfridian Arthurian folklore and so are deserving of consideration here. Such folklore is most fully referenced in

Herman's *De Miraculis Sanctae Mariae Laudensis* ('The Miracles of St Mary of Laon'). This is an account of a journey made in 1113 to Britain by some canons of Laon, in northern France (O.J. Padel, 'The Nature of Arthur', *Cambrian Medieval Celtic Studies*, 27 (1994), pp. 1-31 at pp. 4-6 and pp. 8-10; J.S.P. Tatlock, 'The English Journey of the Laon Canons', *Speculum*, 8 (1933), pp. 454-65). Whilst travelling between Exeter and Bodmin the canons were shown the 'seat' and the 'oven' of King Arthur and were told that this was 'Arthurian country' – 'Arthur's Seat' is otherwise unknown but 'Arthur's Oven' may well be the 'King's Oven' recorded on Dartmoor in 1240. Both would seem to be the same kind of topographic folklore that is found in *Historia Brittonum* §73 (see Padel, 1994, pp. 5-6). A similar piece of topographic folklore is recorded by Lambert of St Omer in the *Liber Floridus* of 1120, who added to the *mirabilia* of the *Historia Brittonum* a building known as 'Arthur's Palace', which is now generally acknowledged to be a circular building of Roman date near Stirling (Scotland) known as 'Arthur's Oven' in the thirteenth century (Padel, 1994, p. 6).

When the Laon canons arrived at Bodmin in Cornwall, they once again encountered the Arthurian legend:

> ...a certain man having a withered hand kept a vigil at the shrine [of Our Lady of Laon] to recover his health. In just the same way as the Bretons are accustomed to arguing with the French about King Arthur, the same man began to bicker with one from our community by the name of Hangello of the community of Lord Guidon, Archdeacon of Laon, saying that Arthur still lived. Then there arose a not a small tumult; many men rushed into the church with arms and if the aforementioned cleric Algardus had not prevented it, it would almost certainly have come to the spilling of blood. (J.B. Coe and S. Young (ed. and trans.), *The Celtic Sources for the Arthurian Legend* (Felinfach, 1995), p. 47)

The text clearly shows that in the pre-Galfridian period a belief in Arthur still living was common to both the Bretons and the Cornish and was a matter of such strong feeling that a riot was only just averted when it was questioned. This should be viewed alongside the reference to Arthur having no grave in the probably ninth-century Welsh *Englynion y Beddau* and William of Malmesbury's statement in his *Gesta Regum Anglorum* (*c.* 1125) that 'Arthur's grave is nowhere to be seen, whence antiquity of fables still claims that he will return'. See on all of this O.J. Padel's 'The Nature of Arthur', *Cambrian Medieval Celtic Studies*, 27 (1994), pp. 1-31 at pp. 8-12, and T. Green, *Concepts of Arthur* (Stroud, 2007), pp. 73-75. For the other piece of Arthurian folklore found in William's *Gesta Regum Anglorum*, relating to Gwalchmai's grave, see above under *Englynion y Beddau*; Green, 2007, pp. 71, 170-71; and

P. Sims-Williams, 'The Early Welsh Arthurian Poems', in R. Bromwich *et al* (edd.) *The Arthur of the Welsh: The Arthurian Legend in Medieval Welsh Literature* (Cardiff, 1991), pp. 33-71 at pp. 49-50.

q. *Trioedd Ynys Prydein*

The 'Early Version' of *Trioedd Ynys Prydein* ('The Triads of the Island of Britain') is found in the mid-thirteenth-century NLW Peniarth 16. This manuscript ends with triad 46 and the remaining triads are found in the fourteenth-century 'White Book of Rhydderch' and the 'Red Book of Hergest' (47-69), Peniarth MS. 47 (fifteenth century; contains most of the triads of the 'Early Version' and triads 70-80) and Peniarth MS. 50 (81-6), with triads 87-96 consisting of 'miscellaneous additions to *Trioedd Ynys Prydein* which appear for the first time in one or other of the late manuscript collections': R. Bromwich (ed. and trans.), *Trioedd Ynys Prydein: The Welsh Triads* (Cardiff, 1978), p. xi. The triads were originally mnemonic devices devised by the 'guardians' of Welsh traditional material to facilitate the recall of this material by systematising it and associating three characters or episodes with one another on the basis of features common to all three. The original collection of these triads, *Trioedd Ynys Prydein*, appears to have first been put together in the eleventh or twelfth century, though obviously the traditions it contained were older than this. With regards to our extant manuscripts, the contents of the 'Early Version' (NLW Peniarth 16) of this corpus can be considered pre-Galfridian in nature, whilst those triads found in the 'Later Version' (WB and RB) do show the influence of Geoffrey of Monmouth at several points, though they are not in the main derived from him.

Many of the triads have Arthurian references and these are particularly prominent in the later versions of the triads, reflecting the growing interest in the Arthurian legend and the drawing of traditional non-Arthurian figures into this cycle – indeed in the 'Later Version' Arthur displaces other characters from their original stories (as in the hunting of Henwen, *TYP* no. 26W). In *Trioedd Ynys Prydein* Arthur seems to be conceived of as the 'lord of Britain', as he is in *Culhwch ac Olwen* and perhaps *Kat Godeu*. Thus in *TYP* no. 1 Arthur is Chief Prince of the Three Tribal Thrones of the Island of Britain: at Mynyw [=St David's] in Wales, Celliwig in Cornwall [his court in *Culhwch ac Olwen* and *Pa gur*], and 'Pen Rhionydd in the North' (see T. Green, 'A Note on Aladur, Alator and Arthur', *Studia Celtica*, 41 (2007), pp. 237-41 in n. 17, for another possible Arthurian occurrence of this court). In some triads *Llys Arthur*, 'Arthur's Court', is used as the frame of reference for the triad rather than *Ynys Prydein*, 'The Island of Britain' (as in *TYP* no. 9); this becomes increasingly common over time). Arthur is not, however, the inactive and ineffectual ruler of later Romances but rather he still possesses 'the hero's destructive energy as his ravaging devastates the land for seven years' wherever he goes: B.F. Roberts, '*Culhwch ac Olwen*, the Triads, Saint's Lives', in R. Bromwich *et al* (edd.) *The Arthur of the Welsh* (Cardiff, 1991), pp. 73-95 at p. 81; *TYP* nos. 20 and 20W.

Arthur's high status in Welsh tradition is made clear by the fact that his name is sometimes added at the end of a triad 'as a fourth and exceptional example of a particular feature' (Roberts, 1991, p. 80) – for example in *TYP* no. 2 Arthur is said to be 'more generous' than the three named 'Generous Men', and in *TYP* no. 52 he is 'more exalted' than the Three Exalted Prisoners (two of which he himself frees in *Preideu Annwfyn* and *Culhwch ac Olwen*). Turning away from the portrayal of Arthur to his deeds, we find references to tales of his final battle at Camlann and conflict with Medraut, though these are late and/or probably influenced by Geoffrey of Monmouth (nos. 51, 53, 54, 59, 84); his imprisonment (no. 52, in the Otherworld?); his attempts to procure/hunt boars (nos. 26 and 26W); and his role as Protector of Britain (no. 37R), when he discloses the 'Head of Brân the blessed from the White Hill, because it did not seem right to him that this island should be defended by the strength of anyone but by his own'. Additionally Arthur is named as one of the Three Frivolous Bards (no. 12) and in no. 18W an *englyn* is attributed to him on his Three Battle-Horsemen.

For an indispensable discussion, text and translation of all the Arthurian triads, see R. Bromwich (ed. and trans.), *Trioedd Ynys Prydein: The Welsh Triads* (Cardiff, 1978), which has recently been updated into a third edition (Cardiff, 2006). See also B.F. Roberts, '*Culhwch ac Olwen*, the Triads, Saint's Lives', in Bromwich *et al* (edd.) *The Arthur of the Welsh* (Cardiff, 1991), pp. 73-95; T. Green, *Concepts of Arthur* (Stroud, 2007), especially throughout chapters three, four and six; and O.J. Padel, *Arthur in Medieval Welsh Literature* (Cardiff, 2000), pp. 84-88.

r. Tri Thlws ar Ddeg Ynys Brydain

Tri Thlws ar Ddeg Ynys Brydain ('The Thirteen Treasures of the Island of Britain') is found in over forty manuscripts, the earliest being NLW Peniarth 51 (*c.* 1460). In all fifteen treasures are named, though each list contains only thirteen. Two of the feeding vessels mentioned in this text – the 'Hamper of Gwyddno Garanhir' and the 'Cauldron of Diwrnach the Giant' – are also mentioned in *Culhwch ac Olwen*, and the late date of the manuscripts of *Tri Thlws ar Ddeg Ynys Brydain* shouldn't be allowed to obscure the fact that we have here an attempt to transmit and preserve genuinely ancient fragments of lost traditional literature of medieval Wales. The origins of these 'treasures' are probably to be sought in stories of magic objects won (or bestowed) from the Otherworld, with this text being simply a list of 13 of these traditional talismans. There are two items of specific Arthurian interest in the list. The first is the cauldron of Diwrnach the Giant, which is undoubtedly the same as that cauldron of Diwrnach Wyddel taken from Ireland (a euhemerisation of the Otherworld) by Arthur in *Culhwch ac Olwen*. Of this it is stated:

> if meat for a coward were put in it to boil, it would never boil; but if meat for a brave man were put into it, it would boil quickly (and thus the brave could be distinguished from the cowardly).
> (J.B. Coe and S. Young (ed. and trans.), *The Celtic Sources for the Arthurian Legend* (Felinfach, 1995), p. 89)

This should obviously be compared with the statement in the perhaps eighth-century poem *Preideu Annwfyn* that the cauldron of the Chief of Annwfyn, which Arthur travels to the Otherworld to seize,

> boils not a coward's food (Coe and Young, 1995, p. 137)

underlining both the relationship between the Preideu *Annwfyn* tale and that in *Culhwch ac Olwen*, and the traditional nature of this 'Treasure'. The second item is:

> The mantle of Arthur in Cornwall: Whoever was under it could not be seen, and he could see everybody. (Coe and Young, 1995, p. 91)

Arthur's mantle again appears to be traditional Otherworldly talisman and treasure. It is mentioned briefly in *Culhwch ac Olwen* and in *Breuddwyd Rhonabwy* it is called Gwenn ('white, pure, sacred, holy'): 'According to the tale, one of the properties of the mantle was "that the man around whom it might be wrapped, no one would see him and he would see everyone. And no colour would ever stay on it except its own colour". Its own colour was white, and it was brought to Arthur by a red man mounted on a red horse. Its Otherworldly origins are clear.' (P.K. Ford, 'On the Significance of some Arthurian Names in Welsh', *Bulletin of the Board of Celtic Studies*, 30 (1983), pp. 268-73 at p. 270).

See on *Tri Thlws ar Ddeg Ynys Brydain,* B.F. Roberts, '*Culhwch ac Olwen*, the Triads, Saint's Lives', in R. Bromwich *et al* (edd.) *The Arthur of the Welsh* (Cardiff, 1991), pp. 73-95 at pp. 85-88; R. Bromwich (ed. and trans.), *Trioedd Ynys Prydein: The Welsh Triads* (Cardiff, 1978); and T. Green, *Concepts of Arthur* (Stroud, 2007), pp. 57, 115. On the Otherworldly possessions of Arthur and the stories surrounding them see P.K. Ford, 'On the Significance of some Arthurian Names in Welsh', *Bulletin of the Board of Celtic Studies*, 30 (1983), pp. 268-73.

s. Breuddwyd Rhonabwy

Breuddwyd Rhonabwy ('The Dream of Rhonabwy') is probably of a late thirteenth- or early fourteenth-century date, though possible composition-dates range from the mid-twelfth century to the mid-fourteenth century (the latter date is provided by a reference to 'Rhonabwy's Dream' by the poet Madog Dwygraig (*fl.* 1370-80)). Interestingly, the tale on the whole seems to be largely independent of Galfridian influence. Although it is normally considered alongside the 'Mabinogion' group of tales, it differs in several ways from the others in this 'group' – it is only contained in the Red Book of Hergest (cols. 555.10-571), not the White Book of Rhydderch; it is separated from the other 'Mabinogion' tales in the Red Book by some 56 columns; and it appears to have been written by one single author and not to have evolved over time like the other tales. Most importantly, traditional material is utilised not as an end in itself but so as to create a completely original Arthurian tale composed in 'a satiric rather than a heroic vein, with a highly complex interplay of ambiguities and ironies' (C. Lloyd-Morgan, '*Breuddwyd Rhonabwy* and Later Arthurian Literature', in Bromwich *et al* (edd.) *The Arthur of the Welsh* (Cardiff, 1991), pp. 183-208 at p. 185), with King Arthur himself being portrayed in a non-heroic light – although, interestingly, he is portrayed as a giant. In effect, the 'Dream of Rhonabwy' breaks all the 'rules' that the other 'Mabinogion' tales stick to while being very familiar with these conventions, and *Rhonabwy* should probably be best seen as a parody of the whole fabric of Arthurian literary conventions in general.

See for a full discussion of *Breuddwyd Rhonabwy*, C. Lloyd-Morgan, '*Breuddwyd Rhonabwy* and Later Arthurian Literature', in R. Bromwich *et al* (edd.), *The Arthur of the Welsh* (Cardiff, 1991), pp. 183-208; J.T. Koch, 'The Celtic Lands', in N.J. Lacy (ed.) *Medieval Arthurian Literature* (New York, 1996), pp. 239-322 at pp. 278-80; O.J. Padel, *Arthur in Medieval Welsh Literature* (Cardiff, 2000), pp. 94-99.

t. The Gogynfeirdd and Cywyddwyr

The Arthurian legend makes a number of appearances in the works of the twelfth- and thirteenth-century *Gogynfeirdd* (the court poets of the Welsh princes) and later Welsh poetry. It is frequently used as a source for positive comparisons with which to honour the subject of a poem, and this usage obviously echoes that of the earlier pre-Galfridian poets. In these twelfth-century and later compositions Arthur appears generally in his pre-Galfridian guise as a 'paragon of military valour', just as he does when used as a comparison in *Y Gododdin* and *Marwnad Cynddylan*. Thus the mid-twelfth century poet Gwalchmai ap Meilyr – who seems to have been named after

Arthur's nephew – praises Madog ap Maredudd, king of Powys (d. 1160) for having *Arthur gedernyd* ('Arthur's Strength'), and Cynddelw (*c.* 1170) compares the fearsome shout of Madog's army to that of Arthur's host. Similarly Prydydd y Moch (who flourished *c.* 1170-1220) refers to 'Generous Arthur, the battle-famous lord' and says that 'he was a whirlwind, attacking beyond measure'.

Other elements of the Arthurian legend which appear in the work of the *Gogynfeirdd* include Medraut (the references to whom are always favourable, for example Meilyr Brydydd, in a lament for the death of Gruffudd ap Cynan (d. 1137), praises his subject for having Medraut's valour in battle, and Meilyr's son Gwalchmai lauds Madog ap Maredudd for possessing the 'good nature of Medrawd'); Arthur's son Llacheu (who appears, like his father, as a paragon of valour, thus Cynddelw's reference to *Llacheu uar*, 'Llacheu's ferocity'); Gwenhwyfar's father Ogrfan Gawr (with Hywel ab Owain, d. 1170, seeming to make a reference to a lost tale of Arthur's suit for Gwenhwyfar); and also, in passing, Gwalchmai, Cai, the Twrch Trwyth, *Kelli wic* and Camlann (which seems, curiously, to be portrayed as a successful battle). On the whole the fragments of Arthuriana that are found in the works of the *Gogynfeirdd* appear to be non-Galfridian in character – the poets making reference to tales and characters known to us from pre-Galfridian materials, such as the Twrch Trwyth and Cai's killing of Dillus the Bearded – and, indeed, seem in some ways to go clearly against the Galfridian narrative, as in the treatment of Medraut and the battle of Camlann. See further O.J. Padel, *Arthur in Medieval Welsh Literature* (Cardiff, 2000), pp. 51-61; R. Bromwich (ed. and trans.), *Trioedd Ynys Prydein: The Welsh Triads* (Cardiff, 1978).

It is instructive to note that although the Arthurian legend clearly had a place in the body of legends drawn upon by the twelfth- and early thirteenth-century *Gogynfeirdd*, it was not nearly so prominent as it was to be in the work of the later poets. This prominence increases over time probably as a direct result of Arthur's growing international fame and the popularity in Wales of Geoffrey of Monmouth's *Historia Regum Britanniae* (which the poets certainly seem to have been aware of and which was translated three times into Welsh in the thirteenth century as *Brut y Brenhinedd*) and *Y Tair Rhamant* ('The Three Romances'), from which many of the late references seem to derive: B.F. Roberts, 'Geoffrey of Monmouth, *Historia Regum Britanniae* and *Brut y Brenhinedd*', in R. Bromwich *et al* (edd.) *The Arthur of the Welsh* (Cardiff, 1991), p. 111; Padel, 2000, pp. 54, 60-61, 99; C. Lloyd-Morgan, '*Breuddwyd Rhonabwy* and Later Arthurian Literature', in R. Bromwich *et al* (edd.) *The Arthur of the Welsh* (Cardiff, 1991), pp. 202-03.

As Lloyd-Morgan points out (1991, p. 198ff.), Welsh writers in general seem to have seen this new material as a valuable resource, extending and enriching their native stock of stories, and it quickly came to dominate, with the writers blending it, where possible, with the native traditions. In contrast to the prose writers, however, the *cywyddwyr* – the poets of the fourteenth, fifteenth and sixteenth centuries – seem to have been somewhat selective in how many of the continental and Galfridian developments they chose to adopt and how closely they followed them. They seem to have been happy to continue to draw on the native and non-Galfridian Arthurian tradition, and when there was any discrepancy between this and the non-native material they frequently sided with the former. Thus in the fourteenth century Llacheu continues to feature as a standard of praise; Medraut remains an honourable and valiant character (rather than the traitor of the *Historia Regum Britanniae*); and the poets' concept of Cai is that of *Culhwch* rather than that of the 'Matter of Britain'. When Dafydd ap Gwilym and Dafydd ab Edmwnd refer to the abduction of Gwenhwyfar by Melwas they are referring not to continental tales of infidelity but to the Otherworldly pre-Galfridian tale that underlies *Ymddiddan Melwas ac Gwenhwyfar* and the *Vita Gildae* of Caradoc of Llancarfan.

Of course, this is not to say that the *cywyddwyr* (or the late *Gogynfeirdd*) routinely rejected the non-native materials. Indeed, they seem to have generally favoured the *Brutiau* and the 'Three Romances' over *Culhwch ac Olwen* and the like as a source for poetic references and comparisons (Lloyd-Morgan, 1991, p. 203, for example the references to Peredur, Geraint and Owain made in the poems of Bleddyn Fardd in the late thirteenth century and the appearance of the grail and characters such as Lancelot in fifteenth-century texts). Additionally we can see that the influence and dominance of the post-Galfridian material on their work did increase over time and that the native traditional material was increasingly eclipsed by or blended with this. For example, the poets' conception of Gwenhwyfar probably changed during the fourteenth century from a victim of abduction to a willing adulterer, and Medraut, though he manages to remain a positive character throughout the middle ages in native tradition, finally becomes the enemy of Arthur/traitor that he is the Galfridian tale in the work of the early sixteenth-century poet Tudur Aled. On the whole, however, the resistance by the poets to obvious changes in the nature of the established native Arthurian characters is notable and surprisingly long-lasting. Reference to the full range of the Matter of Britain did not really appear until very late and only then in the work of certain poets of the later fifteenth and early sixteenth century, such as Siôn ap Hywel and Tudur Aled (Padel, 2000, pp. 99-101, 111, 113-19).

Both this continuing use of native Arthurian tradition and the adoption and co-existence of non-native elements can also be witnessed in the later versions of *Trioedd Ynys Prydein* and related texts such as the mid-fifteenth-century *Pedwar Marchog ar Hugain Llys Arthur* ('Twenty-Four Knights of Arthur's Court'). An awareness of the Galfridian tale of Arthur and Medraut, for example, is clearly the source of several of the later Triads concerning Camlann but it also seems to act as a catalyst for the recording of other apparently non-Galfridian (and sometimes contradictory) traditions regarding the battle (such as *TYP* nos. 53, 59 and 84). Similarly in *Pedwar Marchog ar Hugain Llys Arthur* some of the groups of knights are drawn straight from the pre-Galfridian tradition of *Culhwch ac Olwen* (for example, 'Three Irresistible Knights'), others are largely non-Galfridian in character but betray some influence (for example, 'Three Golden-Tongued Knights'), and yet others are entirely non-native (for example, 'Three Virgin Knights'). See Bromwich, 1978; Padel, 2000, pp. 87-88, 91-2; Lloyd-Morgan, 1991, pp. 200-02.

See further O.J. Padel, *Arthur in Medieval Welsh Literature* (Cardiff, 2000), pp. 51-61, 71, 99-101, 111, 113-19; R. Bromwich (ed. and trans.), *Trioedd Ynys Prydein: The Welsh Triads* (Cardiff, 1978); R. Bromwich *et al* (edd.), *The Arthur of the Welsh* (Cardiff, 1991), particularly the chapters by C. Lloyd-Morgan and P. Sims-Williams; T. Green, *Concepts of Arthur* (Stroud, 2007); and J. Rowlands, *Early Welsh Saga Poetry: a Study and Edition of the Englynion* (Cambridge, 1990), pp. 250-59. On the *Gogynfeirdd* see J.E. Caerwyn Williams, *The Poets of the Princes* (Cardiff, 1978) and A.O.H. Jarman and G.R. Hughes (ed.), *A Guide to Welsh Literature I* (Swansea, 1976).

3

A Gazetteer of Arthurian Onomastic and Topographic Folklore

A Gazetteer of Arthurian Onomastic and Topographic Folklore

Contents

1. Introduction

One aspect of the Arthurian legend which has often received little consideration is Arthur's frequent appearance in the onomastic and topographic folklore of Britain and Brittany. Most usually the attitude has been that we should 'conclude that literature rather than genuine folklore accounts for most of them'.[1] Such notions do not, however, stand up to scrutiny. Instead, as Oliver Padel has recently demonstrated, Arthurian onomastic and topographic tales should probably be seen as central to the legend and its origins. Arthur appears to have been primarily a mythical and/or legendary hero, 'the leader of a band of heroes who live outside

---

1   G. Ashe, 'Topography and Local Legends', in N.J. Lacy (ed.) *The New Arthurian Encyclopaedia* (New York & London, 1996), pp. 455-58 at p. 457.

society, whose main world is one of magical animals, giants, and other wondrous happenings, located in the wild parts of the landscape'. This concept of Arthur was, from at least the ninth century, frequently manifested through tales attached to remarkable features in this landscape. In particular, natural rocks and prehistoric antiquities were often used by these tales, reputedly being the visible local remnants of Arthur's activity, sometimes – but by no means always – called 'Arthur's X' in remembrance of this.[1]

The above concept of Arthur as a local hero of topographic and onomastic folklore can be demonstrated wherever a Brittonic language was once spoken – in southern Scotland, Wales, the Welsh borders, south-west England, and Brittany – and it is present in even the earliest sources (see below). Moreover, such a situation is not, in fact, at all unusual; such local folk-tales, especially place-name tales, are a recurring feature of literature and folklore in Celtic languages. For example, the legend of Fionn mac Cumhaill in early Irish tradition – which Padel and others see as closely analogous to the early Arthurian legend – appears to have originated in just such disparate pieces of local folklore. These usually narrated a single episode in the hero's life and adventures in the wilderness, with a distinctive landscape-feature or place-name serving as the focus for the tale; a coherent account of Fionn's life and exploits only seems to have emerged later as a literary development of this oral tradition.[2] Similarly the Tristan legend, as found in the works of the continental poets such as Béroul, is now generally accepted as deriving from Cornish onomastic and topographic folklore.[3] Indeed, so popular were these stories that they became a genre in their own right, known to the Irish as *dinnsheanchas*, 'place-lore', the Black Book of Carmarthen *Englynion y Beddau* being a specialised Welsh example of this, concerned with the supposed resting places of mythical/folkloric heroes (including several Arthurian characters).

What follows is split into two sections. The first briefly highlights key early literary references to such Arthurian onomastic and topographic folklore. The second comprises a gazetteer of some of this material. With regards to the latter, although the gazetteer itself is restricted largely to that material associated with a name in the form 'Arthur's X', other Arthurian onomastic and topographic lore did, of course, exist. Indeed, it is recorded from the earliest period right through to the nineteenth century, and it is arguably dominant in the non-Galfridian material. Important instances of

---

1   O.J. Padel, 'The Nature of Arthur', *Cambrian Medieval Celtic Studies*, 27 (1994), pp. 1-31, quotation at p. 14.

2   Padel, 'Nature of Arthur', p. 22; D. Ó hÓgáin, *Fionn mac Cumhaill: Images of the Gaelic Hero* (Dublin, 1988).

3   See especially O.J. Padel, 'The Cornish Background of the Tristan Stories', *Cambridge Medieval Celtic Studies*, 1 (1981), pp. 53-81.

this – for example, place-names reflecting the localisation of the various tales in *Culhwch ac Olwen* in the Welsh landscape, such as *Mesur-y-Peir*, 'Measure of the Cauldron', referring to the place where Arthur and his men landed with a captured cauldron – are discussed below and in T. Green, *Concepts of Arthur* (Stroud, 2007). However, the nature of this material, especially the unidentified location of some of the names, means that it is not readily amenable for inclusion in a gazetteer.

For this reason the focus in the catalogue provided below is on the more easily locatable and classifiable subset of the lore which relates to a place or object named after (and by implication, belonging to) Arthur, such as 'Arthur's Stone' and 'Arthur's Chair'. This is, of course, just that material which is most often criticised and subject to scepticism over its origins. In part, this is justified. As Grooms has noted, much of this type of Arthurian topographic and onomastic folklore is only recorded from the sixteenth century onwards, with one class – 'Arthur's Quoits' – certainly unable to have an origin any earlier than this.[1] In consequence, antiquarian invention cannot be discounted for a number of the names. On the other hand, whilst some are late, others are most definitely early. Thus, to give a few examples, we have an 'Arthur's Seat' and an 'Arthur's Oven' recorded as early as 1113, an 'Arthur's Palace' in 1120 (which is also known as 'Arthur's O'en' in the thirteenth century), an 'Arthur's Bower' documented in the 1170s, an 'Arthur's Seat' described in *c.* 1190, and various 'Arthur's Stones' and other similar items referred to from at least the thirteenth century onwards.[2] Indeed, in the perhaps tenth-century poem *Marwnat Cadwallon ap Cadfan* we learn that a seventh-century battle was supposedly fought at *Ffynnawn Uetwyr*, 'Bedwyr's Spring' (Bedwyr being one of Arthur's closest companions in the earliest stratum of the Arthurian legend and having no existence outside of this material).[3] All this would tend to confirm that such items of local folklore had a genuine and early place in Arthurian story. Although the earliest tales (such as those related in *Culhwch ac Olwen*) are apparently dominated by topographic and onomastic folklore which is not in the form 'Arthur's X', this is clearly no reason to dismiss this material. Furthermore, Padel[4] has established a good context for these type of names within the non-Galfridian legend, which makes their existence comprehensible without recourse to wide-spread antiquarian invention. Quite simply, this is exactly

---

1   C. Grooms, *The Giants of Wales. Cewri Cymru*, Welsh Studies vol 10 (Lampeter, 1993), pp. l, 118; Padel, 'Nature of Arthur', p. 27; T. Green, *Concepts of Arthur* (Stroud, 2007), pp. 244-45.

2   See below for some discussion of these; also Padel, 'Nature of Arthur', pp. 4-6, 25-26 and Grooms, *Giants of Wales*, pp. 116, 127.

3   J.T. Koch and J. Carey, *The Celtic Heroic Age: Literary Sources for Ancient Celtic Europe & Early Ireland & Wales*, fourth edition (Aberystwyth, 2003), p. 373; compare the 'Arthur's Fountain' and the 'Arthur's Well' noted in the gazetteer.

4   Padel, 'The Nature of Arthur', *passim.*

the type of folklore that the nature of Arthur in the early Welsh sources would lead us to expect to find in the British landscape.

Indeed, it is worth remembering that both the names and the stories attached to these 'remarkable features' in the landscape – the visible reminders of Arthur's adventures and deeds – are astonishingly consistent across the centuries in their portrayal of the British non-Galfridian Arthur. The stories and place-names recorded by nineteenth- and twentieth-century collectors of oral traditions differ little from those recorded by chance in the twelfth or thirteenth centuries, or even those found in the ninth-century *Englynion y Beddau* and *Historia Brittonum*. This, in itself, does give the lie to the old view that post-Galfridian and, especially, post-medieval Arthurian onomastic and topographic folklore is of no value as it mainly results from (or is contaminated by) the international literary legend.[1] To cite one example of this notable continuity from the perspective of stories, the Welsh *Carreg Carn March Arthur* ('Stone of Arthur's Steed's Hoof', bearing the footprint of Arthur's horse made as he hunted the monstrous Afanc) and the 'Arthur's Stone' in St Columb, Cornwall (which is said to bear the impression of the footprints of Arthur's horse and is associated with the legends of him hunting in this area), bear very close comparison with the Arthurian tale surrounding a remarkable stone atop Corn Gafallt, a hill near Rhaeadr, recorded in the *Historia Brittonum* of 829/30.[2]

In the light of the above, the late recording of some of this lore, especially that where the place-name is in the form 'Arthur's X' (for instance the *Coetan Arthur*, 'Arthur's Quoits'), does not seem so much of a problem as has sometimes been assumed. Whilst allowing that some examples will have been invented by antiquarians and thus not have genuine folk-tales underlying and explaining them, mass invention cannot be seen as the most credible explanation for the corpus as a whole. Place-lore appears to be too central to the early Arthurian legend, and the type and nature of the names and stories are too consistent over the course of more than 1000 years. As Padel has recently observed,

> What interests us, and is so impressive, is not the antiquity of any individual name, but the vitality and consistency of the tradition in the various Brittonic areas… The folklore may in some cases have been boosted by the literary developments… [but] it remained largely unaffected by the literary Arthurian cycle, and retained its character throughout the period.[3]

---

1   Padel, 'Nature of Arthur', pp. 25-30; Green, *Concepts of Arthur*, pp. 242-45.
2   See below and Padel, 'The Nature of Arthur', pp. 2-3, 28; Green, *Concepts of Arthur*, pp. 67-70, 105, 242-43.
3   Padel, 'Nature of Arthur', pp. 27 and 29-30.

Before ending this introduction, three final features of the material categorised and listed in the gazetteer require comment. First, all instances known to the present writer of a name in the form 'Arthur's X' are included, but the level of detail of the material covered varies considerably between instances. In some cases we have a full tale recorded or summarised; in others we have only the name surviving, not the explanatory story that originally accompanied it. In such circumstances the original folk-tale can only be guessed at, through comparison with either Arthurian literary texts or other similar onomastic and topographic lore, Arthurian or otherwise (this is a problem common to all characters who feature in topographic and onomastic folklore).[1] It is, of course, such instances where only the name – not the story – survives that are most open, still, to the suspicion of post-medieval antiquarian invention, though it should be recalled here that we find just the same situation in the medieval period too, so that (for example) only the name 'Bedwyr's Well' survives in the early Welsh poem *Marwnat Cadwallon ap Cadfan*. Scepticism in some of these cases may well be justified, but hyper-scepticism is certainly not.

The second is the fact that Arthur appears to have been seen as a giant and he competes with other giants for prominence in his folkloric connection with various 'quoits' and other 'remarkable' features in the landscape. Such a concept can also perhaps be observed in early Welsh literary sources – including *Historia Brittonum* §73, *Preideu Annwfyn* and *Breuddwyd Rhonabwy* – but it is particularly clear in the onomastic and topographic lore, with folklore collectors such as Myrddin Fardd referring to stories of 'Arthur the Giant' and a large section of Grooms recent survey of Welsh Giant-lore devoted to tales of Arthur. As is noted in the gazetteer, the very nature of many of the 'Arthur's X' names necessarily implies a gigantic size and strength for Arthur.[2]

Finally, it should be noted that the following gazetteer is inevitably biased. Some regions saw their local folklore recorded in detail and from a very early date, whilst in others such antiquarian activity was largely lacking. This fact almost certainly lays at the root of the large number of Welsh sites in this list compared to, for example, the paucity of material from the south-west. That this situation does not reflect reality can be readily seen from the work of the mid-nineteenth-century Cornish folklorist Robert Hunt, who stated that in eastern Cornwall 'all the marks of any peculiar kind found on rocks... are almost always attributed to Arthur' and that 'King Arthur's beds, and chairs, and caves[, and quoits] are frequently to be met with', but who then seems content to describe more fully only one such site, the stone

---

1   Grooms, *Giants of Wales*, *passim*.

2   See further Green, *Concepts of Arthur*, particularly chapter two for Arthur and chapter four for his gigantic companions and family. See also Padel, 'Nature of Arthur', and Grooms, *Giants of Wales*, pp. 113-28.

in St Columb, Cornwall.[1] Another factor which affects the distribution is, naturally, the availability of such records – thus Grooms' material from Brittany is as yet unpublished, and there is therefore very little Breton folklore in the following gazetteer. In consequence, the gazetteer must be considered a provisional list; its compilation, needless to say, owes a considerable debt to Chris Grooms' important study and Geoffrey Ashe's *Traveller's Guide to Arthurian Britain*.[2]

2. Arthurian Folklore: A Brief Guide to Early Literary References

a. *Historia Brittonum §73 and Culhwch ac Olwen*

That one major expression of Arthur's early legend was through local onomastic and topographic folklore is made very clear by the *Historia Brittonum*, written in A.D. 829 or 830. Chapters 67-75 of this work contain a description of various *mirabilia*, 'marvels', from Britain and Ireland that the author had either heard of or had personally experienced; two of these are Arthurian in character. One describes a topographic folk-tale relating to Arthur's murder and burial of his son, Amr:

> There is another wonder in the country called Ergyng (*Ercing*).
> There is a tomb there by a spring, called Llygad Amr (*Licat Amr*);
> the name of the man who was buried in the tomb was Amr. He was
> the son of the warrior Arthur, and he killed him there and buried
> him. Men come to measure the tomb, and it is sometimes six feet
> long, sometimes nine, sometimes twelve, sometimes fifteen. At
> whatever measure you measure it on one occasion, you never find it
> again of the same measure, and I have tried it myself.[3]

This is without a doubt a chance – and exceptionally early; given that most British folklore goes unrecorded before the twelfth century – survival of an onomastic topographic tale drawn from local, popular folklore, here designed to explain the name *Licat Amr* and an associated grave. The story

---

1   R. Hunt, *Popular Romances of the West of England. The Drolls, Traditions and Superstitions of Old Cornwall*, third edition of 1881 (Felinfach, 1993), I, p. 186. Similarly Borlase remarked of Cornwall in the mid-eighteenth century that 'whatever is great, and the use and Author unknown, is attributed to Arthur', although he only identifies a few such sites: Padel, 'Nature of Arthur', p. 29.

2   Grooms, *Giant of Wales*, pp. 113-28; G. Ashe, *The Traveller's Guide to Arthurian Britain* (Glastonbury, 1997).

3   *Nennius: British History and The Welsh Annals,* ed. and trans. J. Morris (Chichester, 1980), p. 42.

of Arthur killing Amr is otherwise unknown, although 'Amhar son of Arthur' appears in *Geraint* as one of Arthur's four chamberlains. Nonetheless, this is sufficient to demonstrate both the early existence of this material and the manner in which remarkable features in the wilds of the landscape had explanatory Arthurian stories attached to them. Even more interesting is the other Arthurian *mirabile*:

> There is another wonder in the country called Builth. There is a heap of stones there, and one of these stones placed on the top of the pile has the footprint of a dog on it. When he hunted Twrch Trwyth, Cafal (*Cabal*), the warrior Arthur's hound, impressed his footprint on the stone, and Arthur later brought together the pile of stones, under the stone in which was his dog's footprint, and it is called Carn Cafal (*Carn Cabal*). Men come and take the stone in their hands for the space of a day and a night, and on the morrow it is found upon the stone pile.[1]

Carn Cabal is a prehistoric cairn which gives its name to Corn Cafallt, a hill near Rhaeadr (Powys). Again we have an unusual and wondrous landscape feature having its existence and name being explained through the attachment to it of an Arthurian onomastic and topographic tale. This 'wonder' is particularly interesting as we know from the eleventh-century prose tale *Culhwch ac Olwen* that the hunting of the giant divine boar *Twrch Trwyth* (more correctly *Trwyd*) was a developed and important Arthurian tale. It is consequently significant that here, at its earliest occurrence, it is thoroughly rooted in local folklore. Indeed, this appears true of the tale even in *Culhwch* too: there the hunt is localised in a number of places across south Wales, such as Cwm Kerwyn, the highest point on the Preselly mountains, and various sites with names mainly associated – either correctly or through folk-etymology – with pigs.[2]

The tale of *Twrch Trwyd* is not the only one in *Culhwch* which appears to have been expressed through and/or had its origins in local onomastic and topographic folklore. For example, the tale of Arthur's raid on Ireland for the cauldron of Diwrnach Wyddel – which is a euhemerism of Arthur's cauldron-seeking raid into the Otherworld related in the early poem *Preideu Annwfyn* – is clearly derivative of a pre-existing onomastic tale in *Culhwch*:

> And they disembarked at the house of Llwydeu son of Cel Coed, at Porth Cerddin in Dyfed. And Mesur-y-Peir [a place-name, 'Measure of the Cauldron'] is there.[3]

---

1 *Nennius*, p. 42.
2 See Green, *Concepts of Arthur*, pp. 67-72.
3 *The Mabinogion*, trans. G. Jones and T. Jones (London, 1949), p. 130.

This place-name is now lost; however, Kenneth Jackson has identified a *Messur Pritguenn* ('Measure of [Arthur's ship] Prydwen') in the twelfth-century charters of the Book of Llandaf, which he considers to be part of this onomastic tale and confirmation of its pre-existence.[1]

Indeed, a deeper investigation implies that many early Arthurian tales may have been expressed, at least partially, through such material. To cite some further examples, the Arthurian killings of the Very Black Witch and Dillus Farfawg in *Culhwch* both look to fall into this category of Arthurian tales which derive from (or are expressed in) local folklore, as does the clearly folklore-derived battle between Arthur and the giant Ritho/Retho in Geoffrey of Monmouth's *Historia Regum Britanniae*.[2]

b. The Latin Saints' Lives

Arthur makes a number of appearances in the eleventh- to thirteenth-century Latin Saints' Lives. There he is most usually 'an arrogant, grasping tyrant who is humbled in ignominious defeat, not in any armed struggle but in his childish greed and even in his failure to fulfil his traditional role as giant or dragon-slayer'. Nonetheless, it has recently been concluded that 'the Arthurian episodes appear to be genuine fragments of Arthurian legend [consistent with the portrayal of Arthur found in *Culhwch ac Olwen* etc.], manipulated so that they may display Arthur in the worst possible light.'[3] In several instances these episodes appear, once again, to be at least in part drawn from local onomastic and topographic lore. Thus in Lifris' *Vita Sancti Cadoci*, written between 1061 and 1104, we find two tales of Arthur unknown from any other source, one seeming to reflect a topographic folktale involving the exchange of magical or Otherworldly animals at a ford, and another that looks to be a similar folktale in which Arthur is a mighty warrior, protector, and defender of the realm/guardian of the border who exists outside of normal society.[4] Also otherwise unknown are the tales of Arthur slaying dragons which have been manipulated by the authors of the Welsh *Vita Prima Sancti Carantoci* (*c.* 1100?) and the twelfth-century Breton *Vita Euflami*. In the case of the latter at least, the story would seem to have already been in existence by *c.* 1110 – judging by the evidence of the

1   See J.T. Koch 'The Celtic Lands', in N.J. Lacy (ed.) *Medieval Arthurian Literature: A Guide to Recent Research* (New York, 1996), pp. 239-322 at pp. 256-57.

2   Green, *Concepts of Arthur*, chapter three for a full discussion and development of these points; for place-names in *Culhwch ac Olwen*, see also *Culhwch and Olwen. An Edition and Study of the Oldest Arthurian Tale*, edd. R. Bromwich and D. Simon Evans (Cardiff, 1992).

3   B.F. Roberts '*Culhwch ac Olwen*, the Triads, Saints' Lives', in R. Bromwich *et al* (edd.) *The Arthur of the Welsh* (Cardiff, 1991), pp. 73-95 at p.83.

4   Padel, 'The Nature of Arthur', pp. 7-8; Green, *Concepts of Arthur*, pp. 128-29, 199-200.

Perros Relief – and it shows very clear signs of deriving from local topographic lore.[1]

c. Englynion y Beddau, De Rebus Gestis Anglorum & Ymddiddan Gwyddno Garanhir ac Gwyn fab Nudd

As noted in the introduction, the mid-late ninth-century *Englynion y Beddau* is effectively an early Welsh catalogue of 'place-lore', concerned with the supposed resting places of mythical/folkloric heroes. Although it claims no knowledge of Arthur's grave, it does refer to that of his nephew, Gwalchmai – 'The grave of Gwalchmai is in Peryddon (*periton*) / as a reproach to men' – and to that of one of his constant companion, Bedwyr – 'the grave of Bedwyr is on Tryfan hill.'[2]

Clearly in these we have further evidence for the very early existence of Arthurian burial-folklore, like that related in the *Historia Brittonum*. Unfortunately no further details are given of the stories attached to these sites in the *Englynion y Beddau*. However, the grave of Gwalchmai is also referred to by William of Malmesbury in his *Gesta Regum Anglorum* of *c.* 1125:

> At this time (1066-87) was found in the province of Wales called R(h)os the tomb of Walwen, who was the not degenerate nephew of Arthur by his sister… [This] was found in the time of King William [the Conqueror, 1066-1087] upon the sea shore, fourteen feet in length; and here some say he was wounded by his foes and cast out in a shipwreck, but according to others he was killed by his fellow-citizens at a public banquet. Knowledge of the truth therefore remains doubtful, although neither story would be inconsistent with the defence of his fame.[3]

This expansion of the *Englynion y Beddau*'s brief reference obviously aids considerably our understanding of the underlying folktale – though much is obviously missing – and both the size of the grave and nature of the tale bear comparison with the grave of Amr, Arthur's son, in the *mirabilia* of the *Historia Brittonum*. With regards to the location of Gwalchmai's grave, the site of the grave recorded in both sources would appear, upon investigation, to be identical, suggesting that the discovery in 'the time of King William' was either an opening or excavation of the traditional site of Gwalchmai's burial recorded in the *Englynion y Beddau*.[4]

---

1 See Green, *Concepts of Arthur*, chapter three for a full discussion.

2 P. Sims-Williams 'The Early Welsh Arthurian Poems', in R. Bromwich *et al* (edd.) *The Arthur of the Welsh* (Cardiff, 1991), pp. 33-71 at p. 50.

3 E.K. Chambers, *Arthur of Britain* (London, 1927), p. 17.

4 Green, *Concepts of Arthur*, pp. 170-71; Sims-Williams, 'Early Welsh Arthurian

Incidentally, another of Arthur's sons, Llacheu, also appears to have a traditional burial site. In the perhaps tenth-century *Ymddiddan Gwyddno Garanhir ac Gwyn fab Nudd* we find evidence for the existence of some story of his death:

> I have been where Llacheu was slain
> the son of Arthur, awful [/marvellous] in songs
> when ravens croaked over blood.[1]

Where this occurred is not stated but we find, in a thirteenth-century elegy by Bleddyn Fardd, the statement that 'Llachau was slain below Llech Ysgar'. Whilst the place is unidentified – though it was the site of one of the courts of Madog ap Maredudd, d. 1160 – Sims-Williams has suggested that there could well have been a local legend underlying the above like those cited previously.[2]

d. *De Miraculis Sanctae Mariae Laudensis, Liber Floridus, Itinerarium Kambrie & Marwnat Cadwallon ap Cadfan*

Herman's *De Miraculis Sanctae Mariae Laudensis*, 'The Miracles of St Mary of Laon', is an account of a journey made in 1113 to Britain by some canons of Laon, in northern France.[3] From the current perspective the primary importance of this text lies with the fact that, whilst travelling between Exeter and Bodmin, the canons were shown the 'seat' and the 'oven' of King Arthur and were told that this was 'Arthurian country'. These are some of the earliest recorded instances of specific sites actually being granted a name of the form 'Arthur's X', although we lack the stories which explained why these sites were so described (see the gazetteer below for some later comparative material that might well allow these to be guessed at).

Similar unexplained pieces of onomastic and topographic folklore are found in other early sources too. Lambert of St Omer, in his *Liber Floridus* of 1120, made additions to the *mirabilia* of the *Historia Brittonum* including a building known as 'Arthur's Palace', which is now generally acknowledged to be a circular building of Roman date near Stirling (Scotland) known as

---

Poems', p. 50.

1 *The Celtic Sources for the Arthurian Legend*, ed. and trans. J.B. Coe and S. Young (Felinfach, 1995), p. 125.

2 Sims-Williams, 'Early Welsh Arthurian Poems', p. 44; O.J. Padel, *Arthur in Medieval Welsh Literature* (Cardiff, 2000), p. 99, suggests that 'below Llech Ysgar' might refer to Crickheath Hill south of Oswestry, Shropshire.

3 Padel, 'Nature of Arthur', pp. 4-6, 8-10; J.S.P. Tatlock, 'The English Journey of the Laon Canons', *Speculum*, 8 (1933), pp. 454-65.

'Arthur's O'en' in the thirteenth century.[1] Gerald of Wales refers, in his *c.* 1190 *Itinerarium Kambrie* (I.2), to a hill 'called Kairarthur, that is Arthur's seat, because of the twin peaks of a projection rising up in the form of a chair', to be identified as Pen y Fan, the highest point of the Brecon Beacons.[2] And in the perhaps tenth-century poem *Marwnat Cadwallon ap Cadfan* we learn that a seventh-century battle was supposedly fought at *Ffynnawn Uetwyr*, 'Bedwyr's Spring', a potentially very early instance of Arthurian naming and one which, once again, naturally implies some kind of lost topographic legend.[3]

3. A Gazetteer of Arthurian Onomastic and Topographic Folklore

a. *Arthur's Stones*

There are numerous 'Arthur's Stones' (usually, in Welsh, *Carreg Arthur* or *Maen Arthur*). The implication is that these are enormous and remarkable stones that Arthur's gigantic strength allowed him to mark his mark upon, or place in their current position, whilst wandering in the wilds of the landscape.[4] Although some may well be antiquarian inventions, Padel has established a convincing context for these names and we have examples back into the medieval period – as such there is little reason to doubt that a large proportion represent the remnants of genuine onomastic and topographic folk-tales, created at various times over the past 1000 years. One example is a Neolithic or Bronze Age burial-chamber found in Herefordshire and first recorded in the thirteenth century (SO318430).[5] Other examples include:

❖ A double megalithic chambered tomb with capstone in Llanrhidian Lower on the Gower peninsula (SS49139055): 'Legend has it that when Arthur was walking through Carmarthenshire on his way to Camlann, he felt a pebble in his shoe and tossed it away. It flew seven miles over Burry Inlet and landed in Gower, on top of the smaller stones of Maen Cetti.'[6]

❖ Two 'Arthur's Stone's are mentioned in Wales in the fourteenth

1   Padel, 'Nature of Arthur', p. 6.
2   Padel, 'Nature of Arthur', p. 25-26.
3   Koch and Carey, *The Celtic Heroic Age*, p. 373.
4   Padel, 'The Nature of Arthur'; Grooms, *The Giants of Wales*.
5   Padel, 'Nature of Arthur', p. 4; Grooms, *Giants of Wales*, pp. 115-16.
6   Grooms, *Giants of Wales*, p. 115.

century.[1]

- ❖ An 'Arthur's Stone' in Bettws, Carmarthenshire (SN6441212)
- ❖ An 'Arthur's Stone' in Manafon, Montgomery (SJ12960496)
- ❖ An 'Arthur's Stone' in Llanfair Caereinion, Montgomery (SJ1006)
- ❖ An 'Arthur's Stone' on Berwyn Mountains, Montgomery (SJ1139)
- ❖ An 'Arthur's Stone' in Llanddwywe-is-y-graig, Merioneth (SH60332283)
- ❖ A stone circle known as 'Arthur's Stones' in Llanaber, Merioneth (SH63161886)
- ❖ The 'Stones of the Sons of Arthur' are a group of standing stones in Mynachlog-ddu, Pembrokeshire (SN11813102) where there are numerous other Arthurian sites. They are apparently meant to represent the site of a battle
- ❖ An 'Arthur's Stone' (in Denbigh, SJ224470) where a giantess called on 'Arthur the Giant' from the Eglwyseg Rocks for help against St Collen
- ❖ The 25 ton capstone of an ancient burial chamber near Reynoldston, north of Cefn Brynis, West Glamorgan (SS490905) is called Arthur's stone and his ghost is occasionally said to emerge from underneath it – it is explained as a stone that was tossed from Arthur's shoe
- ❖ A megalithic burial of c. 3000 BC is known as Arthur's Stone, just north of Dorstone (SD3141)
- ❖ An 'Arthur's Stone' in Llanfechell parish, Anglesey around half a mile from the parish church (SH36849025)
- ❖ An 'Arthur's Stone' near Colomendy Lodge, Denbigh (SJ13226938)
- ❖ An 'Arthur's Stone' in the parish of Dolbenmaen, Caernarvonshire (SH509434)
- ❖ An 'Arthur's Stone' lying at the top of a hill in Maen Arthur Wood near Pont-rhyd-y-groes, Cardiganshire (SN726730), with the name of Arthur's horse present in nearby Rhos Gafallt
- ❖ An 'Arthur's Stone' near Penarthur, Pembrokeshire (SM746267) and related in folklore to a Coetan Arthur (Arthur's Quoit)
- ❖ An 'Arthur's Stone' near Coupar Angus, Perthshire (NO261430)

---

1 Grooms, *Giants of Wales*, p. 116.

❖ 'Stone Arthur' is on top of a mountain in Westmorland (NY348092)

In addition to these, there are several 'Arthur's Stones' whose origin-stories directly referenced Arthur's (gigantic?) horse:

❖ Two instances of *Carreg Carn March Arthur*, the 'Stone of Arthur's Steed's Hoof', one in Llanferres parish, Denbigh (SJ203626) and the other near Llyn Barfog above Aber-tafol, Merioneth (SN65059816).[1] The latter is associated with Arthur's dragging of the demonic *Afanc* from Llyn Barfog, the referenced marks being left on the stone by Arthur's horse's hooves as he undertook this endeavour.

❖ An 'Arthur's Stone' in St Columb, Cornwall (SW913637), near Arthur's Hunting Lodge/Seat, which is said to bear the impression of the footprints of Arthur's horse and is associated with the legends of him hunting in this area

❖ The stone atop Corn Gafallt, a hill near Rhaeadr, in which Arthur's steed left impressions of his hooves whilst Arthur chased the *Twrch Trwyd* (as recorded in the ninth-century *Historia Brittonum* §73 and fully developed in *Culhwch ac Olwen*). Although not actually named as an 'Arthur's Stone', the similarity of this piece of lore to those noted above should be obvious. It may thus provide some indication of the kind of explanatory stories that many of these names once had attached to them, as well as further confirmation that such material had a genuine place in the Arthurian tradition.

b. Arthur's Quoits

The name 'Arthur's Quoit' (Welsh *Coeten Arthur*, 'quoit' meaning 'discus, a solid circular object thrown for sport') is usually applied to a cromlech and probably originally referred to the capstone of such prehistoric structures. Such features, when not being named after Arthur, are frequently associated with giants and reflect the concept of Arthur as a giant referred to above, Arthur having the requisite giant-like strength to fling these enormous stones for sport. It should be noted that these names must all date from after the sixteenth century, given that this is when the word 'quoit' was borrowed into Welsh:. As such they are late coinings, but their relationship to the earlier 'Arthur's Stones' is obvious and they fit well into the context

---

1   Grooms, *Giants of Wales*, p. 117.

which Padel has established for this type of Arthurian folklore. As such they testify to the continued vitality of such Arthurian onomastic and topographic folklore, although antiquarian invention of at least some of the examples below might be suspected.[1] Examples include:

❖ An 'Arthur's Quoit' (SN40553860) with 'a trace of Arthur's thumbmark … plainly seen on it now' was tossed to Llangeler and Penboyr by Arthur from Pen Codfol; 'another of the giant's quoit landed on the land of Llwyn-ffynnon; this place is called Cae Coetan Arthur'.[2]

❖ A cromlech named 'Arthur's Quoit' is found in Myl1teyrn parish, Caernarvonshire (SH22973456). Grooms translates the following from Myrddin Fardd (writing in the nineteenth century), which is worth repeating for its illustration of the local folkloric traditions surrounding these stones:

> A multitude of tales are told about him [Arthur]. Sometimes, he is portrayed as a king and mighty soldier, other times like a giant huge in size, and they are found the length and breadth of the land of stones, in tons in weight, and the tradition connects them with his name – a few of them have been in his shoes time after time, bothering him, and compelling him also to pull them, and to throw them some unbelievable distance… A cromlech recognized by the name 'Coetan Arthur' is on the land of Trefgwm, in the parish of Myl1teyrn; it consists of a great stone resting on three other stones. The tradition states that 'Arthur the Giant' threw this coetan from Carn Fadrun, a mountain several miles from Trefgwm, and his wife took three other stones in her apron and propped them up under the coetan.[3]

❖ Three 'Arthur's Quoits' are mentioned in the nineteenth century in Ardudwy, Merionethshire (SH60852460, SH60322383 and SH58862287), where 'the tradition states that King Arthur threw it [them] from the top of Moelfre to the places where they rest presently. It is believed that marks of his fingers are the indentations to be seen on the last stone that

---

1   Padel, 'Nature of Arthur', pp. 26-27; see further Green, *Concepts of Arthur*, pp. 244-45.
2   Grooms, *Giants of Wales*, p. 118.
3   Grooms, *Giants of Wales*, p. 118-19.

was noted.'[1]

❖ Three 'Arthur's Quoit's mentioned in the nineteenth century in Caernarvonshire, in the parishes of Llanrug (SH536621), Llanystumdwy (SH49894132) and Rhoslan (SH48434096)

❖ An 'Arthur's Quoit' (the remains of a burial chamber) recorded in Newport parish, Pembrokeshire (SN06033935)

❖ An 'Arthur's Quoit' in Llangadog parish, Carmarthenshire (SN73772205) – this is a large rock in the river Sawddwy, which Arthur flung into position from Pen Arthur, a mile distant, and is accompanied by a similar large rock that was tossed from the shoe of a lady acquaintance of Arthur.[2]

❖ An 'Arthur's Quoit' in Llangadog parish, Carmarthenshire (SN69962298)

❖ An 'Arthur's Quoit' in Mynachlog-ddu parish, Pembrokeshire (SN143325), said to have been hurled by Arthur from Henry's Moat parish, where there is a stone circle; associated with Arthur's Grave and Arthur's Cairn

❖ A burial chamber and large capstone lying near St David's Head, Pembrokeshire (SM725281), close-by an Arthur's Hill

❖ A 17 feet long stone known as Arthur's Quoit but now lost, near Llwydiarth, Anglesey (SH43278575)

❖ The capstone of the Llugwy dolmen near Moelfre, Anglesey (SH50138603)

❖ A capstone destroyed in 1845 in Llanllawer parish, Pembrokeshire (SN00683617)

❖ An 'Arthur's Quoit' at Pentre Ifan, Pembrokeshire (SN09943701)

❖ An 'Arthur's Quoit' in Caeo parish, Carmarthenshire (SN656348)

❖ An 'Arthur's Quoit' in Celynin Parish, Caernarvonshire recorded in the seventeenth century (SH786719)

❖ An 'Arthur's Quoit' in Llanjestin parish, Caernarvonshire recorded in the seventeenth century (SH251351)

❖ A lost 'Arthur's Quoit' in Caernarvonshire (SH419490)

❖ An 'Arthur's Quoit' cromlech near Manorbier, Pembrokeshire (SS05939728)

❖ An 'Arthur's Quoit' in Cas-ael parish, Pembrokeshire (SN00953025)

---

1   Grooms, *Giants of Wales*, p. 119.
2   Grooms, *Giants of Wales*, pp. 120-21.

❖ An 'Arthur's Quoit' in Llangwyryfon parish, Cardiganshire (SN60926748)

❖ Two 'Arthur's Quoit's in Clynnog, Caernarvonshire (SH407496)

❖ An 'Arthur's Quoit' recorded in 1838 in Caernarvonshire (SH50894390)

❖ An ?'Arthur's Quoit' cromlech at Carn Penbery, Pembrokeshire (SM766293)

❖ A lost 'Arthur's Quoit' at the Pembroke estuary (SM97/00-1)

❖ A cromlech known as Arthur's Quoit in Pembrokeshire (SM 92)

❖ An 'Arthur's Quoit' in Llanwnda parish, Pembrokeshire (SM919380)

❖ An 'Arthur's Quoit' or 'Giant's Quoit' cromlech in St Columb Major parish, Cornwall (SW923619)

❖ An 'Arthur's Quoit' (a capstone of a cromlech) near Tintagel, Cornwall

❖ An 'Arthur's Quoit' near Llanenddwyn, Monmouthshire (SH588229), sometimes known as 'Arthur's Stone', which is part of a chambered long cairn

❖ Trethevy Quoit in Cornwall (SX259689) is sometimes called 'Arthur's Quoit'

c. Arthur's Dining Sites

There are a number of sites which claim to be associated with Arthur dining in the wilderness. Certainly some of these, at least, ought to be seen to parallel the *fulachta* – ancient cooking places in wild areas – often attributed to Fionn and his men, whose legend closely parallels that of the non-Galfridian Arthur.

Two sites carry the name 'Arthur's Oven'. One of these was seen in 1113 by some canons of Laon, in northern France, who were touring England to try and raise funds for their monastery after a fire the previous year. It is probably the 'King's Oven' (*furnus regis*) recorded on Dartmoor in the next century and beyond (SX674812). This was a feature prominent enough to be used as a marker in the bounds of the royal forest of Dartmoor in 1240, and it is believed to be an ancient tin-smelting furnace, which has been abandoned and (function forgotten) later appropriated by the Arthurian legend to feature in onomastic and topographic lore. Another 'Arthur's Oven' is a circular building of Roman date near Stirling

(NS879827), known as Arthur's O'en (Oven) from at least the thirteenth century and destroyed in the eighteenth century.[1]

Also relevant is *Ffynnon Cegin Arthur*, 'The Spring of Arthur's Kitchen', in Llanddeiniolen parish, Cardiganshire (SH555648), which is mentioned by the Cardiganshire poet Ieuan ap Rhydderch (*fl.* 1430-70) thus: 'Some vapour surrounding Arthur's Kitchen, Rust on every commote of pain, an ugly riddle, phantom's snare'. R.J. Thomas commented that 'The spring is called Ffynnon Cegin Arthur, not because there is any direct connection with Arthur, but because it was a common custom within place-names of connecting Arthur the Giant with everything huge or exceptional' (the spring is coloured red with iron oxide).[2] Related is the *Crochan Arthur*, Arthur's Pot or Cauldron, which was supposedly used by him for cooking and which is near to Arthur's Table in Carmarthenshire (SN170257).

In addition we might also consider whether the Cornish 'Arthur's Cups and Saucers' possibly fall within this category. These are twenty small circular depressions, 5-15 cm across, found on the headland at Tintagel, Cornwall, where there is also an Arthur's Chair, Arthur's Footprint and, nearby, an Arthur's Quoit.[3] Finally, we should note the numerous 'Arthur's Tables' that exist. One very interesting 'table' (a flat topped stone) associated with Arthur is that at the boundary of Gulval, Zennor and Madron in Cornwall, where Arthur is said to have dined before defeating the invading Vikings of far-western Cornwall.[4] A similar legend is also attached to the Table Mên, Sennen (Cornwall).[5] Other examples include:

- ❖ An 'Arthur's Table' from Caernarvonshire (SN170257)
- ❖ An 'Arthur's Table' in the Mynydd Llangyndeyrn (SN487130)
- ❖ An 'Arthur's Table' at Llangynog (SN336161)
- ❖ Bwrdd Arthur (Arthur's Table), Anglesey (SH588816), which is actually a hillfort
- ❖ Bwrdd Arthur (Arthur's Table), Denbighshire (SH961672), a circle of indentations in a rocky hillside recorded in the sixteenth century
- ❖ Caerleon, Monmouthshire (ST339906), where the old Roman amphitheatre was known as the 'Round Table'

---

1   See Padel, 'Nature of Arthur', pp. 5-6 for both of these sites and the possibility that the second was first mentioned in 1120.
2   Grooms, *Giants of Wales*, pp. 114, 127.
3   Initials are cut among them purporting to date from as far back as the seventeenth century, but see Charles Thomas, *Tintagel: Arthur and Archaeology* (London, 1993), p. 49, for doubts as to the folkloric origin of the attribution.
4   M.A. Courtney, *Cornish Feasts and Folklore* (1890), p. 74.
5   Hunt, *Popular Romances of the West of England*, II, pp. 305-06.

❖ Maryborough, Westmorland (NY523284), which is an earthwork known as the 'Round Table'

❖ A 'Round Table' from Stirling, Stirlingshire (NS789936) which is first mentioned *c.* 1478 by William of Worcester

Some of these, of course, may owe their origins to the international literary legend and medieval pseudo-Arthurian events and feasts, rather than topographic folklore.

d. Arthur's Seats

There are a large number of topographic features bearing the name 'Arthur's Seat' (Welsh *Eisteddfa Arthur*). Two of these have been mentioned in section two, being an unlocated feature in Devon shown to the canons of Laon when travelling between Exeter and Bodmin in 1113 and the hill 'called Kairarthur [*sic*], that is Arthur's seat, because of the twin peaks of a projection rising up in the form of a chair', referred to in *c.* 1190 by Gerald of Wales in his *Itinerarium Kambrie* (I.2) and identified as Pen y Fan, the highest point of the Brecon Beacons (SO010214). Another famous 'Arthur's Seat' is that in Edinburgh, first recorded as *Arthurissete* in 1508 (NT275729) but possibly referred to as the site of a mythical battle in the pre-Galfridian poem *Pa gur yv y porthaur?*[1] In all cases, the concept of Arthur would seem to be, once again, that of a giant, with these enormous rock-formations providing him furniture whilst he roamed the wilds of the landscape, just as they do for other giants in the non-Arthurian giant-lore recorded by Grooms. Other instances include the following:

❖ Examples found in north Pembrokeshire (in the modern period) in the parishes of Nevern and Meline

❖ 'Arthur's Seat' as an alternative name for *Cadair Idris* ('Idris's Chair') in Wales

❖ A mountain in the Hart Fell area, Dumfriesshire (NT110126) is known as 'Arthur's Seat'

❖ Certain stones known as *Cadeir Arthur*, 'Arthur's Chair' on the peak Pen-y-fâl (Sugar Loaf) in Monmouthshire (SO273188)

❖ An 'Arthur's Seat' at Dumbarrow Hill, Angus (NO552479)

❖ An 'Arthur's Seat' east of Liddesdale, Cumberland (NY495783), also called Arthur Seat and Arthur's Hill

1 See Padel, 'Nature of Arthur', pp. 25-26; Grooms, *Giants of Wales*, p. 114; and Green, *Concepts of Arthur*, pp. 84, 119-21.

❖ An 'Arthur's Chair' at Tintagel, Cornwall which has initials
  purporting to date back to the seventeenth century cut into it
  and a slit known as the Window.[1]

❖ An 'Arthur's Chair' north-west of Sewingshields,
  Northumberland (NY800700). This is found at King's Crags
  and has its pair in Queen's Crags, where there is Gwenhwyfar's
  Chair. Arthur, clearly conceived of as a giant, supposedly threw
  a boulder from his chair at Gwenhwyfar which bounced off of
  her comb to land on the ground, with the teeth-marks from the
  comb still visible on the rock.

e. Arthur's Residences

A number of sites have been claimed as Arthur's residence in the
wilderness. One of these is mentioned in an encyclopaedia completed in
1120 by Lambert of St. Omer, whose text is related to the *Historia Brittonum*.[2]
In his list of *mirabilia* (wonders, folklore) of the island of Britain he notes a
'palace' of *Arturi militis* which was located in Pictland and had sculpted on it
his deeds and battles. This *mirabile* is now generally accepted as being a
circular building of Roman date near Stirling (NS 879827), known as
Arthur's O'en (Oven) from at least the thirteenth century.[3]

Another site with a claim to be Arthur's court is *Kelli wic*. This site
appears in some of the earliest Arthurian tales, such as the early dialogue
poem *Pa gur yv y porthaur?* and the eleventh century Culhwch *ac Olwen*, and it
has been identified with a number of sites across the country. Certainly it is
a wilderness site, *kelli wic* meaning 'forest grove', but whether it ever had a
real location – to be derived like the above from topographic folklore – is to
be severely doubted: its origins seem more plausibly fictional, or even
mythical.[4] Other claimed sites for Arthur's residence include:

❖ 'Arthur's Hall', Cornwall (SX130777), a stone enclosure on
  Bodmin Moor which was recorded first in the sixteenth
  century. It consists of a rectangular bank (enclosing marshy

---

1   See further Thomas, *Tintagel*, p. 49.

2   D.N. Dumville, 'The *Liber Floridus* of Lambert of Saint-Omer and the *Historia
    Brittonum*', *Bulletin of the Board of Celtic Studies*, 26 (1974-6), pp. 103-22.

3   Padel, 'Nature of Arthur', p. 6.

4   P.K. Ford, 'On the Significance of some Arthurian Names in Welsh', *Bulletin of
    the Board of Celtic Studies*, 30 (1983), pp. 268-73 at p. 271; O.J. Padel, 'Some
    south-western sites with Arthurian associations', in R. Bromwich *et al* (edd.) *The
    Arthur of the Welsh* (Cardiff, 1991), pp. 229-48; Padel, 'Nature of Arthur', pp. 12-
    13.

ground) with a rectangle of upright granite slabs within. It was also known as Arthur's Hunting Lodge. Nearby are Arthur's Bed, Arthur's Troughs and Arthur's Downs.

❖ 'Arthur's Hunting Lodge' (or Hunting Seat) in Castle-an-Dinas, Cornwall, near St Columb, from which Arthur rode in the hunt on Tregoss Moor – a stone in St Columb bears the four footprints that his horse made whilst he was out hunting.

❖ Treryn Dinas, an ancient fort in Cornwall, is claimed to have been a 'castle' of Arthur.

❖ *Llys Arthur*, 'Arthur's Court/Hall/Palace' lies close to the site of Cai and Bedwyr's battle with Dillus Farfog, at SN787784.[1]

❖ Cadbury Castle, Somerset, was recorded as Arthur's Camelot in the sixteenth century by Leland. The name 'Camelot' seems to have only become attached to the Arthurian legend in the late-twelfth century and has no place in British traditions, as indicated by *Trioedd Ynys Prydein*. In 1586, however, it was recorded that locals called Cadbury Castle 'Arthur's Palace' – a name which could conceivably have preceded (and informed) its designation as Camelot, in light of the *Liber Floridus* – and the presence of 'Arthur's Hunting Causeway' beside Cadbury Castle should also be noted, given the Cornish traditions. A 'King Arthur's Well' is found in the lowest rampart of the fort.

❖ There is a prehistoric hill-fort known as *le Camp d'Artus*,. 'Arthur's Camp', at Huelgoat (Brittany), with a *la Grotte d'Artus*, 'Arthur's Cave' nearby.

In addition to Arthur's palaces and halls, we also have a *Burum Arturi*, 'Arthur's Bower', that is probably 'bed-chamber'. This is a topographic feature located in Carlisle and first recorded in the 1170s.[2] Also relevant may be numerous 'Arthur's Caves', particularly as a number of these have stories attached in which he takes temporary refuge there, or slumbers there eternally. Caves, real or legendary, with Arthurian associations include Cadbury Castle, Caerleon, Snowdonia, Ogo'r Dinas, Alderley Edge, Craig-y-Dinas, Melrose, Richmond, Marchlyn Mawr, Sewingshields, Llantrisant (Mid-Glamorgan), Pumsaint (Carmarthenshire), Threlkeld (Cumberland) and Sneep (Northumberland). There is an *Ogof Arthur* in Angelsey, another in Merioneth, and one more two or three miles north of Monmouth above the Wye in Herefordshire (SO545155).

Finally, although perhaps better included with the Arthurian graves, we have several Arthurian beds. 'King Arthur's Bed' is located on Bodmin

---

1   Grooms, *Giants of Wales*, p. 167.
2   Padel, 'Nature of Arthur', p. 25.

Moor, east Cornwall (SX240756). It takes the form of a granite monolith on top of a hill, with a natural hollow in it shaped like a human torso. The first record of it is found in the works of an eighteenth-century Cornish antiquary, William Borlase (writing in 1754), who accompanies his description with the following remarks:

> Round Arthur's Bed, on a rocky Tor in the parish of North-hill, there are many [rock-basins], which the country people call Arthur's Troughs, in which he us'd to feed his Dogs. Near by also, is Arthur's Hall, and whatever is great, and the use and Author of unknown, is attributed to Arthur.[1]

Another 'Arthur's Bed' – *Gwely Arthur* – is near Pen Arthur in Dyfed and yet another is found near Tintagel (see *Arthur's Graves*).

f. Arthur's Graves

Early-recorded graves of Arthurian heroes are discussed in the second section, above. In addition to these, there are several sites either said to be Arthur's grave or called this, despite the *Englynion y Beddau*'s claim (backed up by other early sources) that no grave for Arthur was known. One of these is 'Arthur's (or Giant's) Grave', Warbstowe, Cornwall (SX202908), which is a long barrow mound in the double-ramparted Warbstowe Bury hill-fort. Another site is *Bedd Arthur* in Preselly Mountains, Pembrokeshire (SN130325), which is a cairn on top of a hill that is sometimes known as *Carn Arthur*. The most famous 'grave' is, of course, that found at Glastonbury but this cannot be considered folkloric in origin. Other folkloric sites include:

- ❖ *Bedd Arthur* ('Arthur's Grave') is associated with Arthur's Quoit in Mynachlog-ddu parish (SN10123580).[2]
- ❖ A cromlech near Trébeurden (Côtes-du-Nord, Brittany) is said to be Arthur's grave.[3]
- ❖ First recorded in the thirteenth century, a Neolithic or Bronze Age burial-chamber in Herefordshire (SO318430) is said to be Arthur's grave (or that of a giant he killed), with marks in the stone being made either by the giant's elbows or knees
- ❖ There is a *Carnedd Arthur* ('Arthur's Cairn') at Snowdonia,

---

1 Padel, 'Nature of Arthur', p. 29.
2 Grooms, *Giants of Wales*, p. 116.
3 Padel, 'Nature of Arthur', p. 27.

where the king was supposedly buried after Mordred killed him at Camlann (the battle is reported to have been fought in a nearby valley) and which has a 'cave legend' attached to it

❖ Another cairn, known as 'Arthurhouse', is presumably another grave for Arthur and is the most northerly piece of Arthurian place-lore, located at Garvock, Kincardineshire (NO748718)

A final possible folkloric grave for Arthur is located just outside the chapel at Tintagel, where there would appear to be a rock-cut grave of the medieval period. This was recorded by Leland in the sixteenth century and so has lain open since at least this point, and in the modern period it is variously known as King Arthur's Bed, Elbow Chair and Hip-Bath. The main interest lies with the 'remarkable' properties ascribed to this topographic feature. Thus John Norden wrote *c.* 1600:

> Ther is in this Castle a hole hewed out of a rocke, made in manner of a graue, which is sayde to haue bene done by a Hermite for his buriall; and the gravue will fitt euerye stature, as it is effabuled; but experience doth not so assure me.[1]

This obviously parallels the grave of Arthur's son mentioned in *Historia Brittonum* §73, discussed above, and Padel's comments are worth quoting at length on this matter:

> Variable-length graves are recorded occasionally elsewhere in Celtic folklore, in addition to the *Licat Amr* in the *Historia Brittonum*. What is significant here is finding one in an Arthurian context, and Norden's remark of having tried its length, echoing so closely (though with a different result) the remark in the *Historia Brittonum* almost eight hundred years earlier, in relation to *Licat Amr*: 'et ego solus probavi' ('and I myself have tried it'). Not only the folklore, it seems, but the scepticism of visitors has been remarkably constant over the centuries.[2]

g. Miscellaneous Arthuriana

In addition to the above categories of Arthurian onomastic and topographic folklore, we have a number of other features and places named after Arthur or associated with him. Some of these describe furniture or belongings of

---

1 Padel, 'Nature of Arthur', p. 27.
2 Padel, 'Nature of Arthur', p. 28.

Arthur, or marks made by him on rocks, suggestive of an underlying concept of 'Arthur the giant' similar to that behind the instances of 'Arthur's Seat' and 'Arthur's Quoit':

❖ *Cist Arthur*, 'Arthur's Chest', recorded in the parish of Llandeilo Bertholau, Monmouthshire (SO 3218) by Edward Lhuyd in the seventeenth-century thus: 'There is upon Skerid Vawr a great stone shaped like a house called Cist Arthur'.[1] It is located near an 'Arthur's Seat'

❖ 'Arthur's Footprint/Footstep' – this is found on the headland at Tintagel, Cornwall, on the highest point of the island. It was recorded as 'King Arthur's Footstep' in 1872 and his Footprint in 1901 and 1908, and takes the form of an eroded hollow, the base of which has the shape of a large human footprint. It is reputed to have been imprinted in the solid rock when Arthur 'stepped at one stride across the sea to Tintagel Church' (1889) and thus may be seen to parallel tales from other areas where Arthur is a giant who leaves impressions on various rocks. Thomas has suggested that hollow may actually have had a ceremonial use in the post-Roman period.[2]

❖ Moses Williams (1685-1742) records 'Arthur's Spear' (a thin standing stone) 'close to the Llech at one end of the way that leads from Bwlch-y-ddeufain to Aber' (Caernarvonshire, SH 73867167).[3]

Other instances of 'Arthur's X' would seem to reference the concept of Arthur as someone who hunted in the wild parts of the landscape:

❖ 'Arthur's Hunting Causeway' – this is found beside Cadbury Castle, Somerset, and is an ancient track passing the camp towards Glastonbury. In addition to evidencing 'Arthur the hunter' it would seem to be related the widespread folkloric belief that Arthur led the Wild Hunt, with tales of Arthur and his men riding along this a night-time, invisible except for the glint of silver horse shoes. The riders are said to stop to water their horses at 'the Wishing Well'.[4]

❖ 'Arthur's Troughs' – these are found on Bodmin Moor,

---

1 Grooms, *Giants of Wales*, p. 118.
2 Thomas, *Tintagel*, pp. 96-99.
3 Grooms, *Giants of Wales*, p. 128.
4 K. Palmer, *The Folklore of Somerset* (London, 1976), p. 83; Chambers, *Arthur of Britain*, pp. 184-85.

Cornwall, in the parish of North-Hill. They are reputed to be where Arthur fed his hunting dogs. Nearby are Arthur's Bed, Arthur's Downs, and Arthur's Hall.

Finally, yet others attach his name to a variety of landscape features; what stories underlie these is beyond conjecture, but the liminal locations of some of these reinforce the notion that it is in these untamed, remote or strange parts of the landscape that Arthur was active in British folklore:

❖ 'Arthur's Downs', located just to the north of Arthur's Hall (SX130777) on Bodmin Moor, Cornwall. Perhaps Arthur's hunting grounds?

❖ *Buarth Arthur*, 'Arthur's Enclosure', is the remains of a stone circle in Carmarthenshire (SN142266).

❖ *Fons Arthuri*, 'Arthur's Fountain' – recorded in Crawford parish, Lanarkshire (NS956205) as a landmark in a 1339 land grant

❖ *Pen Arthur*, 'Arthur's Hill'. Numerous instances of this name are recorded – they are perhaps to be related to those Arthurian tales found in the Saints' Lives and *Culhwch ac Olwen* that begin with Arthur and/or his men sat on a hilltop, ready for adventure (a position Fionn and his men are often found in). Several examples come from within the vicinity of an 'Arthur's Quoit' in Llangadog, Carmarthenshire, where there is *Banc Pen Arthur* (SH715240) and two farms, *Pen Arthur* and *Pen Arthur-isaf.* Another example comes from near St David's, Pembrokeshire (SM722279). The two peaks of the Brecon Beacons, recorded in the twelfth century as 'Arthur's Seat' are also known as 'Arthur's Hill' or 'Hill-Top' in the sixteenth century, and there is a *Moel Arthur* (Arthur's Hill) in Flintshire (SJ145660), a *Pencraig Arthur* in Denbighshire (SH815649), a *Ben Arthur* in Argyllshire (NN259059), an 'Arthur's Hill' at Newcastle, and 'Arthur's Seat', east of Liddesdale, Cumberland (NY495783), is also known as 'Arthur's Hill'.

❖ 'Arthur's Slough' – the following is recorded in *Notes & Queries*, volume 10, third series, December 29 1866, p.509:

> On my way from Wells to Glastonbury some years since, I overtook on the road a countryman who pointed out to me a morass which he said was known in those parts as Arthur's Slough. Can 'N. & Q.' inform me whether any tradition of King Arthur, who was buried at Glastonbury, attaches to this marsh?

Unfortunately the correspondent never seems to have received an answer.

❖ *Coed Arthur*, 'Arthur's Wood', is found at ST040715 in South Glamorgan.

❖ 'Arthur's Fold' – a farm in Perthshire, which was near an 'Arthur's Stone' but no longer exists. There is, however, a nearby Arthurbank (NO254427)

❖ 'Arthur's Well'. This is found in the lowest rampart of Cadbury Castle, Somerset. In this area Arthur and his knights are said to ride at night in the Wild Hunt and water their horses either here or at another well by the village church of Sutton Montis.[1] Another Arthur's Well is found near Waltoun-Crags, Northumberland (NY677667).

❖ 'Great Arthur' and 'Little Arthur' – the names of two of the Scilly Isles, off the coast of Cornwall.

❖ 'Loch Arthur' – a loch in Kirkcudbrightshire (NX905690).

---

1   Chambers, *Arthur of Britain*, pp. 184-85.

4

Lincolnshire and the Arthurian Legend

Lincolnshire and the Arthurian Legend

1. Introduction

ARTHUR: *How do you do, good lady? I am Arthur, King of the Britons. Whose*
castle is that?
WOMAN: *King of the who?*
ARTHUR: *The Britons.*
WOMAN: *Who are the Britons?*

('Monty Python and the Holy Grail', 1975, Scene III)

In all but the most eccentric theories about the origins of Arthur it is agreed that he was indeed a Briton, be he a real or imaginary one. Sometimes he is an emperor; more often he is a king, or a general, of the Britons. But inevitably the question follows, which Britons? Who were the Britons that he supposedly led? The following article suggests that, if Arthur existed all, then the answer to this question might be the Britons of Lincolnshire.

This is, of course, something of a departure from the usual theories of a 'historical Arthur' but, unlike many of these popular theories, this conclusion follows from a consideration of the latest historical and archaeological research. It has its genesis both in research into the Late Roman and Early Medieval East Midlands and in a critical examination of hypotheses regarding the supposed historical reality of the most famous legendary inhabitant of Britain during this period. From the latter study several key themes emerged, which are elaborated upon and discussed below. What was particularly striking, however, was the almost complete unwillingness of theorists who believe there actually was a historical Arthur to address one possibility for his area of operations that appears in even the earliest sources that refer to him as a figure of history: specifically, Lincolnshire. This article is intended to rectify this, proceeding from the widely-held assumption of the existence of a genuinely 'historical Arthur', before going on to consider the even more fundamental question of whether we ought to believe in Arthur's existence at all.

2. The Arthur of the *Historia Brittonum*

Before we can even begin to consider where any possible historical Arthur may have been based, if he existed, some essential background must be established. The earliest sources to feature Arthur as a historical figure place him in the period around the end of the fifth century and the beginning of the sixth century. Specifically, he is placed at the Battle of Badon Hill, an event that is also mentioned (though Arthur himself is not) by the near-contemporary writer Gildas in his *De Excidio Britanniae*, §26. Although the exact date of this event is much debated, for our purposes it can be placed with a reasonable degree of confidence around A.D. 500 (see Sims-Williams, 1983; Lapidge and Dumville (edd.), 1984; Higham, 1994; Howlett, 1998. Snyder, 1998: 45, 280-81, has a good summary of recent opinions and their merits).

The first source with such an indisputably historical concept of Arthur is the *Historia Brittonum* of A.D. 829/30, often wrongly attributed to one Nennius (see further Dumville, 1974, 1975-6, 1986 and 1994). Arguably the *Historia* is the only historical source that is of any value to researchers, given that it is the most detailed of the early sources and later sources add little of historical import, often appearing to be derivative of it (Charles-Edwards, 1991; Koch, 1996: 252-53; Green, 1998; Higham, 2002: 201-02; Green, 2007a, chapter 1). It opens its Arthurian section, §56, with the following statement:

> Then Arthur fought against them [*i.e.* the Anglo-Saxon invaders] in those days, together with the kings of the Britons, but he was their battle leader (*dux bellorum*). (Koch and Carey, 2003: 299)

Arthur is clearly here conceived of as a great warrior, not necessarily a king (though this is not explicitly excluded: Jackson, 1959: 9; Snyder, 2005), who won fame by fighting the Anglo-Saxon invaders. Some have seen in this an Arthur who is the leader of *all* the Britons against the invaders, a 'general commanding a combined British force' (Alcock, 1971 and 1972: 15-17; Morris, 1973), with Arthur and his army riding around Britain and fighting in places as far apart as Bath and southern Scotland (based on the identifications of the twelve battles subsequently assigned to Arthur by the author of the *Historia*). Such a notion is, however, rejected by most modern researchers for a variety reasons, including both the fact that it is implausible in the historical context of the time and given the nature and reliability of the *Historia* itself and its battle list (for example, Jackson, 1945-6: 57; Jones, 1964: 8; Bromwich, 1975-6: 168-69; Padel, 1994: 15; Green, 1998; Green, 2007a: chapter 1). In consequence, if we are to have a historical Arthur underlying the *Historia Brittonum*, he must be seen as a character of regional, not national, influence who fought the Anglo-Saxons *c.* 500.

3. The Locality of Arthur in the 'Historical' Sources

In light of the above, the question must become in what (if any) region do the 'historical' sources suggest that Arthur operated, if we are to believe that he genuinely existed and that any coherent information about a single historical figure can be retrieved from the *Historia Brittonum* (on which assumptions, see further below and Green, 2007a). Modern historians do not, it should be remembered, have an overly high opinion of the *Historia* as a repository of accurate information about the post-Roman period. Written over 300 years after Arthur supposedly lived and with its own agenda, its testimony must be treated with considerable caution (see especially Hanning, 1966; Dumville, 1977a, 1986 and 1994; Green, 1998; Higham, 2002; Green, 2007a: 15-38). What that testimony consists of is a list of twelve battles that the author of the *Historia* ascribes to Arthur.

When it comes to using these to locate a single historical Arthur, any brief survey of the various theories that have been propounded will show one thing very clearly: the vast majority of these theorists lack caution. They set out to find Arthur and his battles in a particular place and, lo and behold, here they declare him (and them) found. Collingwood (1929) sought an Arthur who fought Hengest and the Jutes in the south-east, and find him he did. Skeat (1868, I: 52-58) thought Arthur should reside in the Scottish borders, and there indeed he was found. In almost all such cases, the authors appear to indulge in a wilful ignorance of philology. Many of the battle sites in the *Historia* are highly obscure and some cannot be identified if we adhere to sound scholarship; others do have secure identifications, which have been thoroughly and comprehensively investigated by Kenneth Jackson (see especially Jackson, 1945-6). Many, however, prefer to either indulge in logic of the type 'X *sounds* like Tribruit, so X *is* Tribruit' or to make huge leaps in the translation and interpretation of the names in order to get them to fit places in the locality they are interested in.

If the case for Arthur operating in the Lincolnshire region required such ingenuity then this present piece would have made it no further than idle speculation. Fortunately it does not. Indeed, the very idea of such a case has its genesis in the fact that the site of Arthur's alleged second, third, fourth and fifth battles, by the river called *Dubglas* 'which is in the country of *Linnuis* (*in regione Linnuis*)', is one of the few identifications that is secure and based on good philology: *Linnuis* is Lindsey, the northern part of Lincolnshire.

Lindsey was an independent Anglo-Saxon kingdom in the seventh century (Eagles, 1989; Foot, 1993), and the available evidence indicates that this kingdom was the successor to an earlier British one based around the territory of the Romano-British provincial capital of Lincoln (Leahy, 1993; Yorke, 1993; Green, forthcoming and below). The name of this post-

Roman polity survived in the Old English kingdom-name that became modern Lindsey, *Lindesige*, which derives from the Late British folk-and territory-name **Lindēs*, 'the people of Lincoln', plus Old English *ig/eg*, 'an island' (Jackson, 1953: 332, 543; Cameron, 1991: 2-7; Gelling, 1989 – **Lindēs* derives from Romano-British **Lindenses*, of the same meaning). Lindsey is thus the regular English development of **Lindēs*, and the 'country of *Linnuis*' of the *Historia Brittonum* is simply the regular Old Welsh development of the same kingdom-name: **Lindēs* > Archaic Welsh **Linnēs* > Old Welsh *Linnuis* (and so not 'a garbled rendering of a word meaning the people of… Lincoln', as Reavill, 2003, suggests).

The importance of this should be clear – no speculation is necessary with regards to other, hypothetical, post-Roman **Lindēs* that could produce the *Historia*'s *Linnuis*, as we have in the name 'Lindsey' certain evidence for **Lindēs* actually being used as a significant region-name in post-Roman Britain. Given this we can say that, at the very least, the author of this ninth-century text thought that Arthur fought one or more battles in Lindsey (the four battles said to have taken place here could reflect the river *Dubglas* in Lindsey being a particularly contested location, but it is more likely that they are duplications made by the author of the *Historia* for stylistic reasons, see Hanning, 1966: 119-20). Where exactly these battles were considered to have taken place within Lindsey is open to dispute, however, as no river *Dubglas*, 'blue-black (water)', now exists. Perhaps this is unsurprising: most Lincolnshire rivers have been renamed since the fifth century. I would suggest, however, that Reavill's reasoning is probably correct when he tentatively identifies it as an alternative name for the Witham, on account of the peaty composition of the soil it flows through (Reavill, 2003: 4; the river-name Witham is, incidentally, no longer so certainly an early name as it once seemed to be).

We thus have a secure base to build a theory of a Lindsey Arthur around, which has its origins in the earliest and best source for information on any historical Arthur. From this relatively solid foundation we can now look again at the other possible identifications of battles in the *Historia Brittonum* list. We know that at least one battle, and perhaps four, ascribed to Arthur in the ninth century was supposed to have been fought in Lincolnshire. Given the above conclusion that any historical Arthur (assuming he existed) was unlikely to be a figure that fought all across Britain, the question can now be legitimately asked: could any of his other supposed battles have taken place here too?

The most famous battle on the list is, of course, Badon, the culmination of Arthur's campaign in the *Historia* and the only battle whose existence – though not Arthur's involvement – is confirmed by an early and trustworthy source (Gildas' *De Excidio Britanniae* of *c.* 540). Could this too have been fought in the Lincolnshire region? Surprisingly for such a significant victory its location has long been disputed – Bath is one possibility (Burkitt and Burkitt, 1990) but it is by no means a certainty. Jackson (1958) and Gelling (1988: 60-61) have argued that it could equally well be one of several sites whose name might derive from *Badon* + Old English *byrig/burh*, 'fortification, fortified place'. Most of these are located – like Bath – in southern England, for example Badbury Rings in Dorset, leading to a widespread consensus that this is where Badon was fought. However, there is no sound basis to this, other than the fact that this is where the majority of possibilities are found. There is, in fact, one often overlooked alternative: Baumber, near Horncastle in Lindsey, is also considered to be a possible *Badon* + *burh*, taking the form *Badeburg* in the Domesday Book (Gelling, 1988: 60-61; Cox, 1997-8).

Strictly speaking there is no reason why Baumber should be any less likely as a candidate for Badon than any of the others; all rest almost exclusively on etymological arguments. Certainly, as we will see below, the historical context of Lindsey *c*. 500 is no less plausible a place for a battle between Britons and the Anglo-Saxon immigrants than, say, Bath. Indeed, it should be born in mind that nearby Horncastle, a fortified Roman 'small town', is considered to be part of the Late Roman defences of the east coast and 'one of the leading settlements in the Lincoln area' (Field and Hurst, 1983: 85), so a battle at Baumber – at a high point on the Roman road from Lincoln to Horncastle – would not be at all implausible. In this context it may be worth noting that the second element, *burh*, indicates that there was a fortification of some sort – the literal meaning of Old English *burh* – at Baumber in the early Anglo-Saxon period at least, when most Lincolnshire names involving this element were coined (Cox, 1994). A find of an Anglo-Saxon sword pommel dated to *c*. 450-500 from Baumber may or may not be relevant here (Lincolnshire Historic Environment Record, PRN 43147; there have been no detailed archaeological investigations within the parish).

Of course, Badon does not have to be Baumber. However, if we are to see *Linnuis* and Badon as genuinely Arthurian battle sites, then their potential proximity might well be seen as significant, particularly given the fact that *Linnuis* is one of the few securely identifiable battles sites in the *Historia* and the current academic rejection of 'wide-ranging' Arthur theories.

Moving beyond Badon, it is worth considering the site of Arthur's supposed first battle in the *Historia* – mentioned immediately before the four battles *in regione Linnuis* – said to have been fought at 'the mouth of the river which is called *Glein*'. This river-name is unrecorded in Modern Welsh, where it would take the form **Glain*, but it is in fact etymologically identical to the river Glen in south Lincolnshire and an equation has often been made between the two (Jackson, 1945-6: 46). It must, of course, be remembered that *Glein* is simply an Old Welsh word meaning 'pure, clear (water)', and there is at least one other river in England – in

Northumberland – that bears a name which is probably derivative of this. Nonetheless, in light of the above considerations, the coincidence of another of the *Historia*'s battle-names in Lincolnshire is interesting and the historical context for a genuine late fifth- or early sixth-century battle against Anglo-Saxon immigrants – if we are to treat the battle on the *Glein* as such – is arguably far better from Lincolnshire than it is from Northumberland (see below). Indeed, the Lincolnshire Glen appears to have been canalised by the Romans and may well have been a particularly tempting entry-point for the region, something confirmed by late fifth- and sixth-century Anglian archaeological finds from around the point at which the river exits the dry, higher ground to flow into the Fens towards the Wash (Hayes and Lane, 1992: 146-48; 159-61).

Finally, note should also be made of the ninth battle, fought at the City of the Legions (*in urbe Legionis*). Again this is one of those battles which can, at least potentially, have their intended locations identified. Obviously it cannot have been located in Lincolnshire, as there was no Roman legionary city there. Most frequently the 'City of the Legions' is identified with Chester and considered to be an intrusion into the Arthurian battle-list, borrowed from a battle between the Welsh and the Anglo-Saxons fought there in 616 (Jackson, 1945-6: 50, 57; Bromwich, 1975-6: 171). Such borrowings are a frequent occurrence in Welsh battle-lists and this is a convincing interpretation (see Bromwich, 1975-6, especially pp. 171-72, on this mechanism). Nevertheless, the possibility has recently been raised that *in urbe Legionis* may in fact have been intended as a reference to York rather than Chester, although this is hotly contested (Field, 1999; Green, 2007a: 209). If it could be accepted, this proposition certainly has a better historical context for a real battle of *c.* 500 than Chester, and its proximity to Lincolnshire is once more suggestive for the theory being set out here.

Overall we can sum up as follows. Without any special pleading it is clear that four of Arthur's battles (though there may have been some duplication) were claimed to have been fought in Lincolnshire in the first half of the ninth century. From this relatively secure basis, and in light of a rejection of fanciful notions of a historical Arthur riding around the whole of Britain fighting the invaders from Bath to Scotland, the possibility has to be considered that the other battles with less secure identifications may have also been fought in this region, if we are to believe that Arthur did indeed exist and that the *Historia* preserves genuine details of his deeds. In fact, as we have seen, there is potential for as many as three of the other battles to be identified either in Lincolnshire or close-by it, including the important Battle of Badon Hill which seems (in the *Historia*) to be the climax of Arthur's 'career' and the reason for his fame. Of the remaining five battles, three are completely unidentifiable by sound philology; one is either unidentifiable or borrowed from the mid-late sixth-century hero Urien of

Rheged (depending on which recension of the *Historia* we use, as the name of the battle-site varies: see further Green, 2007a: 208-09; Jackson, 1949; Bromwich, 1975-6: 171-72); and the last, *Cat Coit Celidon* – the 'Battle of the Caledonian Forest' – is probably either the misattribution to Arthur of the late sixth-century Battle of Arthuret, which is linked with *Coed Celyddon* in medieval Welsh poetry, or a mythical conflict given a false historicity (Padel, 1994: 18; Green, 1998; Green, 2007a: 62-67).

Obviously the case is not beyond doubt. Badon could easily not be Baumber but somewhere else entirely (Burkitt and Burkitt, 1990, have made a good case for Bath), as too could be the 'City of the Legions' and the river *Glein*; the identifications of all three of these sites remain uncertain and incapable of proof. However, once again, if *Linnuis* is securely located as Lindsey and a wide-ranging Arthur is rejected, then the possibility that the above identifications are correct and that Arthur operated at least mainly in the Lincolnshire and East Yorkshire region is an attractive one, based on the evidence we have. Of course, this only works if we make certain assumptions about the battle-list of the *Historia Brittonum*, namely that, whilst it may have borrowed battles from other leaders and mythology, at its core there is an accurate record of the deeds of a single, genuinely historical, figure named Arthur, who fought the Anglo-Saxons *c.* 500. This is open to very serious debate (see below and Green, 1998 and 2007a). Nevertheless, if we allow these assumptions then it does seem that a potential case exists for seeing this single leader as operating in the region around the Humber. Two further questions must consequently be asked. First, whether other early Arthurian literature provides any clues that can allow us to reject or further support this hypothesis. Second, whether an Arthur based around the Humber has a convincing historical context.

4. The Locality of Arthur in the Legendary Sources

It is an undeniable fact that there is vastly more 'legendary' material on Arthur than there is 'historical', and arguably some of this does ante-date the *Historia Brittonum*. It would consequently be remiss if we did not look to this to further our understanding of the origins of any possible historical Arthur. In doing so we are in good company, for such an approach is that adopted by Rachel Bromwich in her important but underused survey of the Arthurian question (Bromwich, 1975-6). Bromwich sets out a detailed case for considering the Welsh and Cornish versions of the Arthurian legend to be secondary developments. Instead she identifies the legendary Arthur as originally being a hero of *Y Gogledd*, the British 'Old North' (that is northern England and southern Scotland). She proposes that Arthur's later, wider, fame can be set in the context of the well-established movement of early traditions concerning Northern heroes, such as Urien of Rheged and Llywarch Hen, south to Wales by 'at least as early as the ninth century' (Bromwich, 1975-6: 180).

Two pieces of evidence are particularly important in supporting this viewpoint. The first piece is the Arthurian reference in the poem *Y Gododdin*, ascribed to Aneirin. In recent years there has been much written about the statement there that the warrior Gwawddur 'fed black ravens on the rampart of a fort, though he was no Arthur' (B².38). The poem itself is the tale of a battle at *Catraeth* (Catterick) fought in the late sixth century, and it has often been considered to have been composed *c.* 600 in the 'Old North' (Jackson, 1969; Jarman, 1988). Whether the Arthurian stanza belonged to this original core is, however, very much debated. On the one hand, John Koch has recently undertaken a major study of the poem and included the stanza in his reconstruction of the pre-638 text. On the other hand, his conclusions have not been accepted by all commentators, some of whom would prefer a ninth- or tenth-century dating for the stanza (Koch, 1996: 242-45 and 1997; Padel, 1998; Isaac, 1999. See Green, 2007a: 13-15, 50-52 for a thorough discussion of this reference, its dating and import). If Koch is right – and he has as many supporters as detractors – then this is extremely valuable to our present interests. Even if he is not, the reference is still potentially as old as that found in the *Historia Brittonum*. Whatever the case, *Y Gododdin* is – as Jarman has noted – a very self-contained and insular work, concerned largely only with the 'Old North', and thus the mention of Arthur in it has been seen as implying that he was of that region (Jarman, 1989-90: 17-20; cf. Green, 2007a: 13-15, however, for serious doubts on this point).

The second key piece of evidence is the fact that three or four people living in the 'Old North' were named Arthur in the second half of the sixth century and the first quarter of the seventh century. None of these people can be seen as the 'true' Arthur, as Bromwich and others have made very clear, and what exactly these names signify is unclear (Bromwich, 1975-6: 178-80; Padel, 1994: 24; Dark, 2000a; Dooley, 2005; Green, 2007a: 12-13, 48-50, 251). However, it does seems clear that they must reflect in some way a very early local knowledge and interest in Arthur in this region, which Bromwich and her supporters interpret as further support for any historical Arthur having his origins in the 'Old North'.

Other evidence which is often brought to bear includes the fact that the battle list in the *Historia Brittonum* may have its origins in the 'Old North' too, rather than in Wales like the rest of the text (Bromwich, 1975-6: 174-76). Dumville (1976-7) has argued strongly against this notion of a separate 'Northern History' being incorporated into the *Historia*, but it has been supported recently by both Davies (1982: 205-06, 244) and Koch (1996: 247-48; 1997; 2006: 120). If accepted, this would obviously strongly support the notion of a 'Northern Arthur' and the idea that the battles – if we believe them to genuinely belong to an Arthur who really existed – are to be found in northern, not southern, England.

So far we have talked of the 'Old North' in general but this does perhaps need closer definition if the arguments above are to have a particular applicability to our interest in an Arthur who might have fought in Lincolnshire and perhaps the East Riding of Yorkshire. The 'Old North' is usually said to include the entire area from the Humber up to Edinburgh, and most of the evidence marshalled for Arthur as a hero of the 'Old North' has its immediate origins in the most northerly portions of this region. Bromwich has argued that this, however, simply reflects the fact that, by the time the Arthurian legend was written down and recorded, this was the only portion of the 'Old North' still in British hands. Anglian invaders conquered the southernmost portions to create the kingdoms of Deira and Bernicia during the sixth century, and so the far north was the only place where memories of a Northern Arthur could survive and be celebrated (Bromwich, 1963). In support of this potential for an ultimate legendary origin for Arthur in the southern part of the 'Old North', Bromwich has suggested that the *Y Gododdin* reference to Arthur should be read as implying 'that Arthur was regarded as the adversary in a previous generation of the same enemies as those who opposed Mynyddawg's force at Catraeth [Catterick]', that is the 'early Anglian raiders and settlers in the East Riding [of Yorkshire], who were in the process of laying the foundations of the kingdom of Deira' (Bromwich, 1978: 275).

This is, of course, of the utmost importance in the present context. One of the most respectable academic accounts of the early origins of the Arthurian legend points to 'the south-eastern corner of the 'Old North', that is… the East Riding of Yorkshire and possibly…York itself' as the area in which this legend originated (Bromwich, 1975-6: 180; also Bromwich, 1963). Indeed, of all the 'Old North' this is really the only area that can fit with the archaeological and historical evidence in providing a plausible context for any historical Arthur, as only here do we see Anglian immigration and activity in the late fifth century on the kind of scale that make stories of a British war-leader famed for fighting the invaders, with a climax *c.* 500, plausible (see, for example, Dumville, 1989; Hines, 1990; Higham, 1992; Dark, 2000b: 11).

This does, of course, tally quite nicely with the evidence of the *Historia Brittonum* as discussed previously. Both the historical and the legendary material point to the area around the Humber as being potentially the region of operations for any historical Arthur. Indeed, if the 'City of the Legions' can be seen as York, as Field (1999) has argued, then the fit with Bromwich's survey of the Arthurian legend is close indeed. Obviously, once again, it is worth remembering that certain assumptions have been made in reaching these conclusions – in particular, that the *Historia Brittonum* contains a core of fact relating to the victories of a historical figure named Arthur. If these are allowed then the evidence does seem to be reasonably consistent with any such Arthur having his base of operations in Lincolnshire or the East Riding of Yorkshire around the year 500, fighting against the Anglian invaders whose presence in significant numbers in these areas is indicated by large cremation cemeteries such as those at Sancton (East Riding), Cleatham, South Elkington/Louth and Old Bolingbroke (Lincolnshire, the latter near to Horncastle).

5. The Historical Context

No matter how ingenious the theory of a historical Arthur, it must fit within the context of the period. Arthur's only claim to historical fame is that he fought and defeated the invading Anglo-Saxons. All other claims – imperial and foreign adventures; cataclysmic battles with internal, British, enemies – belong to the legendary Arthur and do not appear in the earliest sources (Camlann, for example, would seem to have its origins in the development of the Arthurian legend, not history: Charles-Edwards, 1991: 25-27, 28; Green, 2007a: 75-77). In light of this, Arthur must be placed in a context that would allow him to do this *c.* 500, if we are to accept the *Historia* as a source of any value. This is, however, something that many theorists forget when they try to locate Arthur in Cornwall, North Wales or southern Scotland. So the question is, does Lincolnshire provide a convincing context for a late fifth-century British war-leader?

At the most basic level, as was noted above, the answer must be 'yes'. The East Riding of Yorkshire is the northernmost limit of significant fifth-century Anglo-Saxon settlement and Lincolnshire is, along with East Anglia, one of the most heavily settled areas of Britain, with a large number of cremation cemeteries each containing up to 2000 burials and beginning during the fifth century (Leahy, 1993: 36). As such Lincolnshire would seem to be just the kind of area that we might expect an Arthur-like figure to be operating in.

Looking in more detail at the nature of this settlement, there is a whole host of archaeological, historical, literary, and etymological evidence which suggests that with the departure of the Romans from Britain, the local *curiales* (aristocracy) took over control of Roman Lincoln – one of four provincial capitals in Late Roman Britain – and the territory that it controlled (Eagles, 1989; Leahy, 1993; Yorke, 1993a; Green, 2007a: 210-12; Green, forthcoming). The resulting political unit probably encompassed modern Lindsey (which inherited its name, **Lindēs*, 'the people of Lincoln') and at least some territory to the south of Lincoln (Eagles, 1989: 202), with its centre remaining at Lincoln, where there would seem to have been a

British church and probably bishop through the fifth century and into the sixth century (Jones, 1994; Green, forthcoming). How long this British *Lindēs* survived is uncertain. Lincoln is clearly in Anglian hands by the early seventh century and Cessford has suggested that the *lynwyssawr* who appear in *Y Gododdin* were 'Lindseymen' who fought at Catraeth for Mynyddawg in *c.* 570, after their own kingdom had finally been taken over by the Anglian invaders (Cessford, 1997: 220-21). How this take-over was actually achieved is unclear, but it may be worth noting that the Old English royal genealogy for Lindsey includes a British name, *Cædbæd*, for a man who would have lived in the early-mid sixth century (Dumville, 1977b: 90; Stafford, 1985: 87; Foot, 1993: 133 – this is now generally considered a wholly Brittonic name and not one of mixed origins, as has sometimes been assumed).

The distribution of Anglian archaeology in Lincolnshire supports this notion of a British 'kingdom' based around Lincoln, with the large cremation cemeteries forming a ring around the city, the closest being Lovedon Hill (17 miles to the south) and Cleatham (19 miles to the north). As Leahy (1993: 36) observes, this is unusual in comparison to many Roman cities and towns of the region, such as York, Caistor-by-Norwich, Leicester, and Ancaster. The most plausible explanation for this distribution is that the post-Roman Britons retained control of Lincoln and its territory throughout the fifth century and were able to control and manage the Anglian settlers within their territory (see further Leahy, 1993; Sawyer, 1998; Green, forthcoming).

This, then, would seem to be a very convincing context for any historical Arthur. Here, in the heart of the region that saw mass Anglo-Saxon immigration (see Scull, 1995 on how the evidence from East Anglia, and by extension Lincolnshire, must be interpreted in this light), we have a British-ruled territory. This, unlike other similar territories, seems to have been able to successfully resist pressure from the invaders and prevent them from encroaching on their chief settlement, Lincoln, during the fifth century and probably at least partway into the sixth century. In further support of this it should be noted that the name Lincoln, OE *Lindcolun*, is derived with little change from the Late British form, *Lindgolun*, something that is not true for most other Roman cities in Britain (Cameron, 1985: 1-3).

6. Some Conclusions

This study was prompted by the unwillingness of most historical Arthur theorists to even consider the possibility that he might have fought in the region around Lincolnshire. A detailed examination of the earliest and best source of information on any historical Arthur – the *Historia Brittonum* – suggests that this idea is not as implausible as it might at first seem.

Working with the assumption that chapter 56 of the *Historia*, whilst it may have borrowed battles from other leaders and mythology, has at its *core* an accurate record of a single leader named Arthur who fought the Anglo-Saxons *c.* 500, a reasonably strong case can be constructed from the *Historia* alone for considering the Lincolnshire region (including perhaps the East Riding of Yorkshire) as the main sphere of Arthur's activities. Widening our consideration of the evidence to look at the 'legendary' material results in a strengthening of this conclusion – academic opinion has often indicated that the legendary material points to the very south-east of the 'Old North' for the origins of the Arthurian legend, that is the East Riding of Yorkshire. Taken together, this all suggests that we should see the area either side of the Humber as the likely region of operations for any historical Arthur.

Finally, any theory that is to be in any way plausible must have an appropriate historical context for Arthur. The Arthur of the *Historia*'s fame comes from his supposed victories over the Anglo-Saxons of *c.* 500 and, given that it is now generally agreed that he is unlikely to have rode all around Britain fighting, we therefore need (at the very least) to place him near to where Anglo-Saxon immigrants were at that time. This is where theories that place him in southern Scotland, North Wales and Cornwall fall down. The region around the Humber is, in contrast, one of the primary regions of early Anglo-Saxon settlement, with Lincolnshire in particular containing two of the three largest cremation cemeteries in England. This context is even more appropriate, however, when we realise that a variety of evidence indicates that – despite this heavy immigration – the British rulers of the territory of the former provincial capital Lincoln appear to have been able to control and resist the invaders, at least until the early-sixth century, and in noteworthy contrast to most other British elites in eastern Britain.

Why, if there is so much evidence, has no-one seriously made this case before? One is tempted to suggest that the less-than-ideal methodology that often besmirches historical Arthur studies is to blame: no-one expected any historical Arthur to be found in Lincolnshire, so he wasn't. Furthermore, the contextual evidence discussed above emerges from very recent studies and few Arthurian theorists appear aware of recent trends and discoveries in the academic study of early-medieval eastern England (many still rely upon the now-outdated survey of Alcock, 1971).

All told, this piece has aimed to provide a more methodologically acceptable approach to the question of Arthur's identity, if we choose to believe that he really existed and that the *Historia* is a source of real value. It has tried to avoid the logical leaps-of-faith that many studies employ. It has also tried to use *all* of the available evidence, historical, legendary and archaeological – many theories tend to rely on just one or two of these categories. Thus we end up with theories that fit the literary evidence but fail to find a plausible context for their Arthurs (such as notions that Arthur is to be found in southern Scotland), or theories that have a very good context (such as those based in southern England) but fail to explain the apparent 'northern' bias, observed by many Celticists, in the legendary materials. By placing Arthur around the Humber we avoid these pitfalls: he is far enough south and east to have a plausible historical context but far enough north to explain why he might be famous in the legends of *Y Gogledd*, the 'Old North', and finally – and most importantly – placing him here fits in with the evidence of the only source modern historians are willing to even partially trust (the *Historia Brittonum*) without doing damage to it.

Indeed, I find that I am perhaps not alone in this conclusion. John Koch has also recently considered *Linnuis* to be potentially significant as the only securely identifiable battle-site which is actually in the 'right' area for its victor to have been battling the Anglo-Saxons *c.* 500. He rightly concedes that the *Historia*'s battle-list is very unreliable, but believes that its claim that Arthur existed probably does derive ultimately from Welsh oral tradition. His suggestion, with regards to the appropriateness of the location of *Linnuis* (Lindsey), is that this 'certainly raises the possibility that the same oral tradition also correctly remembered that Arthur fought and won there' (Koch, 2006: 120), a possibility that the present investigation has tried to examine fully.

7. Some Caveats

One final feature of typical theories of a historical Arthur is the unwillingness on the part of their authors to recognise the assumptions they have made and the potential problems with their theories. As was noted earlier, *all* of the above is based around the assumption that there is a single, historical British war-leader called Arthur buried somewhere within the text of the *Historia Brittonum*. This is an assumption with a very respectable pedigree, but it is also highly debatable. Increasingly historians have attacked what David Dumville has termed the 'no smoke without fire' school of thought with regards to Arthur (Dumville, 1977a: 187). We need to recognise that the first reference to Arthur as a figure of history occurs more than 300 years after he is supposed to have lived, in a text that is often rightly treated with extreme caution as a source for the fifth and sixth centuries. In fact, it is becoming increasingly clear that the *Historia Brittonum*'s concept of Arthur as a war-leader, and the battles it ascribes to him, may well not be able to carry the weight of the assumptions and theories that have been attached to it (and them). Rather, most modern research rejects the notion that the *Historia* has any real value as a source beyond telling us that, by the ninth century, some people believed that a historical war-leader called Arthur had once existed, with the battles listed in the *Historia* being too unreliable to allow any sensible reconstructions of the career of this Arthur, even if he did genuinely exist (see Dumville, 1986 and 1994; Charles-Edwards, 1991; Green, 1998; Higham, 2002; Green, 2007a: chapter 1).

In addition to the above concerns, it has also been argued recently that if we look at the whole body of early Arthurian material – as opposed to just the 'historical' sources in isolation – then the weight of the evidence points to Arthur being primarily and originally a figure of pan-Brittonic folklore and mythology, associated with the Otherworld, supernatural enemies and superhuman deeds, not history (Padel, 1994; Green, 1998; Green, 2007a: see also, for example, Bromwich and Evans, 1992: xxviii-xxix). Instead of being a historical figure who was absorbed into folklore and legend, Arthur is more plausibly seen as a folkloric or mythical figure who was occasionally portrayed as historical, in the same manner as Hengest and the Gaelic Fionn mac Cumhaill, a position with which Rachel Bromwich has recently expressed considerable sympathy (Bromwich, 2006: 282-83; see also Higham, 2002. On Hengest and Fionn, see Yorke, 1993b and Ó hÓgáin, 1988).

Indeed, not only does the above argument critically undermine the notion of an originally historical Arthur, it also attacks the idea of a northern bias in the legendary sources: Arthur emerges from the entirety of the early material as a folkloric figure who was known throughout the whole of Britain from the very start, with no identifiable place of origin. Certainly issues with the supposed northern bias of the legendary material have been raised before, if never so powerfully, though Bromwich and others have tried to suggest solutions which preserve their case. With regards to these solutions it must be said that, as long as we see Arthur as a figure of history, the 'Northern Arthur' theory remains a convincing interpretation, given the fact that a historical Arthur can no longer be plausibly seen as a national figure from the very start. On the other hand, when Arthur is freed from his historical bonds, his clear pan-Brittonic nature and the evidence for this can simply be accepted rather than ignored or explained away (see Bromwich, 1975-6: 177ff.; Padel, 1994; Green, 2007a, especially pp. 40 and 78, on all of this).

If we adopt these new perspectives on the early Arthurian sources, it does not mean that the search for a historical Arthur is in vain. The *Historia*'s Arthur may be a secondary creation but its vision and concept of a historical Arthur may not be entirely false: *someone* won the Battle of Badon (it is mentioned in the near-contemporary *De Excidio Britanniae* of Gildas) and thus, to some degree, there *was* a historical 'Arthur', even though he may have borne a different name and had his deeds reattributed to Arthur by the ninth century. Who might this 'Arthur' be? In this context it is worth noting that in Gildas's *De Excidio Britanniae* Ambrosius Aurelianus is given prominence as the initiator of the British counter-attack which, after the fighting of several battles, culminates in the battle of Badon, just as Arthur in the *Historia Brittonum* initiates the British counter-attack which, after the fighting of several battles, culminates in the battle of Badon. On the basis of this we could well be able to say that, to some extent, we do have a historical Arthur – Ambrosius – in the sense that the concept of Arthur as a historical figure and the framework for his historicisation were based on his deeds. Indeed, both Oliver Padel and Michael Wood have argued that a re-examination of the BL Cotton Vitellius A.vi manuscript of Gildas has the Battle of Mount Badon now reading 'naturally as the victory that crowned the career of Ambrosius Aurelianus', which places this contention on an even sounder footing (Padel, 1994: 16-18, at p. 17; Wood, 1999: 34-38; see also Green, 1998 and the full discussion in Green, 2007a: 31-32 and chapter 6).

This is not to say, however, that we can therefore assign all the battles recorded in the *Historia* to Ambrosius Aurelianus. As has already been noted, the reliability of the list of battles has been called seriously into question. Most significantly, the battles ascribed to Arthur and used to historicise him seem to be drawn from many different sources. Badon, we have seen, potentially belonged originally to Ambrosius Aurelianus. The 'battle on the bank of the river called *Tribruit*' and *Cat Coit Celidon* could be actual Arthurian mythic battles, drawn into history at the same time as Arthur's name became attached to Badon, as may be at least one other battle (Green, 1998; Green, 2007a: 62-67, 119-21, 207-08). *Breguoin*'s association with Urien of Rheged has been discussed above, and Jackson thought another (*urbs Legionis*) was a borrowed seventh-century battle (Jackson, 1945-6). The Arthur of chapter 56 of the *Historia Brittonum* would thus appear to be a composite figure, to some degree, when viewed in light of recent research (and as Hogan long ago thought – Hogan, 1933: 43-46).

Where then does this leave the case for a Lincolnshire Arthur? As I see it, there are three possible conclusions. The first involves accepting the above assumption – that a historical war-leader called Arthur does underlie the *Historia* – on the basis of 'no smoke without fire'. There are good arguments for not doing this, but, as was observed a little earlier, it is an assumption with a very respectable pedigree (for example, Bachrach, 1990; Koch, 1997: 148). If we do decide to do this then I think that the Lincolnshire and East Riding Arthur is the most elegant and historically plausible solution to the question of this leader's identity, doing no damage to either the primary historical evidence or the predominant academic opinion on the origins of the legendary material, whilst being in harmony with the archaeological evidence for potential zones of Anglo-British conflict around A.D. 500.

The second and third alternatives accept the validity of recent work on the existence of Arthur and the notion that the historical Arthur was a secondary development of a character from British folklore and myth. The second alternative asks, if there is a historical figure – who fought at Badon – at the heart of the *Historia*, called perhaps Ambrosius Aurelianus rather than Arthur, then could the Lincolnshire 'core' that has been suggested here in the *Historia*'s account represent *his* deeds? Certainly, *if* Baumber is Badon, this would seem a distinct possibility. In this context it is worth noting the following. First, unlike many of the other battles, both *Linnuis* and *Glein* have never been suggested as battles that are borrowed from myth or other historical figures – their very obscurity may thus point to them belonging to any original historical core that might be present in the *Historia Brittonum*. Second, not only would the historical context established above fit such a figure very well, but there is a highly respectable school of academic thought that holds that Gildas was, in his account of the British counter-attack in the late fifth century led by Ambrosius Aurelianus, writing about the region of the East Riding of York (Thompson, 1979: 215-19; Sims-Williams, 1983: 7; Dumville, 1984: 62-66. See, however, Higham, 1994: 90-117 for an alternative perspective). As such, this hypothesis cannot be easily dismissed without discussion, and I have recently offered a very tentative argument in support of it in *Concepts of Arthur* (Green, 2007a: chapter 6).

Finally, there is a minimalist interpretation. Badon could easily have been somewhere other than Baumber. If we reject the idea that a genuinely historical Arthur lay at the core of the *Historia*, then the secure identification of *Linnuis* as Lindsey can no longer privilege the idea that the other battles mentioned may be close by, as argued above. Fundamentally, the historicised Arthur of chapter 56 of the *Historia* appears to be a composite figure, made up of a framework based on the deeds of Ambrosius Aurelianus to which have been gathered various historical and mythical battles. *Linnuis*/Lindsey could be just one of these borrowings.

This does not, however, mean that all is in vain. There is no reason to think that *Linnuis* was a mythical battle and, as such, its presence in the battle-list implies that it is a borrowing of a historical conflict (or conflicts). This in turn suggests that, in the ninth century, memories of a British warrior who fought the Anglians in Lindsey survived and circulated in the British west and were eventually re-used and re-attributed to Arthur by the author of the *Historia* (or his hypothetical source). This may well be the most convincing possibility – it is also one that is of great interest to all those who are interested in the post-Roman history of eastern England and how the native Britons interacted with the immigrants there.

8. Bibliography

Alcock, L. 1971, *Arthur's Britain: History and Archaeology A.D. 367-634* (Harmondsworth)

Alcock, L. 1972, '*By South Cadbury, is that Camelot...' Excavations at Cadbury Castle 1966-70* (London)

Bachrach, B. S. 1990, 'The Questions of King Arthur's Existence and of Romano-British Naval Operations', *The Haskins Society Journal*, 2, pp. 13-28

Bartrum: C. 1965, 'Arthuriana in the Genealogical MSS', *The National Library of Wales Journal*, 14, pp. 243-45

Bromwich, R. 1963, 'Scotland and the Earliest Arthurian Tradition', *Bulletin Bibliographique de la Société Internationale Arthurienne*, 15, pp. 85-95

Bromwich, R. 1975-6, 'Concepts of Arthur', *Studia Celtica*, 10/11, pp. 163-81

Bromwich, R. 1978, *Trioedd Ynys Prydein. The Welsh Triads* (Cardiff: second edition)

Bromwich, R. 2006, *Trioedd Ynys Prydein. The Welsh Triads* (Cardiff: third edition)

Bromwich, R. and Evans, D. S. 1992, *Culhwch and Olwen. An Edition and Study of the Oldest Arthurian Tale* (Cardiff)

Burkitt, T. and A. 1990, 'The frontier zone and the siege of Mount Badon: a review of the evidence for their location', *Proceedings of the Somerset Archaeological and Natural History Society*, 134, pp. 81-93

Cameron, K. 1985, *The Place-Names of Lincolnshire 1* (English Place-Name Society 58, Cambridge)

Cameron, K. 1991, *The Place-Names of Lincolnshire 2* (English Place-Name Society 64/5, Cambridge)

Cessford, C. 1997, 'Northern England and the Gododdin Poem', *Northern History*, 33, pp. 218-22

Charles-Edwards, T. M. 1991, 'The Arthur of History', in R. Bromwich *et al* (edd.) *The Arthur of the Welsh. The Arthurian Legend in Medieval Welsh Literature* (Cardiff, 1991), pp. 15-32

Collingwood, W. G. 1929, 'Arthur's battles', *Antiquity*, 3, pp. 292-98

Cox, B. 1994, 'The pattern of Old English *burh* in early Lindsey', *Anglo-Saxon England*, 23, pp. 35-56

Cox, B. 1997-8, 'Baumber in Lindsey', *English Place-Name Society Journal*, 30, pp. 27-32

Dark, K. R. 2000a, 'A Famous Arthur in the Sixth Century? Reconsidering the origins of the Arthurian Legend', *Reading Medieval Studies*, 26, pp. 77-95

Dark, K. R. 2000b, *Britain and the End of the Roman Empire* (Stroud)

Davies, W. 1982, *Wales in the Early Middle Ages* (London)

Dooley, A. 2005, 'Arthur of the Irish: a Viable Concept?', in C. Lloyd-Morgan (ed.) *Arthurian Literature XXI: Celtic Arthurian Material* (Cambridge), pp. 9-28

Dumville, D. N. 1974, 'Some Aspects of the Chronology of the *Historia Brittonum*', *Bulletin of the Board of Celtic Studies*, 25, pp. 439-45

Dumville, D. N. 1975-6, 'Nennius and the *Historia Brittonum*', *Studia Celtica* 10/11, pp. 78-95

Dumville, D. N. 1976-7, 'On the North British Section of the *Historia Brittonum*', *Welsh History Review*, 8, pp. 345-54

Dumville, D. N. 1977a, 'Sub-Roman Britain: History and Legend', *History*, 62, pp. 173-92

Dumville, D. N. 1977b, 'Kingship, Genealogies and Renal Lists', in P. H. Sawyer and I. N. Wood (edd.) *Early Medieval Kingship* (Leeds), pp. 72-104

Dumville, D. N. 1984, 'The Chronology of *De Excidio Britanniae* Book I', in D. N. Dumville and I. Wright (edd.) *Gildas: New Approaches* (Woodbridge), pp. 61-84

Dumville, D. N. 1986, 'The Historical Value of the *Historia Brittonum*',

Arthurian Literature, 6, pp. 1-26

Dumville, D. N. 1989, 'The Origins of Northumbria', in S. Bassett (ed.) *Origins of Anglo-Saxon Kingdoms* (London), pp. 213-22

Dumville, D. N. 1994, '*Historia Brittonum*: an Insular History from the Carolingian Age', in A. Scharer and G. Scheibelreiter (edd.) *Historiographie im frühen Mittelalter* (Wien/München), pp. 406-34

Eagles, B. 1989, 'Lindsey', in S. Bassett (ed.) *Origins of Anglo-Saxon Kingdoms* (London), pp. 202-12

Field, P. J. C. 1999, 'Gildas and the City of the Legions', *The Heroic Age*, 1, archived at *http://www.heroicage.org*

Field, N. and Hurst, H. 1983, 'Roman Horncastle', *Lincolnshire History & Archaeology*, 18, pp. 47-88

Foot, S. 1993, 'The Kingdom of Lindsey', in A. Vince (ed.) *Pre-Viking Lindsey* (Lincoln), pp. 128-40

Gelling, M. 1988, 'Towards a chronology for English place-names', in D. Hooke (ed.) *Anglo-Saxon Settlements* (Oxford), pp. 59-76

Gelling, M. 1989, 'The Name Lindsey', *Anglo-Saxon England*, 18, pp. 31-32

Green, T. 1998, 'The Historicity and Historicisation of Arthur', archived at *http://www.arthuriana.co.uk/historicity/arthur.htm*

Green, T. 2007a, *Concepts of Arthur* (Stroud)

Green, T. 2007b, 'A Note on *Aladur, Alator* and *Arthur*', *Studia Celtica*, 41, pp. 237-41

Green, T. forthcoming, *A Re-evaluation of the Evidence of Anglian-British Interaction in the East Midlands* (Oxford D.Phil Thesis)

Hanning, R. W. 1966, *The Vision of History in Early Britain* (New York)

Hayes, P. P. and Lane, T. W. 1992, *The Fenland Project Number 5: Lincolnshire Survey, The South-West Fens*, East Anglian Archaeology, Report No. 55 (Sleaford)

Higham, N. J. 1992, *Rome, Britain and the Anglo-Saxons* (London)

Higham, N. J. 1994, *The English Conquest* (Manchester)

Higham, N. J. 2002, *King Arthur, Myth-Making and History* (London)

Hines, J. 1990, 'Philology, Archaeology and the *Adventus Saxonum vel Anglorum*', in A. Bammesberger and A. Wollman (edd.) *Britain 400-600: Language and History* (Heidelberg), pp. 17-36

Hogan, M. G. 1933, *The Legend of Dathi: An Analogue to the Chronicle Story of Arthur* (Washington D.C.)

Howlett, D. R. 1998, *Cambro-Latin Compositions, Their Competence and Craftsmanship* (Dublin)

Isaac, G. R. 1999, 'Readings in the History and Transmission of the *Gododdin*', *Cambrian Medieval Celtic Studies*, 37 (Summer), pp. 55-78

Jackson, K. H. 1945-6, 'Once Again Arthur's Battles', *Modern Philology*, 43, pp. 44-57

Jackson, K. H. 1949, 'Arthur's Battle of Breguoin', *Antiquity*, 23, pp. 48-49

Jackson, K. H. 1953, *Language and History in Early Britain* (Edinburgh)

Jackson, K. H. 1958, 'The Site of Mount Badon', *The Journal of Celtic Studies*, 2, pp. 152-55

Jackson, K. H. 1959, 'The Arthur of History', in R. Loomis (ed.) *Arthurian Literature in the Middle Ages* (Oxford), pp. 1-11

Jackson, K. H. 1969, *The Gododdin: The Oldest Scottish Poem* (Edinburgh)

Jarman, A. O. H. 1988, *Aneirin: Y Gododdin, Britain's Oldest Heroic Poem* (Llandysul)

Jarman, A. O. H. 1989-90, 'The Arthurian Allusions in the Book of Aneirin', *Studia Celtica*, 24/5, pp. 15-25

Jones, T. 1964, 'The Early Evolution of the Legend of Arthur', *Nottingham Medieval Studies*, 8, pp. 3-21

Jones, M. 1994, 'St Paul in the Bail, Lincoln: Britain in Europe?', in K.S. Painter (Ed.) *Churches built in ancient times* (London), pp. 325-47

Koch, J. T. 1996, 'The Celtic Lands', in N. J. Lacy (ed.) *Medieval Arthurian Literature: A Guide to Recent Research* (New York), pp. 239-322

Koch, J. T. 1997, *The Gododdin of Aneirin. Text and Context from Dark-Age North Britain* (Cardiff)

Koch, J. T. 2006, 'Arthur, the historical evidence', in J. T. Koch (ed.) *Celtic Culture, A Historical Encyclopedia* (Oxford), pp. 117-22

Koch, J. T. and Carey, J. 2003, *The Celtic Heroic Age: Literary Sources for Ancient Celtic Europe & Early Ireland & Wales* (Aberystwyth: fourth edition)

Lapidge, M. and Dumville, D. N. (edd.) 1984, *Gildas: New Approaches* (Woodbridge)

Leahy, K. 1993, 'The Anglo-Saxon settlement of Lindsey', in A. Vince (ed.) *Pre-Viking Lindsey* (Lincoln), pp. 29-44

Morris, J. 1973, *The Age of Arthur* (London)

Ó hÓgáin, D. 1988, *Fionn mac Cumhaill: Images of the Gaelic Hero* (Dublin)

Padel, O. J. 1994, 'The Nature of Arthur', *Cambrian Medieval Celtic Studies*, 27, pp. 1-31

Padel, O. J. 1998, 'A New Study of the *Gododdin*', *Cambrian Medieval Celtic Studies*, 35, pp. 45-55

Reavill, J. B. 2003, 'Lincolnshire in the Dark Ages', *Lincolnshire Past & Present*, 53, pp. 3-4

Sawyer, P. H. 1998, *Anglo-Saxon Lincolnshire* (Lincoln)

Scull, C. 1995, 'Approaches to the material culture and social dynamics of the migration period in eastern England', in J. Bintliff and H. Hamerow (edd.) *Europe Between Late Antiquity and the Middle Ages* (Oxford), pp. 71-83

Sims-Williams, P. 1983, 'Gildas and the Anglo-Saxons', *Cambridge Medieval Celtic Studies*, 6, pp. 1-30

Skene, W.F. 1868, *The Four Ancient Books of Wales* (Edinburgh) 2 vols.

Snyder, C.A. 1998, *An Age of Tyrants. Britain and the Britons A.D. 400-600* (Stroud)

Snyder, C. 2005, 'Arthur and Kingship in the *Historia Brittonum*', in N. J. Lacy (ed.) *Fortunes of King Arthur* (Woodbridge), pp. 1-12

Stafford, P. 1985, *The East Midlands in the Early Middle Ages* (London)

Thompson, E. A. 1979, 'Gildas and the History of Britain', *Britannia*, 10, pp. 203-26

Wood, M. 1999, *In Search of England: Journeys into the English Past* (London)

Yorke, B. A. E. 1993a, 'Lindsey: The Lost Kingdom Found?', in A. Vince (ed.) *Pre-Viking Lindsey* (Lincoln), pp. 141-50

Yorke, B. A. E. 1993b, 'Fact or Fiction? The written evidence for the fifth and sixth centuries A.D.', *Anglo-Saxon Studies in Archaeology and History*, 6, pp. 45-50

5

Arthur and Jack the Giant-Killer

Jack & Arthur: An Introduction to Jack the Giant-Killer

The tale of Jack the Giant-Killer is one that has held considerable fascination for English readers. The combination of gruesome violence, fantastic heroism and low cunning that the dispatch of each giant involves gained the tale numerous fans in the eighteenth century, including Dr Johnson and Henry Fielding.[1] It did, indeed, inspire both a farce[2] and a 'musical entertainment'[3] in the middle of that century. However, despite this popularity the actual genesis of Jack and his tale remains somewhat obscure. The present collection of source materials is provided as an accompaniment to my own study of the origins of *The History of Jack and the Giants* and its place within the wider Arthurian legend, published as 'Tom Thumb and Jack the Giant-Killer: Two Arthurian Fairy Tales?', *Folklore*, 118.2 (2007), pp. 123-40.

The curious thing about Jack is that – in contrast to that other fairy-tale contemporary of King Arthur's, Tom Thumb – there is no trace of him to be found before the early eighteenth century. The first reference to him comes in 1708 and the earliest known (now lost) chapbook to have told of his deeds was dated 1711.[4] He does not appear in Thackeray's catalogue of chapbooks in production around 1689, nor is he present in the lists of 'petty books' published in the first years of the eighteenth century, and he was not one of the folk heroes portrayed by puppet showman Robert Powel – as we might have expected him to have been – in Covent Garden at this time.[5] The suspicion must be, in light of this, that Jack is not mentioned before 1708 because he had no existence before this: he was a literary creation of the early eighteenth century, the framing device for a new heroic tale which was created out of pre-existing stories and classic anecdotes.[6] In support of

---

1   I. Opie and P. Opie, *The Classic Fairy Tales* (Oxford: Oxford University Press, 1974), p. 61.

2   *Jack the Gyant-Killer: A Comi-Tragical Farce of One Act* (London: J. Roberts, 1730).

3   *An English Musical Entertainment, called Galligantus* (London, 1758).

4   J. O. Halliwell, *Popular Rhymes and Nursery Tales of England* (London: John Russell Smith, 1849), p. 56 – see below for Halliwell's version of this text.

5   Opie and Opie, *Classic Fairy Tales*, pp. 60-61.

6   See T. Green, 'Tom Thumb and Jack the Giant-Killer: Two Arthurian Fairy Tales?', *Folklore*, 118.2 (2007), pp. 123-40 at pp. 131, 136-37; Opie and Opie,

the this is the fact that Jack, unlike some of his victims, is 'except in story-books, unknown' – he has, for example, no genuine place in Cornish folklore that Robert Hunt could discover, despite Hunt's extensive investigations into this material and the clear localisation of Jack's tale there.[1]

If Jack was a literary creation – rather than a genuine figure of folk-tale – whose tale was woven from earlier non-Jack giant-killings and traditions, this naturally raises some intriguing questions about the origins of both these stories of Welsh and Cornish giants and the actual concept of Jack as the hero who finally rids Britain of these creatures. With regards to this, it is important to note the presence of King Arthur throughout Jack's tale. Thus the *History of Jack and the Giants* is explicitly set from the start in 'the reign of King Arthur', but this is not simply a case of 'In the days of King Arthur…' as a variant of 'Once upon a time…' So, in the course of the tale, Arthur's son becomes both Jack's companion and his master, and the assistance that Jack's renders him leads to a place for Jack as a Knight of the Round Table. Then, after spending a little time as a member of Arthur's court, Jack asks permission to go and rid Britain of all remaining 'blood-thirsty Giants', a proposal which Arthur accepts. Jack – of course – has great success in this endeavour, but he does make sure to send the heads of all the giants he kills to Arthur, along with an account of his deeds. Finally, when the last giant left in Britain is slaughtered, Arthur rewards Jack with an estate and a wife, with whom to live happily ever after.

What all this means is open to debate. Certainly Arthur is not fundamental to the *History*, but his presence is felt throughout much of the narrative. In this context it ought not to be forgotten that the *History* must, after all, have been deliberately written with this role for Arthur planned within it, given its apparent literary origins. The solution, I have argued,[2] may in fact lie with Arthur's well-documented role as the slaughterer of British giants, through a combination of extreme violence, cunning and trickery. This is found in the earliest of Welsh Arthurian tales right through to the folklore of the modern era (see below, pp. 34-44 for a selection of texts illustrative of this). In fact, in Welsh and Cornish folklore of the sixteenth to nineteenth centuries it is repeatedly claimed that Arthur was the greatest of all giant-killers, responsible for finally ridding the land of giants. To quote one old Cornish man (living near Land's End, like Jack), whose reminiscences were collected by Robert Hunt at some point in the early-mid nineteenth century, the whole land at one time 'swarmed with giants, until

---

Classic Fairy Tales, p. 60.

1   R. Hunt, *Popular Romances of the West of England. The Drolls, Traditions and Superstitions of Old Cornwall*, two volumes (reprint of 1881 edition, Felinfach: Llanerch Publishers, 1993), II, pp. 303-04.

2   Green, 'Tom Thumb and Jack the Giant-Killer'.

Arthur, the good king, vanished them all with his cross-sword.'[1]

We thus have a situation wherein Jack – who is 'except in story-books, unknown' – possesses that very same role in British mythical history (the exterminator of all remaining Cornish and Welsh giants in Britain) which belongs to Arthur in Cornish and Welsh folklore. Indeed, not only is this folkloric role for Arthur well-attested before Jack's first appearance in the said 'story-books', but the giant-killings attributed to Arthur and his closest companions are of a very similar character to those of Jack. As can be seen from the materials selected for inclusion below, Jack's initial trickery of the Cornish and Welsh giants he encounters is paralleled by similar cunning in some of the Arthurian giant-killings. For example, Arthur is said (in a piece of folklore recorded in the early seventeenth century) to have killed the three sisters of the giant Cribwr at Cefn Cribwr near Llangewydd, Glamorgan, 'through cunning':

> For Arthur nicknamed himself Hot Soup to the first sister, and Warm Porridge to the second sister (so runs the tale), and to the third sister Piece of Bread. And when the first sister called for help against Hot Soup, Cribwr answered, "Silly girl, let it cool." And in the same manner he answered the second sister when she sought help against Hot Porridge. And the third sister cried out that Piece of Bread was choking her, and he answered as well, "Silly girl, take a smaller piece." And when Cribwr reproached Arthur for killing his sisters, Arthur answered with an Englyn Milwr in this form:

> > Cribwr [Comber] take your combs.
> > Skulk not in silent wrath.
> > Opponents, if to me they come,
> > What they have had you too shall have.

> No one could kill the three sisters together, by reason of the greatness of their strength, but separately and through cunning Arthur killed them.[2]

In the same way, the last Welsh giants that Jack kills are slaughtered through extreme violence, and this too is a feature of Arthur's giant-killing. Thus, for

---

1   Green, 'Tom Thumb and Jack the Giant-Killer', pp. 132-35; T. Green, *Concepts of Arthur* (Stroud: Tempus, 2007), pp. 112-18; C. Grooms, *The Giants of Wales. Cewri Cymru*, Welsh Studies volume 10 (Lampeter: Edwin Meller, 1993); *Culhwch and Olwen. An Edition and Study of the Oldest Arthurian Tale* edited by R. Bromwich and D. Simon Evans (Cardiff: University of Wales Press, 1992), pp. liv-lix; Hunt, *Drolls, Traditions and Superstitions of Old Cornwall*, II, p. 307.

2   Grooms, *Giants of Wales*, p. 311.

example, his killing of the Giant of Mont St Michel bears close comparison with Jack's deeds. So, Jack strikes at the head of the second giant he meets after setting off from Arthur's court, but misses his aim and so cuts into the giant's face, removing his nose. He then avoids the giant's wild attack, inserts his sword up to the hilt in the giant's 'arse', and laughs out loud as the creature suffers and dies, the giant 'crying out' and 'raving' before finally toppling to the ground in a 'dreadful fall'. Jack then cuts off the giant's head as a trophy for King Arthur. Correspondingly, we are told that Arthur,

> fired with rage... lifted up his sword, and gave him a wound in the forehead, which was not indeed mortal, but yet such as made the blood gush out over his face and eyes, and so blinded him; for he had partly warded off the stroke from his forehead with his club, and prevented its being fatal. However, his loss of sight, by reason of the blood flowing over his eyes, made him exert himself with greater fury, and like an enraged boar against a hunting-spear, so did he rush in against Arthur's sword, and grasping him about the waist, forced him down upon his knees. But Arthur, nothing daunted, slipped out of his hands, and so bestirred himself with his sword, that he gave the giant no respite till he had struck it up to the very back through his skull. At this the hideous monster raised a dreadful roar, and like an oak torn up from the roots by the winds, so did he make the ground resound with his fall. Arthur, bursting out into a fit of laughter at the sight, commanded Bedver to cut off his head, and give it to one of the armour-bearers, who was to carry it to the camp, and there expose it to public view...[1]

It may be relevant in this context that some tellings of this same event include a scene in which Arthur stabs the giant in the genitals.[2] Even if there is no direct derivation of Jack's killing described above from this specific one of Arthur's, the two slaughters (and slaughterers) are clearly highly similar in nature. Consequently I think it fair to say that Grooms displayed sound judgement when he remarked that the tales of Arthur the giant-killer constitute 'a tradition that precedes and informs the popular chap-book tales of Jack the Giant-killer.'[3] In Arthur we have a figure of genuine

---

1   See pp. 187-88. In the same way, compare Jack cutting off another giant's legs so that he becomes a more manageable foe, later removing his head to send to Arthur, to Arthur slaying 'a great giant named Galapas, which was a man of an huge quantity and height, he shorted him and smote off both his legs by the knees, saying, Now art thou better of a size to deal with than thou were, and after smote off his head' – see p. 189.

2   See pp. 188-89.

3   Grooms, *Giants of Wales*, p. 1.

folklore and early British story who parallels and pre-dates Jack in both his role and the type of deeds that are ascribed to him. In this light the references to Arthur throughout *The History of Jack and the Giants* – in particular the ritualistic collecting of the giants' heads for return to Arthur – become explicable. I would contend[1] that they ought to be considered as an acknowledgement by the creator of the *History* that Jack's actions were, in fact, ultimately modelled upon those of the Arthur of British mythical history and folklore: Jack was a new final vanquisher of the giants of Britain, designed for an England that was interested such folkloric tales but which would appear to have become bored of Arthur himself by the early eighteenth century (to give one illustrative example, Malory's *Le Morte Darthur* remained out of print from 1634 until the early nineteenth century).

This is not, of course, to say that a knowledge of the Arthurian tradition fully explains Jack's *History* – there are numerous non-Arthurian sources for its incidents and concept of Jack, some of which are referenced in the notes to my transcription of the 1787 text – but rather to suggest that *The History of Jack and the Giants* deserves to be considered as a genuine part of the development of the Arthurian legend, not simply an unrelated fairy tale that happens to be set in 'the reign of King Arthur' as a variant of 'Once upon a time'.

---

1   As in Green, 'Tom Thumb and Jack the Giant-Killer', pp. 135-37.

The History of Jack and the Giants (1787)

Introduction

Jack the Giant Killer's tale, *The History of Jack and the Giants*, would seem to have been first published by 1708, although the earliest known chapbook to contain it dates from 1711. This was transcribed by James Orchard Halliwell (later Halliwell-Phillipps) and his version is given in full after the present text. Unfortunately, Halliwell transcribed this now-lost chapbook 'with a few necessary alterations', which is to say that he thoroughly modernised the text and removed elements which he found distasteful.[1] As a result, later eighteenth-century derivatives of the original chapbook – such as the *c.* 1760-65 Shrewsbury chapbook used by the Opies in their edition[2] – are usually relied upon during detailed analysis of the tale.

The following transcript was made by the present writer from a 1787 unbowdlerised version of the *History*, printed in Falkirk and housed in the Bodleian Library, Oxford, which is very similar in most regards to the Opies' Shrewsbury version.[3] The layout adopted below approximates that of the original chapbook, hence its eccentricities; where letters were difficult to decipher, the probable reading has been added in square brackets.

Text

The History of Jack and the Giants.

Of his birth and Parentage, and what past between him and the Country Vicar, &c.

IN the reign of King Arthur, near the Lands-end of England, namely the country if Cornwall there lived a wealthy Farmer, who had one only Son,

---

1 J. O. Halliwell, *Popular Rhymes and Nursery Tales of England* (London: John Russell Smith, 1849), pp. 56-69 at p.56.

2 I. Opie and P. Opie, *The Classic Fairy Tales* (Oxford: Oxford University Press, 1974), pp. 64-82.

3 It is the earliest version readily available in facsimile, from *Eighteenth Century Collections Online*, accessible via *infotrac.london.galegroup.com*.

commonly known by the name of Jack the Giant Killer.[1] He was brisk and of a ready wit; so that whatever he could not perform by strength he compleated by ingenious wit and policy: Never was any person heard of that could worst him; Nay the very learned many times he baffled the learned by his cunning sharp and ready inventions.[2]

For instance when he was no more than seven years of age his Father, the Farmer, sent him into the field to look after his Oxen, which were then feeding in a pleasant pasture: A country Vicar by chance coming across the field, call'd to Jack, and asked him several questions; in particular, How many commandments were there? Jack told him there were nine. The parson reply'd There are ten. Nay (Quoth Jack.) Master parson, you are out of that, it is true there was ten, but you broke one of them with your own maid Margery. The parson reply'd thou art an arch Wag, Jack. Well Master parson quoth Jack, you have asked me one question, and I have answered it; I beseech you let me ask you another. Who made these Oxen? The parson reply'd, God made them Child. You are out again (quoth Jack) for God made them bulls, but my Father, and his man Hobson, made Oxen of them. These were the witty answers of Jack. The parson finding himself fool'd, truged away leaving Jack in a fit of laughter.

How a Giant *inhabited the Mount of* Cornwall, *spoiled the Country thereabouts,* &c.

IN those days the mount of Cornwall[3] was kept by a Huge and Monstrous

---

1   The Opies consider 'the Land's end' to be a Cornish turn of phrase, which may be significant in determining where Jack's *History* was created: Opie and Opie, *Classic Fairy Tales*, p. 64. A Cornish origin might also be supported by the fact that the two Cornish giants he kills bear names that were also apparently found in the same or similar forms in Cornish folklore: R. Hunt, *Popular Romances of the West of England. The Drolls, Traditions and Superstitions of Old Cornwall*, two volumes (reprint of 1881 edition, Felinfach: Llanerch Publishers, 1993), I, pp. 46-47, 55-60. The name Jack is a common one for English folkloric heroes, see J. Simpson and S. Roud, *The Oxford Dictionary of English Folklore* (Oxford: Oxford University Press, 2001), pp. 196-99.

2   B. C. Spooner, 'Jack and Tom in "Drolls" and Chapbooks', *Folklore*, 87.1 (1976), pp. 105-12 at p. 115 suggests that this section derives from the Merry Tales and Quick Answers genre that was popular in the sixteenth and seventeenth centuries. Halliwell, *Popular Rhymes*, pp. 47-48 includes another similar sequence, attached to the name of 'Jack Hornby'.

3   Hunt, *Drolls, Traditions and Superstitions of Old Cornwall*, (I, pp. 46-47; II, pp. 303-04) could find no tale of Jack killing a giant at St Michael's Mount in Cornish folklore, and the giant who did live there in this material was not killed. Given the relationship of Jack and Arthur suggested on pp. 143-47, one must wonder whether the creator of the *History* was inspired to place an initial fatal battle here because the most famous Arthurian giant-killing took place at Mont St Michel in Brittany (see p. 146 for another possible instance of this story influencing that

Giant, of 27 feet[1] in height, and about three yards in compass, of a fierce and grim countenance, the Terror of all the neighbouring Towns and Villages. His habitation was in a cave, in the midst of the Mount, neither would suffer any leaving creature to inhabit near him; His feeding was upon other mens cattle, which often became his prey: for whensoever he had occasion for food, he would wade over to the main Land, where he would furnish himself with whatever he could find. For the people at his approach would forsake their habitations; then would seize upon their cows and oxen, of which he would make nothing to carry over on his back half a dozen at a time: and as for the sheep and hogs, he would tye them round his waist like a bunch of bandeliers.[2] This he had for many years had practised in Cornwall, which was much impoverished by him.

But one day Jack coming to the Town-Hall, when the Magistrates were sitting in consternation about the Giant; he asked them what reward they would give to any person that would destroy him? They answered He shall have all the treasure in recompence. Quoth Jack, then I myself will undertake the work.

How Jack *slew this* Giant, *and got the name of* Jack *the* Giant *Killer.*

JAck having undertaken this task, he furnished himself with a horn, a shovel, and pick-ax, and over to the Mount he goes, in the beginning of a dark winter evening, where he fell to work, and before morning had digged a pit two and twenty foot deep, and almost as broad, and cover'd the same over with long sticks and straws: then strowing a little of the mould upon it, so it appeared like plain ground.

This done, Jack places himself on the contrary side of the pit, just about the dawning of the day, when putting his horn to his mouth, he then blew, *Tan Twivie, Tan Twivie.* Which unexpected noise rouz'd the Giant, who came roaring towards Jack, crying, thou incorigible villain! are you come here to disturb my rest? You shall dearly pay for it: Satisfaction I will have, and it shall be this; I will take thee wholely and broil you for my breakfast. Which word were no sooner out of his mouth, but he tumbled head-long into the deep pit, whose heavy fall made the very foundation of the mount to shake.[3]

---

of Jack).

1   In the Opie's and Halliwell's earlier versions of the chapbook, the giant is eighteen feet high.

2   *Bandoliers* are, in this case, the twelve small boxes or cases attached to a soldier's belt (also known as a Bandoleer/Bandolier) which contained charges for a musket: *Oxford English Dictionary*, s.v. Bandoleer.

3   The use of a pit appears to have been a traditional method of disposing of giants. Hunt, *Drolls, Traditions and Superstitions of Old Cornwall* (I, pp. 71-72), in the nineteenth century, tells of a giant killed at Morva in Cornwall by a similarly

Oh! Giant where are you now? Faith you are gotten in Lob's pond,[1] where I will plague you for your threatening words. What do you think now of broiling me for your breakfast? Will no other diet serve you but poor Jack? Thus having tantaliz'd the Giant for a while he gave him a most weighty knock upon the crown of his head, with his pick-ax, that he immediately tumbled down and gave a most dreadful moan and died. This done, Jack threw the earth in upon him, and so buried him; the going and searching the cave, he found a great quaintity of treasure.

Now when the Magistrates, who employed him, heard the work was over, they sent for him, declaring, that he should henceforth be call'd, Jack the Giant Killer. And in honour thereof they presented him with a Sword, together with a fine rich embroider'd Belt, on which these words were wrought in letters of gold.

> Here's the right valiant Cornish Man,
> Who slew the Giant Cormilion.[2]

How Jack was taken by a Giant while asleep, and how he got his liberty again.

THE news of Jack's victory was soon spread over all the western parts; so that another huge Giant Named Blunderboar,[3] hearing of it, vow'd to be

---

concealed hole. This was done by a man named Jack the Tinkeard – not another name for our Jack, but a different character, at least in the tales we have of him – who was required to kill this giant by his prospective father-in-law. If this story goes back to before the beginning of the eighteenth century then this story and character, despite their later lack of relation, might well be seen as a source for Jack the Giant-Killer and this specific giant-killing. However, we unfortunately have no way of proving this at present, and the opposite – that the Morva method of dispatch derives from the *History*, attracted to a similarly named character – may be true instead (as noted by B.C. Spooner, 'The Giants of Cornwall', *Folklore*, 76.1 (1965), pp. 16-32 at p. 27). The use of a hole to kill a giant is not, of course, a method confined to just Cornwall, and it is indeed known from the Arthurian legend too; Arthur's men used a similar method to defeat the giant Dillus in *Culhwch ac Olwen* (see p. 186), and this tale appears to have it origins in Welsh folklore: T. Green, *Concepts of Arthur* (Stroud: Tempus, 2007), pp. 115-16; C. Grooms, *The Giants of Wales. Cewri Cymru*. Welsh Studies volume 10 (Lampeter: Edwin Meller, 1993), pp. 167-68; *Culhwch and Olwen. An Edition and Study of the Oldest Arthurian Tale*, edited by R. Bromwich and D. Simon Evans (Cardiff: University of Wales Press, 1992), pp. lvii-lviii, 148.

1 Lob's Pond = Lob's Pound, 'prison, jail'. Lob means in this context a 'lout': *OED*, s.v. Lob's Pound; Lob, n[2].

2 *Cormilan* in the Opie's Shrewsbury chapbook; *Cormelian* in Halliwell's transcript of the 1711 chapbook.

3 *Blunderboar* in the Shrewsbury chapbook; *Thunderbore* in Halliwell's transcript of the 1711 chapbook. This creature is presumably related to the Blunderbuss of

revenged on Jack, if ever it was in his fortune to light upon him. This Giant kept an inchanted Castle, situated in the midst of a lonesome wood: Now Jack about four months after walking neat the borders of the said wood, on his journey towards Wales, he grew very weary and therefore sat himself down by the side of a pleasant fountain,[1] where a deep sleep suddenly seiz'd on him; at which time the Giant coming there for water, found him, and by the Lines written upon his belt, knew him to be Jack that kill'd his brother Giant, and therefore without making any words, he throws him upon his shoulder, for to carry him to his inchanted castle.

Now as they passed through a thicket the rustling of the boughs awak'd poor Jack, who finding himself strangely surprised, yet it was but the beginning of his terrors; for he beheld the ground all cover'd with bones and skulls of dead men. The Giant telling Jack that his bones would enlarge the number that he saw. This said, he brought him into a large parlour where he beheld the bloody quarters of some that were lately slain, and in the next room were many hearts and livers: which the Giant to terrify Jack, told him, "that mens hearts and livers were the choicest of his diet, for he commonly (as he said) eat them with pepper and vinegar: adding, that he did not question but his heart would make him a dainty bit." This said, he locks up poor Jack in an upper room leaving him there, while he went to fetch another Giant, living in the same wood, that he might be partaker in the pleasure which they would have in the destruction of poor Jack.

Now, while he was gone, dreadful shrieks and cries affrighted Jack, especially a voice which continually cried.

> Do what you can to get away,
> Or you'll become the Giant's prey;
> He's gone to fetch his brother, who
> Will kill, and likewise torter you.

This dreadful noise so affrighted poor Jack, that he was ready to run distracted, then seeing from a window afar off, the two Giants coming together; now (quoth Jack to himself,) my death or deliverance is at hand.

There was strong cords in the room by him, of which he takes two, at the end of which he made a noose; and while the Giant was unlocking the iron gate, he threw the ropes over each of their heads, and then drawing the

---

Cornish folklore, whom a certain Tom kills in a Cornish folktale recorded by Hunt: *Drolls, Traditions and Superstitions of Old Cornwall*, I, pp. 55-9.

1   At this point Halliwell quotes the following description directly from the 1711 text: 'o'ercanopied with luscious woodbine' (see p. 168). This description is missing from both the Shrewsbury and Falkirk versions, which indicates that both their texts, whilst certainly closely related to that of the lost 1711 chapbook, are at least one step removed from that of the original *History*.

other end across the beam, where he pulled with all his main strength until he had throatled them; and then fastening the rope to the beam, turn'd towards the window, where he beheld the two Giant's to be black in their faces; Then sliding down by the rope he came close to their heads, where the helpless Giants could not defend themselves, and drawing out his sword, slew them both and delivered himself from their intended cruelty: He then taking the bunch of keys, he unlock'd the rooms, where upon a strict search, he found three fair Ladie's ty'd by the hair of their heads, almost starved to death, who told Jack, That their husbands was slain by the Giant, and that they were kept many days without food: in order to force them to feed upon the flesh of their husbands; which they could not, if they were starved to death. Sweet Ladies, (quoth Jack) I have destroyed this Monster, and his brutish brother, by which I have obtained your liberties. This said,, he presented them with the keys of the casile, and so proceeded on his journey into Wales.

How Jack travelled into Flintshire, and what happened

JACK having but very little money, though it prudent to make the best of his way by travelling as fast as he could, but losing his road was benighted and could not get a place of entertainment; until he came to a valley, placed between two hills where stood a large house in a lon[e]some place, and by reason of his present condition, he took courage to knock at the gate; and to his surprise there came forth a monstrous Giant, having two heads; yet he did not seem so fiery as the others had been, for he was a Welsh Giant, and what he did was by private and secret malice under the false shew of friendship; for Jack telling his condition he bid him welcome shewing him a room with a bed in it, whereupon he might take his night's repose: Therefore jack undresses himself, and as the Giant was walking away to another apartment, Jack heard him mutter these words to himself.

Tho' here you lodge with me this night,
You shall not see the morning light,
My club shall dash your brains out right.

Say'st though so, quoth Jack, that is like one of your Welsh tricks, yet I hope to be cunning enough for you. Then getting out of bed, he put a billet in his stead and hid himself in a corner of the room, and in the dead time of the night, the Welsh Giant came with his great knotty club, and struck several blows upon the bed where Jack had laid his billet, and then returned to his own chamber supposing he had broken all the bones in his body.[1]

---

1   It is often suggested that this sequence derived ultimately from Norse and Germanic mythology/folklore: Opie and Opie, *Classic Fairy Tales*, p. 58;

In the morning Jack gave him a hearty thanks for his lodging. The Giant said to him, how have you rested? Did you not feel something in the night? Nothing (quoth Jack) but a rat which gave me three or four slaps with her tail. Soon after the Giant arose, and went to breakfast with a bowl of hasty pudding, containing near four gallons, giving Jack the like quantity; who, being loath to let the Giant know he could not eat with him, got a large leather-bag putting it artfully under his loose coat, into which he secretly conveyed his pudding, telling the Giant, he could show him a trick; Then taking a large knife, he ripped open the bag, which the Giant supposed to be his belly, when out came the hasty pudding; At which the Welsh Giant, cried out, Cuts plut, hur can do dat trick hurself.[1] Then taking his sharp knife, he ripped up his own belly, from the bottom to the top, and out dropped his tripes and troly bags,[2] so that hur fell down for dead: thus Jack outwitted the Giant, and proceeded on his journey.[3]

How King Arthur's Son met with Jack, &c.

KING Arthur's Son,[4] only desired of his Father to furnish him with a certain sum of money, that he might go and seek his fortune in the principality of Wales, where a beautiful Lady lived, whom he heard was possessed with seven evil spirits; But the King his Father advised him utterly against it, yet he would not be persuaded from it; so that he granted what he requested, which was one horse loaded with money, and another for himself to ride on; thus he went forth without any attendance.

Now after several days travel, he came to a market town in Wales, where he beheld a large concourse of people gathered together; the King's Son demanded the reason of it, and was told, that they had arrested a corpse for many large sums of money, which the deceased owed when he dy'd. The King's Son reply'd it is a pity that creditors should be so cruel, so bury the dead (said he) and let his creditors come to my Lodging, and their debts

---

Halliwell, *Popular Rhymes*, pp. 56-57; H. Weiss, 'The Autochthonal Tale of Jack the Giant Killer', *The Scientific Monthly*, 28.2 (1929), pp. 126-33 at pp. 129-32. However, Weiss notes that such substitution is a common motif found in French, Italian, and Persian tales (p. 132).

1 M. S. Kirch, 'Note on the History of Jack and the Giants', *Modern Language Notes*, 69.1 (1954), p. 44, suggests this is a corruption of 'God's Blood', with the 'hur' being used to suggest an imperfect command of the English language.

2 *OED*, s.v. Trollibags, 'entrails, intestines'. Note that the *OED* records the first print usage as 1824, which this instance obviously significantly predates.

3 This method of trickery and dispatch is paralleled again in Scandinavian folk-tale: Opie and Opie, *Classic Fairy Tales*, pp. 58-59.

4 Numerous sons of Arthur are known from the medieval Arthurian legend – including Amr, Llacheu, Loholt and Gwydre – but there is no reason to think that any specific son is intended here.

shall be discharged. Accordingly they came, and is such great number, that before night he had almost left himself moneyless.

Now Jack the Giant Killer being there, and seeing the generosity of the King's Son, he was taken with him, and desired to be his servant; it was agreed upon the next morning they set forward, when at the town end, an old woman called after them, crying out, he was ow'n me two pence these five years: pray Sir, pay me as well as the rest? He puts his hand into his pocket, and gave it her, it being the last he had left, then the King's Son turning to Jack, said, I cannot tell how I shall subsist in my intended journey. For that (quoth Jack) take you no thought nor care let me alone, I warrant you we will not want.[1]

Now Jack having a small spell in his pocket, which served at noon to give them a refreshment, when done, they had not one penny left betwixt them; the afternoon the spent in travel and familiar friendly discourse, 'till the sun began to grow low, at which time, the King's Son said, Jack, since we have no money, where can we think to lodge this night? Jack reply'd, Master, we'll do well enough. For I have an uncle lives within two little miles of this place, he's a hudge and monstrous Giant[2] with three heads; He'll fight five hundred men in armour, and make them to fly before him. Alas! (quoth the King's Son) what shall we do there, he'll certainly chop us both up at one mouthful! Nay, we are scarce enough to fill one of his hollow teeth. It is no matter for that (quoth Jack,) I myself will go before, and prepare the way for you; therefore tarry here, and wait my return.

He waits, and Jack rides full speed, when coming to the Gates of the castle, he knock'd with such force, that he made all the neighbouring hills resound. The Giant with a voice like thunder, roared out; who's there? He

---

1   This is generally thought to represent a version of The Grateful Dead theme. The earliest version of this appears in the Biblical 'Book of Tobit', but it is frequently to be found in the folklore of many countries. At its core it involves a dead man's corpse being denied burial by his creditors. These are eventually paid-off by someone – the son of Arthur in this instance – with the corpse then becoming the servant of this person; in this telling, Jack takes the dead man's place as the servant. We also find this theme expressed in Peele's sixteenth-century play *The Old Wives Tale*, but here the corpse retains his original role as the servant after the creditors are paid off, with the corpse's name being revealed to be – most intriguingly – Jack. See K. M. Briggs, 'Possible Mythological Motifs in English Folktales', *Folklore*, 83.4 (1972), pp. 265-71 at p. 270; F. H. Groome, 'Tobit and Jack the Giant-Killer', *Folklore*, 9.3 (1896), pp. 226-44. For further possible evidence of some influence from Peele's *Old Wives Tale* on Jack's *History*, see the notes below.

2   Another example of a giant-killer with gigantic relatives is Arthur, whose wife, son, nephew and closest companion all seem to have been considered giants at some point, see Green, *Concepts of Arthur*, pp. 143, 154-55, 170. Indeed, Arthur's father too appears in some Cornish lore as a giant: J. H. Harris, *Cornish Saints and Sinners* (London: Bodley Head, 1906).

answered, none but your poor cousin Jack[1] quoth he, what news with my poor cousin Jack? He replied, dear uncle, heavy news; God wot prithee what heavy news can come to me? I am a Giant, with three heads; and besides thou knows I can fight five hundred men in Armour and make them fly like chaff before the wind. Oh! but (quoth Jack) here's the King's Son coming with a thousand men in Armour to kill you, and so to destroy all that you have. Oh! Cousin Jack, this is heavy news indeed; I have a large vault under the ground, where I will immediately hide myself, and thou shalt lock, bolt and bar me in, and keep the keys till the King's Son is gone.

Now Jack having secured the Giant, he soon returned and fetched his master, and were both heartily merry with the wine, and other dainties which were in the house: So that night they rested in very pleasant lodgings, whilst poor Uncle the Giant, lay trembling in the vault under ground.

Early in the morning Jack furnished his master with a fresh supply of gold and silver, and then set him three miles forward on his journey; concluding he then was pretty well out of the smell of the Giant, and then returned to let his Uncle out of the hole: Who asked Jack what he should give him in reward his castle was not demolished. Why (quoth Jack) I desire nothing but the old coat and cap together with the old coat and slippers, which are at your bed-head. Quoth the Giant, thou shalt have them, and pray keep them for my sake, for they are things of excellent use. The coat will keep you invisible; the cap will furnish you with knowledge; the sword cuts in sunder whatever you strike; and the shoes are of extraordinary swiftness: These may be serviceable to you, and therefore pray take them with all my heart. Jack takes them, thanking his Uncle and follows his master.[2]

How Jack saved his Master's Life and Drove the evil Spirit out of a Lady, &c.

JACK having overtaken his master, they soon after arrived at the Lady's house: who finding the King's Son to be a suitor, she prepared a banquit for him; which being ended, she wiped his mouth with her handkerchief saying, you must shew me this once to morrow morning, or else lose your head: And with that she put it into her own bosom.

The King's Sone went to bed very sorrowful, but Jack's cap of Knowledge instructed him how to obtain it. In the middle of the night she called upon her familiar spirit to carry her to her friend Lucifer, Jack soon put on his coat of darkness, with his shoes of swiftness, and was there as

1 Presumably an early usage of 'Cousin Jack', a 'familiar name for a Cornishman' (*OED*, s.v. Jack, n.¹).

2 These items are often cited as further evidence for the influence of Scandinavian or Germanic mythology on the tale of Jack: Opie and Opie, *Classic Fairy Tales*, p. 59; Weiss, 'Jack the Giant Killer', p. 130.

soon as her, by reason of his coat they could not see him. When she entered the place she gave the handkerchief to old Lucifer, who laid it upon the shelf; from whence Jack took it, and brought it to his master, who shewed it to the Lady the next day, and so saved his Life.

The next night she saluted the King's Son, telling him, he must shew her to morrow morning, the lips that she kissed last, this night, or lose his head. Ah! (reply'd he) if you kiss non but mine, I will, 'tis neither here nor there (said she) if you do not, death's your portion. At midnight she went as before, and was angry with Lucifer for letting the handkerchief go; But now (said he) I will be too hard for the King's Son, for I will kiss thee, and he's to shew thy Lips; which she did, Jack standing near him with his sword of sharpness, cut off the devil's head, brought it under his invisible coat to his master, who was in bed, and laid it at the end of his bolster. In the morning, when the Lady came up, he pulled it out by the horns, and shewed her the devil's lips which she kissed last.

Thus hav[i]ng answered her twice, the enchantment broke, and the evil spirit left her; at which time she appeared in all her beauty, a beautiful and virtuous creature. They were married the next morning, in great pomp and solemnity, and soon after they returned with a numerous company to the court of King Arthur, where they were received with the greatest Joy, and loud acclamation by the whole court. Jack for his many and great exploits he had done for the good of his country, was made one of the knights of the round Table.

Thus we have finished the first part of this History which now leads us to the second part, wherein you have a more full account of the many valiant and wonderful exploits which was done by the bold adventures of this great and valiant HERO, Jack the Giant Killer.[1]

The SECOND Part.

How Jack by King Arthur's leave went in pursuit of Giants yet alive, &c.

JACK having been successful in all his undertakings, and resolved not to be idle for the future; but to perform what service he could for the honour of his King and country; he humbly requested of the King his royal master, to fit him with a horse and money, to travel in search of strange and new adventures: For, said he, there are many Giants yet alive in the remote parts of the kingdom, and the dominions of Wales, to the unspeakable damage of your Majesty's liege subjects; wherefore may it please your Majesty to give me encouragement, and I doubt not but in a short time to cut them of root and branch, and to rid the realm of those cruel Giants, and devouring

---

1   This paragraph is missing in both the 1760s chapbook used by the Opies and Halliwell's transcript of the 1711 text.

monsters of nature.[1]

Now when the King had heard these noble propositions and had duly considered the mischevious practices of those blood-thirsty Giants: He immediately, granted what honest Jack requested, and on the first day of March, being thoroughly furnished with all the necessaries for his progress, he took leave, not only of King Arthur, but likewise of all the trusty and hardy Knights belonging to the round Table,[2] who after much salutation and friendly greeting they parted, the King and his nobles to their courtly palaces, and Jack the Giant Killer to the eager pursuit of fortune's favours, taking with him the cap of knowledge, sword of sharpness, shoes of swiftness, and likewise the invisible coat, the better to perfect and complete the dangerous enterprizes that lay before him.

How Jack slew a Giant, and delivered a Knight and his Lady from death

JACK travelling over vast hills and wonderful mountains, when at the end of three days, he came to a large and spacious wood through which he must needs pass, where on a sudden to his great amazement he heard dreadful shrieks and cries: Whereupon casting his eyes around to observe what it might be, beheld with wonder, a Giant rushing along with a worthy knight and his fair lady, which he held by the hair of their heads in his hands, with as much ease, as if they had been but a pair of gloves; the sight of which melted poor Jack into tears of pity and compassion: wherefore, alighted off from his horse; which he left tied to an oak tree, and then putting on his invisible coat, under which he carried his sword of sharpness, he came up to the Giant and though he made several passes at him: yet nevertheless, it could not reach the trunk of his body, by reason of his height, tho' it wounded his thighs in several places: but at length giving him a swinging stroke, he cut off both his legs, just below the knees,[3] so that the trunk of his body, made not only the ground shake, but likewise the trees to tremble with the force of his fall, at which by mere fortune, the knight and his lady escaped his rage, then had Jack time to talk with him, setting his foot upon his neck said, thou savage and barbarous wretch, I am come to execute upon you the just reward of your villany. And with that running him through and through, the monster sent forth a hideous groan, and yielded

---

1   As discussed on pp. 145-46, although Jack takes this role here, it actually belongs to Arthur in Welsh and Cornish folklore.

2   Interestingly, these two mentions of the 'Round Table' are the only elements of the international 'literary' Arthurian legend found in Jack's History. Compare this situation with that of *Tom Thumbe, His Life and Death*, which includes Merlin, Lancelot, Tristram and a jousting tournament: see Green, 'Tom Thumb and Jack the Giant Killer' for some further comment.

3   Compare here Arthur's treatment of Golopas/Galapas, see p. 189.

up his life, into the hands of the valiant conqueror; Jack the Giant killer, while the noble Knight and virtuous lady were both joyful spectators of his sudden downfall, and their deliverance.

This being done, the courteous Knight and his fair lady, not only returned him hearty thanks fro their deliverance, but also invited him home, there to refresh himself after the dreadful encounter; as likewise to receive some ample reward by way of gratitude for his good service. No quoth Jack, I cannot be at ease till I find out the den which was this monsters habitation. The Knight hearing this, waxed right sorrowful and reply'd, noble stranger, it is too much to run a second risk, for this noted monster lived in a den under yon mountain, with a brother of his, more fierce and fiery than himself; and therefore if you should go hither and perish in the attempt, it would be the heart breaking of both me and my lady, here let me persuade you to go with us and desist from any farther pursuit: Nay, quoth Jack, if there be another; nay, if there were twenty I would shed the last drop of my blood in my body, before one of them shall escape my fury, and when I have finished this task, I will come and pay my respects to you. So taking directions to their habitation, he mounted his horse, leaving them to return home, while he went in pursuit of the deceased Giants brother.

How Jack slew the other Giant, and sent both their heads to King Arthur

JACK had not rode past a mile and a half before he came in sight of the cave's mouth, near to the entrance of which he beheld the other Giant, sitting upon a huge block of timber, with a knotted iron club lying by his side, waiting as, he supposed, for his brother's return with his cruel prey; his gogle eyes appeared like terrible flames of fire, his countenance grim and ugly, and his cheecks appeared like a couple of large fat flitches of bacon: moreover the bristles of his head seem'd to resemble rods of iron wire; his locks hung down upon his broad shoulders, like curled snakes or hissing adders.

Jack alighted from his horse, and put him into a thicket, then with his coat of darkness he come somewhat near to behold his figure, and said softly, Oh! are you there? It will not be long e'er I take you by the beard. The Giant all this time could not see him by reason of his invisible coat, so coming up close to him, valiant Jack fetching a blow at his head with his sword of sharpness, and missing somewhat his aim, cut off the Giant's nose, whose nostrils were wider than a pair of jack-boots; the pain was terrible and so he put up his hand to his nose, and when he could not find it, he rav'd and roar'd louder than claps of thunder: and tho' he turn'd up his large eyes, he could not see from whence the blow came, which had done him that great disaster; nevertheless he took up his iron knotted club, and began to lay about him like one stark mad: Nay, quoth Jack, if you be for that sport, then I will dispatch you quickly, for fear of an accidental blow falling out. Then as the Giant rose from his block, Jack makes no more to do, but runs his sword up to the hilt in the Gant's fundament, where he left it sticking for a while and stood laughing with his hands a kim bow to see the Giant caper and dance the canaries with his sword in his arse, crying out, he should die, he should die, with the gripping of his guts. Thus did the Giant continue raving for an hour or more, and at length fell down dead whose dreadful fall had like to have crushed poor jack, had he not been nimble to avoid the same.

This being done, Jack cut off both the Giant's heads and sent them both to King Arthur by a waggoner, whom he hired for the same purpose, together with an account of his prosperous success in all his undertakings.[1]

How Jack searched their cave, and delivered many men out of captivity.

JACK having thus dispatch'd these two monsters, resolved with himself to enter the cave in search of these Giants treasure; he passed along through many turnings and windings which led him at length to a room paved with free stone, at the upper end of which was a boiling cauldron, then on the right hand stood a large table; where (as he supposed) the Giants used to dine, then he came to an iron gate, where was a window secured with bars of iron, through which he looked, and there beheld a vast many miserable captives; who seeing Jack at a distance, cried out with a loud voice, Alas! young man, art thou come to be one amongst us in this miserable den? Ay, quoth Jack, I hope I shall not tarry long here: but pray tell me what is the meaning of your captivity? why, said one, young man, I'll tell you, we are persons that have been taken by the Giants that keep this cave, and here we are kept until such time as they have occasion for a particular feast, and then the fattest amongst us is slaughtered, and prepared for their devouring jaws: it is not long since they took three of us for the same purpose: nay, many are the times they have dined on murdered men. Say you so quoth Jack, well, I have given them both such a dinner, that it will be long enough e'er they'll have occasion for any. The miserable captives were amazed at his words: You may believe me, quoth Jack, for I have slain them both with the point of my sword, and as for their monstrous heads I sent them in a wagon to the court of King Arthur, as Trophies of my unparallel'd victory. And for testimony of the truth he had said, he unlock'd the iron gate setting the miserable captivity at liberty, who all rejoiced like condemned malefactors at the sight of a reprieve: then leading them all together to the aforesaid room, he placed them round the table, and set before them two quarters of beef, as also bread and wine, so that he feasted them very plentifully, supper

---

1   As noted on p. 146, this incident has a number of points of similarity with Arthur's killing of the giant of Mont St Michel.

being ended, they searched the Giant's coffers, where finding a vast store of gold and silver, Jack equally divided it amongst them: they all returned him hearty thanks, for their treasure and miraculous deliverance. That night they went to their rest, and in the morning they arose and departed, the captives to their respective towns and places of abode; and Jack to the knight's house, whom he had formerly delivered from the hand of the Giant.

How Jack came to the Knight's house, and his noble Entertainment there, &c.

IT was about sun rising when Jack mounted his horse to proceed on his journey, and by the help of his directions he came to the Knight's house some time before noon: where he was received with all demonstrations of joy imaginable by the Knight and his lady, who in honourable respect to Jack prepared a feast, which lasted for many days, inviting all the gentry in the adjacent parts, to whom the worthy Knight was pleased to relate the manner of his former danger, and the happy deliverance, by the undaunted courage of Jack the Giant Killer: And by way of gratitude, he presented him with a Ring of gold on which was engraven by curious art, the picture of the Giant dragging a distressed Knight and his fair Lady by the hair of the head, with this Motto.

> We are in sad distress you see,
>   Under a Giant's fierce command;
> But gain'd our Lives and Liberty,
>   By valiant Jack's victorious hand.

Now amongst the vast assembly there present, were five aged Gentleman who were fathers to some of those miserable captives, which Jack had lately set at liberty; who understanding that he was the person that performed those great wonders, they immediately paid their venerable respects: After which their mirth encreased; and the smiling bowls went freely round to the prosperous success to the victorious conqueror. But in the midst of all mirth, a dark cloud appeared, which daunted all the hearts of the assembly. Thus it was, a messenger brought the dismal tidings of the approach of one Thunderdel,[1] a huge Giant with two heads; who having heard of the death of his kinsmen, the above named Giants; was come from the Northeren poles in search after Jack to be revenged of him for their most miserable downfal, and was within a mile of the Knight's seat, the country people flying before him, from their houses and habitations like chaff before the wind. When they had related this, Jack not a whit daunted, said, let him come, I am prepared with a tool to pick his tooth, and you gentlemen and

---

1   This name is *Thunderdel* in the Shrewsbury chapbook and *Thunderdell* in Halliwell's transcription of the 1711 Newcastle chapbook.

ladies, walk but forth into the garden, and you shall be the joyful spectators of this monstrous Giant's death and destruction. To which they all consented, every one wishing him good fortune in that great and dangerous enterprize.

How Jack overthrew the Giant in the Moat.

THE situation of the Knight's house take as follows: It was placed in the midst of a small island, encompassed round with a vast moat, thirty feet deep, and twenty feet wide, over which lay a draw bridge. Wherefore Jack employed two men to cut it on both sides, almost to the middle; and then dressing himself in his coat of darkness, likewise putting on his Shoes of swiftness, he marches forth against the Giant, with his sword of sharpness ready drawn; yet when he came close to him, the Giant could not see Jack by reason of his invisible coat which he had on, yet nevertheless he was sensible of some approaching danger, which made him cry out in these words.

> Fe, Fi, Fo, Fum,
> I smell the blood of an Englishman;
> Be he living or be he dead,
> I'll grind his bones to mix my bread.[1]

Says thou so quoth Jack, then thou art a monstrous Miller indeed: But how if I should serve thee as I did the two Giants of late, in my conscience I should spoil your practice for the future. At which the Giant spoke with a voice as loud as thunder: Art thou that villian which destroyed my two kinsmen? Then will I tear thee with my teeth, such thy blood and what is more, I will grind thy bones to powder. You must catch me first quoth Jack; and with that he threw off his coat of darkness that the Giant might see him clearly, and then run from him as through fear. The Giant with a foaming mouth, and glaring eyes, following after like a walking castle, making the foundations of the Earth, as it were, to shake at every step, Jack led him a dance three or four times around the moat that belonged to the Knight's house, that the gentlemen and ladies might take a full view of this huge monster of nature, who followed Jack with all his might but could not overtake him by reason of his shoes of swiftness: [which] carried him faster than the Giant could [follow;] at length Jack to finish the work took [over the] bridge, wh[at] with the weight of his bo[d]y [an]d the most dreadful steps that he took, it broke down, and he tumbled into the water, where he

---

1 As the Opies note, this is a formula common to most British blood-thirsty giants, back to Red Etin in 1528: 'Snouk but and snouk ben, / I find the smell of an earthly man; / Be he living or be he dead, / His heart this night shall kitchen my bread' (Opie and Opie, *The Classic Fairy Tales*, p. 78). Interestingly, Peele's *Old Wives Tales*, referred to above, includes a version of this phrase.

roll'd and wallow'd like a whale. Jack standing at the side of the moat, laugh'd at the Giant and said you told me you would grind my bones to powder, here you have water enough, pray where is your mill? The Giant fretted and foamed to hear him scoff at that rate; and tho' he plunged from place to place in the Moat, yet he could not get out to be revenged on his adversary. Jack at length got a cart rope, and cast it over the Giants two heads with a slip-knot, and by the help of a team of horses, dragged him out again, with which he was near strangled; and before he would let him loose, he cut off both his heads with his sword of sharpness, in the full view of all the worthy assembly of knights, gentlemen and ladies, who gave a joyful shout when they saw the Giant fairly dispatched. Then before he would either eat or drink, he sent these heads also after the other to the court of King Arthur: Which being done, then Jack with the knights and ladies, returned to their mirth and pastime, which lasted for many days.

How Jack came to the house of an old Hermit, and what Discourse happened between them.

AFTER some time spent in triumphant mirth and pastime, Jack grew weary of riotous living, wherefore, taking leave of the noble knights and ladies, he set forward in search of new adventures. Thro' many woods and groves he passed, meeting with nothing remarkable till at length coming to the foot of an high mountain late at night he knocked at the door of a lonesome house, at which time an ancient man, with a head as white as snow arose and let him in. Father, said Jack, have you any entertainment for a benighted traveller, that has lost his way? Yes, said the man, if thou will accept of such accommodation as my poor cottage will afford, thou shalt be right welcome. Jack returned him many thanks, for his great civility, wherefore down they sat together, and the old man began to discourse him as follows: Son, said he, I am sensible thou art the great conqueror of Giants, and it is in thy power to free this place of the country from an intolerable burden which we groan under. For behold my son, on the top of this high mountain, there is an inchanted castle kept by a huge monstrous Giant, named Galigantus,[1] who by the help of an old conjuror betrays many knights and ladies into this strong castle; where by Magick Art they are transformed into sundry shapes and forms: But above all, I lament the sad misfortune of a Duke's Daughter whom they fetch'd from her father's garden by Art, carrying her through the air in a mourning chariot, drawn as it were by two fiery dragons, and being secured within the walls of the castle, she was immediately transformed into

---

1   This name is *Galigantus* in the Shrewsbury chapbook and *Galligantus* in Halliwell's transcription of the 1711 Newcastle chapbook. Is there any relationship between this name and that of Galapas from Malory's *Morte Darthur*, who Arthur kills and whose method of dispatch may have been borrowed earlier in the tale?

the real shape of a white Hind: tho' many worthy knights have endeavoured to break the inchantment, and work her deliverance, yet none of them could accomplish this great work, by reason of two dreadful Griffins who were fix'd by magick art at the entrance of the castle gate; which destroys any as soon as they see them.[1] But you my son, being furnished with an invisible coat, may pass by them undiscovered. Whereupon the brazen gates of the castle you find engraven in large characters, by what means the inchantment may be broken.

This old man having ended his discourse, Jack gave him his hand, with a faithful promise, that in the morning he would venture his life to break the inchantment, and free the lady, together with the rest that were miserable partners in her calamity.

How Jack got into the inchanted Castle, broke the inchantment, killed the Giant, put the conjuror to flight, set free the Knights, and Ladies, &c.

HAVING refreshed themselves with a small morsal of meat they laid them down to rest, and in the morning Jack arose and put on his invisible coat, his cap of knowledge, and shoes of swiftness, and so prepares himself for the dangerous enterprise.

Now when he had ascended to the top of the mountain, he soon discovered the two fiery Griffins; he passed on between them without fear, for they could not see him by reason of his invisible coat: now when he was yet beyond them, he cast his eyes around him, where he found upon the gate a golden trumpet, hang in a chain of fine silver, under which these lines were engraven.

> Whosoever shall this trumpet blow.
> Shall soon the Giant overthrow,
> And break the black inchantment straight,
> So all shall be in happy state.

Jack had no sooner read this inscription but he blew the trumpet, at which time the vast foundation of the castle trembled, and the Giant, together with the conjuror, was in horrid confusion, biting their thumbs and tearing their hair, knowing that their wicked reign was at an end. At which time Jack standing at the Giant's elbow as he was stooping to take up his club, he at one blow with his sword of sharpness, cut of[f] his head. The conjuror, seeing this, immediately mounted into the air, and was carried away in a whirlwind. Thus was the whole inchantment broke and every knight and lady who had been for a long time transformed into birds, and beasts, returned to their proper shapes again; and as for the castle tho' it

---

1   Spooner, 'Jack and Tom', p. 107 notes that a 'conjuror' who abducts a princess to his castle appears in Peele's *Old Wives Tale*, again suggesting the possibility of some influence from this play on Jack's *History*.

seemed at first to be of a vast strength and bigness it vanished away like a cloud of smoke; whereupon an universal joy appeared among the released knights and ladies. This being done, the head of Galligantus was likewise (according to his accustomed manner[)] conveyed to the court of King Arthur as a present made to his Majesty. The very next day after having refreshed the knights and ladies at the old man's habitation, who lived at the foot of the mountain, he set forward for the court of King Arthur, with those knights and ladies which he had so honourably delivered.

When coming to his Majesty, and having related all the passages of his fierce encounters, and his fame run thro' the whole court; and as a reward of his good service, the King prevailed with the aforesaid Duke to he bestow his daughter in marriage to honest Jack protesting that there was no man so worthy of her as he; to all which the Duke very honourably consented: So married they were, and not only the court, but likewise the kingdom was filled with joy and triumph at the wedding. After which the king as a reward for his good services done to the nation, bestowed upon him a noble habitation, with a very plentiful estate belonging thereunto, where he and his lady lived the remainder of their days in peace.[1]

F   I   N   I   S.

---

1   Later versions add here that 'His wife and his children were kind, / Friends place him in great reliance; / His boys were at college refined, / His girls told the tale of the giants' – see p. 182.

The 1711 Text of *The History of Jack and the Giants*

Introduction

James Orchard Halliwell (later Halliwell-Phillipps) transcribed, 'with a few necessary alterations', the earliest surviving version of *The History of Jack and the Giants*.[1] The original of this was printed at Newcastle-on-Tyne in 1711, three years after the very first recorded reference to Jack; as such it constitutes our earliest witness to Jack. Unfortunately, the 1711 chapbook has long-since been lost and Halliwell's transcript is modernised throughout, abbreviated in places, and bowdlerised where the action becomes gruesome. As a result, later derivatives of the original chapbook are usually relied upon for detailed analysis. Nonetheless, Halliwell's text is valuable in and of itself. It is thus presented complete, to allow comparison with the unaltered chapbook text provided above.

Text

In the reign of King Arthur, and in the county of Cornwall, near to the Land's End of England, there lived a wealthy farmer, who had an only son named Jack. He was brisk, and of a lively ready wit, so that whatever he could not perform by force and strength, he accomplished by ingenious wit and policy. Never was any person heard of that could worst him, and he very often even baffled the learned by his sharp and ready inventions.

In those days the Mount of Cornwall was kept by a huge and monstrous giant of eighteen feet in height, and about three yards in compass, of a fierce and grim countenance, the terror of all the neighbouring towns and villages. He inhabited a cave in the middle of the mount, and he was such a selfish monster that he would not suffer any one to live near him. He fed on other men's cattle, which often became his prey, for whensoever he wanted food, he would wade over to the main land, where he would furnish himself with whatever came in his way. The inhabitants, at his approach, forsook their

---

1   J. O. Halliwell, *Popular Rhymes and Nursery Tales of England* (London: John Russell Smith, 1849), pp. 57-69.

habitations, while he seized on their cattle, making nothing of carrying half-a-dozen oxen on his back at a time; and as for their sheep and hogs, he would tie them round his waist like a bunch of bandoleers. This course he had followed for many years, so that a great part of the county was impoverished by his depredations.

This was the state of affairs, when Jack, happening one day to be present at the town-hall when the authorities were consulting about the giant, had the curiosity to ask what reward would be given to the person who destroyed him. The giant's treasure was declared as the recompense, and Jack at once undertook the task.

In order to accomplish his purpose, he furnished himself with a horn, shovel, and pickaxe, and went over to the Mount in the beginning of a dark winter's evening, when he fell to work, and before morning had dug a pit twenty-two feet deep, and nearly as broad, covering it over with long sticks and straw. Then strewing a little mould upon it, it appeared like plain ground. This accomplished, Jack placed himself on the side of the pit which was furthest from the giant's lodging, and, just at the break of day, he put the horn to his mouth, and blew with all his might. Although Jack was a little fellow, and the powers of his voice are not described as being very great, he managed to make noise enough to arouse the giant, and excite his indignation. The monster accordingly rushed from his cave, exclaiming, "You incorrigible villain, are you come here to disturb my rest? You shall pay dearly for this. Satisfaction I will have, for I will take you whole and broil you for breakfast." He had no sooner uttered this cruel threat, than tumbling into the pit, he made the very foundations of the Mount ring again. "Oh, giant," said Jack, "where are you now? Oh faith, you are gotten now into Lob's Pound, where I will surely plague you for your threatening words: what do you think now of broiling me for your breakfast? will no other diet serve you but poor Jack?" Thus did little Jack tantalize the big giant, as a cat does a mouse when she knows it cannot escape, and when he had tired of that amusement, he gave him a heavy blow with his pickaxe on the very crown of his head, which "tumbled him down," and killed him on the spot. When Jack saw he was dead, he filled up the pit with earth, and went to search the cave, which he found contained much treasure. The magistrates, in the exuberance of their joy, did not add to Jack's gains from their own, but after the best and cheapest mode of payment, made a declaration he should henceforth be termed *Jack the Giant-killer*, and presented him with a sword and embroidered belt, on the latter of which were inscribed these words in letters of gold:

> Here's the right valiant Cornish man,
> Who slew the giant Cormelian.

The news of Jack's victory, as might be expected, soon spread over all the West of England, so that another giant, named Thunderbore, hearing of it, and entertaining a partiality for his race, vowed to be revenged on the little hero, if ever it was his fortune to light on him. This giant was the lord of an enchanted castle, situated in the midst of a lonely wood. Now Jack, about four months after his last exploit, walking near this castle in his journey towards Wales, being weary, seated himself near a pleasant fountain in the wood, "o'ercanopied with luscious woodbine," and presently fell asleep. While he was enjoying his repose, the giant, coming to the fountain for water, of course discovered him, and recognised the hated individual by the lines written on the belt. He immediately took Jack on his shoulders, and carried him towards his enchanted castle. Now, as they passed through a thicket, the rustling of the boughs awakened Jack, who was uncomfortably surprised to find himself in the clutches of the giant. His terror was not diminished when, on entering the castle, he saw the court-yard strewed with human bones, the giant maliciously telling him his own would ere long increase the hateful pile. After this assurance, the cannibal locked poor Jack in an upper chamber, leaving him there while he went to fetch another giant living in the same wood to keep him company in the anticipated destruction of their enemy. While he was gone, dreadful shrieks and lamentations affrighted Jack, especially a voice which continually cried,—

> Do what you can to get away,
> Or you'll become the giant's prey;
> He's gone to fetch his brother, who
> Will kill, and likewise torture you.

This warning, and the hideous tone in which it was delivered, almost distracted poor Jack, who going to the window, and opening a casement, beheld afar off the two giants approaching towards the castle. "Now," quoth Jack to himself, "my death or my deliverance is at hand." The event proved that his anticipations were well founded, for the giants of those days, however powerful, were at best very stupid fellows, and readily conquered by stratagem, were it of the humblest kind. There happened to be strong cords in the room in which Jack was confined, two of which he took, and made a strong noose at the end of each; and while the giant was unlocking the iron gate of the castle, he threw the ropes over each of their heads, and then, before the giants knew what he was about, he drew the other ends across a beam, and, pulling with all his might, throttled them till they were black in the face. Then, sliding down the rope, he came to their heads, and as they could not defend themselves, easily despatched them with his sword. This business so adroitly accomplished, Jack released the fair prisoners in the castle, delivered the keys to them, and, like a true knight-errant, continued his journey without condescending to improve the condition of his purse.

This plan, however honourable, was not without its disadvantages, and owing to his slender stock of money, he was obliged to make the best of his way by travelling as hard as he could. At length, losing his road, he was belated, and could not get to any place of entertainment until, coming to a lonesome valley, he found a large house, and by reason of his present necessity, took courage to knock at the gate. But what was his astonishment, when there came forth a monstrous giant with two heads; yet he did not appear so fiery as the others were, for he was a Welsh giant, and what he did was by private and secret malice under the false show of friendship. Jack having unfolded his condition to the giant, was shown into a bedroom, where, in the dead of night, he heard his host in another apartment uttering these formidable words:

> Though here you lodge with me this night,
> You shall not see the morning light:
> My club shall dash your brains out quite!

"Say'st thou so," quoth Jack; "that is like one of your Welsh tricks, yet I hope to be cunning enough for you." He immediately got out of bed, and, feeling about in the dark, found a thick billet of wood, which he laid in the bed in his stead, and hid himself in a dark corner of the room. Shortly after he had done so, in came the Welsh giant, who thoroughly pummelled the billet with his club, thinking, naturally enough, he had broken every bone in Jack's skin. The next morning, however, to the inexpressible surprise of the giant, Jack came down stairs as if nothing had happened, and gave him thanks for his night's lodging. "How have you rested," quoth the giant; "did you not feel anything in the night?" Jack provokingly replied, "No, nothing but a rat which gave me two or three flaps with her tail." This reply was totally incomprehensible to the giant, who of course saw anything but a joke in it. However, concealing his amazement as well as he could, he took Jack in to breakfast, assigning to each a bowl containing four gallons of hasty pudding. One would have thought that the greater portion of so extravagant an allowance would have been declined by our hero, but he was unwilling the giant should imagine his incapability to eat it, and accordingly placed a large leather bag under his loose coat, in such a position that he could convey the pudding into it without the deception being perceived. Breakfast at length being finished, Jack excited the giant's curiosity by offering to show him an extraordinary sleight of hand; so taking a knife, he ripped the leather bag, and out of course descended on the ground all the hasty pudding. The giant had not the slightest suspicion of the trick, veritably believing the pudding came from its natural receptacle; and having the same antipathy to being beaten, exclaimed in true Welsh, "Odds splutter, hur can do that trick hurself." The sequel may be readily guessed. The monster took the knife, and thinking to follow Jack's example with impunity, killed himself on the spot.

King Arthur's only son requested his father to furnish him with a large sum of money, in order that he might go and seek his fortune in the principality of Wales, where lived a beautiful lady possessed with seven evil spirits. The king tried all he could do to persuade him to alter his determination, but it was all in vain, so at last he granted his request, and the prince set out with two horses, one loaded with money, the other for himself to ride upon. Now, after several days' travel, he came to a market-town in Wales, where he beheld a vast concourse of people gathered together. The prince demanded the reason of it, and was told that they had arrested a corpse for several large sums of money which the deceased owed when he died. The prince replied that it was a pity creditors should be so cruel, and said, "Go bury the dead, and let his creditors come to my lodging, and there their debts shall be discharged." They accordingly came, but in such great numbers, that before night he had almost left himself penniless.

Now Jack the Giant-killer happened to be in the town while these transactions took place, and he was so pleased with the generosity exhibited by the prince, that he offered to become his servant, an offer which was immediately accepted. The next morning they set forward on their journey, when, as they were just leaving the town, an old woman called after the prince, saying, "He has owed me twopence these seven years; pray pay me as well as the rest." So reasonable and urgent a demand could not be resisted, and the prince immediately discharged the debt, but it took the last penny he had to accomplish it. This event, though generally ridiculed by heroes, was one by no means overlooked by the prince, who required all Jack's assuring eloquence to console him. Jack himself, indeed, had a very poor exchequer, and after their day's refreshment, they were entirely without money. When night drew on, the prince was anxious to secure a lodging, but as they had no means to hire one, Jack said, "Never mind, master, we shall do well enough, for I have an uncle lives within two miles of this place; he is a huge and monstrous giant with three heads; he'll fight five hundred men in armour, and make them flee before him." "Alas!" quoth the prince, "what shall we do there? He'll certainly chop us up at a mouthful. Nay, we are scarce enough to fill his hollow tooth!" "It is no matter for that," quoth Jack; "I myself will go before, and prepare the way for you; therefore tarry and wait till I return." Jack then rides off full speed, and coming to the gate of the castle, he knocked so loud that the neighbouring hills resounded like thunder. The giant, terribly vexed with the liberty taken by Jack, roared out, "Who's there?" He was answered, "None but your poor cousin Jack." Quoth he, "What news with my poor cousin

Jack?" He replied, "Dear uncle, heavy news." "God wot," quoth the giant, "prithee what heavy news can come to me? I am a giant with three heads, and besides thou knowest I can fight five hundred men in armour, and make them fly like chaff before the wind." "Oh, but," quoth Jack, "here's the prince a-coming with a thousand men in armour to kill you, and destroy all that you have!" "Oh, cousin Jack," said the giant, "this is heavy news indeed! I will immediately run and hide myself, and thou shalt lock, bolt, and bar me in, and keep the keys till the prince is gone." Jack joyfully complied with the giant's request, and fetching his master, they feasted and made themselves merry whilst the poor giant laid trembling in a vault under ground.

In the morning, Jack furnished the prince with a fresh supply of gold and silver, and then sent him three miles forward on his journey, concluding, according to the story-book, "he was then pretty well out of the smell of the giant." Jack afterwards returned, and liberated the giant from the vault, who asked what he should give him for preserving the castle from destruction. "Why," quoth Jack, "I desire nothing but the old coat and cap, together with the old rusty sword and slippers which are at your bed's head." Quoth the giant, "Thou shalt have them, and pray keep them for my sake, for they are things of excellent use; the coat will keep you invisible, the cap will furnish you with knowledge, the sword cuts asunder whatever you strike, and the shoes are of extraordinary swiftness. These may be serviceable to you: therefore take them with all my heart."

Jack was delighted with these useful presents, and having overtaken his master, they quickly arrived at the lady's house, who, finding the prince to be a suitor, prepared a splendid banquet for him. After the repast was concluded, she wiped his mouth with a handkerchief, and then concealed it in her dress, saying, "You must show me that handkerchief to-morrow morning, or else you will lose your head." The prince went to bed in great sorrow at this hard condition, but fortunately Jack's cap of knowledge instructed him how it was to be fulfilled. In the middle of the night she called upon her familiar to carry her to the evil spirit. Jack immediately put on his coat of darkness, and his shoes of swiftness, and was there before her, his coat rendering him invisible. When she entered the lower regions, she gave the handkerchief to the spirit, who laid it upon a shelf, whence Jack took it, and brought it to his master, who showed it to the lady the next day, and so saved his life. The next evening at supper she saluted the prince, telling him he must show her the lips tomorrow morning that she kissed last this night, or lose his head. He replied, "If you kiss none but mine, I will." "That is neither here nor there," said she, "if you do not, death is your portion!" At midnight she went below as before, and was angry with the spirit for letting the handkerchief go: "But now," quoth she, "I will be too hard for the prince, for I will kiss thee, and he is to show me thy lips." She did so, and Jack, who was standing by, cut off the spirit's head, and brought it under his invisible coat to his master, who produced it triumphantly the next morning before the lady. This feat destroyed the enchantment, the evil spirits immediately forsook her, and she appeared still more sweet and lovely, beautiful as she was before. They were married the next morning, and shortly afterwards went to the court of King Arthur, where Jack, for his eminent services, was created one of the knights of the Round Table.

Our hero, having been successful in all his undertakings, and resolving not to remain idle, but to perform what services he could for the honour of his country, humbly besought his majesty to fit him out with a horse and money to enable him to travel in search of new adventures; for, said he, "there are many giants yet living in the remote part of Wales, to the unspeakable damage of your majesty's subjects; wherefore may it please you to encourage me, I do not doubt but in a short time to cut them off root and branch, and so rid all the realm of those giants and monsters in human shape." We need scarcely say that Jack's generous offer was at once accepted. The king furnished him with the necessary accoutrements, and Jack set out with his magical cap, sword, and shoes, the better to perform the dangerous enterprises which now lay before him.

After travelling over several hills and mountains, the country through which he passed offering many impediments to travellers, on the third day he arrived at a very large wood, which he had no sooner entered than his ears were assailed with piercing shrieks. Advancing softly towards the place where the cries appeared to proceed from, he was horror-struck at perceiving a huge giant dragging along a fair lady, and a knight her husband, by the hair of their heads, "with as much ease," says the original narrative, "as if they had been a pair of gloves." Jack shed tears of pity on the fate of this hapless couple, but not suffering his feelings to render him neglectful of action, he put on his invisible coat, and taking with him his infallible sword, succeeded, after considerable trouble, and many cuts, to despatch the monster, whose dying groans were so terrible, that they made the whole wood ring again. The courteous knight and his fair lady were overpowered with gratitude, and, after returning Jack their best thanks, they invited him to their residence, there to recruit his strength after the frightful encounter, and receive more substantial demonstrations of their obligations to him. Jack, however, declared that he would not rest until he had found out the giant's habitation. The knight, on hearing his determination, was very sorrowful, and replied, "Noble stranger, it is too much to run a second hazard: this monster lived in a den under yonder mountain, with a brother more fierce and cruel than himself. Therefore, if you should go thither, and perish in the attempt, it would be a heart-breaking to me and my lady: let me persuade you to go with us, and desist from any further pursuit." The knight's reasoning had the very opposite effect that was intended, for Jack, hearing of another giant, eagerly embraced the opportunity of displaying his skill, promising, however, to return to the knight when he had accomplished his second labour.

He had not ridden more than a mile and a half, when the cave mentioned by the knight appeared to view, near the entrance of which he beheld the giant, sitting upon a block of timber, with a knotted iron club by his side, waiting, as he supposed, for his brother's return with his barbarous prey. This giant is described as having "goggle eyes like flames of fire, a countenance grim and ugly, cheeks like a couple of large flitches of bacon, the bristles of his beard resembling rods of iron wire, and locks that hung down upon his brawny shoulders like curled snakes or hissing adders." Jack alighted from his horse, and putting on the invisible coat, approached near the giant, and said softly, "Oh! are you there? it will not be long ere I shall take you fast by the beard." The giant all this while could not see him, on account of his invisible coat, so that Jack, coming up close to the monster, struck a blow with his sword at his head, but unfortunately missing his aim, he cut off the nose instead. The giant, as we may suppose, "roared like claps of thunder," and began to lay about him in all directions with his iron club so desperately, that even Jack was frightened, but exercising his usual ingenuity, he soon despatched him. After this, Jack cut off the giant's head, and sent it, together with that of his brother, to King Arthur, by a waggoner he hired for that purpose, who gave an account of all his wonderful proceedings.

The redoubtable Jack next proceeded to search the giant's cave in search of his treasure, and passing along through a great many winding passages, he came at length to a large room paved with freestone, at the upper end of which was a boiling caldron, and on the right hand a large table, at which the giants usually dined. After passing this dining-room, he came to a large and well-secured den filled with human captives, who were fattened and taken at intervals for food, as we do poultry. Jack set the poor prisoners at liberty, and, to compensate them for their sufferings and dreadful anticipations, shared the giant's treasure equally amongst them, and sent them to their homes overjoyed at their unexpected deliverance.

It was about sunrise when Jack, after the conclusion of this adventure, having had a good night's rest, mounted his horse to proceed on his journey, and, by the help of directions, reached the knight's house about noon. He was received with the most extraordinary demonstrations of joy, and his kind host, out of respect to Jack, prepared a feast which lasted many days, all the nobility and gentry in the neighbourhood being invited to it. The knight related the hero's adventures to his assembled guests, and presented him with a beautiful ring, on which was engraved a representation of the giant dragging the distressed knight and his lady, with this motto:

We were in sad distress you see,

> Under the giant's fierce command,
> But gain'd our lives and liberty
> By valiant Jack's victorious hand.

But earthly happiness is not generally of long duration, and so in some respects it proved on the present occasion, for in the midst of the festivities arrived a messenger with the dismal intelligence that one Thunderdell, a giant with two heads, having heard of the death of his two kinsmen, came from the north to be revenged on Jack, and was already within a mile of the knight's house, the country people flying before him in all directions. The intelligence had no effect on the dauntless Jack, who immediately said, "Let him come! I have a tool to pick his teeth;" and with this elegant assertion, he invited the guests to witness his performance from a high terrace in the garden of the castle.

It is now necessary to inform the reader that the knight's house or castle was situated in an island encompassed with a moat thirty feet deep, and twenty feet wide, passable by a drawbridge. Now Jack, intending to accomplish his purpose by a clever stratagem, employed men to cut through this drawbridge on both sides nearly to the middle; and then, dressing himself in his invisible coat, he marched against the giant with his well-tried sword. As he approached his adversary, although invisible, the giant, being, as it appears, an epicure in such matters, was aware of his approach, and exclaimed, in a fearful tone of voice—

> Fi, fee, fo, fum!
> I smell the blood of an English man!
> Be he alive or be he dead,
> I'll grind his bones to make me bread!

"Say you so," said Jack; "then you are a monstrous miller indeed." The giant, deeply incensed, replied, "Art thou that villain who killed my kinsman? then I will tear thee with my teeth, and grind thy bones to powder." "But," says Jack, still provoking him, "you must catch me first, if you please:" so putting aside his invisible coat, so that the giant might see him, and putting on his wonderful shoes, he enticed him into a chase by just approaching near enough to give him an apparent chance of capture. The giant, we are told, "followed like a walking castle, so that the very foundations of the earth seemed to shake at every step." Jack led him a good distance, in order that the wondering guests at the castle might see him to advantage, but at last, to end the matter, he ran over the drawbridge, the giant pursuing him with his club; but coming to the place where the bridge was cut, the giant's great weight burst it asunder, and he was precipitated into the moat, where he rolled about, says the author, "like a vast whale." While the monster was in this condition, Jack sadly bantered him about the boast he had made of grinding his bones to powder, but at length, having teased him sufficiently, a cart-rope was cast over the two heads of the giant, and he was drawn ashore by a team of horses, where Jack served him as he had done his relatives, cut off his heads, and sent them to King Arthur.

It would seem that the giant-killer rested a short time after this adventure, but he was soon tired of inactivity, and again went in search of another giant, the last whose head he was destined to chop off. After passing a long distance, he came at length to a large mountain, at the foot of which was a very lonely house. Knocking at the door, it was opened by "an ancient man, with a head as white as snow," who received Jack very courteously, and at once consented to his request for a lodging. Whilst they were at supper, the old man, who appears to have known more than was suspected, thus addressed the hero: "Son, I am sensible you are a conqueror of giants, and I therefore inform you that on the top of this mountain is an enchanted castle, maintained by a giant named Galligantus, who, by the help of a conjuror, gets many knights into his castle, where they are transformed into sundry shapes and forms: but, above all, I especially lament a duke's daughter, whom they took from her father's garden, bringing her through the air in a chariot drawn by fiery dragons, and securing her within the castle walls, transformed her into the shape of a hind. Now, though a great many knights have endeavoured to break the enchantment, and work her deliverance, yet no one has been able to accomplish it, on account of two fiery griffins which are placed at the gate, and which destroyed them at their approach; but you, my son, being furnished with an invisible coat, may pass by them undiscovered, and on the gates of the castle you will find engraven in large characters by what means the enchantment may be broken." The undaunted Jack at once accepted the commission, and pledged his faith to the old man to proceed early in the morning on this new adventure.

In the morning, as soon as it was daylight, Jack put on his invisible coat, and prepared himself for the enterprise. When he had reached the top of the mountain, he discovered the two fiery griffins, but, being invisible, he passed them without the slightest danger. When he had reached the gate of the castle, he noticed a golden trumpet attached to it, under which were written in large characters the following lines:

> Whoever doth this trumpet blow,
> Shall soon the giant overthrow,
> And break the black enchantment straight,
> So all shall be in happy state.

Jack at once accepted the challenge, and putting the trumpet to his mouth, gave a blast that made the hill re-echo. The castle trembled to its foundations, and the giant and conjuror were overstricken with fear, knowing that the reign of their enchantments was at an end. The former was speedily slain by Jack, but the conjuror, mounting up into the air, was carried away in a whirlwind, and never heard of more. The enchantments were immediately broken, and all the lords and ladies, who had so long been cruelly transformed, were standing on the native earth in their natural shapes, the castle having vanished with the conjuror.

The only relic of the giant which was left was the head, which Jack cut off in the first instance, and which we must suppose rolled away from the influence of the enchanted castle, or it would have "vanished into this air" with the body. It was fortunate that it did so, for it proved an inestimable trophy at the court of King Arthur, where Jack the Giant-killer was shortly afterwards united to the duke's daughter whom he had freed from enchantment, "not only to the joy of the court, but of all the kingdom." To complete his happiness, he was endowed with a noble house and estates, and his *penchant* for giant-killing having subsided, or, what is more probable, no more monsters appearing to interrupt his tranquillity, he accomplished the usual conclusion to these romantic narratives, by passing the remainder of his life in the enjoyment of every domestic felicity.

Jack the Giant Killer: a *c.* 1820 Penny Book

Introduction

This short book, published in Banbury around 1820 by John Golby Rusher (a leading producer of chapbooks), provides a good illustration of the later popular versions of this tale. The book itself is housed – as a single uncut sheet – in the de Grummond Children's Literature Research Collection at the University of Southern Mississippi.[1]

Text

> Kind Reader, Jack makes you a bow,
>   The hero of giants the dread;
> Whom king and the princes applaud
>   For valour, whence tyranny fled.
>
> In Cornwall, on Saint Michael's Mount,
>   A giant full eighteen feet high,
> Nine feet round, in cavern did dwell,
>   For food cleared the fields and the sty.
>
> And, glutton, would feast on poor souls,
>   Whom chance might have led in his way;
> Or gentleman, lady, or child,
>   Or what on his hands he could lay.

He went over to the main land, in search of food, when he would throw oxen or cows on his back, and several sheep and pigs, and with them wade to his abode in the cavern.

> Till Jack's famed career made him quake,
>   Blew his horn, took mattock and spade;

1   'The Jack and the Beanstalk and Jack the Giant-Killer Project', edited by Michael N. Salda, at *www.usm.edu/english/fairytales/jack/jackhome.html*.

Dug twenty feet deep near his den,
    And covered the pit he had made.

The giant declared he'd devour
    For breakfast who dared to come near;
And leizurely did Blunderbore
    Walk heavily into the snare.

Then Jack with his pickaxe commenced,
    The giant most terribly did roar;
He thus made an end of the first–
    The terrible Giant Blunderbore.

His brother, who heard of Jack's feat,
    Did vow he'd repent of his blows,
From Castle Enchantment, in wood,
    Near which Jack did shortly repose.

This giant, discovering our hero, weary and fast asleep in the wood, carried him to his castle, and locked him up in a large room, the floor of which was covered with the bones of men and women. Soon after, the giant went to invite his friend Rebecks, to make a meal of Jack; who saw the monsters approaching, and put on his cap of knowledge, to consider how he might best extricate himself from portending dangers.

The giant and friend, arm in arm,
    John liked not the look of Rebecks;
He found a strong cord with a noose,
    And briskly slipt over their necks.

He fastened the cord to a beam,
    And boldly slid down with his sword;
He severed their heads in a trice;
    To free all confined he gave word.

History informs us that he took the keys of the castle from the girdle of Giant Blunderbore, and made search through the building; where he found three ladies tied up by the hair of their heads to a beam; they told him their husbands had been killed by the giants, and themselves were condemned to death, because they would not partake of the remains of their deceased husbands. Ladies, said Jack, I have put an end to the wicked monster and his giant friend Rebecks!

Great lords and fine ladies were there,
    Suspended or tied to great hooks;
Most heartily thanked our friend John;
    Recorded his fame in those books.

The ladies all thought him divine,
    The nobles invited him home:
The castle he gave for their use,
    And he for adventures did roam.

At length John came to a handsome building, he was informed was inhabited by an enormous Welchman, the terror of the surrounding neighbourhood, not very likely to prove friendly to our hero, and gave a genteel rat, tat, too, at the door.

At this Giant-castle, most grand,
    The Welchman meets John at the door;
Gives welcome, and food, and a bed,
    But Jack saves his life on the floor.

The old account of the difficult season informs us that John overheard the giant Welchman utter the following not very agreeable lines:–

Though here you lodge with me this night,
    You shall not see the morning light;
My club shall dash your brains out quite!

John's considering cap is again in request, and finding a log of wood he placed it between the sheets, and hid himself, to witness the giant's anger and club law.

Mid darkness, the giant his bed
    Belabours the post John put there;
And safe in the corner he crept,
    Behind the great giant's arm chair.

Early in the morning Jack walked into the giant's room, to thank him for his lodging. The giant surprised to see him, so early he appeared to say, and continued–

You slept well, my friend, in your bed?
    Did nought in your slumbers assail?

John did to his querist reply,
    A rat gave some flaps with his tail.

Jack thanked the giant for his excellent night's sleep, and although the Welchman was surprised that he had not killed him, he did not express more, but fetched two large bowls of pudding, for his own and his lodger's repast, thinking Jack never could empty one of them.

Hasty pudding for breakfast was brought,
    And John took much more than his friend;
Which slipt in his large leather bag,
    The giant could not comprehend.

Says Jack, Now I'll shew you a trick–
    "A tat" for a giant's trap-door!
He ript up his large leather bag,
    And breakfast bespatter'd the floor.

Ods splutter hur nails, says his host,
    Hur can do that too, without dread;
But Taff made a fatal attack,
    And Jack in a trice doff'd his head.

John seized all his riches and house,
    And bountiful was to the poor;
The pris'ners released from their chains,
    Which bound them in pain to the floor.

In search of new adventures, our hero beheld a relative of the late highlander, dragging to the abode Jack had made his own by stratagem, a noble Knight and his affianced lady, and soon determined his mode of deliverance for them.

A cousin, not heard of his fate,
    Seized Sir Knight and a lady so fair,
When coming to see giant friend,
    And dragg'd them with force by the hair.

Jack donn'd his invisible coat,
    Sharp sword and swift shoes for the fray;
He rescued the knight and the fair,
    And great mighty giant did slay.

His cap for much knowledge and skill,
 He used in encounters most rare;
His sword all the giants did kill,
 For speed none his shoes could compare.

Jack having hitherto been successful,determined not to be idle; he therefore resolved to travel, and to take his horse of matchless speed, his cap of knowledge, his sword of sharpness, his elastic shoes of swiftness, and invisible coat, over hill and dale.

Tradition states, that Jack passed through the counties of Oxford, Warwick, and Northampton; and visited the University, Crouchhill, Banbury-cross and Castle, the Amphitheatre in Bear-garden, Wroxton, Edge-hill, &c.

He travelled the country around,
 East, west, north and south, far and near;
Abroad or at home he was found,
 Where he of a giant could hear.

Jack was informed by an old hermit, at the foot of a high mountain, of an enchanted castle, at the top of the mount inhabited by Galligantus and a magician, where they had imprisoned a duke's daughter and her companions: he soon climbed to the summit, and read these lines:–

Whoever can this trumpet blow,
 Shall cause the giant's overthrow.

Jack blew a loud shrill blast, having on his invisible dress, with his trusty sword by his side: the giant and magician looked for the intruder, but soon exhibited each an headless trunk, when he released the inmates, whom he wished to share the vast riches of the magician's treasury. The duke's daughter plainly informed him that she would willingly do so on one condition, which was speedily arranged on the arrival of the duke and his duchess.

St. George the great dragon did slay,
 Hunters wild boars make compliant,
And beasts of the forest way-lay;
 Jack is the dread of the giant.
Pray who has not heard of his fame?
 His actions so bold and unpliant;
The friend of the rich and the poor,

But never afraid of a giant.

A monster had heard of his fame,
   And vowed he would render him pliant;
He sat on a stone at his door,
   Jack cut off the nose of the giant.

He soon found the edge of his blade,
   Became a most humble suppliant;
And, while he complained of the pain,
   Jack took off the head of the giant.

Jack threatens,–all braggarts beware!
   And coward poltroons he makes pliant;
And thus all vain-glorious puffs
   Are silenced as Jack served the giant.

The Castle-enchantment he razed,
   Magician is made more compliant,
Duke's daughter he rescues from harm,
   Lords, ladies, he saves from the giant.

Duke's daughter, with riches in store,
   To admire our hero not slack;
In marriage they soon did unite,
   The king gave great riches to Jack.

His wife and his children were kind,
   Friends place in him great reliance;
His boys were at college refined,
   His girls told the tale of the giants.

FINIS.

Some Arthurian Giant-Killings

Introduction

Presented below are a number of Arthurian giant-killings, ranging from those belonging to the earliest stratum of the legend through to Welsh folklore of the seventeenth century. In general, Arthur and his men – like Jack – killed their gigantic enemies through a mixture of cunning and extreme violence. Indeed, as both I and others have argued, such tales as these ought to be considered essential source material for Jack's role as the exterminator of all Britain's giants.[1] Certainly, this seems to have been originally a role assigned to Arthur in Welsh and Cornish folklore, with Jack only taking it over in English chapbooks from the early eighteenth century. As one old Cornishman put it, the whole land at one time 'swarmed with giants, until Arthur, the good king, vanished them all with his cross-sword'.[2]

Texts

a. *Culhwch ac Olwen* [3]

[Arthur's men[4] go in search of the first item that they need to complete their

---

1   T. Green, 'Tom Thumb and Jack the Giant-Killer: Two Arthurian Fairy Tales?', *Folklore*, 118.2 (2007), pp. 123-40; C. Grooms, *The Giants of Wales. Cewri Cymru.* Welsh Studies volume 10 (Lampeter: Edwin Meller, 1993), who says of Arthur's giant-killing that it is 'a tradition that precedes and informs the popular chapbook tales of Jack the Giant-killer' (p. 1).

2   R. Hunt, *Popular Romances of the West of England. The Drolls, Traditions and Superstitions of Old Cornwall,* two volumes (reprint of 1881 edition, Felinfach: Llanerch Publishers, 1993), II, p. 307. It should be noted that Arthur as a giant-killer was present in the early to mid-nineteenth-century folklore collected by Hunt, but Jack was nowhere to be found.

3   *The Mabinogion,* translated by C. Guest (London: Bernard Quaritch, 1877), pp. 243-45, 249-50; Wrnach's name has been put into its correct form, rather than Guest's 'Gwrnach'.

4   In *Culhwch ac Olwen* Arthur is not present at this killing, but it seems likely that he was in fact present in the underlying tale that was being used by the author of *Culhwch* and has been simply omitted; thus in the arguably earlier poem *Pa gur?*

quest, the sword of Wrnach the Giant]

All that day they journeyed until the evening, and then they beheld a vast castle, which was the largest in the world. And lo, a black man, huger than three of the men of this world, came out from the castle. And they spoke unto him, "Whence comest thou, O man?" "From the castle which you see yonder." "Whose castle is that?" asked they. "Stupid are ye truly, O men. There is no one in the world that does not know to whom this castle belongs. It is the castle of Wrnach the Giant." "What treatment is there for guests and strangers that alight in that castle?" "Oh! Chieftain, Heaven protect thee. No guest ever returned thence alive, and no one may enter therein unless he brings with him his craft."

Then they proceeded towards the gate. Said Gwrhyr Gwalstawd Ieithoedd ['Interpreter of Tongues'], "Is there a porter?" "There is. And thou, if thy tongue be not mute in thy head, wherefore dost thou call?" "Open the gate." "I will not open it." "Wherefore wilt thou not?" "The knife is in the meat, and the drink is in the horn, and there is revelry in the hall of Wrnach the Giant, and except for a craftsman who brings his craft, the gate will not be opened to-night." "Verily, porter," then said Kai, "my craft bring I with me." "What is thy craft?" "The best burnisher of swords am I in the world." "I will go and tell this unto Wrnach the Giant, and I will bring thee an answer."

So the porter went in, and Wrnach said to him, "Hast thou any news from the gate?" "I have. There is a party at the door of the gate who desire to come in." "Didst thou inquire of them if they possessed any art?" "I did inquire," said he, "and one told me that he was well skilled in the burnishing of swords." "We have need of him then. For some time have I sought for some one to polish my sword, and could find no one. Let this man enter, since he brings with him his craft." The porter thereupon returned and opened the gate. And Kai went in by himself, and he saluted Wrnach the Giant. And a chair was placed for him opposite to Wrnach. And Wrnach said to him, "Oh man! is it true that is reported of thee that thou knowest how to burnish swords?" "I know full well how to do so," answered Kai. Then was the sword of Wrnach brought to him. And Kai took a blue whetstone from under his arm, and asked him whether he would have it burnished white or blue. "Do with it as it seems good to thee, and as though wouldest if it were thine own." Then Kai polished one half of the blade and put it in his hand. "Will this please thee?" asked he. "I would rather than all that is in my dominions that the whole of it were like unto this. It is a marvel to me that such a man as thou should be without a companion."

Arthur is described as fighting in 'Awarnach's hall', this Awarnach almost certainly being *Culhwch*'s Wrnach: see T. Green, *Concepts of Arthur* (Stroud: Tempus, 2007), pp. 84, 109, 112-15.

"Oh! noble sir, I have a companion, albeit he is not skilled in this art."
"Who may he be?" "Let the porter go forth and I will tell him whereby he
may know him. The head of his lance will leave its shaft, and draw blood
from the wind, and will descend upon its shaft again." Then the gate was
opened, and Bedwyr entered. And Kai said, "Bedwyr is very skilful,
although he knows not this art."

And there was much discourse among those who were without, because
that Kai and Bedwyr had gone in. And a young man who was with them,
the only son of Custennin the herdsman, got in also. And he caused all his
companions to keep close to him as he passed the three wards, and until he
came into the midst of the castle. And his companions said unto the son of
Custennin, "Thou hast done this! Thou art the best of all men." And
thenceforth he was called Goreu ['best'], the son of Custennin. Then they
dispersed to their lodgings, that they might slay those who lodged therein,
unknown to the Giant.

The sword was now polished, and Kai gave it unto the hand of Wrnach
the Giant, to see if he were pleased with his work. And the Giant said, "The
work is good, I am content therewith." Said Kai, "It is thy scabbard that
hath rusted thy sword, give it to me that I may take out the wooden sides of
it and put in new ones." And he took the scabbard from him, and the sword
in the other hand. And he came and stood over against the Giant, as if he
would have put the sword into the scabbard; and with it he struck at the
head of the Giant, and cut off his head at one blow. Then they despoiled
the castle, and took from it what goods and jewels they would. And again
on the same day, at the beginning of the year, they came to Arthur's Court,
bearing with them the sword of Wrnach the Giant.

*

[The obtaining of the leash made from Dillus' beard]

As Kai and Bedwyr sat on a beacon carn on the summit of Plinlimmon [*i.e.*
Carn Gwylathyr on Pumlumon], in the highest wind that ever was in the
world, they looked around them, and saw a great smoke towards the south,
afar off, which did not bend with the wind. Then said Kai, "By the hand of
my friend, behold, yonder is the fire of a robber!" Then they hastened
towards the smoke, and they came so near to it, that they could see Dillus
Varvawc ['the Bearded'] scorching a wild boar. "Behold, yonder is the
greatest robber that ever fled from Arthur,"[1] said Bedwyr unto Kai. "Dost

---

1   Again Arthur is not present in the telling of this tale in *Culhwch*, but this phrase
     makes reference to the existence of other tales of Dillus in which Arthur was
     involved: on this tale, which was also told in Welsh folklore, see Green, *Concepts
     of Arthur*, pp. 115-16 and Grooms, *Giants of Wales*, pp. 167-68. Furthermore, it is

thou know him?" "I do know him," answered Kai, "he is Dillus Varvawc, and no leash in the world will be able to hold Drudwyn, the cub of Greid the son of Eri, save a leash made from the beard of him thou seest yonder. And even that will be useless, unless his beard be plucked alive with wooden tweezers; for if dead, it will be brittle." "What thinkest thou that we should do concerning this?" said Bedwyr. "Let us suffer him," said Kai, "to eat as much as he will of the meat, and after that he will fall asleep." And during that time they employed themselves in making the wooden tweezers. And when Kai knew certainly that he was asleep, he made a pit under his feet, the largest in the world, and he struck him a violent blow, and squeezed him into the pit. And there they twitched out his beard completely with the wooden tweezers; and after that they slew him altogether.

And from thence they both went to Gelli Wic, in Cornwall, and took the leash made of Dillus Varvawc's beard with them, and they gave it into Arthur's hand.

b. Geoffrey of Monmouth's Historia Regum Britanniae [1]

In the meantime Arthur had news brought him, that a giant of monstrous size was come from the shores of Spain, and had forcibly taken away Helena, the niece of Duke Hoel, from her guard, and fled with her to the top of that which is now called Michael's Mount; and that the soldiers of the country who pursued him were able to do nothing against him. For whether they attacked him by sea or land, he either overturned their ships with vast rocks, or killed them with several sorts of darts, besides many of them that he took and devoured half alive.

The next night, therefore, at the second hour, Arthur, taking along with him Caius the sewer, and Bedver the butler, went out privately from the camp, and hastened towards the mountain. For being a man of undaunted courage, he did not care to lead his army against such monsters; both because he could in this manner animate his men by his own example, and also because he was alone sufficient to deal with them.

As soon as they came near the mountain, they saw a fire burning upon the top of it, and another on a lesser mountain, that was not far from it. And being in doubt upon which of them the giant dwelt, they sent away Bedver to know the certainty of the matter. So he, finding a boat, sailed

---

clearly related to the tale of Arthur's killing of Ritho/Retho, found in Geoffrey of Monmouth's *Historia Regum Britanniae* and Welsh folklore (Green, *Concepts of Arthur*, p. 116).

1   *Historia Regum Britanniae*, X.3, translated by J. A. Giles in *The British History of Geoffrey of Monmouth* (London: James Bohn, 1842), pp. 205-08. See the following on the two tales contained within this chapter: Green, *Concepts of Arthur*, pp. 116-18, and Grooms, *Giants of Wales*, pp. 214-18.

over in it first to the lesser mountain, to which he could in no other way have access, because it was situated in the sea. When he had begun to climb up to the top of it, he was at first frightened with a dismal howling cry of a woman from above, and imagined the monster to be there: but quickly rousing up his courage, he drew his sword, and having reached the top, found nothing but the fire which he had before seen at a distance. He discovered also a grave newly made, and an old woman weeping and howling by it, who at the sight of him instantly cried out in words interrupted with sighs, "O, unhappy man, what misfortune brings you to this place? O the inexpressible tortures of death that you must suffer! I pity you, I pity you, because the detestable monster will this night destroy the flower of your youth. For that most wicked and odious giant, who brought the duke's niece, whom I have just now buried here, and me, her nurse, along with her into this mountain, will come and immediately murder you in a most cruel manner. O deplorable fate! This most illustrious princess, sinking under the fear her tender heart conceived, while the foul monster would have embraced her, fainted away and expired. And when he could not satiate his brutish lust upon her, who was the very soul, joy, and happiness of my life, being enraged at the disappointment of his bestial desire, he forcibly committed a rape upon me, who (let God and my old age witness) abhorred his embraces. Fly, dear sir, fly, for fear he may come, as he usually does, to lie with me, and finding you here most barbarously butcher you."

Bedver, moved at what she said, as much as it is possible for human nature to be, endeavoured with kind words to assuage her grief, and to comfort her with the promise of speedy help: and then returned back to Arthur, and gave him an account of what he had met with. Arthur very much lamented the damsel's sad fate, and ordered his companions to leave him to deal with him alone; unless there was an absolute necessity, and then they were to come in boldly to his assistance. From hence they went directly to the next mountain, leaving their horses with their armour-bearers, and ascended to the top, Arthur leading the way.

The deformed savage was then by the fire, with his face besmeared with the clotted blood of swine, part of which he had already devoured, and was roasting the remainder upon spits by the fire. But at the sight of them, whose appearance was a surprise to him, he hastened to his club, which two strong men could hardly lift from the ground. Upon this the king drew his sword, and guarding himself with his shield, ran with all his speed to prevent his getting it. But the other, who was not ignorant of his design, had by this time snatched it up, and gave the king such a terrible blow upon his shield, that he made the shores ring with the noise, and perfectly stunned the king's ears with it. Arthur, fired with rage at this, lifted up his sword, and gave him a wound in the forehead, which was not indeed mortal, but yet such as made the blood gush out over his face and eyes, and so blinded him;

for he had partly warded off the stroke from his forehead with his club, and prevented its being fatal. However, his loss of sight, by reason of the blood flowing over his eyes, made him exert himself with greater fury, and like an enraged boar against a hunting-spear, so did he rush in against Arthur's sword, and grasping him about the waist, forced him down upon his knees. But Arthur, nothing daunted, slipped out of his hands, and so bestirred himself with his sword, that he gave the giant no respite till he had struck it up to the very back through his skull. At this the hideous monster raised a dreadful roar, and like an oak torn up from the roots by the winds, so did he make the ground resound with his fall Arthur, bursting out into a fit of laughter at the sight, commanded Bedver to cut off his head, and give it to one of the armour-bearers, who was to carry it to the camp, and there expose it to public view, but with orders for the spectators of this combat to keep silence.

He told them he had found none of so great strength, since he killed the giant Ritho, who had challenged him to fight, upon the mountain Aravius. This giant had made himself furs of the beards of kings he had killed, and had sent word to Arthur carefully to flea off his beard and send it to him; and then, out of respect to his pre-eminence over other kings, his beard should have the honour of the principal place. But if he refused to do it, he challenged him to a duel, with this offer, that the conqueror should have the furs, and also the beard of the vanquished for a trophy of his victory. In this conflict, therefore, Arthur proved victorious, and took the beard and spoils of the giant; and, as he said before, had met with none that could be compared to him for strength, till his last engagement. After this victory, they returned at the second watch of the night to the camp with the head; to see which there was a great concourse of people, all extolling this wonderful exploit of Arthur, by which he had freed the country from a most destructive and voracious monster. But Hoel, in great grief for the loss of his niece, commanded a mausoleum to be built over her body in the mountain where she was buried, which, taking the damsel's name, is called Helena's Tomb to this day.

c. *Malory's Le Morte Darthur* [1]

[Arthur comes upon the giant of Mont St Michel]

Then the glutton anon started up, and took a great club in his hand, and smote at the king that his coronal fell to the earth. And the king hit him again that he carved his belly and cut off his genitours, that his guts and his

---

1   Modernised version of Malory's *Le Morte Darthur*, Book V, chapters five and eight, translated by E. Strachey and A. W. Pollard, made available online by the Project Gutenberg: *http://www.gutenberg.org/dirs/etext98/1mart10.txt*

entrails fell down to the ground. Then the giant threw away his club, and caught the king in his arms that he crushed his ribs. Then the three maidens kneeled down and called to Christ for help and comfort of Arthur. And then Arthur weltered and wrung, that he was other while under and another time above. And so weltering and wallowing they rolled down the hill till they came to the sea mark, and ever as they so weltered Arthur smote him with his dagger.

And it fortuned they came to the place whereas the two knights were and kept Arthur's horse; then when they saw the king fast in the giant's arms they came and loosed him. And then the king commanded Sir Kay to smite off the giant's head, and to set it upon a truncheon of a spear, and bear it to Sir Howell, and tell him that his enemy was slain; and after let this head be bound to a barbican that all the people may see and behold it; and go ye two up to the mountain, and fetch me my shield, my sword, and the club of iron; and as for the treasure, take ye it, for ye shall find there goods out of number; so I have the kirtle and the club I desire no more. This was the fiercest giant that ever I met with, save one in the mount of Araby, which I overcame, but this was greater and fiercer. Then the knights fetched the club and the kirtle, and some of the treasure they took to themselves, and returned again to the host.

*

[At the Battle of Soissons]

Then the battles approached and shoved and shouted on both sides, and great strokes were smitten on both sides, many men overthrown, hurt, and slain; and great valiances, prowesses and appertices of war were that day showed, which were over long to recount the noble feats of every man, for they should contain an whole volume. But in especial, King Arthur rode in the battle exhorting his knights to do well, and himself did as nobly with his hands as was possible a man to do; he drew out Excalibur his sword, and awaited ever whereas the Romans were thickest and most grieved his people, and anon he addressed him on that part, and hew and slew down right, and rescued his people; and he slew a great giant named Galapas, which was a man of an huge quantity and height, he shorted him and smote off both his legs by the knees, saying, Now art thou better of a size to deal with than thou were, and after smote off his head.

d. John Leland's Itinerary [1]

The first River be side *Tyne* that I passid over was Clardue [Claerddu], that is to say *Blak Clare*, no great Streame but cumming thorough Cragges. In the farther Side of hit I saw ii. veri poore Cotagis for Somer Dayres for Catel. and hard by were ii. Hillettes, thorough the wich *Clarduy* passith, wher they fable that a Gigant striding was wont to wasch his Hondes, and that *Arture* killid hym. The Dwellers say also that the Gigant was buried therby, and shew the Place.

e. Siôn Dafydd Rhys on Cewri Cymru ('Welsh Giants') [2]

And all these Giants were of enormous size, and (they were) in the time of Idris Gawr, which Idris was king and chief over them. And in the land of Meirionydd also, and close to Penn Aran in Penllyn, and under the place called Bwlch-y-groes, is a grave of great size, where they say Lytta or Ritta or Rithonwy or Itto Gawr was buried; whose body some of the tribe of Giants moved from Eryri to somewhere near Mynydd Aran Fawr in Penllyn. This Ricca Gawr was the one with whom Arthur had fought and killed in Eryri. And this Giant had made for himself a mantle (pilis) of beards of the kings he had killed. And he sent to Arthur to order him to cut off his own beard and send it to him. And as Arthur was chief of the kings, he would place his beard above the other beards as an honour to Arthur. And if he would not do that, he asked Arthur to come and fight with him, and that the strongest of them should make a mantle from the beard of the other. And when they went to fight, Arthur obtained the victory, and he took the Giant's beard and his mantle.

---

1   John Leland, *The Itinerary of John Leland the Antiquary, in Nine Volumes*, third edition (Oxford: James Fletcher and Joseph Pote, 1770), V, p. 83.

2   R. Bromwich and D. Simon Evans (ed.), *Culhwch and Olwen. An edition and study of the oldest Arthurian tale* (Cardiff, 1992), p. lvii. Further Arthurian giant-killings recorded from Welsh folklore by Rhys can be found above (p. 145) and in C. Grooms, *The Giants of Wales. Cewri Cymru*, Welsh Studies volume 10 (Lampeter: Edwin Meller, 1993), pp. 300-05, 310-13, 316.

6

Miscellaneous Arthuriana

An Arthurian FAQ: Some Frequently Asked Questions

1. Was there a historical Arthur?

Yes, and no. If by Arthur you mean the person who supposedly led the British counter-attack against the Anglo-Saxons in the later 5th century, culminating in the famous Battle of Badon Hill, then the answer is simply 'yes'. Such a character did indeed exist – we have the evidence for his existence (and that of his most famous battle) in Gildas' *De Excidio Britanniae*, written *c.* 540 AD. However, if you mean something else then the answer is probably 'no'.

> ➤ Was Arthur one of the four or five people named Arthur that we have in southern Wales and southern Scotland, born between *c.* 550-625 AD? No, it seems most unlikely – they are born too late to fight Badon (the only specific element of the Arthurian legend which can be confirmed as genuinely historical and which is present in the earliest 'historical' Arthurian sources) and their characters and known deeds seem implausible for such a role as the founder of a great legend.

> ➤ Was 'Arthur' a title? No, there is absolutely no reason to think that this is the case. This is simply many historical-Arthur theorists' way of getting around the awkward fact that whomsoever they wish to claim is Arthur – Urien of Rheged, Cuneglasus, Cerdic – was never actually called Arthur.

> ➤ Was the British leader at Badon actually called Arthur then? No, he was probably called Ambrosius Aurelianus, as Padel has demonstrated. Arthur looks to be the name of a folkloric or mythical Hero and monster-killer whose tales got mixed up with the above historical deeds in the early 9th century, leading to these being re-attributed to this folkloric hero. (This was, it must be stressed, a surprisingly common occurrence in medieval literature and pseudo-history).

➤ Finally, was the British leader at Badon anything like the Arthur of medieval legend, or did he just contribute the historical framework and the battle of Badon to the later legend? The latter is almost certainly the case. There is virtually no trace of history in the early Arthurian legend (see, for example, *Culhwch ac Olwen*), whilst the familiar later medieval stories of Arthur are just that: stories, not history. Bizarre notions of the victor of Badon as someone who rode with a band of knights all around late 5th-century/early 6th-century Britain are a modern academic fantasy.

2. If the historical victor at Badon was called Arthur, where would he have been based?

An interesting question. Many historians have preferred to place such a figure in southern Britain, on the basis of an assumption that this is where Badon was fought (usually it is equated with Bath or Badbury Rings). Many Celticists have preferred to place him in northern Britain, somewhere in the east between the River Humber and Edinburgh, on the basis of *Y Gododdin* and other legendary material. Many enthusiasts continue to place him in Cornwall, north Wales, Cumbria, Essex, Glasgow, Shropshire and almost anywhere else you can think of. The only possible way of locating such a 5th-century figure would be to use the battles listed in the *Historia Brittonum*, in particular the only one of these which can be confirmed as historical, Badon. This battle is, unfortunately, unlocated – all suggestions are more or less speculation, with there being little solid evidence available to go on. To quote J.N.L. Myres, 'the site of *Mons Badonicus* in the absence of any early topographical information... remains anyone's guess.' However, given that it is a battle against the invading Anglo-Saxons, it does seem only reasonable that it (and thus any such Arthur) should be placed somewhere in Britain where there were Anglo-Saxons in significant numbers *c.* 500 AD – that is to say, in southern Britain across to roughly Bath, or in eastern Britain up to the East Riding of Yorkshire.

3. If the historical victor at Badon was called Arthur, was he a king, emperor or battle-leader?

Arthur is certainly described as a 'leader of battles' (*dux bellorum*) in the *Historia Brittonum* but, as Jackson and others have pointed out, this doesn't necessarily mean he wasn't a king. Nonetheless, the earliest sources to describe him as a king come from the 11th century and are legendary in character, so cannot be relied upon. One early poem does call him 'emperor', *ameraudur* (< Latin *imperator*), which might foreshadow Geoffrey of Monmouth's Arthur in the *Historia Regum Britanniae*. On the other hand, we must be cautious, as the strict meaning of the word is probably closer to 'general, commander' in Welsh usage. To be honest, if he was a sub-Roman emperor of Britain then he has left remarkably few traces of his existence and status in the early sources. Given all this it is probably best to stick with the *Historia Brittonum*'s description of him as a battle-leader, though even this is uncertain and may be Biblically-derived by the author of the *Historia*, rather than a genuine reflection of any such Arthur's status. If it was a genuine description of his status, it should be taken to simply mean what it says – theories that make *dux bellorum* not a literal statement but an official title or position, analogous to the known Late Roman *Comes Britanniae*, are more 'colourful' than plausible. To quote Myres once more, 'if we add anything to the bare statement that Arthur may have lived and fought the Saxons, we pass at once from history to Romance.'

4. Was Arthur Riotamus? Can we use Geoffrey of Monmouth to reconstruct 'Arthurian history'?

No. Geoffrey is a highly inventive historian whose claim to possess a now-lost 'ancient book' cannot be in any way trusted. He rather seems to be indulging in the 'old book' claim to try and enhance the reputation of his work. His *Historia Regum Britanniae* looks to have taken themes, motifs, names and narrative elements from a great variety of sources, with Geoffrey weaving them together into a work that is undoubtedly his own creation. Where we can identify his sources, he has manipulated and altered them to a very great degree. As to Riotamus, if Ashe is right in identifying him as one of the sources of Geoffrey's portrayal of Arthur, this has little meaning from an insular perspective. There is no hint that Riotamus was Arthur in the Welsh sources and the theory has been recently dismissed as nothing more than 'straws in the wind', with Riotamus clearly being a name, not a title. If he is reflected in Geoffrey's work then this is either Geoffrey's own contribution to the Arthurian legend or, just possibly, a Breton historicisation of Arthur with the deeds of Riotamus (though the latter depends on the highly dubious evidence of the *Life of Saint Goueznou*, which does itself paraphrase the *Historia Brittonum* and may be influenced by Geoffrey).

5. What is the earliest reference to the Arthurian legend?

The *Y Gododdin* reference, which describes Arthur as a military superhero (to whom a man who killed 300 cannot compare), may go back to before 638 AD, but this is not certain. The *Marwnad Cynddylan* mention of Arthur, which seems to have the same concept of Arthur as *Y Gododdin*, is generally admitted to have its origins in the mid-7th century, if the emendation of *artir* to *artur* is correct (as it almost certainly is). The tales of Arthur raiding the Otherworld in *Preideu Annwfyn* probably go back to before the late 8th century, and the features used to date them thus would also be present in compositions of the 7th century. The folklore in chapter 73 of the *Historia Brittonum* (which includes a reference to Arthur's 'Wild' hunt of the divine, destructive and enormous boar *Twrch Trwyd*) has been recently considered 'already ancient' by the 9th century. These would seem to be some of the earliest Arthurian references and they are discussed in detail, along with other potential members of the 'earliest stratum' of the Arthurian legend, in chapter two of *Concepts of Arthur*.

6. What is the earliest reference to Arthur as a historical figure?

The earliest source which demonstrably possesses a concept of Arthur as a historical figure is the *Historia Brittonum*, sometimes known as 'Nennius'. This is now generally agreed to have been a work of synthetic pseudo-history, unassociated with Nennius and written in the early 9th century – either in 829 or 830 AD (not the 7th century, or '*c.* 800' as some older books state). Thus the first reference to a historical Arthur comes from over 300 years after he is supposed to have fought Badon; he is not mentioned in any of the contemporary or near-contemporary sources that we possess. Although there is a theory that an Old Welsh battle-listing poem underlies the *Historia*'s account, this is both purely hypothetical and would help us little even if this weren't the case (see now chapter one of *Concepts of Arthur* for a very full discussion). Speculation that the *Annales Cambriae* ('Welsh Annals') mentions of Arthur have their origins in 6th-century Easter tables is also now dismissed as nonsense – these entries look to be solidly 10th century in origin and most probably derivative in their concept of Arthur of the *Historia Brittonum*.

7. What do you mean by 'Galfridian', 'pre-Galfridian' and 'non-Galfridian'?

'Galfridian' comes from the name of Geoffrey of Monmouth, which is in Latin *Galfridus Monemutensis*. Galfridian and post-Galfridian literature refers to Geoffrey's own works and those later sources which are clearly derivative of his work, most especially his *Historia Regum Britanniae*. Pre-Galfridian literature is that which is generally agreed to date from before Geoffrey wrote his *HRB*, that is *c.* 1138. Non-Galfridian literature is that which, though it may be later in date than *c.* 1138, shows no signs of being derivative of, or even aware of, Geoffrey's work.

8. Is all continental Arthurian literature post-Galfridian?

To some degree, yes – most continental sources show an awareness of Geoffrey, or the work of one of his translators and adaptors (such as Wace). However, there is much in continental literature that shows no indebtedness to Geoffrey. The majority of this is undoubtedly the result of the imagination of continental writers such as Chrétien de Troyes, or classical and other non-Arthurian sources that have been utilised by them. Nonetheless, some elements may represent a continental take on genuinely non-Galfridian Arthurian tradition, such as the abduction of Gwenhwyfar or the killing of Arthur by *Cath Paluc*. It should not be forgotten that in places such as Spain and Italy there is evidence for a knowledge of the Arthurian legend by perhaps *c.* 1100.

9. Is Cornwall really 'King Arthur Country'?

Certainly Cornwall knew of Arthur. In the 18th century it could be said that 'whatever is great, and the use and Author unknown, is attributed to Arthur' – Arthurian folklore, including his halls, his seats, his chairs, his caves and his tables, filled the countryside. However, this was equally true in Wales too. Going back to the pre-Galfridian period we do not, in fact, find Cornwall dominating the record. In the 11th-century *Culhwch ac Olwen* and the pre-Galfridian Early Version of *Trioedd Ynys Prydein* we find Arthur's court placed in Cornwall – though it is at the unlocated, possibly unlocatable, *Kelli wic* ('forest-grove') not Camelot, or Tintagel. We also find evidence for a belief in Arthur as still alive being so strong in Cornwall that riots could be started when his ever-lasting nature was denied. However, other early sources associate his legend with Wales, or Somerset, or Scotland. This is true even at the level of the 'earliest stratum' of material, that dating before *c.* 900 AD. Here we find knowledge of Arthur and the Arthurian legend in Brittany, south Wales, the Welsh Marches, Shropshire, north Wales and southern Scotland – essentially across the entire Brittonic-speaking world. Indeed, if we go back to the very earliest hints of the existence of the Arthurian legend, the two men born *c.* 550 AD and named Arthur, one was from southern Wales and one from southern Scotland. The Arthurian legend looks to have been pan-Brittonic (common to all British speakers) and unlocalised from the very first.

10. How many children did Arthur have in non-Galfridian Welsh tradition?

Many, it would seem. His son Amr is mentioned in the early 9th-century *Historia Brittonum* and the *Dream of Rhonabwy*, though in the *Historia* he is said to have been killed by Arthur. Another son, Llacheu, is mentioned in *Pa gur*, early poetry and the Triads – he appears to have been a martial hero, just like his father. One late Welsh text has him being killed by Cai, but this is unlikely to be part of the insular tradition, belonging to the French *Perlesvaus* (where the son is Loholt) of which the Welsh *Y Seint Greal* is a translation. Gwydre is another pre-Galfridian Welsh son, named only in *Culhwch ac Olwen* as being killed by the *Twrch Trwyd*, at a site not too far from the later-recorded rock-formation known as *Cerrig Meibion Arthur*, the 'Stones of Arthur's Sons', in Mynachlog-ddu. Finally, we find in one late manuscript another apparently non-Galfridian son, named Duran, who seems to have died at Camlann. In addition to these four pre- or non-Galfridian sons, Arthur also had two nephews: one (Gwalchmai) perhaps by a sister named Gwyar, the other (Eliwlod) by a brother named Madawc (Madog).

The Monstrous Regiment of Arthurs:
A Critical Guide

1. Introduction

Whilst it can certainly be argued that the 'original' Arthur is probably a non-historical (folkloric or mythical) figure who became associated with historical deeds by the ninth century via a process of historicisation (Padel, 1994; Green, 1998a; Green, 2007), it has to be recognised that the opposing view has often been taken too. With regards to this, it is fair to say that a vast literature has been generated by the search for historical characters who 'fit the facts' – that is to say, by the quest to identify the 'original' historical Arthur. The present piece is intended as a guide to the four of the most popular theories which have been proposed by those who choose to make the *a priori* assumption that there really was a historical Arthur at the core of the Arthurian legend. It is felt that such a guide is necessary due to the continuing popularity of this assumption, particularly outside of the academic community, and the potential difficulties for the interested reader in discriminating between the various theories propounded. The value of these theories in general, and of the search itself, is fully discussed elsewhere (Green, 1998a; Green, 2007) and needs no further elaboration here, other than to simply say that an enormous number of theories can and have been proposed. In order for the following guide to work, the question of whether the search for a historical Arthur is a useful one is ignored. Similarly, the notion of 'no smoke without fire' – which is criticised heavily elsewhere – is treated as reasonable, *i.e.* the analyses below follow the theories they discuss in assuming that there probably was a historical Arthur.

2. Arthur, the Post-Roman War-leader

The notion that Arthur could have been a post-Roman war-leader has it origins in a study of one of the earliest and most important Arthurian sources, chapter 56 of the *Historia Brittonum* (written *c.* 829-30 A.D.), in particular the section which says 'Arthur fought against them [the Anglo-Saxon invaders] in those days, together with the kings of the Britons, but he was the leader in battles [*dux bellorum*].' In the most basic and popular form of this theory, the above sentence is treated as a literal statement that the historical Arthur was a great warrior and war-leader (with an implication, it is often suggested, that Arthur was not a king himself), who led the fight against the Anglo-Saxon invaders. The rest of the text lists a number of his supposed battles, although only one of these – the Battle of Badon – can be proven to have definitely taken place in the post-Roman period (Gildas' *De Excidio Britanniae* of *c.* 540 A.D. mentions the battle, but not Arthur). This theory is essentially the 'default' concept of a historical Arthur for the academic community, and is used by those researchers who believe that Arthur probably existed but think that we can know nothing more of him without entering into the realms of speculation. This view takes the *Historia Brittonum* chapter 56 as (to some degree) evidence of the existence of Arthur and his basic nature and role, but frequently doesn't trust the contents of this chapter to provide reliable evidence with regards to the battles he fought (aside from Badon) or the region he operated in (see especially Green, 1998a and 2007, and Higham, 2002, on the reasons for this general academic scepticism about the reliability of the *Historia Brittonum*, particularly with regards to the battles ascribed by it to Arthur). Proponents of this theory of Arthur as a war-leader include Jackson (1959; 1969), who explicitly rejects any localisation of Arthur on the basis of the *Historia* battles, and Charles-Edwards (1991), who concluded his recent survey of the evidence for a historical Arthur by saying that:

> it cannot be ruled out *a priori* that some useful information about the sixth century may, some day, be surmised on the basis of the [*Historia Brittonum*] text; but, at the moment, the prospects are poor. At this stage of the enquiry, one can only say that there may well have been an historical Arthur [but] that the historian can as yet say nothing of value about him. (Charles-Edwards, 1991: 29)

The advantages of this theory are (1) that it is based firmly on a critical appreciation of the early Arthurian sources, usually focussing on the *Historia Brittonum* as the only text worthy of serious consideration as a plausible source of useful information on the nature of the historical Arthur (see, for example, Charles-Edwards, 1991 and Green, 1998a with regards to this); (2) that it recognises the problems inherent in the use of the *Historia* and other sources; and (3) that, although it does require an *a priori* assumption that Arthur existed, otherwise this theory refuses to go beyond what can be established from these sources by a correct historical methodology. It does, however, leave us with a somewhat indistinct portrait of the historical Arthur.

Whilst many might accept the above as the most we can legitimately say of any historical Arthur, if we must have one and given the quality of the sources available to us, some have sought to expand this through various means. Jones (1964), for example, argues that the notice regarding Arthur's death at the Battle of Camlann in the *Annales Cambriae* should be treated as authentic and early and thus added to the above concept of a historical Arthur. Alcock (1971) would argue the same, seeing the *Annales Cambriae* entries (it also records the Battle of Badon as being fought by Arthur) as the most reliable source of information on any historical Arthur, rather than the *Historia Brittonum* account, arguing that they derive from sixth-century Easter tables. Both notions have, however, been hotly contested by more recent research into the *Annales Cambriae* (see for example Dumville, 1977 and Grabowski and Dumville, 1984, which indicate a probable early to mid-tenth-century date for the Arthurian annals) and no academic researcher now accepts the *Annales* notices as witnesses to the historical Arthur that can be relied upon.

Other attempts to fill-out the above concept of Arthur have focussed on trying to localise this Arthur. The most successful (and perhaps the most methodologically sound) of these is the 'Northern Arthur' theory of Bromwich and others, discussed below, which places the war-leader of the *Historia Brittonum* in the 'Old North' of Britain on the basis of a consideration of regional bias in the earliest stratum of Arthurian evidence (both historical and literary: see especially Bromwich, 1975-6). Many other theories try to identify and locate the battles of the Historia Brittonum in a particular region – for example, the south-east; the Midlands; southern Scotland – in order to localise Arthur there (something the 'Northern Arthur' theory scrupulously avoids indulging in), but these are seriously undermined by Jackson's (1945-6; 1959) warnings about the impossibility of doing this – such attempts rely mainly on linguistic 'ingenuity' rather than sound scholarship – and the general and serious academic scepticism over the trustworthiness of the Historia's list of battles (see Bromwich, 1975-6; Green, 1998a and 2007; and Higham, 2002). Lastly, some attempt to argue from identifications of the battles in the *Historia* that Arthur was not associated with any particular locality but rather fought battles all over Britain from southern Scotland to south-western England (for example, Alcock, 1971 and 1972). This theory runs into major problems, however, with regards to both plausibility and (once again) the nature and reliability of the *Historia Brittonum* list of twelve battles, of which, it is worth noting once more, Badon is the *only* battle mentioned that we know actually took place in the post-Roman period (see Jackson, 1959, especially pp.7-8; Bromwich, 1975-6, especially p. 168ff.; Bromwich *et al*, 1991: 2-3; Padel, 1994; and Green, 2007 for (1) far better and less 'romantic' explanations of why *Historia Brittonum* chapter 56 ascribes to its historical Arthur battles in, for example, southern Britain, Chester and *Coed Celyddon* in southern Scotland, and (2) full discussions of why the *Historia*'s list of battles cannot at all be treated as historically reliable). The simple fact of the matter is that it is now generally agreed that the *Historia Brittonum*'s account is not trustworthy or reliable enough to allow any conclusions about the extent and area of activity of its supposedly historical Arthur to be drawn from it.

Finally, there are those who would return to the *Historia Brittonum*'s statement that 'Arthur fought against them in those days, together with the kings of the Britons, but he was the leader in battles [*dux bellorum*]' for further inspiration. For them, the above statement indicates something more than simple war-leadership and, perhaps, an implied non-royal status for Arthur (see Jackson, 1959: 9 for an argument that this statement does not rule out Arthur having been a king, and further below): it is rather suggested that what is being described by the *Historia Brittonum* is Arthur being appointed to the control of some kind of combined British army – a general, if you will, appointed by the British kings to lead the fight against the invaders wherever he is required. Alcock (1971; 1972: 15-18) certainly seems to take this view, having Arthur as a 'general commanding a combined British force', with Arthur and his army riding around Britain and fighting in places as far apart as Bath and southern Scotland (see above on the latter part of this). Some would go even further, making the phrase *dux bellorum*, 'leader in battles', not a literal statement but an official title or position and analogous to the known Late Roman *Comes Britanniae* (for example, Rhys, 1884 and 1891: 6-8). Collingwood (1937: 321ff.) sees this post-Roman *Dux* being placed in charge of a roving Roman-style cavalry unit, whilst Bachrach (1990) favours – on an analysis of (again) the *Historia Brittonum* battles – having him in control of a fifth-century version of the Roman naval forces in the north and east of Britain.

Certainly these last suggestions offer a much more 'colourful' vision of any historical Arthur but they can be (and have been) accused of going far beyond – sometimes very far beyond – what can reasonably be inferred from the sources as to Arthur's status and his role in the defence of Britain. In conclusion, most researchers who believe that a historical Arthur is at least possible have preferred to stick with the concept of Arthur described at the beginning of this section as the most that can be legitimately said (especially given the poor quality of our sources): that is, a concept of Arthur as a late fifth-/early sixth-century war-leader, famed for leading the fight against the invading Anglo-Saxons and winning a great victory at Badon, without any of the above speculations about appointed generalships, areas of operation and what-not. To quote Myres (1986: 16), 'if we add anything to the bare statement that Arthur may have lived and fought the Saxons, we pass at once from history to Romance.'

See further, for example, Jackson (1959: 8-9) for a critique of attempts to make Arthur an appointed general and *dux bellorum* a title, and Charles-Edwards (1991: 24-5, 28) for a discussion of the meaning of *dux bellorum*, where he argues that the phrase was coined by the author of the *Historia*

Brittonum to reflect his view that Arthur's role was much like that of Penda, king of Mercia, at the mid-seventh-century Battle of *Winwæd*, when Penda led a force of thirty other kings and leaders against the Northumbrians, a suggestion that re-opens the question of Arthur's royal status (or lack thereof) and is clearly incompatible with any speculation about 'appointed generals'. Charles-Edwards' comments do, of course, very powerfully raise the question of the extent to which we can really rely upon *any* of the statements of *Historia Brittonum* chapter 56 as a useful guide to the supposed fifth/sixth-century reality of Arthur's status and role; in this light, the sentence discussed above would instead represent an anachronism on the part of the author of the *Historia Brittonum*, projecting his ninth-century ideas about war-leadership onto an earlier age (Charles-Edwards, 1991: 28; see also Higham, 2002: 16-57, 164-5 and chapter one of *Concepts of Arthur* on this topic).

3. The Northern Arthur

The Northern Arthur theory is one of the most respectable theories of a historical Arthur, being supported by Thomas Jones, Rachel Bromwich and A.O.H. Jarman, amongst others. This model takes its concept of a historical Arthur from chapter 56 of the *Historia Brittonum* – that is, it sees him as a late fifth-/early sixth-century warrior famed for leading the fight against the invading Anglo-Saxons (see above). It then uses the nature and perceived regional bias of the very earliest stratum of Arthurian sources to argue that these sources imply that this Arthur was originally a hero of *Y Gogledd*, the 'Old North' (that is northern England and southern Scotland), and that his later fame throughout Britain was a later secondary development of his legend. The Arthurian reference in *Y Gododdin* (a poem from the 'Old North') is seen as particularly significant in this theory, as is the concentration of three or four early (*c.* 550-650 A.D.) 'Arthur' names in the 'Old North', including a prince of the royal house of Dalriada. Other important elements of the evidence for a 'Northern Arthur' include a possible northern British origin for chapter 56 of the *Historia Brittonum* and the Arthurian references in the *Annales Cambriae* (these elements are controversial, however: see on the *Historia*, for example, Bromwich, 1975-6; Dumville, 1977; Dumville, 1986; Koch, 1996: 247-8). Jarman has commented with regards to the *Y Gododdin* reference (often seen as the earliest reference to Arthur, dating from perhaps as early as *c.* 600 A.D.) that the poem is a very self-contained and insular work, concerned only with the 'Old North', and thus the mention of Arthur in it can be seen as implying that he was of that region (Jarman, 1989-90: 17-20). The most detailed examination of the evidence for a 'Northern Arthur' is that of Bromwich

(1975-6), in which she strongly argues for such an identification and provides a context for Arthur's later, wider, fame by associating the proposed shift of the Arthurian legend to Wales with the well-established movement of early traditions concerning Northern heroes such as Urien Rheged and Llywarch Hen south to Wales by 'at least as early as the ninth century' (Bromwich, 1975-6: 180).

One very major advantage over similar theories of Arthur's geographical origins that this 'Northern Arthur' theory has is, of course, its scholarly rigour and the fact that it is grounded firmly in a detailed and learned analysis of the very earliest Arthurian sources. Another, as Bromwich notes, is its deliberate avoidance of getting tied up in the futile games many authors play in trying to identify the exact location of the battles mentioned in chapter 56 of the *Historia Brittonum* (Skene, 1868: I, 52-8 is one example of this tendency which might, if correct, support the Northern Arthur hypothesis; see though Jackson, 1945-6, for both criticisms of Skene and the general futility of all attempts to identify and locate more than a handful of the battles recorded in the *Historia*). Also counting in its favour is the proponents willingness to admit to problems with their theory (something that less reliable theorists hardly ever do), principally the fact that a member of the royal house of Dyfed in south Wales – who was probably born in the late sixth century – was named Arthur, and the reference to Arthur in the mid-seventh-century East Powys poem *Marwnad Cynddylan* (Bromwich, 1975-6: 177, 179; Jarman, 1981: 5; Jarman, 1989-90: 19. Bromwich offers possible solutions to both of these issues but these are not really satisfactory and do not resolve the issue: see further for discussion and alternative explanations chapter two of *Concepts of Arthur*, Green, 1998a; and Padel, 1994; and below).

Finally, two things must be noted. First, the 'Northern Arthur' theory does naturally depend to some large degree upon the dating, nature and interpretation of the evidence mentioned above, and in this context it is worth noting the controversies surrounding this (Green, 1998a and 2007, and the references therein). Second, the 'Northern Arthur' theory does have questions to answer with regards to the Battle of Badon if – as is generally accepted – this battle was fought somewhere in *southern* England against the invading Anglo-Saxons. If this 'Northern Arthur' is associated with areas of the 'Old North' such as Rheged or Gododdin, then we have to assume that either (1) Badon was not in the south (which causes problems with both the archaeology and Gildas, though these may not be insurmountable); (2) Arthur ranged widely all over Britain (in which case the dubious and methodologically flawed theories of non-localised Arthur – such as Alcock, 1972 – are in fact correct and he was not an originally solely Northern figure as Bromwich *et al* argue the sources indicate); or (3) Badon was not originally fought by Arthur. If the latter is true then the entire case for

Arthur as a historical personage and defeater of the Saxons starts to collapse, as this case (whatever you may think of its merits) is fundamentally based around the Arthur/Badon connection, with Badon supposedly being the reason for Arthur's fame amongst the Britons and, furthermore, the only thing that ties the *Historia Brittonum* account of Arthur to known history, with the *Historia*'s account being the mainstay of the case for a historical Arthur (see Green, 1998a, and above).

One possible solution to this issue (other than being forced to make the difficult argument for a northern Badon) may be to follow Bromwich in associating Arthur with 'the south-eastern corner of the "Old North", that is with the East Riding of Yorkshire and possibly with York itself' (the later Anglian kingdom of Deira), rather than the more northerly regions. This would put Arthur far enough south to fight fifth-century Anglian invaders (see, for example, the large early-Anglian cremation cemetery at Sancton in the East Riding of Yorkshire) and it is reasonably close to the most northerly of the candidates for Badon, Baumber in northern Lincolnshire. Then, when this area was lost to the invaders, the traditions of a great defender might have been passed northwards to the surviving 'Old North' kingdoms (see Bromwich, 1963; 1975-6: 180-1; 1978: 275; and Thompson, 1979: 215-9 for an argument that the East Riding – or the Vale of York – was in fact the area Gildas was talking about when he gave details of the settlement and rebellion of the Anglo-Saxon federates: this is highly debatable though, for example Wright, 1984; Higham, 1991; Dark, 1993: 260-66; Higham, 1994). Overall, this seems to be the most plausible variant of the 'Northern Arthur' theory.

4. Arthur the Emperor

The notion that Arthur was some sort of emperor has its origins firmly in the Middle Ages. Geoffrey of Monmouth, in his *Historia Regum Britanniae*, has Arthur as the ruler of an empire that eventually encompassed Britain, Brittany, Ireland, Iceland, Gaul and Norway, and even challenged Imperial Rome itself, and there may be traces of this conception in earlier texts such as the Old Welsh poem *Gereint fil[ius] Erbin*, where Arthur is called 'emperor, leader in toil [*i.e.* battle]', though the term translated as 'emperor', *ameraudur*, may be better read in this context as 'general' or 'commander' (Jarman, 1983: 106). In the twentieth and twenty-first centuries, however, the notion that the historical Arthur was genuinely an emperor, ruling over the whole of Britain, has not – to say the least – achieved widespread assent amongst academics. In fact the theory had its only serious modern champion in John Morris, who saw Arthur as the dominant figure of his age. Morris made an extensive study of 'The Age of Arthur' (as he termed it) and his main conclusions on Arthur's identity from this research were as follows:

> He was the emperor, the all-powerful ruler of the whole of Britain, and the seat of his power was in the lowlands [Colchester, according to Morris, was Camelot]... [He restored] the government of [the] Roman emperor, equipped with a hierarchy of civil and military officers, on the model of that which had existed in the earlier fifth century... These institutions endured for at least thirty years after Badon ... With Arthur died the unity of Britain, and all hope of reviving it under British rule... The rule of Arthur had been an age of order, truth and justice, to be praised in retrospect... Arthur dominates and unites the history of two centuries; his victory was the climax and consummation of the fifth-century struggles; and his undoing shaped the history of the sixth century, the mould wherein the future of the British Isles was formed. He was at once the last Roman emperor in the west, and the first medieval king of the country now called England ... He left a golden legend, and he rescued a corner of the Roman world from barbarian rule for a short space. (Morris, 1973: 132-141)

Unlike some of the other theories of a historical Arthur discussed here, few would now be tempted to describe Morris' 'Arthur the Emperor' theory as a respectable work of scholarship in its totality, and especially with regards to Arthur. As has been argued at length by two distinguished reviewers, it is 'an outwardly impressive piece of scholarship' which 'crumbles upon inspection into a tangled tissue of fact and fantasy which is both misleading and misguided' (Kirby and Williams, 1975-6). This view is supported to some very large degree by David Dumville in his justly famous attack on both Morris and Alcock (1971), 'Sub-Roman Britain: History and Legend', where he demonstrates the utter invalidity of Morris' approach to the sources which renders his 'reconstruction' of events almost completely worthless (Dumville, 1977). Another reviewer, James Campbell, is slightly more generous, recognising the good hidden in amongst the bad, but he too admits that *The Age of Arthur* is a book so misleading, so idiosyncratic, so full of problems, difficulties, and traps for the unwary, that it should be used only by professional scholars – already familiar enough with the ongoing debates and the primary sources to ignore the many unreliable theories and passages in the book – and that it is manifestly not a work appropriate for amateurs or newcomers to the subject (Campbell, 1975). Unfortunately, this seems to be just the category of readers who make most use of the book nowadays, with very few professional researchers ever now returning to the tome due to these immense problems.

5. The South-Western Arthur

The belief that the historical Arthur belongs to the south-west of Britain has been supported recently by authors such as Ashe (1968: 50-1) and Dunning (1988), but it is an ancient and popular association. Thus, for example, he is called *penn kadoed Kernyw*, 'chief of the battalions of Cornwall', in the *c*. 1150 non-Galfridian poem *Ymddiddan Arthur a'r Eryr*, and in Herman's *De Miraculis Sanctae Mariae Laudensis* ('The Miracles of St. Mary of Laon') a visit to Cornwall in 1113 by some canons from Laon almost ended in violence and rioting when one of the visitors dared to argue that the people of Bodmin were wrong in their belief that Arthur 'still lived', indicating the great strength of interest and feeling amongst the local Cornish population of the early twelfth century towards Arthur (see Coe and Young, 1995: 44-7, and Padel, 1994: 8-9, on this). Another south-western association for Arthur is the fact that *all* the early native sources – the twelfth-century Welsh poets, the non-Galfridian *Trioedd Ynys Prydein* (the 'Welsh Triads'), and *Culhwch ac Olwen* (which has been variously dated from the mid-tenth century to the late eleventh century) – agree that Arthur's court was called *Kelli wic* ('the forest grove') and was to be found in Cornwall. Indeed, *Kelli wic* also seems to appear in the Arthurian poem *Pa gur yv y porthaur?*, which may date from as early as the ninth century, and as such there is a strong suggestion that the tradition of *Kelli wic* as Arthur's court was one of considerable antiquity (in the poem it is not, however, stated where this place was to be found but, given that *Kelli wic* is never located anywhere other than Cornwall in native tradition, a Cornish location can reasonably be assumed; see further on all the above Bromwich, 1978: 3-4; Padel, 1991: 234-40; Koch, 1994: 1127). Other evidence for an association of Arthur with south-western Britain includes the mid-late ninth-century poem *Gereint fil[ius] Erbin;* the *Vita Prima Sancti Carantoci* (*c*. 1100?), which mentions a dragon-slaying episode in Somerset; the story of Gwenhwyfar's abduction and imprisonment at Glastonbury (and Arthur's summoning of the men of Cornwall and Devon to help free her) in the *Vita Gildae* of Caradoc of Llancarfan (1120s or 1130s); the belief that Glastonbury was Arthur's last resting place and Avalon (see below); and Geoffrey of Monmouth's story of Arthur's conception at Tintagel, Cornwall (many of these sources are discussed further in Green, 1998b and 2007).

These are the kinds of materials upon which the theory of a south-western Arthur has often been built (for example, Wilson, n.d.: 96-7). The problem with all of this is, of course, that it stems mainly from sources reflecting the Arthurian legend, rather than those, such as the *Historia Brittonum*, which are generally felt to reflect, to some degree, the Arthurian reality. Naturally, this does raise some very important methodological issues. Fundamentally this theory proceeds from the same basis as the 'Northern Arthur' theory, that is an attempt to locate the war-leader of *Historia*

Brittonum chapter 56 by looking at the regional bias of the Arthurian sources. However, two things need to be noticed here. First, we have to recognise that the above sources for a 'South-Western Arthur' are generally far more 'legendary' in nature than those used by the 'Northern Arthur' theory. Second, whilst there are more of them, they are also largely later – sometimes much later – in date than those used by the 'Northern Arthur' theory (especially if the *Y Gododdin* reference can be dated to before *c.* 638 A.D., as Koch, 1997 has recently argued; see, however, Green, 1998a and 2007). If we are to see the development of the Arthurian legend as a general movement from sober history to fantastical (and increasingly popular) legend, then both of these features would tend to add weight to Bromwich's notion that the presence of the legend in the south-west reflects a secondary development of an originally northern legend and hero, though there are issues with this theory (Bromwich, 1975-6 and above).

Given the above considerations, the case for a 'South-Western Arthur' would seem to require further support if it is to be considered plausible. If the supposed discovery of Arthur's grave in the 1190s by the monks at Glastonbury Abbey (and their claim that Glastonbury was Avalon) could be proven to be genuine then this would obviously significantly alter the situation. C.A. Ralegh Radford (1968) and L. Alcock (1971) have attempted to, at least partially, argue this case, but they fail to convince (see Rahtz, 1993; Carey, 1999; Carley, 1999). Another possible link with reality comes from the Alcock's excavations at Cadbury Castle, Somerset, which showed that this important Iron-Age hill-fort was reoccupied and heavily refortified in the late fifth or sixth century by a very powerful war-lord (Alcock, 1972 and 1995), the Arthurian link being Leland in the sixteenth century who records that the local people thought that this site was Arthur's Camelot. Certainly the possibility is interesting, but the Arthurian link is based on very late traditions, first recorded more than 1000 years after the historical Arthur is supposed to have lived, which severely limits their value in constructing any theory of a historical Arthur; Cadbury-Camelot therefore cannot be taken as proof of a 'South-Western Arthur'.

The question must therefore be asked, is there any good reason to believe that the 'South-Western Arthur' theory is worth supporting? I think that we can cautiously answer 'yes, perhaps' here, on the following basis. Working with the critical study of the early materials as our foundation, we can say that most serious researchers – if they believe in Arthur at all – would argue that the *Historia Brittonum* is the only plausible source of information on any historical Arthur that we possess, and that the most that can be inferred from this source with any degree of confidence is that Arthur was a late fifth-/early sixth-century war-leader, famed for leading the fight against the Anglo-Saxon invaders and winning a great victory at the Battle of Badon. Now, given that the victory over the Anglo-Saxons at

Badon is supposedly the main reason for Arthur's fame – and the fact that it is the *only* battle associated with Arthur in the *Historia Brittonum* (the source of the main academic concept of any historical Arthur) which we know from other historical sources actually took place in the post-Roman period – it does not seem unreasonable to take its location as some sort of a guide to the region of operation of any historical Arthur; it is the only remotely reliable clue that our 'historical' sources can provide for us. Of course this does require a degree of assumption, mainly that Badon would have been fought in *roughly* the region Arthur operated within, but this does not seem unreasonable either. The notion that any historical Arthur was a general or even an emperor(!) who led a combined British army in fighting battles all over Britain – as Alcock (1971 and 1972) and Morris (1973) make him –, not just his own general *region* (wherever that might have been), is no longer supported by serious researchers and can be dismissed on the grounds of both plausibility and the nature and reliability of the *Historia Brittonum* list of twelve battles, upon which it largely rests (as noted above; see the other references there for further details, especially Bromwich, 1975-6: 168ff., and above). One would not wish to claim that an identification of Badon might closely localise Arthur – it cannot be denied that post-Roman war-leaders might have ranged over a reasonably wide area, even if the notion of them travelling all over Britain can be dismissed – but it *may* give us some idea about the *general region* that he operated within (I am, of course, leaving to one side here the question of whether Badon was actually fought by Arthur, for the very good reasons set out above).

So, where was Badon? Most researchers agree that this battle was fought somewhere in southern Britain, with Jackson writing that 'no amount of ingenuity can make Badon, the most probably genuine of [Arthur's battles], anything but a battle against the Saxons or the Jutes in southern England' (Jackson, 1959: 10 – see also, for example, Bromwich, 1975-6: 172). Some dissenting voices have been raised against this consensus, preferring to argue the difficult case for a location of Badon in the *north* of Britain (Thompson, 1979: 215-19 and Dumville, 1984: 70-2), but this suggestion is highly contentious and has not received widespread support (see for example Higham, 1991; Dark, 1993: 260-6; Higham, 1994; Wright, 1984). Further, the general consensus that Badon probably belongs to southern Britain is supported and supplemented by the archaeology of fifth-century Anglo-Saxon settlement, which indicates that the earliest and most extensive settlements and conquests by the invading Anglo-Saxons occurred in the south and east of Britain, making this the most plausible region for the operation of a British war-leader fighting the invaders (good modern summaries and introductions to the archaeology include Carver, 1989; Hawkes, 1989; Hines, 1990; Higham, 1992; Welch, 1993; Scull, 1995; and Arnold, 1997, chapter 2).

If we can thus say that Badon probably belongs to southern Britain, where in southern Britain was it? There are two main theories with regards to this. The first theory argues that the name *Badon* would, when it was taken into Old English and if the site was a fortified hill, regularly become the modern English place-name 'Badbury' and variants (see Jackson, 1953-8; Gelling, 1988: 60-1). There are a number of 'Badbury' names in southern and eastern England that might thus have their origins in *Badon,* including Badbury Rings (Dorset), Liddington Castle (Wiltshire, this site being once known as Badbury Camp), Badbury Hill (Berkshire), and Baumber (Lincolnshire), with Badbury Rings in Dorset often being the favoured above the others (see especially Jackson, 1953-8). Another favoured 'Badbury' identification is Liddington Castle, but recent archaeological excavations there seem to cast doubt on the plausibility of any identification of this site with Badon, despite support for it from Chambers (1927), Myres (1986: 159) and others (see Hirst and Rahtz, 1996). The second theory follows Geoffrey of Monmouth's *Historia Regum Britanniae* in identifying Badon with Bath, an identification that has been taken up in modern times by Alcock (1971: 70-71) and the Burkitts (1990) on both philological and archaeological grounds. On the whole it cannot yet be said to be clear which of these competing theories should command our support. However, as the most recent survey of the evidence has commented, we can say on the most general level that the balance of probabilities and current scholarly opinion indicates that 'the battle probably took place in the south-west' (Hirst and Rahtz, 1996: 17).

In conclusion, if we assume (as it does not seem unreasonable to do) that the location of Badon can be seen as a *rough* guide to the general region that the Arthur of the *Historia Brittonum* chapter 56 operated in, then it follows that Arthur was quite possibly a figure from the southern portion of Britain and most probably the south-west. This notion has the major advantage of being based around what can be reasonably assumed from the 'historical' sources about any possible genuinely historical Arthur, rather than a perceived regional bias in the 'non-historical' material concerning Arthur, and if it is accepted then it does go a long way towards making the 'South-Western Arthur' theory the plausible theory that the later legendary material on its own cannot.

There are, naturally, a number of issues with this theory: First, by its very nature in arguing for a 'South-Western Arthur', this theory ignores or sets-aside the evidence for a northern bias in the early Arthurian material such as *Y Gododdin,* as observed by Bromwich (1975-6) and others (see above). To this we can add that there is also early evidence for a knowledge of Arthur and his legends in Wales, including *Historia Brittonum* chapter 73 (the traditions related here are considered to pre-date the ninth century: Bromwich and Evans, 1992: lxvi); the poem *Preideu Annwfyn* (which Koch argues should be dated to before the late eighth century: Koch, 1996: 263-

5); the mid-seventh-century East Powys poem *Marwnad Cynddylan*; and the existence of Arthur map Petr of the Dyfed royal house, born *c.* 570 A.D. (Bromwich, 1975-6: 178-9). This is, of course, part of a wider issue which seriously affects the 'Northern Arthur' theory too: even the very earliest and most reliable evidence for the distribution of a knowledge of the Arthurian legend – the use of the name Arthur in the mid-late sixth century by the royal houses of both Dyfed and Dalriada – indicates that this knowledge was extremely widely spread, from south Wales to southern Scotland. The explanation of all this is very difficult, especially given that theories of the historical Arthur as an age-defining figure who fought all around Britain are no longer considered plausible or methodologically defensible, as noted above (for possible solutions to this problem, see Bromwich, 1975-6: 177ff.; Padel, 1994, especially p.24; Green, 1998a and chapter two of *Concepts of Arthur*. Bromwich's is the only solution that has been offered which would maintain Arthur as a historical figure, and it forms part of her 'Northern Arthur' theory). Of course, as formulated above, the 'South-Western Arthur' theory is primarily based around the 'historical' sources, not materials reflecting the growth of the Arthurian legend, but this does not mean that these considerations can be discounted or ignored; the question still has to be asked, if we argue that the historical Arthur belonged to the south-west, what then are we to make of this very early evidence for a knowledge of his legend in Wales and southern Scotland?

Second, the above argument for a 'South-Western Arthur' is based around an assumption that Badon would have been fought in roughly the same region that any historical Arthur operated within. Whilst this is not at all unreasonable, it is an assumption and it should be remembered that early medieval war-bands could be very mobile, raiding deep into enemy territory. Given, however, that we are only looking for a rough general region for Arthur's operation, rather than an exact location, this is much less of a concern and an issue than it might have been. And third and finally, we should not forget that Badon has not actually been securely identified. Whilst most agree that it was fought in southern Britain and most likely in the south-west, there are dissenting voices. It ought not to be forgotten that one of the 'Badbury'-style place-names which may derive from *Badon* is located in Lincolnshire, still south of the Humber but in the East Midlands rather than the south-west. Furthermore, Badon may not, of course, have been any of the places so far suggested but rather some as-yet-undiscovered site elsewhere in Britain, where perhaps a new English or Scandinavian place-name has silently replaced and erased the earlier name 'Badon'.

6. Bibliography

L. Alcock, *Arthur's Britain: History and Archaeology A.D. 367-634* (London, 1971)

L. Alcock, *'By South Cadbury, is that Camelot...' Excavations at Cadbury Castle 1966-70* (London, 1972)

C.J. Arnold, *An Archaeology of the Early Anglo-Saxon Kingdoms*, second edition (London, 1997)

G. Ashe, 'The Arthurian Fact', in G. Ashe (ed.) *The Quest for Arthur's Britain* (London, 1968), pp. 27-57

B.S. Bachrach, 'The Questions of King Arthur's Existence and of Romano-British Naval Operations', *The Journal of the Haskins Society*, 2 (1990), pp. 13-28

R. Bromwich, 'Scotland and the Earliest Arthurian Tradition', *Bulletin Bibliographique de la Société Internationale Arthurienne*, 15 (1963), pp. 85-95

R. Bromwich, 'Concepts of Arthur', *Studia Celtica*, 10/11 (1975-6), pp. 163-81

R. Bromwich (ed. and trans.), *Trioedd Ynys Prydein*, second edition (Cardiff, 1978)

R. Bromwich *et al*, 'Introduction', in R. Bromwich *et al* (edd.) *The Arthur of the Welsh. The Arthurian Legend in Medieval Welsh Literature* (Cardiff, 1991), pp. 1-14

R. Bromwich and D. Simon Evans (edd.), *Culhwch and Olwen. An Edition and Study of the Oldest Arthurian Tale* (Cardiff, 1992)

T. Burkitt and A. Burkitt, 'The frontier zone and the siege of Mount Badon: a review of the evidence for their location', *Proceedings of the Somerset Archaeological and Natural History Society*, 134 (1990), pp. 81-93

J. Campbell, 'The Age of Arthur', *Studia Hibernica*, 15 (1975), pp. 177-85

J. Carey, 'The Finding of Arthur's Grave: A Story from Clonmacnoise?', in J. Carey *et al* (edd.) *Ildánach Ildírech. A Festschrift for Proinsias Mac Cana*

(Andover & Aberystwyth, 1999), pp. 1-14

J.P. Carley, 'Arthur in English History', in W.R.J. Barron (ed.) *The Arthur of the English* (Cardiff, 1999), pp. 47-57

M.O.H. Carver, 'Kingship and material culture in early Anglo-Saxon East Anglia', in S. Bassett (ed.) *The Origins of Anglo-Saxon Kingdoms* (London, 1989), pp. 141-58

E.K. Chambers, *Arthur of Britain* (London, 1927)

T. Charles-Edwards, 'The Arthur of History', in R. Bromwich *et al* (edd.) *The Arthur of the Welsh. The Arthurian Legend in Medieval Welsh Literature* (Cardiff, 1991), pp. 15-32

J.B. Coe and S. Young (ed. and trans.), *The Celtic Sources for the Arthurian Legend* (Felinfach, 1995)

R.G. Collingwood and J.N.L. Myres, *Roman Britain and the English Settlements* (Oxford, 1937)

K.R. Dark, *Civitas to Kingdom: British Political Continuity, 300-800* (London, 1993)

D.N. Dumville, 'On the North British Section of the *Historia Brittonum*', *Welsh History Review*, 8.3 (1977), pp. 345-54

D.N. Dumville, 'Sub-Roman Britain: History and Legend', *History*, 62 (1977), pp. 173-92

D.N. Dumville, 'The chronology of *De Excidio Britanniae*, Book 1', in M. Lapidge and D.N. Dumville (edd.) *Gildas: New Approaches* (Woodbridge, 1984), pp. 61-84

D.N. Dumville, 'The Historical Value of the *Historia Brittonum*', *Arthurian Literature*, 6 (1986), pp. 1-26

R. Dunning, *Arthur: King in the West* (Gloucester, 1988)

M. Gelling, 'Towards a chronology for English place-names', in D. Hooke (ed.) *Anglo-Saxon Settlements* (Oxford, 1988), pp. 59-76

L.M. Gowans, *Cei and the Arthurian Legend*, Arthurian Studies XVIII (Cambridge, 1988)

K. Grabowski and D.N. Dumville, *Chronicles and Annals of Medieval Ireland and Wales* (Woodbridge, 1984)

T. Green, 'The Historicity and Historicisation of Arthur' (1998a), archived at *http://www.arthuriana.co.uk/historicity/arthur.htm*

T. Green, 'A Bibliographic Guide to Welsh Arthurian Literature' (1998b), archived at *http://www.arthuriana.co.uk/notes&queries/N&Q1_ArthLit.pdf*

T. Green, *Concepts of Arthur* (Stroud, 2007)

S.C. Hawkes, 'The South-East After the Romans: The Saxon Settlement', in V.A. Maxfield (edd.) *The Saxon Shore. A Handbook* (Exeter, 1989), pp. 78-95

N.J. Higham, 'Old light on the Dark Age landscape: the description of Britain in the *De Excidio Britanniae* of Gildas', *Journal of Historical Geography*, 17 (1991), pp. 363-72

N.J. Higham, *Rome, Britain and the Anglo-Saxons* (London, 1992)

N.J. Higham, *The English Conquest: Gildas and Britain in the Fifth Century* (Manchester, 1994)

N.J. Higham, *King Arthur, Myth-making and History* (London, 2002)

J. Hines, 'Philology, Archaeology and the *Adventus Saxonum vel Anglorum*', in A. Bammesberger and A. Wollman (edd.) *Britain 400-600: Language and History* (Heidelberg, 1990), pp. 17-36

S. Hirst and P. Rahtz, 'Liddington Castle and the Battle of Badon: Excavation and Research 1976', *The Archaeological Journal*, 153 (1996), pp. 1-59

K.H. Jackson, 'Once Again Arthur's Battles', *Modern Philology*, 43 (1945-6), pp. 44-57

K.H. Jackson, 'The site of Mount Badon', *Journal of Celtic Studies*, 2.2 (1953-8), pp. 152-55

K.H. Jackson, 'The Arthur of History', in R. Loomis (ed.) *Arthurian Literature in the Middle Ages* (Oxford, 1959), pp. 1-11

K.H. Jackson, *The Gododdin* (Edinburgh, 1969)

A.O.H. Jarman, 'The Delineation of Arthur in Early Welsh Verse', in K. Varty (ed.) *An Arthurian Tapestry: Essays in Memory of Lewis Thorpe* (Glasgow, 1981), pp. 1-21

A.O.H. Jarman, 'The Arthurian Allusions in the Black Book of Carmarthen', in P.B. Grout *et al* (edd.) *The Legend of Arthur in the Middle Ages* (Cambridge, 1983), pp. 99-112

A.O.H. Jarman, 'The Arthurian Allusions in the Book of Aneirin', *Studia Celtica*, 24/25 (1989-90), pp. 15-25

T. Jones, 'The Early Evolution of the Legend of Arthur', *Nottingham Medieval Studies*, 8 (1964), pp. 3-21

D.P. Kirby and J.E.C. Williams, 'Review of *The Age of Arthur*', *Studia Celtica*, 10-11 (1975-6), pp. 454-86

J.T. Koch, 'Review of R. Bromwich *et al* (edd.), The Arthur of the Welsh', *Speculum*, 69.4 (October, 1994), pp. 1127-9

J.T. Koch, 'The Celtic Lands', in N.J. Lacy (ed.) *Medieval Arthurian Literature: A Guide to Recent Research* (New York), pp. 239-322

J.T. Koch, *The Gododdin of Aneirin. Text and Context from Dark-Age North Britain* (Cardiff, 1997)

J. Morris, *The Age of Arthur* (London, 1973)

J.N.L. Myres, 'Review of *The Age of Arthur*', *English Historical Review*, 90 (1975), pp. 113-6

J.N.L. Myres, *The English Settlements* (Oxford, 1986)

O.J. Padel, 'Some south-western sites with Arthurian associations', in R. Bromwich *et al* (edd.) *The Arthur of the Welsh. The Arthurian Legend in Medieval Welsh Literature* (Cardiff, 1991), pp. 229- 248

O.J. Padel, 'The Nature of Arthur', *Cambrian Medieval Celtic Studies*, 27 (Summer 1994), pp. 1-31

P. Rahtz, *Glastonbury* (London, 1993)

C.A. Ralegh Radford, 'Glastonbury Abbey', in G. Ashe (ed.) *The Quest for Arthur's Britain* (London, 1968), pp. 97-110

J. Rhys, *Celtic Britain* (London, 1884)

J. Rhys, *Studies in the Arthurian Legend* (Oxford, 1891)

C. Scull, 'Approaches to material culture and social dynamics of the migration period in eastern England', in J. Bintliff and H. Hamerow (edd.) *Europe Between Late Antiquity and the Middle Ages* (Oxford, 1995), pp. 71-83

W.F. Skene, *The Four Ancient Books of Wales* (Edinburgh, 1868)

E.A. Thompson, 'Gildas and the History of Britain', *Britannia*, 10 (1979), pp. 203-26

M. Welch, 'The archaeological evidence for federate settlement in Britain in the fifth century', in F. Vallet and M. Kazanski (edd.) *L'Armée Romaine et les barbares du IVe au VIIe siècles* (Paris, 1993), pp. 269-77

C. Wilson, 'Search for the Real Arthur', in B. Duxbury *et al, King Arthur Country in Cornwall* (St Teath, n.d.)

N. Wright, 'Gildas's Geographical Perspective: Some Problems', in M. Lapidge and D.N. Dumville (edd.) *Gildas: New Approaches* (Woodbridge, 1984), pp. 85-106

An Arthurian Reference in *Marwnad Gwên?* The Manuscript Evidence Examined

Although the early Welsh poetic references to Arthur are now frequently discussed and utilised, there is one possible reference that is only very rarely mentioned, and only then in non-academic works. This is the apparent reference to Arthur in the *Canu Llywarch Hen* poem *Marwnad Gwên*, noted by the *Myvyrian Archaiology of Wales*, p.93b, and Skene's *Four Ancient Books* II, p.436. The poem itself has recently been dated by Rowland (in *Early Welsh Saga Poetry*, pp.388-9) to the late 8th to mid-9th century, and its Arthurian version runs as follows:

> *Gwen wrth lawen yd welas neithwyr*
> *arthur ny techas*

> Gwên watched last night by the Llawen;
> Arthur did not retreat.

The reason for the absence of this reference from recent academic discussions of the early Arthurian legend is the fact that it is not found in the Red Book of Hergest (RB) text of the poem, which is the primary basis of all modern editions. The second line of the *englyn* in the RB reads:

> *athuc ny techas*

The version which substitutes *arthur* for *athuc* is only noted as a variant reading in the editions of Williams, Ford and Rowland, with no further comment. The question addressed in the present article is simply whether this current rejection of the *arthur* reading is fully justified.

Unfortunately, the *Myvyrian Archaiology*, which treats the *arthur* reading as primary, does not reveal its source for this line. Aside from this, the *arthur* reading is known only from two 'texts' within a single manuscript, National Library of Wales 4973, collected and copied by Dr John Davies of Mallwyd before 1631. The *athuc* version, on the other hand, is found in the late 14th-century RB, the 1607 Peniarth Ms. 111, BL. Addl. Ms. 31055, and (again) NLW 4973 (the pages from the White Book of Rhydderch (WB) which should have contained this poem are unfortunately missing). The RB is clearly a much older manuscript than any of the others and there are more examples of the *athuc* reading than the *arthur*. Nevertheless, it is worth examining these manuscripts further to see whether the *arthur* version of the *englyn* can be completely dismissed from consideration.

First let us deal with the main *athuc* readings. The RB is, of course, famous as one of our main sources of medieval Welsh literature. It has been described as a one volume library, containing almost the whole body of Welsh literature known to have been committed to writing before 1400. As such it is easy to see why it has been given priority. However, the RB text cannot be considered to be completely reliable. It should not be forgotten that it is only a late 14th-century copy of a poem which was composed up to 600 years earlier, and editorial work by Williams and others indicates that emendations to the text of the Llywarch Hen *englynion* are necessary and readings in other manuscripts are sometimes superior.

Two of the other *athuc* readings are related, as both Peniarth Ms. 111 and BL. Addl. Ms. 31055 derive from a lost 1573 copy of the lost WB portions of the *Canu Llywarch Hen*. As such we can assume that the 14th-century WB version of Marwnad Gwên also read *athuc*, not *arthur*. This, naturally, greatly supports the notion that *athuc* is correct, though not to such a great extent as might be at first thought. The WB is, of course, famous in its own right as the other major repository of medieval Welsh literature aside from the RB, and it is indeed a little earlier in date than the RB (mid-14th century). However, it is not independent of the RB – they both seem to derive, at least in the case of their *englynion* poetry, from an earlier common single source (Rowland, 'The Red Book *englynion*', pp.80-2). As such, the main witnesses to the *athuc* reading of line 14b of the *Canu Llywarch* do not in fact represent discrete pieces of evidence for the correctness of this reading; rather they are representative of a single manuscript tradition (although the fact that both the WB and the RB contained *athuc* indicates that this tradition could well go back beyond the mid-14th century).

Next we come to NLW 4973. This manuscript is most interesting, containing copies of a number of different, earlier Welsh manuscripts. Briefly, it includes: a copy of a lost manuscript of the works of the *Gogynfeirdd* (including 27 poems not found anywhere else); a copy of the Book of Taliesin; the oldest extant copy of *Marwnad Cynddylan* (a genuinely mid-7th-century poem which includes one of the earliest references to Arthur); a unique version of the '*englynion Llywarch*', termed by Rowland 'NLW 4973a' in her study of the *englynion* poetry; a copy of miscellaneous poetry from the RB; and a second unique copy of the '*englynion Llywarch*', termed by Rowland 'NLW 4973b'.

From the perspective of *Marwnad Gwên*, the important thing to note here is that neither 4973a nor 4973b can be seen as a simple composite copy of extant versions. Instead they both appear to be genuinely medieval in origin and independent from the RB and the 'WB' texts (and each other) – indeed, in some readings they are clearly superior to the RB and the 'WB' and confirm some of the emendations to the text proposed by Williams and others (Rowland, 'Red Book *englynion*'; Rowland, *Early Welsh Saga Poetry*, p.397ff.). So how do they treat the second line of the *englyn*? In fact, both contain both readings of this line. NLW 4973a reads *ath hug*, changed above to *arthur*, whilst 4973b reads *Arthur*, with '*Ll. C* [=RB] *Athug / ath ddug*' added in the margin. Presumably Davies copied 4973a's *athuc* reading and then went back, after discovering 4973b's reading, and 'corrected' it to *arthur* (whilst noting, in 4973b, the fact that RB – which Davies had available to him – disagreed with this reading).

Thus we effectively have three discrete witnesses to the line in question. One, NLW 4973b, uses *arthur* and probably goes back to at least the time of the RB, though it is not derived from this. The other two, NLW 4973a and the RB/WB text, use *athuc/ath hug*, and probably go back beyond the 14th century, though by how much isn't clear. The fact that none of these texts give us a definitive version of the Llywarch Hen *englynion*, all containing some readings which are superior and some which are inferior to those found in the other manuscripts, means that we cannot be completely certain that the *arthur* reading of NLW 4973b and *Myvyrian Archaiology* is a mistake through a consideration of the manuscripts alone. However, the combined 'weight' of the RB, 'WB' and NLW 4973a texts certainly pushes us strongly in this direction, and it is not impossible that whilst NLW 4973a and b do not derive from either the RB or the WB, they could derive from the lost source of the RB/WB text (which would remove the status of the *arthur* version as a discrete witness to the lost original text and make it simply a mistake in transmission).

Can a consideration of context help clear this up any further? *Marwnad Gwên* is a lament by Llywarch Hen for his son Gwên, who has been killed. If the *arthur* reading is correct then the *englyn* in question and the two that follow it would translate as follows:

> Gwên by Llawen kept watch last night.
> Arthur did not retreat.
> Sad is the tale on the green bank.

> Gwên by Llawen kept watch last night.
> with his shield on his shoulder.
> Since he was my son he was ready.

> Gwên by Llawen kept watch last night
> with his shield against his chin.

Since he was my son he did not escape.

As should be clear, a reference to Arthur does not really seem to fit here with the context of the piece. The only way we can really accommodate it is if we assume that Gwên is being honoured as a mighty warrior by the poet, either through making Arthur present at his last battle or by calling him Arthur (just as we find Arthur being used in the mid-7th-century *Marwnad Cynddylan* and the possibly mid to late 9th-century *Gereint fil[ius] Erbin*).

On the other hand, if we choose the *athuc* reading we run into problems as the text can only be made sense of by emendation. Two such emendations have been proposed. Sir Ifor Williams (*Canu Llywarch Hen*) suggested that the line should read *cat gaduc nu techas* rather than the *athuc* [/*ath hug*] *ny techas* we find in all the manuscripts which contain the *athuc* reading, giving:

> Gwên by Llawen kept watch last night.
> In the fight he fled not.
> Sad is the tale on the green bank.

Whilst arguably giving better sense than the *arthur* version, the requirement of serious emendation is troubling because it posits that the RB/'WB'/4973a texts are all corrupted, when it is on the basis of the 'weight' of these texts that the *arthur* reading (which requires no emendation) is dismissed. The other proposed emendation (by both Caerwyn Williams, *BBCS*, 21 (1964), pp.26-7, and Rowland, *Early Welsh Saga Poetry*) is far more elegant and satisfactory, adding only *yr* to the beginning of the line as it appears in the RB, giving:

> Gwên by Llawen kept watch last night.
> Despite the onslaught he did not retreat.
> Sad is the tale on the green bank.

Whilst it does still assume that the RB/'WB'/4973a text is corrupt (though to a lesser degree), it provides an explanation of this corruption via the fact that the word preceding *athuc* in the manuscripts was *neithwyr*, which, as it ends in -*yr*, would have made it easy for scribes to skip across a following *yr* before *athuc*.

To sum up, it seems highly likely that the reference to Arthur in the *Myvyrian Archaiology* and NLW 4973b versions of *Marwnad Gwên*, despite both these texts treating it as primary, is in fact a corruption and not 'genuine'. However, given the nature of the manuscript evidence we cannot be completely certain of this, particularly as the non-Arthurian versions of *Marwnad Gwên* are all assumed to be themselves corrupt, even if primary, and in need of some degree of emendation to make sense (something which is not true of the Arthurian version).

The Other Early Arthurian Cycle: the Tale of Tristan and Isolt

1. Introduction

The medieval Arthurian legend, as found in the Romances, is not solely (or even chiefly) about Arthur, a fact too many Arthurian enthusiasts forget. Those who believe in and argue for a historical Arthur are legion, whilst Myrddin and others are often neglected, lacking their own band of cheerful supporters to argue about the smallest detail in their legends. This brief study aims to slightly redress the balance. There are two key insular story-cycles that inform the international Arthurian legend – that about Arthur himself, with which the majority of this website is concerned, and that about the love-triangle between King Mark, Tristan and Isolt. This latter is one of the great medieval tales, inspiring Wagner, and it is the focus for the present investigation.

Though it is found in a number of medieval versions, hardly any of which are actually complete, a brief summary of the key elements might run as follows (the following is, of course, a composite of these various versions). The tale in general tells of the adventures of a prince named Tristan, the nephew of King Mark of Cornwall. As might be expected, Tristan eventually finds his way to his uncle's court at Tintagel, where he is praised for his manliness – he, like Arthur, was a great warrior. Tristan, by way of various adventures (including the killing of a dragon), then ends up being responsible for transporting the fair Isolt from Ireland to Cornwall to marry his uncle, accompanied by a potion that Isolt's mother had prepared to ensure her daughter and Mark would not have a loveless marriage. As is the way with love potions, it ends up being mistakenly drunken by those it was not intended for – Tristan and Isolt, who become instantly besotted with each other.

The tale then becomes one of deception through a variety of episodes. Thus Isolt substitutes her maid for herself on her wedding night, though Mark knows nothing of this and is simply grateful to his nephew for bringing his wonderful new wife to him. Similarly, in the summer Mark's court moves to Lancien, supposedly in south Cornwall. The two continue their illicit relations, using the king's chamber when he is out hunting, until one day Mark discovers them and exiles Tristan from his court. Not discouraged, the obsessed pair contrive new ways to meet, Tristan throwing twigs into the stream that runs beneath Isolt's window to tell her to hasten to an apple orchard to meet him. Unfortunately for them, an evil dwarf discovers them via magic and informs Mark. Mark spies on them from the branches of a tree, trying to find proof of their guilt, though he leaves convinced of their innocence when he is unknowingly revealed to Tristan and Isolt by the light of the moon, allowing them to make a play of the meeting.

Although this falsified innocence of their meetings allows Tristan's reinstatement to court, Mark's conviction does not last. Tristan is given a favoured retainer's sleeping position, next to the king's bed, whilst the dwarf, angry at his mistreatment after his supposed lies about the orchard, sets a trap so that Tristan is caught visiting Isolt whilst Mark is away from his bed by flour on the floor. Tristan and Isolt are sentenced to be burnt, though Tristan escapes by jumping from a chapel – known as 'Tristan's Leap' – over a cliff to safety. Isolt is then sentenced to be ravished by lepers, a fate she is rescued from by her lover, who takes her into hiding in the forest of Morrois.

After further adventures, Isolt and Mark are reconciled at the ford of Mal Pas as the potion-inspired obsession begins to wane (though her and Tristan's love remains), and Tristan is once more banished, though he actually goes again into hiding. Meanwhile, Isolt is required by unfriendly lords to prove her innocence of adultery by a public Trial by Ordeal – she agrees on the condition that King Arthur is present and it should take place at Blancheland, Mark's high hunting ground. On the appointed day she proves her innocence through trickery with the help of Tristan, with whom she then consents to continue cuckolding Mark with! This lasts but a short while, this time, and Tristan eventually accedes to her pleas to go far away for the safety of them both. He ends his life in Brittany, married to another Isolt. On his death-bed he asks for the original Isolt to come to him and provide a cure for his wounds, which she does – unfortunately the second Isolt succumbs to jealousy and tells him that the other is not coming, causing Tristan's death. When his lover finally reaches him, she lies down in his arms and dies too.

2. The Tristan of the Welsh

This, then, is the legend we are concerned with – how much, if anything, is this tale prefigured in insular Celtic sources? Where do its origins lie? Our evidence for an insular Tristan tradition is highly fragmentary but there clearly was some kind of tale circulating before the Romances were written. Thus there are allusions to Tristan in the Welsh Triads, *Trioedd Ynys Prydein*

(*TYP*). Although these only survive in 13th- and 14th-century manuscripts, their origins lie in the 11th or 12th centuries and they are largely independent of continental developments (Bromwich, 1978). In these *Drystan* (the Welsh form of Tristan) is named as one of the *Tri Galofydd*, 'Enemy Subduers, lords of hostility' (*TYP* 19), and one of the *Tri Thaleithiog Cad*, warriors who wore a ?coronet in battle as a mark of distinction (*TYP* 21), indicating that he held an accepted place in early heroic tradition.

This is true also of *March* (the Welsh form of Mark), who is named in *TYP* 14 as one of the *Tri Llynghesawg*, 'Seafarers'. He also appears in the mid-late 9th-century Black Book *Englynion Y Beddau* as a folkloric hero whose burial place is commemorated by tradition. This latter reference is particularly interesting as he is collocated with Arthur himself in this text. Although minimal, the Arthurian associations of at least March/Mark may thus go back to a very early stage. Furthermore, in this context it is worth noting that that all three heroes linked with Drystan in *TYP* 21 are Arthurian heroes or members of Arthur's court in *Culhwch ac Olwen*. Indeed, in *Culhwch* (line 191) Drystan is himself listed as a member of Arthur's court (surnamed *Hayarn*, Iron-Fist), as is, separately, Isolt (*Esyllt*) herself, though this may be an addition to the court-list (Bromwich, 1991a: 211; Bromwich and Evans, 1992: 110).

What is most interesting in all of this is that Drystan, March and Esyllt are never named together in any of the above, which raises the question of whether we can actually demonstrate the existence of the Tristan tale itself – rather than the participants – in Welsh materials that pre-date the Anglo-Norman versions of the story. There are two or three sources that may be relevant here. The first is the description of Drystan as one of the *Tri Gwrddfeichiad*, 'Mighty (or Powerful) Swineheards' (*TYP* 26), where he is associated with both March and Esyllt. This alludes to a curious tale of the protection of March's pigs, which Arthur is trying to steal. Unfortunately Bromwich suggests that this is an untraditional episode and an ironic fabrication, perhaps actually inspired by the Anglo-Norman tales (Bromwich, 1991a: 219-20).

Aside from this we only have a poem (or fragments of two poems). This is found in the 13th-century Black Book of Carmarthen and names *D(i)ristan* and *March* (without patronymics) in a highly dramatic context:

> Drystan is enraged at your coming:
> I will not accept my casting out (by you?),
> For my part, I have sold (or 'betrayed') March for you.
> To avenge Kyheic would be my desire
> because of his sweet words;
> Alas, dwarf, your anger was hostile to me.
> (Bromwich, 1991a: 213)

The above, with its linking of the names Drystan and March, a hostile dwarf and a 'casting out', has been seen (probably rightly) as reflecting some of the episodes found in continental and Anglo-Norman versions of the Tristan legend. This impression is strengthened by the fact that earlier in the poem we find an earlier allusion that runs 'we two were companions in the place where the water carries the leaves', which is suggestive of the 'twigs/chips in the stream' incident, which did indeed involve a hostile dwarf (Bromwich, 1991a: 218). If such associations are legitimate then it is crucial to know how old this poem actually is. Bromwich dates them certainly to pre-1100, which would seem to put them securely out of the reach on continental influence (Bromwich, 1991a: 214). Indeed, given that the verbal noun ending -*iu* is retained in the poem, proved by internal rhyme, this can be tentatively extended back even further: as Koch has noted, -*iu* seems to have become shortened to -*i* in the second half of the 9th century or the first half of the 10th century, implying that the composition of this poem pre-dates this development (Koch, 1996: 276; Koch, 1997: cxxviii).

The notion of the Anglo-Norman and continental versions of the Tristan legend having at least part of their origins in a Welsh story thus rests largely on the above poem. Other than this we can only demonstrate with certainty the existence of the characters in Wales, not the love-story that binds them together. Indeed, aside from *TYP* 26, this situation is maintained through the 12th century and into the 14th century, with March and Drystan's names being used as heroic standards of comparison. Only from the mid-14th century do we find explicit references in Welsh poetry to the love-story itself, in the works of Gruffudd ap Maredudd and Dafydd ap Gwilym – indeed, the love potion first appears in the 15th century, when Dafydd ab Edmwnd refers to 'the drink of Trystan'.

A 15th-century version of *TYP* (though one which has archaic features indicating an earlier written exemplar) may also be relevant in this context. Here we find Drystan not simply as the hero he is in earlier Triads but also now as a lover. He is one of the Three Lovers, Three Stubborn Men and Three Peers of Arthur's Court (*TYP* 71, 72, 73). Later in the same manuscript *Esyllt Fyngwen* (Esyllt Fair-hair), Drystan's mistress, is named as one of the Three Faithless Wives (*TYP* 80) with the same epithet as she has in the 11th-century *Culhwch ac Olwen*. Finally, *Trystan ap Tallwch* is named in the mid-15th-century triadic *Pedwar Marchog ar Hugain Llys Arthur* (the 'Twenty-four Knights of Arthur's Court'), where he is grouped as one of the 'Three Enchanter Knights of Arthur's Court' with the Arthurian *Menw ap Teirgwaedd* and *Eddilig Cor*, 'the Dwarf'. These all probably point to an increasing interest in the figure of Drystan and Esyllt in light of the continental romances, as Bromwich has noted, though with this being combined with the insular treatment of Drystan (1991a: 215-16).

In fact, the only really plausible independent Welsh reference, beyond the Black Book poem, is found in the *Ystorya Trystan*, 'The Tale of Trystan', which is a mixed prose and verse (*englynion*) text found in manuscripts of the 16th to 18th centuries (although the verse passages are certainly older than this). The key characters in this are, of course, Trystan, Esyllt and March, though Arthur, Cai and Gwalchmai play a part. In this tale Trystan and Esyllt are in exile in *Coed Celyddon* whilst Arthur goes with his warband to seek 'denial or compensation' on behalf of March ap Meirchiawn. Trystan's magical abilities (compare *Pedwar Marchog ar Hugain Llys Arthur*) prevent Arthur *et al* from directly confronting him and instead Arthur makes peace between Trystan and March, ruling that one of them should have Esyllt whilst the leaves were on the trees and the other when they are leafless. Esyllt then states:

> Three trees are of good kind:
> Holly and Ivy and Yew
> which keep their leaves while they live –
> Trystan will possess me while he lives!
> (Bromwich, 1991a: 217)

There is little to indicate direct influence on the *Ystorya* by the French Tristan romances – there are, in fact, sharp differences in treatment and nature – and rather it has its greatest affinity with the Triads, the Black Book of Carmarthen poem and some lines of the medieval poet Dafydd ap Gwilym (who may actually refer to Arthur's solution to the dispute in the *Ystorya*), with there being suggestions that some portions of the tale (such as the *ymddiddan* between Gwalchmai and Trystan) are not only perhaps much older than the present manuscripts but were originally separate (see Bromwich, 1991a: 216-19; Bromwich, 1978: 332, 383-4; Rowland, 1990: 252-4).

To sum up, there is clear evidence that, as characters, Drystan, March and Esyllt were known to Welsh tradition, and from an early period. However, the ties that bind them together are surprisingly rarely found in the early material, with only the fragmentary poem being free of any suspicion of contamination from the Anglo-Norman and continental Romance versions. If the poem is taken as proof of an early Welsh knowledge of the love-story, then the *Ystorya Trystan* and *TYP* 26 references can be seen as derivative of this, rather than continental or Anglo-Norman tales. Nonetheless, whilst there might thus seem to be a reasonable case for the love-story having been known to Welsh tradition, it has to be said that it does not seem to have been a particularly central part of it. The interest in the tale of Tristan, Isolt and Mark in Wales from the 14th century onwards would seem to owe less to a native fascination with this and more to the external stimulus of the French Romances.

3. The Tristan of the Cornish

Given the relative weakness of the evidence for a pre-Romance tradition of the Tristan love-story in Wales, the question must naturally be asked what evidence there is for a 'Celtic' background to the Anglo-Norman and continental Romances. Certainly there must be some Celtic background to these, if only because of 'twigs/chips in the stream' incident appears to be present in the Black Book poem/poems and the fact that the names Tristan, Isolt and Mark all stem from an insular context – thus both the French forms *Tristan* and *Brengain* (Isolt's maid) must have come, in fact, from a written Old Welsh source (Bromwich, 1978: 329; Bromwich, 1991b: 280). The question is, was all else invention, or is there any further evidence to suggest an insular background to the Tristan legend?

A major landmark in our understanding of this is Oliver Padel's 'The Cornish Background of the Tristan Stories' (1981). Padel has convincingly demonstrated that the Continental poets – and Béroul especially, writing in the last third of the 12th century – derived their knowledge of the tale of Drystan/Tristan *et al* from Cornish folkloric sources. In fact, in Béroul's version there is a detailed and still identifiable Cornish localisation of almost all the major events, including the ford of *le Mal Pas* (which is south of Truro), and the hunting-ground of *la Blanche Lande*, near Mal Pas and west of Truro. Similarly Mark's court at *Lancïen* is now generally accepted as being that Lantyan near Fowey and the forest of *Morrois* in which Tristan and Isolt hide is the woodland attached to the manor of Moresk, outside Truro (which Béroul rightly identifies as being a night's ride from *Lancïen*). Indeed, Béroul demonstrates his detailed local knowledge of Cornwall when the hermit in the story 'goes off to the Mount, for the fineries that are there', clearly referencing the fact that two markets were found in the 12th century opposite St Michael's Mount. Most interesting of all, his comments such as 'it is still at St Samson's; those who have seen it say so' and 'Cornishmen still call that rock Tristan's Leap' imply a solid familiarity with Cornwall, and that the Tristan tale was part of Cornish onomastic/topographic folk-legend (see Padel, 1981: 58-65).

Clearly the best explanation of this is that many of the events of the Tristan legend, as found in Béroul, were actually derived directly from Cornish stories current in the 12th century (before the Tristan legend was widely popular on the continent) and thus that the legend itself may be, in fact, Cornish in origin. Further support for this contention comes from an unexpected angle – a Cornish charter. An Anglo-Saxon charter-boundary dated 967 AD names a *hryt eselt*, 'Isolt's Ford' in Cornish, with the stream crossed by this emerging at Porthallow on the Lizard peninsula (south of *Blanche Lande*). Given the extreme rarity of the name *Eselt/Esyllt*, Padel convincingly sees this as representing a piece of onomastic folklore like that recorded for Arthur and apparently lying behind 'Tristan's Leap' – in this case it is best seen as representing an alternative localisation of the events that Béroul placed at *le Mal Pas* (Padel, 1981: 65-8). As such it would appear that not only was Béroul's account derived apparently from 12th-century Cornish folk-tale, but that the tale of Tristan and Isolt was being told, at least with regards to the events at the ford, in Cornwall by the mid-10th century.

These Cornish connections, so obvious in Béroul, are not confined to this text. All the medieval poets – Thomas, Marie de France, Eilhart, and Gottfried – place Mark's court in Cornwall, as Bromwich too has now recognised (1991: 220). Further, they show Cornish local knowledge beyond that mentioned by Béroul. Thus Eilhart mentions *Blanchelande* and accurately identifies it as a hunting-ground, which is what names such as Chacewater indicate it actually was. Clearly, for the medieval Romancers, the Tristan legend was a legend set in Cornwall, this unanimity being arguably highly significant and these conclusions remaining relevant whether one believes in some continental 'ur-*Tristan*' narrative or not. The evidence of Béroul and *hryt eselt* would suggest that this was not simply an idle or meaningless localisation but rather it represented the region from which these Anglo-Norman and continental authors ultimately derived their knowledge of this legend, which was current there from at least the 10th century.

4. The Origins of the Tristan Legend

So, where did the Tristan legend and its characters ultimately come from? We have two branches of evidence. One suggests that the Tristan and Isolt love-story, though not particularly popular in Wales, was known there (in at least one episode) by the middle of the 10th century, if the evidence of our Black Book poem(s) can be trusted. The other suggests that all the widely known Anglo-Norman and continental Romance treatments of Tristan had their origins in Cornwall and most probably in a tale which was tied to the Cornish landscape and derived from Cornish folk-lore. This Cornish version too would seem to have been in existence by the mid-10th century. Which version has priority?

It must be admitted that it is impossible to make a decisive judgement on this question. Nonetheless, given the detailed localisation found in Béroul's version, the continental unanimity on the location of the legend's action, and the fact that the 10th-century boundary-description looks to reference local (and presumably reasonably ancient and well-known, for it to be used in such a description) onomastic Cornish folklore, a suggestion of an ultimate Cornish origin must have priority – especially in light of the apparent relative unpopularity of the love-story in Wales until the 14th century. There is simply no convincing reason to recommend treating the

Tristan legend as either pan-Brittonic or Welsh in origin, given all this. Rather than indicating a Welsh origin, the Black Book poem(s) might, instead, be seen as evidence of the popularity and fame of a specifically Cornish legend from an early date, which allowed knowledge of it to spread to even Wales by the mid-10th century.

The above scenario would seem, at present, to be the best explanation for the evidence that we have. Even if there is still a little doubt as regards how the Welsh references emerged, it can in any case be said that Cornwall was the place from which the story of Tristan and Isolt's love came into the repertoire of Continental romance and thus that Padel is correct in concluding that the 'Tristan stories, then, are Cornwall's most significant, and best-known, gift to the literary world' (1981: 80). Certainly such a Cornish origin fits the evidence a lot more satisfactorily than the Pictish and Irish genesis invoked by previous generations (Bromwich, 1953; Newstead, 1959). The foundations of this latter theory are unsound and rest largely on the following arguments.

First, that the names of both Drystan (Tristan) and his father in Welsh tradition, *Tallwch*, are probably of Pictish origin. Certainly *Drosten/Drostan*, the Pictish name cognate with the Welsh *Drystan*, is a common name in Pictland. It appears, for example, on a 9th-century inscription at St Vigeans, Angus and in the Pictish regnal lists (which also include the shorter form *Drust* or *Drest*). However, the name is clearly derived from Celtic *Drustagnos*. As such Welsh *Drystan* is a perfectly good Brittonic name and, in fact, the earliest occurrence of this name is on a 6th-century inscribed stone from Cornwall (see further below; Bromwich, 1978: 329; Padel, 1981: 54-5; Bromwich, 1991a: 210; Koch, 1996: 275).

With regards to the name of Drystan's father (first found in the Triads), the Welsh *Drystan vab Tallwch* is often compared with the *Talorcan filius Drostan* and *Drest (Drust) filius Talorgen* in the Pictish king-list, with the result that *Tallwch* and *Talorc(-)* have often been equated. The former has often been assumed to derive from the latter, thus 'proving' the Pictish origins of Drystan. However, there are two difficulties here: (a) nothing like *Tallwch/Talorc* appears in the Romances (indeed, the name of his father is notably variable) and we thus cannot be at all certain that the patronymic was attached to Drystan in the earliest Welsh/Cornish material (it could be an invention, in light of its etymology, *tal*, 'brow' + *hwch*, 'swine, sow', reflecting its first appearance in *TYP* 26) (b) *Talorc* and *Tallwch* cannot be said to be cognates – they are, in reality, entirely different names. At best a partial loan translation is involved (Koch, 1996: 275). As Caerwyn Williams notes, 'any idea that the name *Tallwch* represents the Pictish *Talorc* or its diminutive *Talorcan* would seem to be unfounded, especially in view of the forms *Talorg, Talorgg, Talorggan*, etc' (quoted in Bromwich, 1978: 564).

Second, it is frequently argued that the basic content of the Tristan/Isolt/Mark love-triangle derives from Irish storytelling, the closest parallel being in the Fenian story of Diarmaid and Gráinne. This tells how the young heroine Gráinne is destined to be the wife of Fionn mac Cumhaill but, rather than marry him, she instead elopes with Diarmaid, a member of his warband (and occasionally his nephew). The couple live in the wilderness in fear of Fionn who succeeds in killing Dairmaid through treachery. Against seeing this as the origin of the Tristan story we have to recognise the following: (a) the outstanding points of detail between the two stories are first apparent in the mid-17th-century version of the 'Pursuit of Diarmaid and Gráinne' (b) as both Padel and Bromwich note, the Diarmaid story seems to have been considerably influenced by the Continental Tristan tradition in many points of detail and thus the relationship between this and the Tristan stories is likely to be the reverse of that generally assumed (see Padel, 1994: 56-7; Bromwich, 1991a: 222-3). As such, comparison between the story of Diarmaid and Gráinne and the Tristan legend can tell us nothing certain of the origins of the tale and of its characters.

A second suggested Irish analogue involves an Irish monster-slaying episode in the Middle Irish *Tochmarc Emire*, 'The Wooing of Emer'. This is a mainly 10th-century tale but the striking similarities between this and *one* preliminary part of Tristan's story in Eilhart, Gottfried, *Tristrams saga*, and *Sir Tristrem* (the dragon-slayer episode) may be as late as the 12th century – as such French influence cannot be excluded as a possibility. Additionally it must be remembered that this sequence has no echoes in the Welsh Tristan material (it is also absent from Béroul's poem, which would seem to have the closest affinities with Cornish folkloric material) and 'at the very most, the episode represents only one part of the preliminaries to the main Tristan story, and thus again does not represent proof of an Irish, or a Pictish, origin for the main story' (Padel, 1981: 56).

In light of all this there is no cogent reason to believe that the tale of Tristan and Isolt was of Pictish or Irish origins, particularly given the very strong Cornish links of the Continental material and the probable presence of the tale in local Cornish topographic folklore in the 10th century. The case is simply not convincing. Indeed, as was noted above, it cannot be forgotten that the earliest occurrence of the name Tristan is in fact Cornish, dating from probably the 6th century. This is found on a memorial stone near Castle Dore, Cornwall, which reads (assuming that the ligatured *AV* of the inscription should expanded to *ANV) DRVSTA[N]VS HIC IACIT CVNOMORI FILIUS*, 'here lies Drystan (Old Cornish **Drostan/*Drestan*) son of Cynfawr (OC **Kenvör*)'.

The exact significance of this is to be debated. Certainly, when historical enthusiasts have cared to consider Tristan, this has been treated as evidence for a historical origin to the Tristan tale, or at least for Tristan himself (for example, Ashe, 1997). The stone itself is found at a site around a mile and a half to the south of Castle Dore in Cornwall, this site being itself a mile and a half to the south of a farm named Lantyan (*Lancïen*), King Mark's palace in Béroul. Purely from a geographical perspective one can see why a connection between the stone and the Tristan legend has been attractive. The presence of an early form of the name Tristan close by Lantyan is, nevertheless, not the only reason that this stone has been seen as significant – the second name on the stone, *CVNOMORI*, is often claimed to 'be' Mark himself. This is done on the basis of the fact that Wrmonoc, in the 9th-century Breton *Life of St Paul Aurelian*, has St Paul encountering one King Marcus ruling somewhere in Britain (Cornwall or Glamorgan), *quem alio nomine Quonomorium vocant*, 'whom by another name they call Quonomorius' (Welsh tradition does indeed, it should be observed, give the name Cynfawr/*Kenvör to a member of the Brittonic royal family of Dumnonia: Padel, 1981: note 60). So, what are we to make of all this?

Now, the later name is a common one in Wales, Brittany and Cornwall and so we must be cautious – a coincidence is not impossible, and is even likely according to Bromwich (1991a: 221 and 1978: 445-6; note that Tristan is Marks' nephew, not son, in Béroul). Nonetheless, there could be some link between the stone, Lantyan and Wrmonoc's remarks. There is, however, 'no reason why the relationship between it and the stories should not be reverse of that assumed by those who wish to read historical fact into the stories' (Padel, 1981: 78). Padel suggests that the presence of the stone may have been itself responsible for Béroul's, or his source's, localisation of Mark's palace at Lantyan. Similarly, Padel suggests that Wrmonoc's comment, written in a monastery with close links to Cornwall, might have been due to a knowledge of the stone and a desire on his part to connect the Tristan of legend with the *DRVSTA[N]VS* of the stone.

All told Padel sees this as the most likely explanation, with the legend of Tristan and Isolt being purely folkloric in origins. He does, however, leave open the possibility that 'the Cornish stories had grown up around an historical figure, the man commemorated on the stone', with the proviso that 'they would still not be historical events, of course' – Béroul was writing more than half a millennium after the stone was set up and is not a historical source, whilst popular claims that Castle Dore was any historical Mark's palace of *Lancïen* must be rejected given that a re-examination of the archaeology of this place shows that there was no significant re-occupation in the 5th to 7th centuries (Padel, 1981: 78-9 and note 66; Padel, 1991: 241-3). With regards to all this, it may be worth noting that the ultimate etymological meaning of Old Cornish *Eselt*, Welsh *Esyllt*, 'she-who-is-worth-looking-at', is very appropriate for the character of Isolt. As such it may be suggested that 'Eselt/Esyllt as a beautiful woman of storytelling might go back to a time when the name was understood, in the 5th century or earlier' (Padel, 1981: 66). If so, then Isolt's origins as a romantic character of folklore would pre-date the *DRVSTA[N]VS* of the stone, something which might well be seen as weighing in favour of Padel's theory that the story of

Tristan and Isolt was ancient folk-tale, unrelated to any historical figures (*DRVSTA[N]VS* could, indeed, have been named after the character, rather than vice-versa, if any explanation of this name is felt necessary).

5. Bibliography

Ashe, A. 1997, *The Traveller's Guide to Arthurian Britain*, third edition (Glastonbury)

Bromwich, R. 1953, 'Some Remarks on the Celtic Sources of "Tristan"', *Transactions of the Honourable Society of Cymmrodorion*, pp.32-60

Bromwich, R. 1978, *Trioedd Ynys Prydein. The Welsh Triads* (Cardiff: second edition)

Bromwich, R. 1991a, 'The Tristan of the Welsh', in R. Bromwich *et al* (edd.) *The Arthur of the Welsh: The Arthurian Legend in Medieval Welsh Literature* (Cardiff), pp.209-28

Bromwich, R. 1991b, 'First Transmission to England and France', in R. Bromwich *et al* (edd.) *The Arthur of the Welsh: The Arthurian Legend in Medieval Welsh Literature* (Cardiff), pp.273-98

Bromwich, R. and Evans, D.S. 1992, *Culhwch and Olwen. An Edition and Study of the Oldest Arthurian Tale* (Cardiff)

Koch, J.T. 1996, 'The Celtic Lands', in N.J. Lacy (ed.) *Medieval Arthurian Literature: A Guide to Recent Research* (New York), pp.239-322

Koch, J.T. 1997, *The Gododdin of Aneirin. Text and Context from Dark-Age North Britain* (Cardiff)

Newstead, H. 1959, 'The Origin and Growth of the Tristan Legend', in R.S. Loomis (ed.) *Arthurian Literature in the Middle Ages* (Oxford), pp.122-33

Padel, O.J. 1981, 'The Cornish Background of the Tristan Stories', *Cambridge Medieval Celtic Studies*, 1, pp.53-81

Padel O.J. 1991, 'Some south-western sites with Arthurian associations', in R. Bromwich *et al* (edd.) *The Arthur of the Welsh: The Arthurian Legend in Medieval Welsh Literature* (Cardiff), pp.229-248

Rowland, J. 1990, *Early Welsh Saga Poetry: a Study and Edition of the Englynion* (Cambridge)

Myrddin & Merlin: A Guide to the Early Evolution of the Merlin Legend

The Merlin legend and its associated prophecies can be split into two main phases. The first is the definitely pre-Galfridian Welsh stage in which Merlin (Welsh *Myrddin*) is conceived of as a legendary prophet. The second is the transformation of this Myrddin, by Geoffrey of Monmouth, into an internationally renowned wizard and vaticinator named Merlin who plays a crucial role in bringing about the conception of Arthur and who is prominent in later Arthurian story.

We do not possess a prose version of the Myrddin legend in Middle Welsh, but it has been argued that a general idea of its contents can be deduced from a number of allusions found in six medieval poems which, combined with Scottish and Irish versions of the tale, make possible a reconstruction of its main outline. These poems are *Yr Afallennau* ('The Apple-trees'); *Yr Oianau* ('The Greetings'); *Ymddiddan Myrddin a Thaliesin* ('The Dialogue of Myrddin and Taliesin'); *Cyfoesi Myrddin a Gwenddydd ei Chwaer* ('The Conversation of Myrddin and his Sister Gwenddydd'); *Gwasgargerdd fyrddin yn y Bedd* ('The Diffused Song of Myrddin in the Grave'); and *Peirian Faban* ('Commanding Youth'). The first three can be found in the thirteenth-century Black Book of Carmarthen and the remaining three occur in manuscripts dating from succeeding centuries. However, all the poems contain material that is probably considerably older than the dates of the written texts and they all furthermore include both legendary and prophetic material (with the legendary matter being undoubtedly older than the prophetic), the proportions of which vary from poem to poem.

In most of these poems the subject – who is either named as Myrddin or is generally assumed to be him – is portrayed as a Wild Man of the Woods living in *Coed Celyddon* (the 'Caledonian Forest'), where he has fled to after losing his reason ('wandering with madness and madmen') in the northern battle of Arfderydd, fought between rival chieftains *c.* 573 A.D.; with this lapse into madness Myrddin is said to have acquired the gift of prophecy. The antiquity of these traditions is however suspect, at least in their attachment to Myrddin. In Scottish sources there is a virtually identical tale of a Wild Man to that summarised above, but in these he is named Lailoken rather than Myrddin. It has been convincingly argued by Jarman that the above traditions of a prophetic wild man, which are attached to the name

Myrddin, originally belonged to this Lailoken alone; it was only when the legend of Lailoken was transported to Wales, along with other northern saga material, that these traditions were attached to the name Myrddin. Jarman suggests that this occurred in ninth or tenth century; Padel, in contrast, has recently contended that this happened in the mid-twelfth century, but equally agrees that these tales originally belonged to Lailoken (see further below).

The question therefore must become 'who was the original Welsh Myrddin, if he is not the prophetic Wild Man of the poems?' The solution to this problem lies in the name Myrddin itself. The name *Myrddin* derives from the place-name *Caer-fyrddin*, 'Carmarthen' (Dyfed), and this clearly puts Myrddin in the same category as such figures as Port (a personal name derived the place-name Portsmouth), that is an eponymous founder-figure invented to explain a place-name – there is no possibility that *Caer-fyrddin* was named because of Myrddin, despite medieval speculation to the contrary. It further seems very likely that this figure was credited with some powers of prophecy previous to his association with the legends of Lailoken, the prophetic Wild Man. This is necessary both to account for the substitution of Myrddin's name in the Lailoken material, and also because of those few references to Myrddin that occur outside of the six poems mentioned above: most important of these is the ascription of a prophecy to Myrddin in the *c.* 930 Dyfed poem *Armes Prydein*. With the above in mind we can now turn to the accounts of Geoffrey of Monmouth.

Geoffrey of Monmouth first mentions Merlin (*Merlinus*, based on the variant form of Myrddin, *Merddin*, adjusted by Geoffrey to avoid a unfortunate similarity in form to French *merde*) in his *Historia Regum Britanniae* of *c.* 1138, in which the mid-fifth-century British king Vortigern finds that the only way for the foundations of his fortress to be made secure is to sprinkle the blood of a fatherless youth onto the stones. Such a youth is found at Carmarthen named Merlin, whose mother, Geoffrey tells us, was the daughter of the king of Dyfed. She, living with the nuns at a local convent, had been impregnated by an incubus demon *i.e.* Merlin was fatherless. This child was further found to have prophetic powers and Geoffrey makes him utter the *Prophetiae Merlinus*, a long series of obscure prophecies. The essentials of this tale were not products of Geoffrey's imagination, but had rather been lifted bodily from the *Historia Brittonum* (written *c.* 829-30), with contractions and expansions here and there, including the addition of the *Prophetiae Merlinus*. There are however two major changes that give the story an entirely new direction. Firstly, in the *Historia Brittonum* the fatherless youth is named as Ambrosius, not Myrddin/Merlin. Secondly, in the *Historia Brittonum* the youth is found in *Glywysing* (*i.e.* Glamorgan), not at Carmarthen in Dyfed. Thus it seems clear that the Merlin of Geoffrey's *Historia Regum Britanniae* was a result of Geoffrey identifying the *Historia Brittonum's* Ambrosius with Myrddin in his earliest form as the prophetic eponymous founder-figure of Carmarthen. Of course Geoffrey didn't simply leave his portrayal of Merlin with this – he can be seen to have added various other elements, such as Merlin's involvement with the conception of Arthur and with the transportation of the Stonehenge stones, which have no parallel in the pre-Galfridian material, thus transforming how later generations would view this figure.

Geoffrey's interest in Merlin appears to have continued after the completion of his *Historia* and in his Latin poem of *c.* 1150, *Vita Merlini*, he presents a portrait of Merlin totally at variance with that in the *Historia*. The Merlin of this poem is clearly the same person as the Myrddin of the Welsh poems: both are Wild Men of the woods who have lost their reason in battle and subsequently live in the forest of *Calidon* or *Celyddon*; both converse with the famed poet and reputed vaticinator Taliesin; both are associated with animal companions and apple-trees; and the characters that figure in the Welsh poems (Gwenddolau, Rhydderch and Gwenddydd) are clearly present in the *Vita Merlini*. There are, naturally, many points of divergence, but the general relationship is clear. The key question is what does this mean? How did this come about? Jarman holds that, when writing his *Historia c.* 1138 Geoffrey was only slightly acquainted with the Myrddin legends and this acquaintance merely amounted to knowledge of the belief at Carmarthen in an eponymous prophetic founder-figure named Myrddin/Merddin. However, at some time subsequent to the publication of the *Historia* he encountered pre-existing legends of Myrddin the prophetic Wild Man and thus set about composing a new 'life' of Merlin, which showed indebtedness to both the Welsh poems and the Lailoken tales. On the other hand, Padel has recently suggested that the reverse is true – rather than believing that the *Vita Merlini* was influenced by the Welsh poems in which Myrddin appears as a Wild Man, he suggests that the *Vita* was in fact the first text to conflate the Dyfed prophetic Myrddin with tales of a northern Wild Man that originally belonged to Lailoken. As such the Welsh poems which name Myrddin as this figure would, in his opinion, date from after the *Vita Merlini* and be derivative of it.

Which of these competing models ought to be adopted is a complex issue. Some of the six poems mentioned above would certainly appear to pre-date the composition of Geoffrey's *Vita Merlini*, including *Yr Afallennau* and *Ymddiddan Myrddin a Thaliesin*. However, in these cases either the Wild Man of the poem is not named at all (as in *Yr Afallennau*, with his common identification as Myrddin being simply an assumption based on the other poems), or Myrddin is named but it is not clear that he was considered to have been the Wild Man of *Coed Celyddon* in the poem rather than merely a famous prophet (as is the case with the *Ymddiddan*). In fact, the only one of the Welsh poems which can be credibly considered pre-Galfridian and in which a concept of Myrddin as the Wild Man does definitely appear is the

Cyfoesi Myrddin a Gwenddydd ei Chwaer, where Myrddin refers to his madness after the battle of Arfderydd. Both Jarman and Jackson consider that the *Cyfoesi* had its origins before the *Vita Merlini* was written, perhaps even as early as the tenth century; on the other hand, Padel notes that the earliest manuscript of the poem dates to *c*. 1300 and he expresses doubts over whether we can be entirely certain that this poem's composition must have occurred before *c*. 1150.

Whatever the case may be, the fact that Geoffrey produced two very different portraits of Merlin seems not to have unduly worried this most inventive of medieval British authors. Geoffrey solved the problem to his satisfaction by presenting Merlin's career as lasting from Vortigern's reign to the late-sixth century, though it has to be said that this solution appears to have strained even medieval credulity (see Giraldus Cambrensis, for example). The view thus developed after Geoffrey that there had been two Merlins, the first that of the *Historia* and the second that of the Welsh poems and the *Vita Merlini*, named respectively *Merlinus Ambrosius* (*Myrddin Emrys*) and *Merlinus Silvester* (*Merlinus Celidonus*, *Myrddin Wyllt*).

Bibliography and Further Reading

Any investigation into Merlin must rely to a great extent on the published works of A.O.H. Jarman, the leading authority on the early Welsh literature relating to the figure Myrddin for the past four decades, the most recent of which is 'The Merlin Legend and the Welsh Tradition of Prophecy', in R. Bromwich, A.O.H. Jarman and B.F. Roberts (edd.) *The Arthur of the Welsh. The Arthurian Legend in Medieval Welsh Literature* (Cardiff 1991), pp. 117-145, on which the above is largely based – his earlier publications on this topic include 'The Welsh Myrddin Legend', in R.S. Loomis (ed.) *Arthurian Literature in the Middle Ages: A Collaborative History* (Oxford 1959), pp. 20-30; *Ymddiddan Myrddin a Thaliesin* (Cardiff 1951; 1967); and 'Early Stages in the Development of the Myrddin Legend', in R. Bromwich and R.B. Jones (edd.) *Astudiaethau ar yr Hengerdd, Studies in Old Welsh Poetry* (Caerdydd 1978), pp. 326-349. O.J. Padel's suggested revision to Jarman's chronology for the development of the Myrddin legend can be found in 'Geoffrey of Monmouth and the development of the Merlin legend', in *Cambrian Medieval Celtic Studies*, 51 (2006), pp. 37-65.

It is sometimes suggested that Myrddin was a historical 'bard' of the sixth century, the main proponents being Nikolai Tolstoy in *The Quest for Merlin* (London 1985) and Rachel Bromwich in her 'Y Cynfeirdd a'r Traddodiad Cymraeg', in *The Bulletin of the Board of Celtic Studies*, 22 (1966), pp. 30-7. This contention is based entirely upon the apparent strength of the medieval tradition concerning him, according to which he is almost the equal of Taliesin. The case is, however, fatally weakened by the following:

(1) the name Myrddin derives from the place-name *Caerfyrddin*; (2) Myrddin is absent from the list of renowned Welsh poets added to the *Historia Brittonum* (written A.D. 829/30), which mentions both Aneirin and Taliesin; (3) Myrddin is absent from northern and Scottish tradition in general in pre-Geoffrey forms; and (4), unlike Aneirin and Taliesin, no known early works are ascribed to Myrddin. As such the case must be rejected – the arguments are discussed in detail by Professor Jarman in 'A oedd Myrddin yn Fardd Hanesyddol?', in *Studia Celtica*, 10/11 (1975-6), pp. 182-97 and Dr Bromwich has conceded the debate in light of the above derivation of the name Myrddin: Rachel Bromwich (ed. and trans.) *Trioedd Ynys Prydein. The Welsh Triads* (Cardiff 1978), pp. 559-60.

'But Arthur's Grave is Nowhere Seen': Twelfth-Century and Later Solutions to Arthur's Current Whereabouts

1. Introduction

The belief that Arthur never truly died and will return is one of the best known aspects of his legend, and the focus of the present piece. The key statement of this concept of Arthur is to be found in Geoffrey of Monmouth's *Historia Regum Britanniae* (*c.* 1138), where it is asserted that, although Arthur 'was mortally wounded' at the battle of Camlann, he – unlike the other warriors who fell at that battle – did not die of his deadly injuries, but was instead carried off to the Isle of Avalon to be somehow miraculously cured. This brief claim is further elaborated in Geoffrey's own *Vita Merlini* (*c.* 1151), where the *Historia*'s implication that Arthur was at some point cured – and thus still lived and might one day return from Avalon to rule Britain – is made explicit when Telgesinus suggests to Merlinus that a ship be sent to bring Arthur back from Avalon (see Padel 1994: 11-12; Clarke 1973).

However, this notion of Arthur's continued existence and future return was apparently not a purely literary motif. For example, we learn from the Anglo-Norman poetic text *The Description of England* (1140s) that the Welsh can be heard talking about how they will, 'by means of Arthur' – that is, by means of Arthur's military prowess exercised on behalf of the Welsh after his return – expel the English and the Normans from Britain. Similarly, both Peter of Blois (*c.* 1190) and Giraldus Cambrensis (*c.* 1191) compare the *Britones* mockingly with the Jews, 'awaiting their messiah' (Arthur). In the same way, William of Newburgh (1196-8) says how 'most of the Britons are thought to be so dull that even now they are said to be awaiting the coming of Arthur', and they will not hear that he is dead. Furthermore, the belief appears to have been both wide-spread and long-lived: the Italian Boncampagno da Signa (*c.* 1200) refers to it in a letter; John Lydgate in his *Fall of Princes* (1431-8) noted the belief that Arthur 'shall resorte as lord and sovereyne Out of fayrye and regne in Breteyne'; and a late sixteenth-century Spanish chronicler related that Philip II swore at the time of his marriage to Mary Tudor in 1554 that he would resign the kingdom if Arthur should return (see Bullock-Davies 1980-2; Loomis 1959: 64-5; Padel 1994: 11).

Although the earliest of the above references imply an active Brittonic oral tradition 'of Arthur's survival and future return, it will nevertheless be observed that they are all effectively 'post-Galfridian', and thus that their claims may reflect Geoffrey of Monmouth's concept of Arthur to some greater or lesser degree. Furthermore, Arthur is curiously absent from the Old and Middle Welsh prophetic poetry – which refers to a variety of 'messianic' heroes of the Welsh, such as Cadwaladr, who will supposedly return to defeat their enemies – that might be used to counter this concern and offer direct confirmation of a widespread Welsh belief in Arthur's return for the specific purpose of expelling the English and the Normans (see Padel 2000: 61-3; Jones 1974: 183). However, this is not to say that we can consider the *core concept* of Arthur as unkillable to be ultimately the invention of Geoffrey: whilst there is no hint of a link between Arthur's return and the expulsion of the English in pre-Galfridian literature, both his deathlessness and potential return (for an unclear purpose) are referred to. Thus a belief in Arthur's continued life was sufficiently powerful in 1113 to almost cause a riot in Cornwall when it was contradicted by sceptical French canons: 'many men rushed into the church with arms' and, if local passions had not been calmed, 'it would certainly have come to the spilling of blood'. Similarly, William of Malmesbury remarked in *c.* 1125 that 'Arthur's grave is nowhere seen, whence antiquity of fables still claims that he will return'. Indeed, the idea of Arthur's continued life – though not his return – seems to be recorded as early as the ninth century, with the *Englynion y Beddau* commenting on the impossibility of finding/achieving 'a grave for Arthur' (Coe and Young 1995: 47; Padel 1994: 10; Green 2007: 72-5, 196 – the latter includes a more detailed discussion of this concept of Arthur in Brittonic tradition).

All told then, this is – in some form or another – an ancient and enduring aspect of the Arthurian legend. The aim of the following piece is simply to provide a guide to the pressing question that inevitably must accompany any assertion of Arthur's continued vitality such as those noted above: if Arthur still lived, then where is he now? And if he is to return as some claimed, from whence will he be coming?

2. The Isle of Avalon

When the concept of Arthur's survival and return extends beyond a simple statement of the existence of the belief, the explanation for his current absence takes a number of forms, the best known of which is that Arthur was biding his time on the Isle of Avalon, to return when his people needed him. The earliest references to this Arthurian residence on the Isle of

Avalon are found in the works of Geoffrey of Monmouth. In *Historia Regum Britanniae* XI.2 (*c.* 1138) he asserted that Arthur 'was mortally wounded' at Camlann, but was then 'carried off to the Isle of Avalon (*insulam Auallonis*), so that his wounds might be attended to'. In this ambiguous statement we can probably see Geoffrey's attempt to reconcile tales in which Arthur died at Camlann (Arthur is 'mortally wounded') with the belief that Arthur still lived (his wounds would be attended to in Geoffrey's Avalon), and thus satisfy all his possible audiences (Jarman 1983: 112; Padel 1994: 11-12).

Further details of Arthur's destination are given by Geoffrey in his *Vita Merlini*, lines 908-40 (*c.* 1151). In this text Geoffrey has two seers, Merlinus (Merlin, Myrddin) and Telgesinus (Taliesin), engaging in lengthy conversation. Telgesinus reminds Merlinus, in his first speech, that they two, with their steersman Barinthus, conveyed the mortally wounded Arthur over the sea to be healed by Morgen at the blissful, ever-green 'Island of Apples, which is called the Fortunate Isle' (*insula pomorum que fortunata vocatur*). This Morgen was the chief of nine sisters who presided over the island kingdom, and she was possessed of magical powers, such as the ability to change shape, heal wounds and fly. She put Arthur in her chamber on a golden bed, telling him that health could be returned to him, if only he stayed with her a long while and accepted her treatment. Telgesinus then declares that a message should, in view of the oppression of the Britons, be sent to Arthur asking him to return, a suggestion Merlinus resists in favour of awaiting the return of Cadwaladr and Cynan (*Cadualadrus* and *Conanus*), the heroes of the tenth-century poem *Armes Prydein* (see Jarman 1983; Clarke 1973).

The *Vita Merlini*'s 'Island of Apples' is undoubtedly the same place as the 'Island of Avalon' that Arthur is taken to in Geoffrey's *Historia*. Although there has been some debate over the meaning of *insulam Auallonis* (rendered *enys Auallach* in the Welsh *Brut*), on the whole it seems clear that it should be seen as a Welsh common noun meaning 'a place (island) of apples/fruit-trees' rather than – as Loomis and others suggested on the basis on medieval speculation – reflecting the personal name *Aballac, Avallach*. As such *insula pomorum* appears to be a literal translation of *insulam Auallonis/Ynys Avallach* (Bromwich 1978: 266-8; Bullock-Davies 1969: 133-4; Loomis 1959: 66). The origins of the name Avalon do, naturally, raise the question of whether the tale of Arthur's current location that Geoffrey relates was entirely his own invention. Whilst Geoffrey undoubtedly drew upon classical models of 'Fortunate Isles' in his description of Avalon, in its fundamental characteristics – such as the abundant apple trees, the perpetual youth, and the unending fertility – Avalon presents all the features of the Celtic Otherworld islands found in early Irish literature, for example *abhlach*, the elysian island of the sea-god Manannan mac Lir (Bromwich 1978: 267, 461-2; Loomis 1959: 66). Furthermore, Geoffrey's description of Avalon as an island ruled over by nine magical virgins is reminiscent of the stories told of the nine virgin enchantresses of the island of Sena, off the coast of Brittany – skilled in magic, medicine, divination and shape-shifting – recorded most fully by Pomponius Mela (*c.* 41-50 AD), and the nine maidens who reside in an overseas fortress and have in their charge the cauldron of the Chief of *Annwfyn* (the Otherworld) in the pre-Galfridian Welsh poem *Preideu Annwfyn*. Finally, the ruler of Avalon is named as *Morgen*, a Welsh-name meaning 'sea-born', whom later writers indicate was considered by some at least to have been a goddess; note, for example, Giraldus Cambrensis description of *Morganis* as 'a certain imaginary goddess' and later references to her as *Morgain le deesse*, *Morgne the goddes* (Bromwich 1978: 461-2).

Given the above, it is difficult to believe that the Otherworldly 'Isle of Avalon' was the ultimate invention of Geoffrey of Monmouth, though certainly Avalon with its inhabitants becomes a literary place used for literary purposes in later texts – for example, Morgen becomes Arthur's sister, the mother of Yvain, and she takes on, in the romances, the aspect of a wicked enchantress. Arthur's association with the Isle is more questionable, but it does not seem *entirely* implausible that it pre-dates Geoffrey; indeed, the theme of a select few resting in the ever-fertile Isles of the Blessed is at least as old as ancient Greece. In support of this, both Giraldus Cambrensis and Gervase of Tilbury attribute the belief that Arthur was still alive and being attended to by Morgen in Avalon to the 'vulgar traditions' (that is, folklore) of the *Britones*. As such it *may* be that we have, in the accounts given by Geoffrey, a reflection of a genuine pre-Galfridian 'vulgar tradition' which sought to explain Arthur's current absence through a claim that he was presently residing on a 'Celtic' Otherworld island. Nevertheless, even if this is the case, the question of how much of the detail of Geoffrey's version of events can be trusted is to be very much debated: thus the involvement of Merlinus and Telgesinus in the translation of Arthur is likely to be a Galfridian addition, as is probably the linking of Arthur's presence in Avalon with his injury at the battle of Camlann. Indeed, as Budgey has pointed out, it could easily be that the Galfridian narrative of Arthur's sojourn in Avalon was Geoffrey's own imaginative re-working of an Arthurian raid on an overseas Otherworld, similar to those found in *Preideu Annwfyn* (see Budgey 1992: 394).

Finally, any discussion of Arthur and Avalon must make at least some mention of the famed burial and cross 'found' by the monks of Glastonbury in 1191. The primary witness for this event is Giraldus Cambrensis's *De Principis Instructione* of *c.* 1193-9 and his *Speculum Ecclesiae* of *c.* 1216, but accounts are also to be had from Ralph of Coggeshall (*c.* 1225) and Adam of Domerham (1291), amongst others. These accounts differ in several important aspects from one another, in particular the reasons why the excavations were conducted; the nature of the coffin and its contents; and the inscription on the lead cross (at least five different versions are known). The only major points of agreement in the texts are to be had in the description of where the monks dug, and in the belief that the monks 'found' an inscribed lead cross with some graves which recorded that here was located the 'renowned King Arthur', buried 'in the Isle of Avalon'. This episode has been much discussed but there now seems to be a general agreement that the story that the monks had uncovered Arthur's grave, with Glastonbury being Avalon, is a late twelfth-century fraud committed by the Glastonbury community, with the cross which attested these claims is now seen as a product of the twelfth century – not the tenth or eleventh century, as some have tried to claim – and its text is derivative of Geoffrey of Monmouth's *Historia Regum Britanniae* (there was a copy of this at Glastonbury from *c.* 1170). The fraud may have been perpetrated to attract pilgrims to help fund the rebuilding of the monastery, or for the benefit of the king of England – for whom it would seem to have had several possible advantages – or indeed for a combination of these two reasons (see on all of this Rahtz 1993; Carley 1999: 47-57). Whatever the reason for the fraud, the 'discovery' of Arthur's supposed grave did nothing to dampen the widespread 'vulgar' belief that Arthur lived on and would return, though it did influence later medieval Arthurian literature. As a whole then, the incident tells us little about popular traditions regarding Avalon or about Arthur's association with this Otherworldly 'Fortunate Isle', but it does demonstrates two things for us. Firstly, that the belief that Arthur was still alive and would return was sufficiently well-known to make it worthwhile the Glastonbury community engineering such a fraud. Secondly, that the belief in Arthur still being alive was powerful enough to survive this attempt to deny it by making the Otherworldly home of Arthur merely his grave at Glastonbury.

Whilst the Glastonbury monks attempted to make Avalon simply the final resting place of Arthur, literary accounts retained the notion that Arthur was still alive and Avalon was a elysian place where he was staying until it was time for him to return, though they too tried to give Avalon a worldly location. Thus, for example, the author of the *Flouriant et Florete* (*c.* 1250) identified Avalon with Sicily, with the chief fortress of Morgan being *Mongibello* (Mount Etna), and this belief passed into Sicilian folklore, with the mirage phenomenon in the Straits of Messina being called the *Fata Morgana* in the fourteenth century. The Mallorcan author Guillem Torroella, in his *La Faula* (1360-70), also still considered Arthur to be waiting in Avalon (again perhaps identified as Sicily), describing how he travelled to Avalon on the back of a whale and found Arthur and Morgen awaiting the 'messianic return'. Jean d'Outremeuse similarly points to a Mediterranean locality for Avalon in *Ly Myreur des Histors* (written before 1400), relating how Ogier the Dane in the year 896 was shipwrecked on Avalon, which was nine days' sail from Cyprus. Here Ogier fights with, amongst others, *capalus* (the Palug's Cat of pre-Galfridian Arthurian legend) and Arthur himself before *Morghe* (Morgen) conducts him to her palace, surrounded by fruit-trees and pools, and grants him, like Arthur, perpetual youth and immortality. Jean's account drew on, at least partly, a fourteenth-century French poem about Ogier (*Roman d'Ogier le Danois*). This however placed Avalon in the Far East near the Earthly Paradise, with a Danish redactor of this poem identifying Avalon with India, and eastern locations for Avalon are provided by other sources too. For example, *Le Batard de Bouillon* (*c.* 1350) describes how Baudouin learns from the princes of Mecca that beyond the Red Sea lay the land of faerie where Arthur and Morgen dwelt (see Loomis 1959: 67-8; Lacy 1996: 25-6, 458). Needless to say, all of these are purely literary imaginings and there is no reason to think that they reflect genuine Brittonic beliefs.

3. Arthur's Subterranean Kingdom

Whilst the Avalon tale is well known from medieval Arthurian literature, inspired a notable fraud, and just possibly may have its origins in genuine non-Galfridian folklore, in the recorded modern 'vulgar traditions' it very much took second-place to another account of Arthur's whereabouts as he waits to return, which made little impact on the medieval Arthurian romances: the legend that Arthur was biding his time in his magical subterranean kingdom/abode which could only be entered through a cavern in the side of a hill/mountain.

One of the earliest certain references to this explanation of Arthur's present whereabouts can be found in Gervase of Tilbury's *Otia Imperialia* (*c.* 1211). Gervase was familiar with the Galfridian account of Avalon and Morgen but he also notes, on the authority of natives, how a groom of the Bishop of Cantania, pursuing a runaway horse, entered the side of Mount Etna in Sicily via a narrow path and came upon a fair plain with all manner of delights. Here he found Arthur lying on a couch in a marvellous palace, who, after telling him the story of his fight with Mordred and of his wounds that opened afresh each year, sent him away with presents to the bishop. Gervase was in Sicily with the Norman King William around 1190 and his story dates from this period; although its origins are perplexing, they may perhaps lie in an undocumented transplantation of Breton folk-legends to Sicily as a result of the conquest of Sicily by the Normans and their Breton followers (Chambers 1927: 221-2; Loomis 1941: 297-9; Loomis 1958: 12-13). In support of this position can be cited Étienne de Rouen's *Draco Normannicus*. Writing a little earlier than Gervase, in *c.* 1169, Étienne de Rouen confuses the tale of Arthur in Avalon with what would appear to have been a similar tale of Arthur's underground kingdom to that recounted by Gervase, whilst making a mock of the 'Breton Hope'. In this text Arthur is said to have gone to Avalon to be with *Morganis* (Morgen, made here his sister), who then grants him earthly immortality as ruler of the lower hemisphere; from here, in Étienne's account, Arthur then returns to protect the Bretons from Henry II. As Loomis long ago pointed out, the natural implication of such a ridiculing of the notion that Arthur was waiting in an antipodean kingdom is that the Bretons did actually believe such a story (Loomis 1941; Loomis 1959: 69). Thus it appears that the tale that Arthur was alive in a subterranean kingdom from which he would return was established in Brittany, at least, from the mid-twelfth century, and formed sufficient part of the 'Breton Hope' for it to be worth satirising.

Other references to this belief in Arthur's subterranean Otherworldly dwelling are to be had, for example, from the thirteenth-century compilation of poems *Der Wartburgkrieg*, where there is an allusion to Arthur dwelling *in dem berge*, where he lived in delight – supplied with abundant food and drink – with hundreds of his knights, and in the English poem *A Dispute between a Christian and a Jew* (*c.* 1375), which describes Arthur and his knights residing in a magnificent manor reached by a path under a hill (Loomis 1959: 69). The most significant body of evidence comes from post-medieval folklore however. In this Arthur is similarly found in an Otherworldly hollow hill/mountain, but in many of the tales he and his men are asleep – rather than awake and living in splendour – in their magical abode. These legends are most frequent in Wales, and Chambers quotes the example of Craig-y-Dinas as typical:

A Welshman is guided by an English cunning man/wizard to a hidden enchanted cavern leading deep underground. In this passage hangs a bell which must not be touched for, if it is, the inhabitants of the subterranean chamber will awake and ask 'Is it day?'. If this happens the answer must be given 'No, sleep thou on', as the inhabitants of this cavern are the still-living Arthur and thousands of his men, asleep in a circle, waiting until the bell is tolled for them to rise and lead the Cymry to victory. Within the circle lay a heap of gold and a heap of silver and the Welshman is told by the magician that he can take from only one pile – this he does, but on his way out he accidentally strikes the bell, having to give the required answer in order to escape with his treasure. He is warned that he must not squander what he has stolen from the magical dwelling of Arthur, but when it is all spent he pays a second visit to the cavern. This time however he forgets to give the correct formula when he accidentally rings the bell and several knights awake, beat him, and send him forth a cripple. For the rest of his days he is poor and could never again find the entrance (summarised from Chambers 1927: 222-3; Ashe 1996: 76).

The story is similar elsewhere, though it varies in minor respects from place to place, for example, the bell may be replaced by a bugle, or the cave leading to Arthur's abode is discovered by a shepherd seeking his sheep. On

Snowdon Arthur's men lie in the cave but not Arthur himself; he fell at Camlann and is buried in a cairn (this obviously represents an attempt to reconcile the legend of Arthur still being alive with the folk-tale that he died at Camlann, which may have originated in this area: see Sims-Williams 1991: 51).

This concept of Arthur is also to be found in England and Scotland. One early example is from South Cadbury hill, Somerset, which is probably first recorded by the Welsh antiquary Elis Gruffudd, who died in 1552. He records two versions of the legend of Arthur magically sleeping inside a hill, one 'in the region of Gloucester' and one where Arthur is 'asleep in a cave under a hill near Glastonbury', which is probably South Cadbury – this belief persisted into the nineteenth century, when a party of antiquaries were asked on their visit to South Cadbury by an old man 'Have you come to take the king out?' (Padel 1991: 240; Loomis 1959: 69-70; other tales give the hollow Cadbury Castle iron or golden gates, see Chambers 1927: 185). Other instances are to be had from Alderly Edge in Cheshire, the Eildon Hills in Scotland, St Michael's Mount in Cornwall, and Freeborough Hill in Yorkshire, for example (Simpson 1986; Loomis 1958: 14-15). In the English and Scottish versions of the tale the intruder is sometimes tested and fails through confusion or panic. Thus beneath the Castle of Sewingshields Arthur sleeps with his wife and court, waiting for a horn to be blown and a garter to be cut with a sword of stone. A farmer follows, by accident, a crevice to find them and cuts the garter with the sword, whereupon Arthur awakes uttering the words:

> O woe betide that evil day
> On which this witless wight was born,
> Who drew the sword – the garter cut,
> But never blew the bugle horn.

He then falls back into his enchanted slumber. Similarly at Richmond Castle in Yorkshire Potter Thompson, who finds Arthur's hidden subterranean waiting-place, fails to complete the ritual:

> Potter Thompson, Potter Thompson, hadst thou blown the horn,
> Thou hadst been the greatest man that ever was born.
> (Chambers 1927: 224-5)

While there are clear differences, the above tales are all clearly related and testify to a strong popular belief (found apparently in Brittany, Wales, England and southern Scotland) that the reason Arthur was not presently to be found was that he was waiting/sleeping in his magical subterranean kingdom/abode, the entrance to which was often elusive and could only be found on rare occasions. It is worth noting that there is no possible Galfridian or romance source for this tale of Arthur's underground residence and, as discussed above, the earliest references point to it having its origins at least as early as the mid-twelfth century as part of the much-mocked Brittonic belief in Arthur's 'messianic return'. As such, it seems not unreasonable to treat it as a genuine example of non-Galfridian Brittonic folklore, this being a development of the belief that Arthur could never be slain found in the *Englynion y Beddau*, despite the fact that it is not recorded from British or English folklore until after the medieval period.

Ultimately this tale, like that of Arthur in Avalon, would seem to be one of Arthur's present absence being ascribed to the fact that he was currently residing, still alive – though sometimes asleep – in the Celtic Otherworld, from which he would at some point return. Arthur's subterranean abode/kingdom is certainly of a magical/Otherworldly character in these tales, and it is clearly reminiscent of the Celtic tradition that located the Otherworld or Fairyland underground, with elusive caverns in the side of hills/mountains acting as the entrance to it (Rees & Rees 1961: 38-40, 45, 303-5; Ross 1995: 441; Loomis 1941; Loomis 1959: 71). It is also associated with the common folk-motif of the hero asleep in an Otherworldly mountain, first recorded by Plutarch of an unnamed British deity asleep in a deep enchanted cavern in an island near Britain (Thompson 1955-8, numbers A.571 and D.1960.2; Ashe 1996: 76, 77; Padel 1994: 30-1; Padel 1995: 110-11; Chambers 1927: 225-7, 230). The main difference from the Avalon tale is simply one of the conception of the Otherworld that Arthur was currently residing in, and the fact that, in this less literary tale, the owner/ruler often appears to be Arthur himself, not the supposed-goddess Morgen. It ought, incidentally, to be noted that the notion that the tale of a subterranean sleeper was only attached to genuinely historical figures, and therefore that this tale 'proves' that Arthur really existed (as proposed by Geoffrey Ashe), is a false one, as can be seen from its attachment to a British deity in Plutarch and to the Gaelic Fionn mac Cumhaill (Ashe 1995: 7-8; Padel 1994: 30-31; Padel 1995: 110-11). In addition to the definite examples of the legend, there are several *Ogof Arthur*, 'Arthur's cave', known from Wales, which have no extant hollow hill/cave legend attached to them but which may be related. Similarly, Hunt (1865: II.186) notes that in the mid-nineteenth century, Arthur's Caves were 'frequently to be met with' in western Cornwall, although he fails to elaborate any further on these.

4. The Wild Hunt

At South Cadbury, Somerset, the legend of Arthur asleep in an underground 'Otherworld' is joined by another fascinating explanation of Arthur's current whereabouts, recorded here in the modern period: there is an old track near Cadbury Castle called 'Arthur's Hunting Causeway' and spectral riders and hunting-dogs can be heard rushing along it on rough winter nights, these being Arthur and his hounds – usually invisible except for glint of his horse's silver shoes – riding in the Wild Hunt (Palmer 1976: 83). This 'Wild Hunt' is an widespread and ancient folk-belief found across Europe, which would seem to at least partly owe its origins to an explanation of the strange noises made by storms and high winds. It is a phantom chase with a spectral/Otherworldly host (often said to be the souls of the dead), coursing through a forest or the air at night with bugles or horns blowing and accompanied by the cries of the hunting pack. One of the earliest-recorded leaders of this Otherworldly hunt was Odin/Woden, the Germanic god, and the leadership of the hunt seems to have been originally part of the role of the Indo-European Männerbund-gods, Odin being the classic example of this type (Kershaw 2000, especially 20-40), although it was attached over the centuries to many personages, both mythical and historical, such as Charlemagne, the Devil, Herla (possibly Odin under another name), Arawn (King of *Annwfyn*, the Welsh Otherworld), and Gwyn ap Nudd.

Given all of the above, the South Cadbury folklore is consequently suggestive of a concept of Arthur in which his present absence is explained as a result of his taking on the leadership of this mythical and spectral host. Moreover, the South Cadbury tale is not the earliest reference to this role for Arthur: as with the reference to Arthur's subterranean faery kingdom, Gervase of Tilbury (*c.* 1211) provides one of the earliest accounts of this belief. After finishing his Sicilian story he recounts that he has heard foresters from the woods of both Britain and Brittany tell of companies of knights who meet for hunting beneath the full moon, with hounds and a din of horns; when questioned they reveal themselves to be of 'Arthur's household' (Chambers 1927: 228). This belief is also mentioned in the Didot Perceval (*c.* 1220-30), and the preacher Étienne de Bourbon in his *Tractatus de diversis materiis praedicabilibus* (*c.* 1250-60) says how on a moonlight night a woodcutter met the Wild Hunt – composed, says Étienne, of devils – near the Mont du Chat in Savoy (where, it should be noted, the Welsh folktale of Arthur and *Cath Paluc* became localised) and he was told that the hunting-party was of Arthur's household and his court was nearby. The woodcutter then follows the party into Arthur's faery palace, filled with knights and ladies, dancing and feasting, and lays as directed with a beautiful lady, only to wake up the next morning on a bundle of faggots (Loomis 1958: 11).

There are numerous other references to Arthur's leadership of the Wild Hunt. It is most interesting to note that in Brittany and western France the Wild Hunt is referred to as *la Chasse Artu*, references to this apparently going back to at least the twelfth century and continuing right through until the twentieth (Loomis 1959: 70; Taylor 1921: 287-9). These accounts assign various origins to the chase but the most usual is that, in order to join in a hunt, Arthur left the service of the mass at the moment of the elevation of the host and for this sacrilegious act he is condemned to chase forever. A version from Fougères (between Brittany and Maine) relates how Arthur on that occasion pursued the hare through the forest to the verge of an enormous cliff, from which the hare leaped; however, instead of falling it floats on before the chase, which followed and continues to pursue it, unsuccessfully, for eternity. Another famous reference to the legend of Arthur and the Wild Hunt is to be had from the sixteenth-century *Complaynt of Scotland*. In amongst a list of medieval romance-titles to be told for recreation we find:

> Arthour knycht he raid on nycht
> Viht gyltin spur and candil lycht

Bruce took this entry as indicative of a lost ballad based on the folk-tale of the Wild Hunt, though its text has also been compared to charms found in later folklore with the suggestion that it was nothing more than this (Bruce 1912: 192; Taylor 1921: 286-7). A final interesting example of the legend comes in a letter from William Wordsworth to Allen Cunningham, dated November 23, 1823:

> Do not say I ought to have been a Scotchman. Tear me not from the country of Chaucer, Spenser, Shakespeare and Milton; yet I own that since the days of childhood, when I became familiar with the phrase 'They are killing geese in Scotland, and sending the feathers to England' (which every one had ready when the snow began to fall), and when I used to hear in the time of a high wind, that
>
> > Arthur's bower has broken his band,
> > And he comes roaring up the land;
> > King o' Scots wi' a' his power
> > Cannot turn Arthur's bower,
>
> I have been indebted to the North for more than I shall ever be able to acknowledge.

This clearly underlines the fact that the Wild Hunt would seem to have been originally an explanation for the strange noises made by storm-winds. The rhyme quoted by Wordsworth from his childhood also finds its way, in a slightly different form, into Beatrix Potter's *The Tale of Squirrel Nutkin* (p. 50):

Nutkin began again –

> 'Arthur O'Bower has broken his band,
> He came roaring up the land!
> The king of Scots with all his power,
> Cannot turn Arthur of the Bower!'

Nutkin made a whirring noise to sound like the wind, and he took a running jump right onto the head of Old Brown!

Taken together, this all indicates that the concept of Arthur in which he is leader of the Wild Hunt was a strong and long-lived one. Just how early it developed is impossible to say with certainty. The French references to the *Chasse Artu*, which apparently begin in the twelfth century, presumably spread from Brittany to the other areas, and a Brittonic origin for the folklore is further indicated by Gervase of Tilbury's early thirteenth-century attribution of the belief to foresters from both Britain and Brittany (see Green 2007: 259). Indeed, it has recently been suggested that Arthur's leadership of the Wild Hunt may go back to the earliest stratum of the legend. Not only has Arthur's hunting of the giant supernatural boar *Twrch Trwyth*, which appears in the ninth-century *Historia Brittonum* and the eleventh-century *Culhwch ac Olwen*, been considered to be a form of the Wild Hunt (Westwood 1985: 275, 448; Green 2007: 237), but if Arthur was *originally* a Männerbund-god, as has recently been very tentatively suggested, then leadership of the hunt will have always been a role of his (Green 2007: 233-40).

5. Arthur the Bird

The above represents the final concept of Arthur in which he was still alive in a human form. In addition to these explanations for his current absence, one further concept of Arthur's fate is especially strange in character. This holds that Arthur still lives but that he has been transformed into a bird and roams the earth in this form. The first reference to this belief is found in Julian del Castillo's 1582 Spanish chronicle *Historia de los Reyes Godos* (Loomis 1958: 16-17). This asserts that in England it was common talk (*fama comun*) that Arthur had been enchanted into the form of a crow and that many penalties were inflicted on anyone who killed one of these birds. This belief is also famously referred to by Miguel de Cervantes Saavedra, who actually mentions the belief three times in his *Don Quixote* (1605 & 1615) and his posthumously published *Persiles y Sigismunda* (1617). The following is from *Don Quixote*, I, ii.5:

What! said Don Quixote, have you never read the annals and history of England, which treat of the famous exploits of Arthur, whom, at present, in our Castilian language, is called king Artus, and of whom, there is an ancient tradition, generally believed all over Great-Britain, that he did not die, but was, by the art of enchantment, metamorphosed into a raven: and, that the time will come, when he shall return, and recover his sceptre and throne. For which reason, it cannot be proved, that from that period to this, any Englishman has killed a raven. (Smollett 1755: 77)

The above was quoted by an eighteenth-century correspondent, Edgar MacCulloch, in *Notes & Queries* (First Series, VIII, p. 618), who added his own observations on this matter. These were in turn quoted by Robert Hunt in his *Drolls, Traditions and Superstitions of Old Cornwall* (1865: II.308-9) with further remarks:

> "My reason for transcribing this passage [from Don Quixote] is to record the curious fact that the legend of King Arthur's existence in the form of a raven was still repeated as a piece of folk-lore in Cornwall about sixty years ago. My father, who died about two years since, at the age of eighty, spent a few years of his youth in the neighbourhood of Penzance. One day he was walking along Marazion Green with his fowling-piece on his shoulder, he saw a raven at a distance, and fired at it. An old man who was near immediately rebuked him, telling him that he ought on no account to have shot at a raven, for that King Arthur was still alive in the form of that bird. My father was much interested when I drew his attention to the passage which I have quoted above.
>
> "Perhaps some of your Cornish or Welsh correspondents may be able to say whether the legend is still known among the people of Cornwall or Wales. Edgar MacCulloch
>
> "Guernsey."

I have been most desirous of discovering if any such legend as the above exists. I have questioned people in every part of Cornwall in which King Arthur has been reported to have dwelt and fought, and especially have I inquired in the neighbourhood of Tintagel, which is reported to have been Arthur's stronghold. Nowhere do I find the raven associated with him, but I have been told that bad luck will follow the man who killed a Chough, for Arthur was transformed into one of these birds.

THE CORNISH CHOUGH.

The tradition relative to King Arthur and his transformation into a raven, is fixed very decidedly on the Cornish Chough, from the colour of its beak and talons. The–

'Talons and beak all red with blood!'

are said to mark the violent end to which this celebrated chieftain came.

Hunt's comments with regards to the attachment of the legend to the Cornish Chough – a red-legged and red-billed crow – are confirmed by other sources, and in Welsh *bran Arthur* ('Arthur crow') is an alternative name for the Chough (otherwise known as *bran goesgoch*, 'red-legged crow'); Chambers further notes of the bird that Arthur is said to have been transformed into that a 'recent enquirer was told by a Delabole quarryman that it was a nath or puffin.' (Chambers, 1927: 229).

This strange concept of an undying Arthur would seem to be a relatively late explanation of Arthur's current whereabouts in popular tradition (it clearly belongs to this), given that the concept is unrecorded before the sixteenth-century, though the fact that without the chance record of this belief by Julian del Castillo and Miguel de Cervantes Saavedra we would have no evidence of it until the eighteenth or nineteenth century suggests that a more ancient origin is not impossible. The disagreement between the sources over the type of bird that Arthur was turned into is interesting: the legend has been attached to the raven, the crow, the Chough, and the puffin. All but the puffin, which is only once associated with the legend, are corvids and thus the disagreement must at least partly represent a confusion between large black birds of the crow family. With regards to the raven, this is a bird strongly associated with myth and legend and it is probably significant in the present context that, in Wales and the West Country, it was held to be a royal bird, and in Somerset men tipped their hats to it as it flew by.

Whilst the belief that Arthur survives as a corvid is not recorded in the medieval period, certain aspects of the early Arthurian legend may help elucidate it. Firstly, Arthur himself is associated with the raven or crow in medieval Welsh literature (for example in *Y Gododdin*). Secondly, his family seem to have been, in early Brittonic tradition, shape-shifters. For example, his father Uthyr Pendragon would seem to have been a renowned enchanter and shape-shifter, with Triad 28 indicating that Uthyr taught his skills to Menw son of Teirgwaedd, who is one of Arthur's men in the eleventh-century *Culhwch ac Olwen* and in this text transforms himself into a bird (see

Green 2007: 146; Bromwich 1978: Triad 28 and pp. 520-3). Similarly Arthur's nephew, Eliwlod m. Madawg m. Uthr, is transformed posthumously into an eagle in the non-Galfridian (*c.* 1150?) *Ymddiddan Arthur a'r Eryr* (which displays knowledge of Cornwall), in which form he now lives and talks to Arthur. Whilst such references cannot prove that the idea of Arthur being transformed into a bird was part of medieval Brittonic folklore, they do provide a context in which such a situation would be plausible.

6. Arthur in the Stars

The last concept of Arthur's current whereabouts considered here explains that his present absence is due to the fact that he has been bodily removed from the earth and placed in the sky, specifically in the constellation of Boötes. The only explicit reference to this occurs in John Lydgate's *Fall of Princes* (1430s), where after the battle of Camlann Arthur is transported to *Arthuris constellacioun*, 'Arthur's constellation' (Boötes), where he resides still in a magnificent crystalline palace:

> Wher he sit crownid in the heuenly mansioun
> Amyd the paleis of stonis cristallyne,
> Told among Cristen first of þe worthi nyne.
> (Dwyer 1978: 159)

Although this story is found nowhere else, that there was indeed some sort of close relationship between Arthur and this constellation in the medieval period is strongly indicated by the fact that *Arcturus*, the name of a star in the constellation of Boötes, was a genuine medieval form of Arthur's name, used apparently independently by Ailred of Rievaulx (*Speculum Charitatis*, *c.* 1141) and Geoffrey of Monmouth (*Vita Merlini*, *c.* 1151) amongst others (Bromwich 1978: 544-5). In this light it is worth considering whether this concept of Arthur's survival might have been more widespread than the available evidence indicates. Certainly, as has been discussed elsewhere, a link between Arcturus and Arthur has the potential to be very ancient indeed, and such a situation may additionally help explain some very puzzling concepts of Arthur that existed in the medieval period (Green 2007: 188, 191-4, 243; Anderson 2004; Green forthcoming).

7. Conclusion

The above perhaps demonstrates something of the richness and vitality of the legends surrounding Arthur's survival. By the twelfth century the concept of Arthur in which he could not be killed – as found in the *Englynion y Beddau* – had developed into one of his return, and had furthermore begun to take on certain specific forms in its attempts to explain away Arthur's current very-obvious absence. According to some,Arthur was waiting on an island or subterranean Otherworld, of which he is sometimes lord. Other explanations, some later than others, held that he presently led an Otherworldly hunt through the air; had been transformed into a crow, raven or Chough; was residing in the stars like the classical heroes of old; or was even currently resting in an underwater Otherworld (the last is referred to only by Godfrey of Viterbo in *c.* 1190 – see Loomis 1959: 70-1, cf. Westwood 1985: 287). One has to ask how many more such concepts once existed, whether literary or folkloric? It is sobering to reflect how fragile our knowledge of some of the above actually is.

8. Bibliography

Anderson, G. 2004, *King Arthur in Antiquity* (London)

Ashe, G. 1996, 'Cave Legend', in *The New Arthurian Encyclopedia*, ed. N.J. Lacy (New York), pp. 76-7

Ashe, G. 1995, 'The Origins of the Arthurian Legend', *Arthuriana*, 5.3, pp.1-24

Bromwich, R. (ed. and trans.) 1978, *Trioedd Ynys Prydein. The Welsh Triads* second edition (Cardiff)

Bromwich, R., Jarman, A. O. H., and Roberts, B. F. (edd.) 1991, *The Arthur of the Welsh. The Arthurian Legend in Medieval Welsh Literature* (Cardiff)

Bromwich, R. and Evans, D. S. (edd.) 1992, *Culhwch and Olwen. An Edition and Study of the Oldest Arthurian Tale* (Cardiff)

Bruce, J. D. 1912, 'Arthuriana', *Romanic Review*, 3, pp. 173-193

Budgey, A. 1992, '"Preiddeu Annwn" and the Welsh Tradition of Arthur', in *Celtic Languages and Celtic People*, edd. C. J. Byrne *et al* (Halifax, Nova Scotia), pp. 391-404

Bullock-Davies, C. 1969, 'Lanval and Avalon', *Bulletin of the Board of Celtic*

Studies, 23, pp. 128-42

Bullock-Davies, C. 1980-2, '"Exspectare Arthurum", Arthur and the Messianic Hope', *Bulletin of the Board of Celtic Studies*, 29, pp. 432-40

Carley, J. P. 1999, 'Arthur in English History', in *The Arthur of the English*, ed. W. R. J. Barron (Cardiff), pp. 47-57

Chambers, E. K. 1927, *Arthur of Britain* (London)

Clarke, B. (ed. and trans.) 1973, *Life of Merlin: Vita Merlini* (Cardiff)

Coe, J. B. and Young, S. (ed. and trans.) 1995, *The Celtic Sources For the Arthurian Legend* (Felinfach)

Dwyer, R. A. 1978, 'Arthur's Stellification in the *Fall of Princes*', *Philological Quarterly*, 57, pp. 155-71

Ford, P. K. 1983, 'On the Significance of some Arthurian Names in Welsh', *Bulletin of the Board of Celtic Studies*, 30, pp. 268-73

Green, T. 2007, *Concepts of Arthur* (Stroud)

Green, T. forthcoming, 'King Arthur and the Arctic'

Hunt, R. 1865, *Popular Romances of the West of England. The Drolls, Traditions and Superstitions of Old Cornwall* third edition, reprint (Felinfach)

Jarman, A. O. H. 1983, 'The Arthurian Allusions in the Black Book of Carmarthen', in *The Legend of Arthur in the Middle Ages*, edd. P. B. Grout *et al* (Cambridge), pp. 99-112

Jones, B. L. 1974, 'Review of *Armes Prydein*, ed. I. Williams & trans. R. Bromwich', *Medium Aevum*, 43, pp. 181-5

Kershaw, K. 2000, *The One-Eyed God: Odin and the (Indo-)Germanic Mannerbunde* (Washington D.C.)

Lacy, N. J. (ed.) 1996, *The New Arthurian Encyclopedia* (New York)

Loomis, R. S. 1941, 'King Arthur and the Antipodes', *Modern Philology*, 38.3, pp. 289-304

Loomis, R. S. 1958, 'Arthurian Tradition and Folklore', *Folklore*, 69, pp. 1-25

Loomis, R. S. 1959, 'The Legend of Arthur's Survival', in *Arthurian Literature in the Middle Ages*, ed. R. S. Loomis (Oxford), pp. 64-71

Padel, O. J. 1991, 'Some south-western sites with Arthurian connections', in *The Arthur of the Welsh*, edd. R. Bromwich *et al* (Cardiff), pp. 229-248

Padel, O. J. 1994, 'The Nature of Arthur', *Cambrian Medieval Celtic Studies*, 27, pp. 1-31

Padel, O. J. 1995, 'Recent Work on the Origins of the Arthurian Legend: A Comment', *Arthuriana*, 5.3, pp. 103-14

Padel, O. J. 2000, *Arthur in Medieval Welsh Literature* (Cardiff)

Palmer, K. 1976, *The Folklore of Somerset* (London)

Rahtz, P. 1993, *English Heritage Book of Glastonbury* (London)

Rees, A. & Rees, R. 1961, *Celtic Heritage. Ancient Tradition in Ireland and Wales* (London)

Ross, A. 1995, 'Ritual and the Druids', in *The Celtic World*, ed. M. Green (London), pp. 423-44

Simpson, J. R. 1986, 'King Arthur's Enchanted Sleep: Early Nineteenth Century Legends', *Folklore*, 97.2, pp. 207-9

Sims-Williams, P. 1991, 'The Early Welsh Arthurian Poems', in *The Arthur of the Welsh*, edd. R. Bromwich *et al* (Cardiff), pp. 33-71

Smollett, T. (trans.) 1755, *The History and Adventures of the Renowned Don Quixote* reprint (Ware)

Taylor, A. 1921, 'Arthur and the Wild Hunt', *Romanic Review*, 12, pp. 286-9

Thompson, S. 1955-8, *Motif-Index of Folk Literature* (Bloomington)

Westwood, J. 1985, *Albion. A Guide to Legendary Britain* (London)

A Bibliographic Guide to the Characters of the Pre-Galfridian Arthurian Legend[*]

1. Arthur

Bromwich and Evans have recently written that the Arthur of pre-Galfridian literature was:

> above all else... a defender of his country against every kind of danger, both internal and external: a slayer of giants and witches, a hunter of monstrous animals – giant boars, a savage cat monster, a winged serpent (or dragon) – and also, as it appears from *Culhwch* and *Preiddeu Annwn,* a releaser of prisoners. This concept [of Arthur] is substantiated from all the early sources: the poems *Pa Gur* and *Prieddeu Annwn,* the Triads, the Saint's Lives, and the *Miribilia* attached to the *Historia Brittonum...* in early literature he belongs, like Fionn, to the realm of mythology rather than to that of history. (R. Bromwich and D. Simon Evans (edd.), *Culhwch and Olwen. An edition and study of the oldest Arthurian tale* (Cardiff, 1992), pp. xxviii-xxix)

Only in the *Historia Brittonum* of 829/30, the mid-10th-century *Annales Cambriae,* and the 12th-century *Gesta Regum* is a non-Galfridian 'historical' concept of Arthur as the victor of Badon and defeater of the Saxons found, and the latter two texts appear to be related genetically to the first and consequently cannot act as independent witnesses to this concept of Arthur. The vast majority of the sources make no reference whatsoever to this notion, and this has been seen as very significant when it comes to determining the origins of Arthur (see further 'The Historicity and Historicisation of Arthur'; O. J. Padel, 'The Nature of Arthur', *Cambrian Medieval Celtic Studies,* 27 (1994), pp. 1-31; T. Green, *Concepts of Arthur* (Stroud, 2007)).

---

[*] This brief guide to the characters who appear in the pre-Galfridian Arthurian legend was first placed online in 1998 in much the same form as it is presented here. An up-to-date expansion, development and revision of all of the material found below is contained in my *Concepts of Arthur* (Stroud, 2007), particularly chapter four.

By the 12th century the Arthurian legend achieves extensive written form in Welsh as narratives and allusions and Arthur is an imposing character, granted fantastic titles and the lordship of the whole of Britain. As a figure Arthur becomes too strong and too clearly established to be anything other than central in any context he appears in and, as a consequence, the Arthurian legend attracts figures and episodes of unrelated story-cycles: 'In this lay the seeds of decline as the story setting, the hero a story-telling device, and the Arthurian scene an opportunity for parody. Arthur, not integral in story-telling context, never achieves, in Continental romance, the active central role which he has in the earliest Welsh, and even the later Welsh texts fail to maintain his real pre-eminence.' (B. F. Roberts, 'Culhwch ac Olwen, the Triads, Saint's Lives', in R. Bromwich *et al* (edd.), *The Arthur of the Welsh: The Arthurian Legend in Medieval Welsh Literature* (Cardiff, 1991), pp. 73-95 at p. 85).

2. Cai and Bedwyr

Later medieval representations of Cai (= Kay) make boastfulness and mockery his most prominent characteristics and often use him as an excuse for a humorous or moralising interlude at his expense. This Cai is, however, very different to that attested by the non-Galfridian evidence. One important early view of Cai is provided by the poem *Pa gur yv y porthaur?*, in which Cai is presented as one of the chief companions of Arthur, a magnificent heroic figure of epic poetry:

> Vain was a host
> compared with Cai in battle.
> (Lines 52-53; P. Sims-Williams, 'The Early Welsh Arthurian Poems', in R. Bromwich *et al* (edd.), *The Arthur of the Welsh: The Arthurian Legend in Medieval Welsh Literature* (Cardiff, 1991), pp. 33-71 at p. 43)

> Cai would entreat them,
> while he struck them three at a time.
> When Celli was lost,
> there was fury.
> Cai would entreat them
> as he cut them down. (Lines 31-36; Sims-Williams, 1991, p. 41)

> Heavy was his vengeance,
> painful was his fury.

When he would drink from a horn
he would drink enough for four.
When he came into battle,
he would slay enough for a hundred.
Unless it were God who accomplished it,
Cai's death were unattainable. (Lines 68-75; Sims-Williams, 1991, p. 43)

Whilst other figures do appear in this work, Cai's exploits dominate: more than a third of the poem is devoted to the praise of Cai and to a catalogue of his feats. Other pre-Galfridian materials, including *Culhwch ac Olwen* and the *Life of St Cadog* (both works datable to *c.* 1100), extend our knowledge of this figure, confirming him as one of Arthur's main companions and a heroic figure possessing superhuman powers. Thus in *Culhwch* it is said that:

Kai had this peculiarity, that his breath lasted nine nights and nine days under water, and he could exist nine nights and nine days without sleep. A wound from Kai's sword no physician could heal. Very subtle was Kai. When it pleased him he could render himself as tall as the highest tree in the forest. And he had another peculiarity,—so great was the heat of his nature, that, when it rained hardest, whatever he carried remained dry for a handbreadth above and a handbreadth below his hand; and when his companions were coldest, it was to them as fuel with which to light their fire. (C. Guest, *The Mabinogion* (London, 1877), p. 229)

These references can perhaps point us to the origins of this figure. Arthur himself was probably not originally a historical figure but rather a folkloric, heroic one, 'the leader of a band of heroes who live outside society, whose main world is one of magical animals, giants, and other wonderful happenings, located in the wild parts of the landscape' (see 'The Historicity and Historicisation of Arthur'; O. J. Padel, 'The Nature of Arthur', *Cambrian Medieval Celtic Studies*, 27 (Summer 1994), pp. 1-31 at p. 14; T. Green, *Concepts of Arthur* (Stroud, 2007)). Cai with his magical attributes, his heroic characteristics, and his superhuman powers – see further L. M. Gowans, *Cei and the Arthurian Legend* (Cambridge, 1988) – would fit very well into such a folkloric cycle. Moreover, his ability to change his height, and other traditions which make it clear that Cai was thought to be a giant, is strongly reminiscent of folkloric suggestions that Arthur and his relatives were giants/could alter their height (see Padel, 1994 and C. Grooms, *The Giants of Wales. Cewri Cymru* (Lampeter, 1993) on this). With regards to the name Cai, nothing certain can be said. Some favour deriving it from Latin *Caius* but others would instead see it as a native name perhaps meaning 'path' or 'way' (see Rachel Bromwich (ed. and trans.), *Trioedd Ynys Prydein. The Welsh Triads* (Cardiff, 1978), pp. 303-4, 547; Gowens, 1988, pp. 2-3).

Bedwyr (= Bedivere) is also presented in early texts as one of the chief companions of Arthur and as a heroic figure of epic poetry, second only to Cai; in the early references Cai and Bedwyr are nearly always named in close conjunction, though Bedwyr is usually shown as subordinate in importance to Cai:

> they fell by the hundred
> before Bedwyr the Perfect [or Perfect-Sinew].
> On the shores of Tryfrwyd,
> fighting with Rough Grey [a werewolf],
> furious was his nature
> with sword and shield.
> (*Pa gur yv y porthaur?* lines 46-51: Sims-Williams, 1991, p. 42)

> Arthur called upon Bedwyr, who never shrank from an enterprise upon which Cei was bound. It was thus with Bedwyr, that none was so handsome [the text in the Red Book of Hergest reads 'so swift'] as he in this Island, save Arthur and Drych son of Cibdar, and this too: that though he was one-handed no three warriors drew blood in the same field faster than he. Another strange quality was his: one thrust would there be of his spear, and nine counter-thrusts. (*Culhwch ac Olwen*: G. Jones and T. Jones (trans.), *The Mabinogion* (London, 1949), pp. 107-8)

Bedwyr, as a great heroic warrior who wielded a magic spear, who fought a renowned werewolf and who was, along with Cai, the close companion of Arthur, would seem to lend himself also to the interpretation suggested above for Cai, that is that he was a heroic figure of folklore associated from a very early date with the Arthurian cycle. Of particular interest in this context is the reference to 'Bedwyr's Well/Spring' as a place-name in the 9th- or 10th-century poem *Marwnat Cadwallon ap Cadfan*, which would seem to parallel Arthur's early associations with such topographic features (see Padel, 1994 and chapter two of *Concepts of Arthur*). We can also cite here the reference, in an Arthurian *englyn*, to 'the grave of Bedwyr...on Tryfan hill' (Sims-Williams, 1991, p. 50) in the mid-late 9th-century Black Book of Carmarthen version of *Englynion y Beddau* (for the date see J. Rowland, *Early Welsh Saga Poetry: a Study and Edition of the Englynion* (Cambridge, 1990), p. 389), the *Englynion y Beddau* being a specialised Welsh record of pre-existing antiquarian topographic folklore which was specifically concerned with the supposed resting places of mythical/folkloric heroes. In the light of both of these references we can feel confident in treating Bedwyr as a folkloric hero of some considerable antiquity and the same type as Arthur. Cai similarly seems to be associated from an early date with topographic lore. Thus the place-name *gwryt kei* is attested as early as the 12th century and seems to refer to a pass across which the gigantic Cai could stretch his arms (see Grooms, 1993, pp. 148-150). On Bedwyr see further L. M. Gowans, *Cei and the Arthurian Legend* (Cambridge, 1988), pp. 32-36, and R. Bromwich (ed. and trans.), *Trioedd Ynys Prydein. The Welsh Triads* (Cardiff, 1978), pp. 279-80.

3. Gwalchmai m. Gwyar

Gwalchmai m. Gwyar appears to have been Arthur's sister's son and a hero in the mould of Bedwyr and Cai:

> Arthur called on Gwalchmei son of Gwyr, because he never came home without the quest he had gone to seek. He was the best of walkers, and the best of riders. He was Arthur's nephew, his sister's son, and his first cousin. (*Culhwch ac Olwen*: R. Bromwich (ed. and trans.), *Trioedd Ynys Prydein. The Welsh Triads* (Cardiff, 1978), p. 369)

This Gwalchmai is the same person as Geoffrey of Monmouth's *Gualgu(i)nus* (*Gualgwinus, Walwan(i)us*), Arthur's nephew by his sister Anna (*Historia Regum Britanniae* IX, 9), the *Gauvains* of French romance (English *Gawain*), and the *Walwen* mentioned by William of Malmesbury in 1125 (see Bromwich, 1978, pp. 369-375):

> At this time (1066-87) was found in the province of Wales called *R(h)os* the tomb of Walwen, who was the not degenerate nephew of Arthur by his sister. He reigned in that part of Britain which is still called Walweitha... But the tomb of Arthur is nowhere beheld, whence ancient ditties fable that he is yet to come. The tomb of the other, however, as I have said, was found in the time of King William upon the sea shore, fourteen feet in length; and here some say he was wounded by his foes and cast out in a shipwreck, but according to others he was killed by his fellow-citizens at a public banquet. Knowledge of the truth therefore remains doubtful, although neither story would be inconsistent with the defence of his fame. (E. K. Chambers, *Arthur of Britain* (London, 1927), p. 17)

The 'historical' details in the above, such as the claim that Walwen ruled in *Walweitha* (Galloway) can be safely dismissed as later antiquarian speculation (for example, the placing of Walwen in Galloway is clearly due to a later comparison of the two names, not any real association). Our main interest in the passage stems from the fact that William's account clearly preserves a folk explanation of a remarkable feature in the natural landscape, in this case an enormous tomb. Such topographic folktales (see particularly O. J. Padel, 'The Nature of Arthur', *Cambrian Medieval Celtic Studies*, 27 (1994), pp. 1-31) are a distinguishing feature of the earliest Arthurian material and, indeed, the 14 feet long grave is strongly reminiscent of the variable and great length of the grave of Arthur's son, *Amr* – recorded in chapter 73 of the early 9th-century *Historia Brittonum* – and the numerous references which suggest that Arthur and his chief companions were believed to have been giants (see Padel, 1994; L. M. Gowans, *Cei and the Arthurian Legend* (Cambridge, 1988); Grooms, in his *Giants of Wales. Cewri Cymru* (Lampeter, 1993), p. 230, considers Gwalchmai to have been a giant and notes that he appears as such in local folklore). Unfortunately, the section already quoted from *Culhwch* is Gwalchmai's only significant appearance in that tale and he entirely absent from the (admittedly incomplete) poem *Pa Gur?*. However he is present in the Black Book of Carmarthen version of *Englynion Y Beddau*, dated to the mid-late 9th century by Rowland (in J. Rowland, *Early Welsh Saga Poetry: a Study and Edition of the Englynion* (Cambridge, 1990), p. 389), indicating that topographic folklore was attached to his name by this point, the *Englynion* being a specialised record of such pre-existing folklore. He is also to be found in the pre-Galfridian Early Version of *Trioedd Ynys Prydein*, No. 4, 'Three Well-Endowed Men of the Island of Britain', alongside Arthur's son Llacheu, and he is used by Cynddelw in the 12th century as a paragon of heroic qualities. Given all of this it seems clear that Gwalchmai was a folkloric hero of some antiquity and the same type as Arthur, but also that he perhaps occupied a lesser role in the non-Galfridian Arthurian tradition than did either Bedwyr or Cai.

With regards to Gwalchmai's parentage it should be noted that there is some confusion as Geoffrey makes him Arthur's nephew by Anna and Lot of Lothian, but in *Culhwch* and the Early Version of the Triads he is 'Gwalchmai son of Gwyar'. It seems safe to assume that the Welsh tradition is the earlier one, with later Welsh writers being seen to struggle with the differing accounts given by Geoffrey and the native tradition, but the substitution of Anna's name with that of Gwyar in the 14th-century *Birth of Arthur* raises the possibility that Gwyar could be a matronymic, a rare but not unknown situation (see Bromwich, 1978, pp. 372-3). In Culhwch he is given a brother, Gwalhauet mab Gwyar, who is also referred to in a *marwnad* by the 13th-century poet Llygad Gwr, suggesting that this brother might have been a traditional rather than an invented character. The name Gwalchmai may mean something like 'The Hawk of the Plain(s?)' or 'Hawk-Beak' with Gwyar literally meaning 'blood' (Bromwich, 1978, p. 552; Bromwich rejects completely Loomis' derivation of the forms *Gauvains* etc. from *Gwrvan gvallt auvyan* rather than *Gwalchmai*, see pp. 370-71), although Koch has suggested that it could be from an early **Wolcos Magesos*, 'Wolf' or

'Errant Warrior of the Plain' ('The Celtic Lands', in N. J. Lacy (ed.), *Medieval Arthurian Literature: A Guide to Recent Research* (New York, 1996), pp. 239-322 at p. 267).

4. Gwenhwyfar

Gwenhwyfar (= Guinevere) is first named as Arthur's queen in *Culhwch ac Olwen* (*c.* 1100) but a fuller account of her role in the pre-Galfridian tradition is to be had from Caradog of Llancarfan's *Vita Gildae*, written in the 1120s or 1130s for the monks of Glastonbury:

> Glastonbury....was besieged by the tyrant Arthur with an innumerable host because of his wife Gwenhwyfar, whom the aforesaid king Melwas had violated and carried off bringing her there for safety, because of the invulnerable position's protection, provided by the thicketed fortifications of reed, rivers and marshes. The war-like king had searched for the queen throughout the cycle of one year, and at last heard that she resided there. Thereupon he called up the armies of the whole of Cornwall and Devon and war was prepared between the enemies.
>
> When the abbot of Glastonbury – attended by the clergy and Gildas the Wise – saw this, he stepped in between the contending armies, and peacefully advised his king Melwas, that he should restore the kidnapped lady. And so, she who was to be restored was restored in peace and good will. When these things had been done, the two kings gave to the abbot many territories; and they came to visit the church of St Mary to pray; the abbot sanctioning the dear fraternity in return for the peace they enjoyed and the benefits which they had bestowed and which they were about to bestow yet more plentifully. Then, reconciled, the kings left, swearing reverently to obey the most venerable abbot of Glastonbury, and not to violate the holiest part nor even the lands bordering on the land of its overseer. (J. B. Coe and S. Young (ed. and trans.), *The Celtic Sources for the Arthurian Legend* (Felinfach, 1995), pp. 25-7)

There are several subsequent references to this tale of the abduction of Gwenhwyfar by Melwas, for example in Chrétien de Troyes's *Le Chevalier de la Charette*, in which a certain Meleagant abducts Arthur's queen Guenièvre, wounding Keu in the process, and takes her to the Otherworldly kingdom of *Go(i)rre* (OFr. *voirre*, 'glass'; Welsh *gwydr*, 'glass'); on the Modena archivolt, where there appears to be a representation of some version of this story; in the 14th-century poetry of Dafydd ap Gwilym; and in the non-Galfridian

Ymddiddan Melwas ac Gwenhwyfar, a dialogue poem which appears to be between Arthur's queen and Melwas 'from *Ynys Wydrin* (Isle of Glass)' (Cai may also have a part at the end). While this latter work only survives in post-medieval manuscripts, the original poem should probably be regarded as very much older (*i.e.* 12th century: R. Bromwich (ed. and trans.), *Trioedd Ynys Prydein. The Welsh Triads* (Cardiff, 1978), p. 383). It has been convincingly suggested that behind these tales lies a pre-Galfridian Welsh story concerned with the rescue of Gwenhwyfar from an Otherworld Island of Glass controlled by Melwas (who appears in other works as a magician who went to the 'end of the world'), similar to *Preideu Annwfyn* and its analogues. The version presented in *Vita Gildae* would seem to be being an adaptation of this story with the Isle of Glass being identified – spuriously – as Glastonbury by Caradog (the name actually means 'island, or fortress, of the Glastings', not 'Isle of Glass' as Caradog asserts, though he may not have been the first to make the identification) thus allowing him to introduce the abbot of Glastonbury as peacemaker and beneficiary of 'many lands' from Arthur and Melwas (see P. Sims-Williams, 'The Early Welsh Arthurian Poems', in R. Bromwich *et al* (edd.), *The Arthur of the Welsh: The Arthurian Legend in Medieval Welsh Literature* (Cardiff, 1991), pp. 33-71 at pp. 58-61).

The above abduction theme remains at the centre of the tales concerning Gwenhwyfar, though the abductor changes: in Geoffrey of Monmouth's *HRB* the abductor is Arthur's nephew Mordred; in Ulrich's *Lanzelet* it is Valerin; in *Diu Crone* it is Gasozein and, finally, in the Vulgate romances it becomes Lancelot. It should of course be noted that some of these may not be changes but rather variant versions of the abduction tale. The resemblances between the Fenian and Arthurian cycles have often been noted (for example, A. G. Van Hamel 'Aspects of Celtic Mythology', *Proceedings of the British Academy*, 20 (1934), pp. 207-48) and, as such, Geoffrey's account of Mordred's abduction of Gwenhwyfar could represent an early tradition since it is closely paralleled by the abduction of Fionn's wife Grainne by his nephew Diarmaid. That said however, this requires us to identify Mordred as Arthur's nephew, an identification not confirmed by texts independent of Geoffrey of Monmouth, whose authority in this matter is to be doubted (see note on Medraut; on the recurrent idea that Gwenhwyfar was somehow involved in the Battle of Camlann, see the discussion in chapter four of T. Green, *Concepts of Arthur* (Stroud, 2007)).

With specific regard to Gwenhwyfar herself, a number of points need to be made. First, her name is generally agreed to mean 'white/sacred fairy/enchantress' (see M. Richards, 'Arthurian Onomastics', *The Transactions of the Honourable Society of Cymmrodorion* (1969), pp. 250-64 at p. 257), and as Ford has shown, the first element of this name, *gwen* 'white, holy', points clearly to her Otherworldly origins (P. K. Ford, 'On the Significance of some Arthurian Names in Welsh', *The Bulletin of the Board of Celtic Studies*, 30 (1983), pp. 268-273). This name, Gwenhwyfar, is cognate with the Irish *Finnabhair* and Richards has pointed out that the division in the Triads into *Gwenhwy* + *fawr*, 'great', in contrast with her supposed sister *Gwenhwy* + *fach*, 'little', is a transparent folk etymology. Second, Geoffrey of Monmouth's forms of her name include *G(u)anhumara* and the -*m*- here is best explained as deriving from a misreading of a written Old Welsh (9th-11th century) source (Bromwich, 1978, p. 381), which is obviously of interest. Third, in early Welsh tradition (for example, in *Brut y Brenhinedd* and *Trioedd Ynys Prydein*) Gwenhwyfar's father is Ogfran *Gawr* ('the Giant') and she herself appears as a giantess (understandably, given her parentage) in British folklore – thus Sir John Rhys records the following popular rhyme: *Gwenhwyfar, ferch Ogrfan Gawr / Drwg yn fechan, gwaeth yn fawr*, 'Gwenhwyfar daughter of Ogfran the Giant, bad when little, worse when big' (*Studies in the Arthurian Legend* (Oxford, 1901), p. 49).

5. Lancelot du Lac

Lancelot du Lac is a non-insular figure – his name is clearly a foreign importation and he was unknown to the *Gogynfeirdd*, the references to him by Welsh poets of the 15th and later centuries owing their origin to a knowledge of the French *Vulgate Cycle*. Lancelot first appears in the late 12th-century poems *Le Chevalier de la Charette* by Chrétien de Troyes and *Lanzelot* by Ulrich von Zatzikhofen. Both of these poems contain elements of mythology and folklore which are obviously 'Celtic' in origin, but there is no reason to think that Lancelot is one of these elements. As a major Arthurian hero Lancelot is late on the scene, finally superseding the earlier hero Gawain (= Gwalchmai, see note) as the peer of Arthur's knights in the 13th-century Vulgate romances (see R. Bromwich (ed. and trans.), *Trioedd Ynys Prydein. The Welsh Triads* (Cardiff, 1978), pp. 414-16, who rejects completely any association between Lancelot and the god Lug, arguing instead that the name *Lancelot* is most probably a variant of the Breton *Lancelin*, recorded in 11th century, with an altered suffix).

6. Llacheu m. Arthur

Llacheu features frequently in the early poetry, although he is only mentioned once in the Early Version of the *Triads*, which were originally compiled in the 11th or 12th century: Triad 4 'Three Well-Endowed Men of the Island of Britain:.. Llacheu son of Arthur...'. In the Black Book of Carmarthen there are two important references to him. The first comes from the perhaps 10th-century poem *Ymddiddan Gwyddno Garanhir ac Gwyn fab Nudd*, the last section of which contains a catalogue of earlier heroic warriors at whose deaths the speaker claims to have been present:

> I have been where Llacheu was slain
> the son of Arthur, awful [/marvellous] in songs
> when ravens croaked over blood.
> (J. B. Coe and S. Young (ed. and trans.), *The Celtic Sources for the Arthurian Legend* (Felinfach, 1995), p. 125)

The 'marvellous songs' probably refer to Llacheu, not Arthur (see A. O. H. Jarman, 'The Delineation of Arthur in Early Welsh Verse', in K. Varty (ed.), *An Arthurian Tapestry: Essays in Memory of Lewis Thorpe* (Glasgow 1981), pp. 1-21 at p. 18, n.26). The second is in the early poem *Pa gur yv y porthaur?*, where Llacheu appears alongside Cai in the list of warriors and their deeds that Arthur narrates:

> Cai the fair and Llachau,
> they performed battles
> before the pain of of blue spears (ended the conflict).
> (Lines 76-8: P. Sims-Williams, 'The Early Welsh Arthurian Poems', in R. Bromwich *et al* (edd.) *The Arthur of the Welsh: The Arthurian Legend in Medieval Welsh Literature* (Cardiff, 1991), pp. 33-71 at p. 43)

There are continuing references to him in later Welsh verse (*i.e.* after *c.* 1150), in which he is used as a standard of heroic comparison (for example, Cynddelw refers to *Llacheu uar*, 'Llacheu's ferocity'), and he is mentioned in *Breuddwyd Rhonabwy*. As Bromwich says, 'These allusions in poetry indicate that Llacheu was a figure of considerable importance in the early Arthurian saga, and that like Kei and Bedwyr he belonged to the oldest stratum of Arthurian tradition...' (R. Bromwich (ed. and trans.), *Trioedd Ynys Prydein. The Welsh Triads* (Cardiff, 1978), p. 416). Certainly he would appear to be present in local topographic folklore, like Arthur *et al*, if the evidence of a 13th-century elegy can be trusted (see Sims-Williams, 1991, p. 44).

It is worth noting that early Arthurian tradition gave Arthur more than one son. In the early 9th-century *Historia Brittonum* Arthur is said to have slain his son Amr. This Amr failed, however, to achieve later fame beyond a mention of 'Amhar son of Arthur' in *Geraint* (he appears as one of Arthur's four chamberlains along with Bedwyr's son, Amhren – see G. Jones and T. Jones (trans.), *The Mabinogion* (Dent, 1949), p. 231). Another son, one Loholt, is mentioned in the continental romances. *Y Seint Greal* identifies Llacheu with this Loholt, thus having Cai slay Llacheu rather than Loholt as he does in the *Perlesvaus*. There is, however, no reason to believe in any early association between Llacheu and Loholt (or indeed, in a traditional origin for Loholt – he first appears in Chrétien's *Erec* and the name is Breton-French) and thus no reason to think that there was a tradition of Cai slaying Arthur's son which is not recorded in the Welsh sources. Rather the equation of Llacheu with Loholt is best viewed as the result of the translation of the continental material into Welsh and the consequent substitution of Welsh traditional material for the unfamiliar continental names (see Bromwich, 1978, pp. 417-18; C. Lloyd-Morgan, 'Bruddwyd Rhonabwy and Later Arthurian Literature', in R. Bromwich *et al* (edd.), *The Arthur of the Welsh: The Arthurian Legend in Medieval Welsh Literature* (Cardiff, 1991), pp. 183-208 at p. 197). Other sons granted to Arthur in Welsh materials include Gwydre, named in *Culhwch ac Olwen* as having been killed by the giant boar *Trwyd* at *Cwm Kerwyn* in the Preselly mountains, and Duran, who appears in an *englyn* and prose fragment from MS Mostyn 131, p. 770, which, though late (perhaps 15th century?), is clearly working in the native non-Galfridian tradition of Arthur.

7. Madog m. Uthyr

In the 'Dialogue of Arthur and the Eagle' (*Ymddiddan Arthur a'r Eryr*), a work drawing on traditions earlier than Geoffrey of Monmouth though the text itself cannot be dated before *c.* 1150, the eagle reveals himself as Arthur's deceased nephew *Eliwlat vab Madawc vab Uthyr* (this genealogy is repeated in the mid-15th-century *Pedwar Marchog ar Hugain Llys Arthur*), thus making Madawg and Arthur brothers. This Madog son of Uthyr is known from another pre-Galfridian text, *Madawg drut ac Erof* in the Book of Taliesin:

> *Madawc mur menwyt.*
> *Madawc kyn bu bed,*
> *Bu dinas edryssed*
> *o gamp a chymwed.*
> *Mab vthyr kyn lleas*
> *Oe law dywystlas.*

> Madog, the rampart of rejoicing.
> Madog, before he was in the grave,
> he was a fortress of generosity
> [consisting] of feat(s) and play.
> The son of Uthyr, before death
> he handed over pledges.
> (P. Sims-Williams, 'The Early Welsh Arthurian Poems', in R.

Bromwich *et al* (edd.), *The Arthur of the Welsh: The Arthurian Legend in Medieval Welsh Literature* (Cardiff, 1991), pp. 33-71 at pp. 53-4)

and from a late 12th-century religious poem, where he is mentioned ironically in a list of former worthies:

Madog, famous leader, was false;
he had great profit: wretched sorrow! (Sims-Williams, 1991, p. 54)

From these references it is evident that there were stories current in early Welsh tradition regarding Arthur's 'brother', but unfortunately nothing more survives of these than the above and Geoffrey made no use of such traditions.

8. Medraut

Medraut (= Modred) makes his first appearance in the *Annales Cambriae*, in an annal of probably mid-10th-century origin (see 'The Historicity and Historicisation of Arthur'; T. Green, *Concepts of Arthur* (Stroud, 2007)):

The Battle of Camlann, in which Arthur and Medraut fell: and there was plague in Britain and Ireland (*s.a.* 537)

This annal makes it clear that, by the 10th century, Medraut was seen as playing an important part in the pre-Galfridian Welsh tales, and this conclusion is confirmed – if confirmation is needed – by the references made to him by the 12th century and later bards. For example, Meilyr Brydydd, in a lament for the death of Gruffudd ap Cynan (d. 1137), praises his subject for having Medraut's valour in battle, and Meilyr's son Gwalchmai lauds Madog ap Maredudd (d. 1160) for possessing the 'good nature of Medrawd'. Going beyond this simple statement of fact is, however, difficult, as no source uninfluenced by Geoffrey of Monmouth or the *Bruts* makes Medraut Arthur's nephew or his betrayer/opponent – in fact they seem rather to contradict these claims. Thus the references to him by the 12th-century Welsh court poets, including those noted above, seem to indicate that Medraut was thought of as a paragon of valour, courage and good nature to whom their patrons could be favourably compared (see R. Bromwich (ed. and trans.), *Trioedd Ynys Prydein. The Welsh Triads* (Cardiff, 1978), pp. 454-55; O. J. Padel *Arthur in Medieval Welsh Literature* (Cardiff, 2000), pp. 113-15), and the native Welsh tradition on this point seems to have remained remarkably vigorous to a very late date – no references to any conflicts or acts of treachery between Arthur and Medraut are made by the Welsh poets until the early 16th century, when they first appear in the work of Tudur Aled. Similarly, on the matter of parentage, no non-Galfridian account supports Geoffrey's claims and we have to recognise that the parents attributed to Medraut by Geoffrey are the same as those given by him to Gwalchmai – sources earlier than Geoffrey make it clear that this parentage is false for Gwalchmai at least, and post-Galfridian authors who do make use of Geoffrey appear to indicate that the parentage given in his *Historia* to both Gwalchmai and Medraut was at variance with that found in the traditional materials. As such it is now generally accepted that there is no reason to believe that either notion is any older than the *Historia Regum Britanniae* itself (see for example Bromwich, 1978 and Padel, 2000).

In the later Vulgate *Mort Artu*, Morguase – Arthur's supposed half-sister – is made to be Medraut's mother and this incest motif is preserved in the romances based upon the *Mort Artu* (for example, Malory's *Morte Darthur*). Both this parentage and the incest motif are, however, clearly inventions of the *Mort Artu*, despite their modern popularity, and in all unrelated accounts the portrayal of Medraut is solidly Galfridian. Geoffrey's form of the name, *Mordredus*, was derived from a Cornish or Breton source and the name is known from the Cornish *Domesday* returns and in the Bodmin manumissions of A.D. 960-1000 (Bromwich, 1978, p. 455).

9. Uthyr Pendragon

Uthyr is, of course, famous as the father of Arthur in Geoffrey of Monmouth's *Historia Regum Britanniae* (*c.* 1138), but he was known to Welsh tradition prior to the publication of this work (*pace* Geoffrey Ashe: see A.O.H. Jarman 'Emrys Wledig; Amlawdd Wledig; Uthr Bendragon', in *Llên Cymru* 2 (1952)). So, for example, in the early poem *Pa gur yv y porthaur?* from the Black Book of Carmarthen one of Arthur's band of men is named as:

> Mabon son of Myrdon,
> Uthr Pendragon's servant;
> (Lines 13-14: P. Sims-Williams, 'The Early Welsh Arthurian Poems', in R. Bromwich *et al* (edd.), *The Arthur of the Welsh: The Arthurian Legend in Medieval Welsh Literature* (Cardiff, 1991), pp. 33-71 at p. 40)

One of the most interesting questions is, naturally, whether Uthyr was viewed as Arthur's father previous to Geoffrey. The answer to this is probably 'yes'. In the 'Dialogue of Arthur and the Eagle' (*Ymddiddan Arthur a'r Eryr*), which is independent of Geoffrey's work, the eagle reveals itself to be Arthur's deceased nephew, Eliwlod son of Madawg son of Uthyr (stanzas 7-9), *i.e.* Arthur and Madog are both sons of Uthyr (the above relationship between Uthyr and Madog is confirmed by another reference in the Book of Taliesin – see note on Madog). In addition to this, in the Book of Taliesin poem *Marwnat vthyr pen[dragon]* (another piece of evidence, incidentally, for a pre-Galfridian Uthyr) the speaker, who would appear to be Uthyr, boasts 'I have shared my refuge, a ninth share in Arthur's valour', that is, perhaps, that he has passed on his qualities (or his kingdom) to Arthur, and later that 'The world [or 'battle'] would not exist if it were not for my progeny' (see Sims-Williams, 1991, p. 53).

Accepting the above, it must therefore be asked what was the nature of this Uthyr beyond being perceived as Arthur's father? The crucial piece of evidence is provided by Triad 28, which tells us that Uthyr was a great and renowned enchanter/magician who teaches one of the 'Three Great Enchantments of the Island of Britain' to Menw son of Teirgwaedd, a character who is one of Arthur's men and has the ability to shape-shift and to become invisible in *Culhwch ac Olwen*. This fits, of course, very nicely with the episode in Geoffrey's text in which Uthyr shape-shifts in order to lie with Gorlois' wife, and Bromwich's suggestion that Geoffrey was here drawing on a native tradition, just as he did in making Uthyr Arthur's father, appears to have been accepted (see R. Bromwich (ed. and trans.), *Trioedd Ynys Prydein. The Welsh Triads* (Cardiff, 1978), p. 56, and Sims-Williams, 1991, p. 53; it is generally agreed that British traditions and stories lie behind many elements of Geoffrey's work, though the Arthurian sections taken as a whole are Geoffrey's alone and owe little to prior narrative: see B. F. Roberts, 'Geoffrey of Monmouth, *Historia Regum Britanniae* and *Brut y Brenhinedd*', in R. Bromwich *et al* (edd.), *The Arthur of the Welsh: The Arthurian Legend in Medieval Welsh Literature* (Cardiff, 1991), pp. 97-116). As such, Uthyr was probably originally perceived as a magician and shape-shifter who was/became known as Arthur's father; for the view that Uthyr was originally a 'Celtic' god, see K. Malone, 'The Historicity of Arthur', *Journal of English and Germanic Philology*, 23 (1924), pp. 463-91.

With regards to the name, *uthr* can be both an adjective ('terrible') or a proper name, a fact which has caused some confusion in the past. However, in the light of the evidence for pre-Galfridian traditions about this figure, and the fact that Uthyr appears as a personal name in Welsh and Irish sources, there is no reason to look for the origins of the name Uthyr Pendragon – or his association with Arthur – in an early gloss on the name Arthur (see Jarman, 1952 and Bromwich, 1978, pp. 521-22). *Pendragon* means literally 'Chief Dragon' but *dragon* occurs in the oldest poetry (for example, in *Y Gododdin*) as a euphemism for warriors; thus *Pendragon* should be taken as something like 'foremost leader' or 'chief of warriors' (see Bromwich, 1978, pp. 520-23).

A Guide to Arthurian Archaeology[*]

1. *Duodecimum fuit bellum in monte Badonis*

'The twelfth battle was on Badon hill' (*Historia Brittonum*, chapter 56). The battle of Badon is probably the most famous of Arthur's alleged battles, largely because it is also recorded by Gildas in his *De Excidio Britanniae* §26.1 (*obsessio Badonici montis*), where it is described as the culmination of the British counter-attack against the Saxons, thus making its historicity certain. The battle is undated in the *Historia Brittonum* and the date that Gildas gives to this event is obscure also, depending to a great extent upon the dating of Gildas' text, though somewhere around A.D. 500 is generally agreed to be likely (the evidence of the mid-10th-century *Annales Cambriae* is of no real value in determining the date of the battle, for the reasons discussed in T. Green, *Concepts of Arthur* (Stroud, 2007), chapter one, and 'The Historicity and Historicisation of Arthur').

Before going any further it must be pointed out that the association of this battle with Arthur can be evidenced no earlier than the 9th century, with recent research into the earliest manuscript of Gildas' *DEB* (British Library, Cotton Vitellius A.vi) concluding that, rather than not identifying the battle with any particular British leader, Gildas in fact identifies the victor of Badon as Ambrosius Aurelianus (O. J. Padel, 'The Nature of Arthur', *Cambrian Medieval Celtic Studies*, 27 (1994), pp. 1-31 at pp. 16-18; M. Wood, *In Search of England: Journeys Into the English Past* (London, 1999), pp. 34-38). This confusion over the victor fits into the picture described elsewhere of a process by which a non-historical folkloric figure named 'Arthur' was historicised, partly with great battles from the past fought by genuine leaders of the 'Heroic Age' (see Green, 2007, chapter six; Padel, 1994). This does not, of course, lessen the desire to identify the site of this battle, and this question has long been a source of controversy.

---

[*] This brief guide to the various locations which have been connected with the pre-Galfridian Arthurian legend was first placed online in 1998 in much the same form as it is presented here. An up-to-date discussion of Badon and its attribution to Arthur can be found in T. Green, *Concepts of Arthur* (Stroud, 2007), chapters one and six. The notes on the other locations are in need of some revision, particularly to take full account of recent excavations, but it is hoped that they nonetheless continue to provide a useful discussion of the Arthurian associations of these sites.

One possible location for Badon might be at one of the many 'Badburys', as these place-names may derive from *Badon* plus Old English *byrig/burh*, 'fortification, fortified place' (see M. Gelling, 'Towards a chronology for English place-names', in D. Hooke (ed.) *Anglo-Saxon Settlements* (Oxford, 1988), pp. 59-76 at pp. 60-61; K.H. Jackson, 'The site of Mount Badon', *Journal of Celtic Studies*, 2.2 (1958), pp. 152-55). Another possible location is Bath, if this was earlier known as Badon (see T. Burkitt and A. Burkitt, 'The frontier zone and the siege of Mount Badon: a review of the evidence for their location', *Proceedings of the Somerset Archaeological and Natural History Society*, 134 (1990), pp. 81-93; L. Alcock *Arthur's Britain* (Harmondsworth, 1971)). The problem is that the philological arguments can take us no further than this – one can accept a British origin for the name of Bath or one for the name Badbury, but it is a subjective judgement with nothing to argue conclusively for either side. Indeed, if the Badbury suggestion is adopted, then there is the further problem of 'which Badbury was Badon?', as there are many Badburys and related names located across southern Britain from Dorset through to Lincolnshire.

Unfortunately the other available evidence for the location of Badon (both historical and archaeological) is similarly subjective and inconclusive (see S. Hirst and P. Rahtz, 'Liddington Castle and the Battle of Badon: Excavation and Research 1976', *The Archaeological Journal*, 153 (1996), pp. 1-59 at pp. 8-19 for a good summary of the 'search' for Badon). Overall, the weight of archaeological evidence points to somewhere in southern or eastern Britain as the area where such a battle is likely to have been fought – as this is where the Anglo-Saxons were in the fifth and earlier sixth centuries – but beyond this it is difficult to progress. There is simply insufficient evidence to allow us to decide between the competing cases: 'the site of *Mons Badonicus* in the absence of any early topographical information... remains anyone's guess' (J. N. L. Myres, in *The Antiquaries Journal*, 25 (1945), p. 84).

2. Castle Killibury, Cornwall

The Arthurian associations of Castle Killibury stem from attempts to discover the location of *Kelli wic*, the name given in both *Culhwch ac Olwen* and *Trioedd Ynys Prydein* to Arthur's residence in Cornwall. In 1900 Castle Killibury was suggested as *Kelli wic* for three main reasons: firstly that a hill-fort would be the most appropriate identification; secondly that the names *Kelli wic* and Killibury are similar; and thirdly because it was near Tregeare Rounds. This last argument is the one that tipped the balance in favour of this site, when the name alone gave it no better case to be *Kelli wic* than, say, Callington and Calliwith. This argument is, however, false. Its origins lie in attempts to discover the Dimilioc that Geoffrey of Monmouth has Gorlois, Duke of Cornwall, being besieged at whilst Uther was fathering Arthur at Tintagel. Geoffrey's Dimilioc is obviously the hill-fort close by Domellick, but eighteenth-century antiquarians, reading Geoffrey's text, believed that Dimilioc had to be within a night's ride of Tintagel (Domellick is twenty miles away), though Geoffrey never states this. They thus looked for a hill-fort near Tintagel which might be Dimilioc instead, and they settled on Tregeare Rounds, leading to the invalid argument – which seemed cogent at the time – that Killibury was near to Tregeare Rounds and was thus likely to be *Kelli wic*. However, 'in the light of the re-identification of Dimilioc, there is now no reason for maintaining the suggestion [that Killibury = *Kelli wic*], other than the vague similarity of the names' (O. J. Padel, 'Some south-western sites with Arthurian associations', in R. Bromwich *et al* (edd.) *The Arthur of the Welsh. The Arthurian Legend in Medieval Welsh Literature* (Cardiff, 1991), pp. 229-48 at p. 236).

The question thus becomes, where was *Kelli wic* if it was not Castle Killibury? Given the testimony of *Culhwch ac Olwen* and *Trioedd Ynys Prydein*, it seems clear that the early medieval Welsh considered it to have been located in the Cornwall or the south-west. There is some additional evidence which may help in the attempt to further narrow down the area meant, such as the reference in 1302 to a *Thomas de Kellewik* from the far west of Cornwall, but beyond this it is difficult to say. It is, however, worth pointing out that the name *Kelli wic* itself would seem to mean 'forest grove', and there is thus no pressing reason to believe that Arthur's *Kelli wic* was based on any real place. Indeed, as Ford points out, it may have originally been envisaged as somewhere Otherworldly (sacred groves being common in Celtic myth) and only later might a specific location have been ascribed to it (see O. J. Padel, 'The Nature of Arthur', *Cambrian Medieval Celtic Studies*, 27 (1994), pp. 1-31 at pp. 12-13; P. K. Ford, 'On the Significance of Some Arthurian Names in Welsh', *Bulletin of the Board of Celtic Studies*, 30 (1983), pp. 268-73).

3. Glastonbury, Somerset

There are two areas of interest in Glastonbury, namely the Abbey (ST 500388) and the Tor (ST 512386). Ralegh Radford's excavations at the Abbey in the 1960s aimed to discover the earliest religious activity on the site, and they uncovered an ancient cemetery of stone-lined graves near traces of a small timber structure thought to be the original church of St Mary (C. A. Ralegh Radford, 'Glastonbury Abbey', in G. Ashe (ed.) *The Quest for Arthur's Britain* (London, 1971), pp. 97-110). Along with this building were found post-holes interpreted as traces of wattled oratories and all of this was bounded on the east by a great bank and ditch interpreted as a monastic *vallum*. While there was no dating evidence these features, all lay below later Anglo-Saxon features and thus it seemed likely that they were 'Celtic' in date. More recent excavations on the precinct ditch uncovered wooden stakes which yielded radiocarbon dates centred on the late sixth and seventh centuries. Also found in this area was an eastern Mediterranean copper censer, again of late sixth- or seventh-century date, which has been taken to suggest that Glastonbury was a British Christian site which maintained Byzantine ecclesiastical contacts (C. Snyder, 'A Gazetteer of Sub-Roman Britain (AD 400-600): The British sites', *Internet Archaeology*, 3 (1997)).

Philip Rahtz's excavations on the Tor have uncovered much more evidence of post-Roman activity (dating from the late fifth century onwards – there is no sign of earlier activity): structures were found on the summit of the Tor and on the terrace platforms, and there were certainly wooden buildings upon these, although little remained of them. Associated with these buildings were charcoal, burnt stones and large quantities of food remains, mainly animal bones. These were not the remains of animals slaughtered on the spot, but rather of meat brought to the Tor as joints (P. Rahtz, 'Glastonbury Tor', in G. Ashe (ed.) *The Quest for Arthur's Britain* (London, 1971), pp. 111-22 at p. 116). Several post-holes around an eastern hollow have been interpreted as some sort of fence or protective barrier, and in the the hollow there was a variety of evidence, including an iron lamp-holder, suggestive of the presence of a building. Also found in this area was a mysterious stone cairn which defies solid interpretation but might be seen as building foundations, a bench or even an alter. The most important area was the south platform, an artificially cut platform which has been partly destroyed by erosion, where traces of a large timber building were found along with two hearths, crucibles and other evidence of metal working; a dozen pieces of imported post-Roman Mediterranean amphorae (providing dating evidence); and a carved bronze head (stylistically 'Celtic') which may have been enameled. The exact nature of the post-Roman activity on the Tor is, however, difficult to assess. The excavator favoured the explanation of the Tor as a secular fortress of a lesser British chieftain (he ruled out the idea that the Tor may have been a signalling station as part of a defensive network), due to the large numbers of animal bones, the evidence for metal-working and the presence of imported Mediterranean pottery. However, the Tor could just as easily have been a ecclesiastical site – the main argument against this was that the large numbers of animal bones were contrary to the ascetic lifestyle of monks of this period, but recent excavations at monastic centres such as Whithorn have revealed large numbers of animal bones, thus negating this argument and making the interpretation of the Tor as an early hermitic monastic site equally as valid as the interpretation of this site as a secular fortification (see further P. Rahtz,

English Heritage Book of Glastonbury (London, 1993); C. Snyder, 'A Gazetteer of Sub-Roman Britain (AD 400-600): The British sites', *Internet Archaeology*, 3 (1997); P. Hill, *Whithorn and St Ninian. The Excavation of a Monastic Town 1984-91* (Stroud, 1997)).

What then of the Arthurian associations? Arthur's connection with Glastonbury is first recorded in the *Vita Gildae* ('Life of St Gildas') by Caradoc of Llancarfan, which was written in the 1120s or 1130s:

> Glastonbury... was besieged by the tyrant Arthur with an innumerable host because of his wife Gwenhwyfar, whom the aforesaid king Melwas had violated and carried off bringing her there for safety, because of the invulnerable position's protection, provided by the thicketed fortifications of reed, rivers and marshes. The war-like king had searched for the queen throughout the cycle of one year, and at last heard that she resided there. Thereupon he called up the armies of the whole of Cornwall and Devon and war was prepared between the enemies.
>
> When the abbot of Glastonbury – attended by the clergy and Gildas the Wise – saw this, he stepped in between the contending armies, and peacefully advised his king Melwas, that he should restore the kidnapped lady. And so, she who was to be restored was restored in peace and good will. When these things had been don, the two kings gave to the abbot many territories; and they came to visit the church of St Mary to pray; the abbot sanctioning the dear fraternity in return for the peace they enjoyed and the benefits which they had bestowed and which they were about to bestow yet more plentifully. Then, reconciled, the kings left, swearing reverently to obey the most venerable abbot of Glastonbury, and not to violate the holiest part nor even the lands bordering on the land of its overseer. (J. B. Coe and S. Young (ed. and trans.), *The Celtic Sources for the Arthurian Legend* (Felinfach, 1995) pp. 25-27)

This story, despite its obvious aim of justifying the privileges of Glastonbury Abbey, would appear to have ancient origins, as it is referred to in a number of other sources. However, Glastonbury was probably not part of the original tale which, it has been convincingly argued, was a story about the rescue of Gwenhwyfar from an Otherworld 'Island of Glass' similar to *Preideu Annwfyn* and its analogues. The version presented in *Vita Gildae* was probably an adaptation of this story, with the 'Isle of Glass' being identified spuriously as Glastonbury by Caradoc (the name actually means 'island, or fortress, of the Glastings', though he may not have been the first to make the identification) thus allowing him to introduce the abbot of Glastonbury – the Glastonbury community being the recipients of his *Life* – as peacemaker and beneficiary of 'many lands' from Arthur and Melwas (see P. Sims-Williams, 'The Early Welsh Arthurian Poems', in R. Bromwich *et al* (edd.) *The Arthur of the Welsh: The Arthurian Legend in Medieval Welsh Literature* (Cardiff 1991), pp. 33-71 at pp. 58-61).

A far more significant Arthurian connection emerged in the 1190s, with the excavation at the Abbey of a grave containing a lead cross which proclaimed that the monks had found the burial-place of Arthur. This episode has been much discussed but it is now generally held to be a late twelfth-century fraud on the part of the Glastonbury monks, possibly for the benefit of the king rather than themselves. The case against a fraud is mainly based upon the researches of C. A. Ralegh Radford (in G. Ashe (ed.), *The Quest for Arthur's Britain* (London, 1971)), who demonstrated that the monks did indeed 'find' a grave and who believed that the Latin of the cross was earlier than the twelfth century, which would indicate that there was no late twelfth-century fraud. This latter suggestion has, however, now been widely rejected, and the cross is seen instead as solidly twelfth century in origins; indeed, it has been noted that the inscription derives in part from Geoffrey of Monmouth's *Historia Regum Britanniae*, a copy of which was present at Glastonbury from the 1170s. As such, the fact that the monks did find a grave only indicates that they chose a spot to excavate which they knew to contain an ancient grave, and the spot in question does appear to have been marked in the graveyard as such previous to their excavations. It might, of course, be proposed that while the cross is a product of the twelfth-century fraud, it was based on a genuine remembrance of Arthur being buried in the Abbey graveyard, but this can be nothing more than wishful thinking. It is worth pointing out that, previous to the 'discovery' of Arthur's 'grave', it appears to have been generally held that no-one knew where Arthur's grave was and, moreover, that he might still be alive: see T. Green, *Concepts of Arthur* (Stroud, 2007), chapter two, and O. J. Padel, 'The Nature of Arthur', *Cambrian Medieval Celtic Studies*, 27 (1994), pp. 1-31 at pp. 8-12, for a full discussion of the belief that Arthur was not dead and would return.

In consequence, it seems clear that there is no reason to think that anyone did actually believe that Arthur was buried at Glastonbury before the 1190s, and the 'discovery' of Arthur's grave is thus almost certainly a monastic fraud of the type with which historians are familiar – truly 'early' Arthurian associations at Glastonbury are only to be found in Caradoc's account, for what this is worth. See further P. Rahtz, *English Heritage Book of Glastonbury* (London, 1993); J. Carey, 'The Finding of Arthur's Grave: A Story from Clonmacnoise?', in J. Carey *et al* (edd.) *Ildánach Ildírech. A Festschrift for Proinsias Mac Cana* (Andover & Aberystwyth, 1999), pp. 1-14; J. P. Carley, 'Arthur in English History', in W. R. J. Barron (ed.) *The Arthur of the English* (Cardiff, 1999), pp. 47-57; A. Gransden, 'The Growth of

Glastonbury Traditions and Legends in the Twelfth Century', *Journal of Ecclesiastical History*, 27 (1976), pp. 337-58; and *Somerset and Dorset Notes & Queries* for 1984 for discussion of this burial and its status as a fraud.

4. South Cadbury, Somerset

This important Iron-Age hill-fort (ST 628252) was reoccupied and refortified in the late fifth or sixth century, but occupation ceased in the seventh century. The hill-fort itself is enormous and it has been estimated that around 870 men would have been needed to defend it. The nature of the evidence for post-Roman activity consists of a massive re-fortification of the defences, including a timber gate-tower (this re-fortification would have represented a formidable undertaking – it spans 1.2 km – and could only have been carried out by someone in command of extensive resources); post-built timber structures in the interior of the hill-fort, one of which is 19 metres long by 10 metres wide and is interpreted as a feasting hall, perhaps modelled on the villa complexes of Late Roman Britain; and a large quantity of imported post-Roman Mediterranean pottery, which is associated with both the buildings and the fortifications. The scale of the occupation and the large amounts of imported pottery make it clear that this was a very high-status site, and the excavator (Leslie Alcock) would see it as an administrative centre of a large British territory.

The nature of the Arthurian connection of this site is difficult to assess. The first reference to such a connection occurs in the sixteenth century, when John Leland – a noted apologist for a historical Arthur, writing *c.* 1540 – wrote that:

> At the very southe ende of the chirch of South-Cabuyri standith Camallate, sumtyme a famose toun or castelle, apon a very torre or hille, wunderfully enstrengtheid of nature... The people can telle nothing ther but that they have hard say that Arture much restorid to Camalat.

Although another sixteenth-century source is suggestive of a tradition that Arthur was asleep under South Cadbury hill-fort, these are very late traditions indeed, from a period in which many sites in both England and Wales were claiming a link with Arthur. As such, whilst this site was undoubtedly very important in the post-Roman period, there seems no good reason to think that these Arthurian associations are of much greater antiquity than the sixteenth century, in the absence of evidence to the contrary. For the site and traditions see L. Alcock, *'By South Cadbury is that Camelot...', The Excavation of Cadbury Castle 1966-1970* (London, 1972); L.

Alcock, 'Cadbury-Camelot: a Fifteen-year Perspective', *Proceedings of the British Academy*, 68 (1982) pp. 355-88; O. J. Padel, 'Some south-western sites with Arthurian associations', in R. Bromwich *et al* (edd.) *The Arthur of the Welsh. The Arthurian Legend in Medieval Welsh Literature* (Cardiff, 1991), pp. 229-48 at pp. 238-40; and now L. Alcock, *Cadbury Castle: Somerset. The Early Medieval Archaeology* (Cardiff, 1995). See also 'A Gazetteer of Arthurian Onomastic and Topographic Folklore'.

5. Tintagel, Cornwall

Tintagel (SX 049891) is first associated with the Arthurian legend in Geoffrey of Monmouth's *Historia Regum Britanniae* (*c.* 1138), where it features as the site of Arthur's conception, and Geoffrey's description suggests that he had seen the place himself. Whilst there is no evidence for pre-Roman occupation of the site, there is reason to believe that Tintagel was a reasonably important place in the Roman period. Two inscribed Roman milestones have been found in the Tintagel neighbourhood and it seems likely that they represent a late Roman (trading?) route passing near Tintagel. In addition Charles Thomas has suggested that Tintagel was the **Durocornovio* ('Fort of the *Cornovii*') of the *Ravenna Cosmography*, something which may be supported by finds of Roman coins (from Tetricus I (270-73) to Constantius II (337-61)) and both commercial and locally made pottery of the third and fourth centuries. The exact nature of Late Roman Tintagel is, nevertheless, elusive and the main focus of activity for this site was in the centuries after the Romans left.

Since the major excavations of the 1930s opinions as to the function of post-Roman Tintagel have altered considerably. The original excavator, C. A. Ralegh Radford, claimed that the site was an early Christian monastery from the fifth through to the eighth century. This interpretation has, however, been shown to be incorrect, and as a result a new historical explanation for the site is required: Tintagel is now usually seen as a very important fifth- to seventh-century secular site (a fortress or royal seat) belonging to the post-Roman kings of Dumnonia. The occupation of this site is likely to have been only seasonal given the inhospitable climate in winter months, but this fits in very well with what we know of early medieval kingship – this was itinerant and worked on the theory that it was easier to take the large royal household to the food than it was to maintain them in one permanent location (see T. Charles-Edwards, 'Early Medieval Kingships in the British Isles', in S. Basset (ed.) *The Origins of Anglo-Saxon Kingdoms* (London, 1989), pp. 28-39). As such, Tintagel was probably visited by the post-Roman kings of Dumnonia to receive tribute and possibly also for the investiture of a new king: 'King Arthur's Footprint', an island-top feature, may have been the site for such a ceremony. Moreover, analysis suggests that Tintagel was the leading centre in Cornwall for trade with the eastern Mediterranean merchants, receiving tin from many places in Cornwall as 'tribute', with this then being traded for luxury goods – including, perhaps, fine silks and other such items which are archaeologically invisible – which were in turn redistributed outwards, via gifting by the rulers, to favoured subjects (see C. Thomas, *Tintagel: Arthur and Archaeology* (London, 1993)). Given this, it seems possible that, when Tintagel – Cornish *din, 'fort' (variant *tin), plus *tagell, 'constriction', that is 'the fort of the narrow neck' – is referred to as a royal residence or defensive site in medieval literature (King Mark's in the Tristan legends; Gorlois' in the *Historia Regum Britanniae*), this represents a much-distorted 'folk-memory' of historical fact.

After Geoffrey's *Historia*, Tintagel plays very little part in the Arthurian cycle and the earliest evidence of the site being locally known as 'King Arthur's Castle' dates from 1650 – indeed, it is usually seen in the medieval literature as the castle of King Mark, a king of Dumnonia, and Geoffrey only places Arthur's conception here, making it clear that Tintagel was the property of a local ruler (Gorlois). It is thus probable that the Arthurian associations are 12th century in origin and result from Geoffrey attaching Arthur to pre-existing folkloric material which associated Tintagel with the post-Roman rulers of the region. See further Charles Thomas, *Tintagel: Arthur and Archaeology* (London, 1993), for a full discussion of the site and its Arthurian connections; it should be noted that the sixth-century inscribed stone which has recently been found at Tintagel has nothing to do with King Arthur, despite media speculation to the contrary (see 'The Historicity and Historicisation of Arthur', note two).

Made in the USA
San Bernardino, CA
20 December 2015